Preliminary Edition Notice

You have been selected to receive a copy of this book in the form of a preliminary edition. A preliminary edition is used in a classroom setting to test the overall value of a book's content and its effectiveness in a practical course prior to its formal publication on the national market.

As you use this text in your course, please share any and all feedback regarding the volume with your professor. Your comments on this text will allow the author to further develop the content of the book, so we can ensure it will be a useful and informative classroom tool for students in universities across the nation and around the globe. If you find the material is challenging to understand, or could be expanded to improve the usefulness of the text, it is important for us to know. If you have any suggestions for improving the material contained in the book or the way it is presented, we encourage you to share your thoughts.

Please note, preliminary editions are similar to review copies, which publishers distribute to select readers prior to publication in order to test a book's audience and elicit early feedback; therefore, you may find inconsistencies in formatting or design, or small textual errors within this volume. Design elements and the written text will likely undergo changes before this book goes to print and is distributed on the national market.

This text is not available in wide release on the market, as it is actively being prepared for formal publication. Accordingly, the book is offered to you at a discounted price to reflect its preliminary status.

If you would like to provide notes directly to the publisher, you may contact us by e-mailing studentreviews@cognella.com. Please include the book's title, author, and 7-digit SKU reference number (found below the barcode on the back cover of the book) in the body of your message.

D1712279

Construction of Social Problems

An Anthology

Revised Preliminary Edition

Edited by Moushumi Roy, Ph.D

Michigan State University

Bassim Hamadeh, CEO and Publisher
Jennifer Codner, Senior Field Acquisitions Editor
Michelle Piehl, Senior Project Editor
Alia Bales, Production Editor
Jess Estrella, Senior Graphic Designer
Stephanie Kohl, Licensing Coordinator
Natalie Piccotti, Director of Marketing
Kassie Graves, Vice President of Editorial
Jamie Giganti, Director of Academic Publishing

Cover image copyright© Depositphotos/photographee.eu.

Printed in the United States of America.

ISBN: 978-1-5165-2521-8 (pbk) / 978-1-5165-2522-5 (br)

Table of Contents

The Editor's Note

The editor is indebted to her family for their support in every step of her life. The editor would also like to thank the Cognella publishing team for extending their support toward publishing an anthology of Social Problems.

The Construction of Social Problems is intended for use in college-level sociology courses. This reader is designed with the understanding that several students enrolled in undergraduate sociology courses are just introducing themselves to the discipline, and is therefore made up of comprehensible readings with simplistic language use, explaining complex sociological concepts and constructs. Following this strategy, my publishing team's and my intentions were to reach out to students of different majors and assist them in developing their sociological understanding of everyday experiences.

We often tend to seek and provide quick-fix solutions to our problematic experiences. In most cases, the nature of these quick-fixes requires instinct-based answers that we settle for as the ultimate resolution. Social problems, on the other hand, claim exception to this rule and speak to the natural tendency of cultivating a sociological frame of reference that is collective in nature. The collective claim is far-reaching, and formulated when we attempt to move away from an individual's pain to a groups' consensus over the pain, which ultimately leads to a collective outcry over the issue. The shift from individual to group consciousness makes the problem at hand social in nature.

The *Construction of Social Problems* anthology is compiled using assorted readings, with the intention of creatively, concisely, and comprehensively captured the social constructionist dimension of social problems. The readings explore perspectives expanding from individuals to groups, as well as from local to global measures.

Sociologist Joel Best (2016) has rightly said that constructionists' view of social problems is aptly explained by social problems process, hence featuring the dynamic embodiment of social problems. The dynamic representation of social problems, which is manifested through a process, is appropriated by collective experiences and movement.

Due to its focus on social constructionism, the anthology develops itself through the lens of an advocacy framework that forms the introductory chapter of the *Construction of Social Problems*. The Introduction to Social Problems identifies the makeup, cause, and resolution of the problems. The chapter maintains that the final and most sought-after stages of the social problem lie in its outcome, which is the agenda of the advocate group. Without the advocacy-consciousness, social problems would neither be social nor have the potential to be acknowledged as a problem. The interest groups frame the primary focus of this anthology; hence, the remaining chapters carry the undertone of the advocacy framework, acknowledging the social problems at hand. The critical examination of the construction process of social problems builds and foreshows the course of social action.

The rest of the book discusses various topics and explains how some major life trajectories are socially constructed to become a problem. Accordingly, chapter three addresses how class or economic conditions are constructed as socially developed problems by separating economic inequality into income and wealth. The essay indicates that wealth is a better measure of inequality.

The chapters following the discussion of economic health present social construction of race, ethnicity, and gender. The other topical areas include health and human behavior.

Within human behavior, discussion of drug and gun use (with the understanding that gun violence also implies possessing or owning a gun) are given special emphasis because of their overwhelming public concerns. Because of the deviant connotations, active debate and controversies associated with these issues, the selection of drug and gun use are important topical areas contextualizing social problems. Additionally, each of the phenomena have been widely recognized due to their criminal nature, which means going over and beyond our discomforts. While drug use has filled up our jail system, gun use has contributed to discontent killings by public gunmen. In the current sociopolitical climate, the use of guns has become a common practice, whereby gun possessors spill out emotional discontent. Nonetheless, as paradoxical as it can be, gun violence and "human rights" issues, in the context of gun ownership, continue to exist as inseparables. The common factor across drugs and guns is that they both potentially target the school system; hence, young citizens of the nation experience unforeseen death. Due to the issue's gravity, both drug and gun use have been called into public action.

The last two chapters focus on the ways that social problems should be addressed to ensure a safety net is developed through the collective claim of the justice system. The final chapter advances the most required and essential ingredients in organizing a mass movement. We expect that students will find these critical and analytical discussions interesting and engaging.

WHAT IS A SOCIAL PROBLEM?

SARA TOWE HORSFALL

⠿ SIX INGREDIENTS OF SOCIAL PROBLEMS

Everyone notices things in the world that need to be improved. But a social problem is more than a personal opinion about something. It has social components. For instance, those affected by a social problem will be a group (collectivity or category), not just one or two people. Also, a social problem is recognized as a problem by a group of people who feel strongly enough to take steps toward change.

Put another way, if people are suffering but no one recognizes it, there is no social problem. It becomes a social problem only when people agree that something is wrong and organize themselves to resolve it. That doesn't mean that people aren't suffering if no one recognizes it. But it does mean that their suffering hasn't filtered into social consciousness, so no one is willing to stop it.

Even those who are suffering may not consider their situation to be a social problem. They may conclude that it is due to their own failing—sin, lack of ability, bad luck, and so on. They may not be aware anyone else is suffering as they are. Or they may be resigned to their fate, believing that the effort to change things is too great and that no one cares about them. But what is defined as a social problem changes over time. Things that are not recognized as social problems today may be considered problems in the future. Recognizing something as a problem is the first step in the social change process.

How can it be that something is not a social problem if no one recognizes it? Consider child abuse. There is evidence that large numbers of children were battered in the eighteenth century and earlier. Yet it was not until the twentieth century that child abuse became a public issue. In 1962 a medical journal published a report by a pediatric radiologist stating that multiple injuries at different stages of healing indicate abuse. Almost immediately professional organizations began to campaign, and twelve years later legislation outlawing child abuse was passed (Kadushin and Martin 1980; Pfohl 1977). Today child abuse is a public issue addressed by social agencies and law enforcement.

Sociologists believe that we create society. We organize ourselves, establish the rules and regulations necessary to make things work, and collectively identify goals. An early sociologist, Emile Durkheim, said that these social norms are as important as, or more important than, instinct. These consensual beliefs tell us what to do and guide our daily lives. Collective recognition and resolution of social problems is part of that creative social process.

To understand the process of defining and resolving issues, we need to know the six ingredients of social problems. First, there are those who are suffering. This is the *target group*: a collection of individuals who are treated unfairly, don't get their fair share of social and/or material resources, or face serious threats to their well-being. In short, their personal well-being (life chances, e.g., satisfaction or emotional happiness) or their social well-being (equality, representation, and other social situations) is threatened. People in the target group may not know each other, so it is more correct to call them a target category or collectivity. For simplicity's sake, I use the term *target group* to mean collectivity, category, or group.

The second ingredient is the *adverse social situation* that affects the target group. It can be changed by human effort and probably has a human or social cause. A physical disaster—a tornado or a tsunami—is not in itself a social problem but can quickly develop into one. The tsunami in Southeast Asia in 2004 created many social problems. In the immediate aftermath, large numbers of people needed food, shelter, and medical assistance. Others suffered long-term needs, such as children without parents, unemployed persons, and persons unable to locate their relatives. These and other problems were addressed by local and international governments (Korf 2007; Tang 2007). Similarly, the 9.0 earthquake that hit Japan in 2011 affected a nuclear power plant. Residents in a nearby farming community were evacuated and, because of high levels of radioactivity, will not be able to return to live there for many years, if ever.

In contrast, several tornados blew through the Fort Worth, Texas, area in 2000 and 2001. There was substantial damage but surprisingly little loss of life (Letchford, Norville, and Bilello 2000). The only real social problem that developed was concern to create a better warning system in the future.

A preventable disaster is almost always a social problem. In 1984 in Bhopal, India, a Union Carbide pesticide factory leaked forty tons of methyl isocyanate gas into the air, killing an estimated 4,000 people, many of whom lived in makeshift houses next to the power plant.[1] There had been little public recognition of the danger to these people before the disaster. Afterward, individuals, groups, and governments debated the risks of dangerous engineering defects and human error in such factories (Perrow 1984; Jasanoff 1994; Hatvalne 2010). The original event was only one part of the problem. There was also concern about the potential for future leaks and the suffering they would cause.

The third ingredient is the group of people who recognize a social problem: the *advocate group*. These individuals are motivated for different reasons, including self-interest, altruism, and idealism. If their own social or physical well-being is threatened, they are heavily invested in the solution. Or they may be moved by the suffering of others. Or they may believe that something about the situation is wrong or sinful and needs to be changed because it offends their belief system. Whatever the reason, they decide that the target group's situation should be changed. They organize themselves to bring the issue into the public arena for discussion and action. They become claims makers (more about that later).

The fourth ingredient of a social problem is the *ameliorating action*—the proposed change—and the fifth ingredient is the *action group*—the group that puts the proposed change into effect.[2] After the Fort Worth tornado in 2000, neighborhood groups (advocate groups) complained that the warning sirens were not sufficient. The complaints were persistent enough and numerous enough that the city governments (action groups) in the surrounding communities took

---

1. Subsequently 11,000 more died from aftereffects of the substance. According to the Indian government some 500,000 people were affected, including thousands of babies born with defects. In June 2010, seven former employees were convicted by an Indian court for their role in the incident.

2. Again, the terminology of "group" is not strictly correct here. The action group is usually an organization or an institution. But for simplicity's sake, when the term *action group* is used, it will mean group, organization, institution, or collectivity—whichever is appropriate.

action. The sirens were tested and upgraded, and in some cases new ones were installed (ameliorating action).

A sixth ingredient is a *will to act* to solve the social problem. Social problems often arise because people find it easier not to act. There is usually a cost attached to the action—if not a monetary cost, then a cost in personal effort or sacrifice of personal interest. To bring change, people must be willing to bear the cost. Replacing the warning sirens was relatively inexpensive, and the will to act was sufficient. Within a few weeks they were replaced or repaired. But in the case of the fertilizer factory in Bhopal, India, there was less will to act. One question that arose was, Who is responsible? When no group or agency is willing to take responsibility or has the necessary resources, the will to act falls to the government.

In sum, then, the six ingredients of a social problem are (1) an advocate group that identifies the problem, (2) an adverse social situation, (3) a victim or target group or target category, (4) an ameliorating action, (5) an action group (organization or institution), and (6) the will to act. Subsequently we can define a social problem as *a situation judged by an advocate group to be adversely affecting the personal or social well-being of a target group (or collectivity) to the extent that it needs to be redressed by means of an ameliorating action to be taken by an action group/organization or institution.* An action group will take such action once there is sufficient will to act.

▪▪ HOW DO SOCIAL PROBLEMS OCCUR?

Looking to the cause, it is easy to blame social problems on people who are irresponsible, selfish, immoral, or deviant in some way—the "nuts, sluts, and perverts" (Liazos 1972). This is the tendency to blame the powerless. Legal offenders are often held to blame. Although innocent people are sometimes convicted, offenders in the criminal justice system are generally assumed to be guilty. And crime is one of the most prominent and important social problems.[3]

---

3. The Innocence Project is an organization of lawyers, students, and others who work to assist prisoners who can be proven innocent by means not available at the time of sentencing—DNA testing. Since 1992, a total of 242 people, who served an average of twelve years in prison, have been exonerated and released. For more information, go to www.innocenceproject.org.

But criminal activity is only one of many causes. Social problems arise because a society is developing or there is general ignorance of a particular situation. Some social problems arise because people pursue their own self-interest at the expense of others. Or there are competing interests. Serious social problems are associated with racism and group discrimination. There are unresolved problems whenever there is a long history of enmity and conflict between groups. This list of causes is not exhaustive, but it is diverse enough to be representative. We will examine each of these possible causes separately.

Development

Chudacoff and Smith's (2000) fascinating account of U.S. urban growth at the turn of the last century highlights problems caused by *development.* Fear of disease (unprotected water supplies were becoming contaminated by seepage from privies and graves) and fear of fire spurred city officials to protect public water supplies. Congestion and dangerous transportation issues in nineteenth-century cities led to complaints that drivers were intentionally reckless; thus traffic regulations and fines were devised for everyone's safety and comfort. Creative solutions to these and other social problems led to the development of the modern urban infrastructure, and the early twentieth century saw "the highest standards of mass urban living in the world" (Chudacoff and Smith 2000, 136, 87, 50). Sometimes developmental problems persist, indicating the existence of factors that erode the social will, such as lack of resources, an inadequate infrastructure, or an insufficient political structure.

Technological advances also bring problems. They create new conditions and issues not addressed by existing regulations or conventions. The rapid and amorphous growth of computers and the Internet during the late twentieth century illustrates this point. Issues of censorship and control are still being discussed—nationally and worldwide.

Aftermath of a Natural Event

A very different kind of social problem comes after a *natural event.* Hurricane Katrina in 2005 was one of the worst natural disasters to hit the United States during the twentieth century. Half a million people were evacuated, 1,600 people lost their lives, and more than 1,000 went missing (Kessler et al. 2006). From a social problems perspective, what is of interest is the way people organize themselves to respond to the possibility of disaster and the human needs arising from it. In the case of Katrina, the most publicized situation involved the low-income, primarily black residents who survived the hurricane but lacked food and shelter (Brodie et al. 2006). Many groups responded with assistance, including the local police, firemen, and Coast Guard, as well as federal agencies—FEMA (Federal Emergency Management Agency) and the Department of Homeland Security. A host of church groups, nonprofits such as the Red Cross, local organizations, and individuals in other cities also helped with shelter, basic necessities, and financial assistance during the subsequent evacuation.

The immediate outpouring of assistance was followed by several years of effort to rebuild the neighborhoods, the city, and the lives of those affected: home owners (Elliott and Pais 2006), those with increased mental health issues (Kessler et al. 2006), those who lost confidence in government officials, especially regarding issues surrounding waste disposal (Allen 2007). Other concerns focused on how the public was informed about environmental and public health threats, as well as preparedness at the local, state, and federal levels (Frickel and Vincent 2007).

Inequality

The most prominent *inequality* is poverty, which affects close to 13 percent of the U.S. population. People who are poor suffer from a lack of basic necessities and from their relationships within the social structure (Myers-Lipton 2006). Minorities are disproportionately affected by poverty and often have reduced access to social resources because of discrimination.[4] Personal, societal, and structural factors are compounded by the underlying ideological beliefs that perpetuate the inequality. A minority child from a low-income family is less likely to attend college or university than a nonminority child from a wealthy family—even if he or she has the intelligence to succeed academically.

---

4. According to the U.S. Census Bureau, 8.3 percent of non-Hispanic whites lived in poverty, as compared with 24.9 percent of African Americans, 24.7 percent of American Indians, and 21.8 percent of Hispanics.

Sociologists call this *stratification*—organization of people according to differential access to resources and the consequent social positions in society. Problems associated with stratification have to do with health care, high rates of drug abuse, high crime areas, educational issues, political representation, and many others (Myers-Lipton 2006).

Self-interest

Self-interest is a major reason that stratification develops in the first place, and an important source of other social problems. The problem is that economic theories today stress self-interest and commonly assume that "individuals in a society always act according to their self-interest or private economic incentive" (Sen 1977). Rational choice theories used by social scientists and economists also assume self-interest. This view of human nature became acceptable around the time of the Industrial Revolution, when rational self-interest for men in the business world was legitimized. The eighteenth-century doctrine of "separate spheres" had women as keepers of religion and morality, whereas men managed the political, legal, and economic affairs outside the home (Coontz 2005). These two sets of values—the moral, "feminine" values inside the home and the rational, self-oriented "masculine" values outside the home—are in conflict. The popular character Tom Sawyer highlights this discrepancy.

> The late 19th century cliché of the mischievous boy was, like the sentimentalization of women and children, an attempt to deal with one aspect of the era's central discomfiture. The very attributes that would make a man occupationally successful were unwelcome in the domestic environment of his own creation. In a situation of conflict, especially when resolution is not forthcoming, a common human response is to try to laugh; hence the mischievous boy and his exasperated female "superior." The image allowed just enough caricature of the rule-breaker and the rule maker to afford the populace a laugh, but few, it appears, truly understood the joke. The final effect of this phenomenon was perhaps its most subversive: the perception of boys' mischievous antics as masculine behavior invited reversal, so that immature or illicit activities of men could, in time, be construed as mischief that is natural and harmless. (Heininger 1984, 27–28)

Self-interest is widespread. It is the norm in a for-profit business world. There is nothing natural or harmless about the activities of senior officials at the Enron Corporation, who created a network of offshore companies to make the company look more profitable than it actually was. After the company collapsed, it became apparent who benefited at the expense of shareholders, employees, pensioners, customers, and suppliers. Even though it is generally accepted that top executives work to perpetuate their own interests (Egeberg 1995), there was an outcry about the actions of Enron officials who became a "visible symbol of the dangers of excessive self-interest" (Finkelstein et al. 2008). Dangerous self-interest, *greed* to Marxists, is a major reason for Marxist opposition to the capitalist system (Walker 2008).

Racism and Discrimination

Racism is the belief that people with different biological traits (e.g., skin color) have different social value. Discrimination is the differential treatment of categories of people. *Racism and discrimination* involve both personal and group self-interest in noncommercial areas. After the U.S. Civil War, the South was associated with white supremacy—local residents believed that theirs was and should be a "white man's country." Fears that the newly freed slaves would upset the balance of political power were supported by theories of scientific racism and "survival of the fittest" Social Darwinism—ideas popular in the late nineteenth century.[5] When Northerners did not react to court decisions that denied protection to blacks (between 1873 and 1898), disaffected Southerners pursued their own ends (McMillen 1990). The so-called Jim Crow laws created a segregated society, depriving African Americans of the right to vote (unless they owned property), the right to be educated in the same schools as whites, and free access to public facilities. Enforcement of the Jim Crow laws was supported by an atmosphere of fear created by lynching.

---

5. Ideology contributes to racism and discrimination. Nineteenth-century eugenicists concluded that Caucasians (in particular Caucasian males, since females weren't included in the top rank) were the most developed of all the races. In *Mismeasure of Man* Stephen J. Gould documents the bias in their "scientific" studies of intelligence used to support their theories. A less obvious ideology of racism today is the common impression that Hispanic children are less likely to do well at school than white children.

Let's analyze this situation using the social problems theory presented here. Disaffected whites in the South after the Civil War considered themselves victims. In their eyes, they were the *target group*. The *adverse situation* they faced was the loss of their way of life, as well as social and political power, to people who had once been their social inferiors. During Reconstruction, in addition to having the right to vote, 2,000 blacks served in federal, state, and local offices (Foner 1993). A racist *advocate group*, the Ku Klux Klan, was formed in Pulaski, Tennessee, in 1866 to oppose the social and political changes (Martinez 2007). It soon spread to other states.

> Fear convinces Klansmen that others, somehow different from them, have negatively affected their lives. They yearn for halcyon days when no one questioned their unbridled authority. Anything or anybody challenging the status quo threatens the established order, and threats must be handled through extra legal means, if necessary. (Martinez 2007, x)

As Martinez noted, the *ameliorating action* of the KKK was to handle the threat by any means that worked. The Jim Crow laws were intended to restrict the social and political power of southern blacks and keep them disadvantaged. Fear was a means of preventing blacks from reasserting themselves. The white supremacists' *will to act* came from the political threat and economic competition they felt from African Americans and fueled their desire to maintain caste boundaries (Beck and Tolnay 1990).

The KKK is uniquely a *target group* (according to its own assessment), an *advocate group,* and an *action group*—all at the same time. They saw themselves as the victim. They worked to draw attention to their situation among others in the South and worked out a solution themselves, rather than turn to the government to resolve the issue. From their point of view, they were successful—at least for a while.

From an African American point of view—and from the view of most people today—the actions of those associated with the KKK created a segregated society that was not legally redressed until the 1960s. It took that length of time for another *advocate group* (or movement, as it turned out) to form and to develop the *will to act* on a national scale. We will revisit this problem later in the section on opposition groups.

Stratification problems (stemming from inequality or discrimination) created by self-interest usually require government intervention, since those in power do not easily give up their position of advantage. Whether they are forced to reevaluate the situation by law or they choose to do so of their own free will, the concerned parties in power often lack a global perspective of the issue. Putting their own well-being on the same level as the other parties involved is one part of a solution. This usually requires relinquishing resources, potential resources, position, or prestige.

Competing Interests

Competing interests may technically be self-interest on a group level but can have other dimensions as well. Territorial claims are an important aspect of political interests, especially when natural resources such as water, energy, and minerals, geostrategic claims, and/or control of a population within territorial boundaries are at stake (Diehl 1999).

Competing territorial claims lie at the core of the Arab-Israeli conflict. In the late nineteenth century, Jews from Russia and eastern Europe began to conceive of the idea of a Jewish homeland to resolve their centuries-long existence as an oppressed minority scattered through many different countries (the diaspora). They began purchasing land in the Middle East—land that they thought, perhaps erroneously, was more or less unoccupied. Their secret intention was to become so numerous in the area that they could eventually claim the country as theirs. The conflict, then, came not from misunderstanding, but from the "conflicting interests and goals of the two populations. The Arabs sought instinctively to retain the Arab and Muslim character of the region and to maintain their position as the rightful inhabitants; the Zionists sought radically to change the status quo, buy as much land as possible, settle on it, and eventually turn an Arab populated country into a Jewish homeland" (Morris 2001, 49). The Jewish people received support from western forces in the region, and ultimately the modern state of Israel was born.

From a social problems perspective, Jewish and Arab *advocate group*s differ in terms of who is the victim. They propose different solutions that involve different organizations or countries to be part of the solution. In short, there are two different social problems here rather than one. Of course, most of us see it as one issue—not two. Part of the difficulty in resolving the conflict is agreeing on who is the victim, and why, and subsequently what kind of action should be taken, by whom.

Northern Ireland is another example of competing claims. Historically the roots of the problem go back to the sixteenth and seventeenth centuries, when Britain sought to reassert its control over Ireland by sending officers, soldiers, administrators, and clergy to settle and establish the country as a self-supporting contributor. The native Catholic population resisted this intrusion. The resulting conflict between the Protestant Unionists and the Catholic Nationalists has continued until today (Ruane and Todd 2000).

Yet another example of competing claims is Cyprus, where Turkish Cypriots and Greek Cypriots claim dominance of the island. The result is that the 3,571-square-mile island (approximately 40 miles across) has been divided since 1974. In 1983 the northern 1,300 square miles became the Turkish Republic of Northern Cyprus, whereas the southern part of the island is the Greek Cypriot Republic of Cyprus. A thin green line crosses the island and divides the capitol of Nicosia and has been patrolled by UN forces since 1964.

History of Enmity and Conflict

Sometimes problems between two peoples continue long after the specific issues have been resolved. Once people have been killed, the grief of the families and friends deepens hostility to the point where even the mention of the other side stirs up animosity and suspicion. After years of conflict in the Middle East, this is true for many Jews and Arabs. It has also been true in Northern Ireland, where there has been enmity between the two sides for hundreds of years— although currently there have been several years of relative peace. It was true in Cyprus, although happily here too the situation has vastly improved.

But there are other places where a history of enmity and conflict has not been resolved. As the former Yugoslavia was breaking apart in the 1990s, Serbs, Kosovar Albanians, Croats, and Bosnian Muslims "each claimed to be defending themselves against annihilation" (MacDonald 2002, 2). Yet a century earlier, they had worked together to form the Kingdom of Serbs, Croats, and Slovenes. They were rebelling against the centuries of domination by the Byzantines, the Ottomans, and the Hapsburg Empire. And in modern times the domination continued. The Germans occupied the area during World War II, and then the communist state of Yugoslavia was formed. The Balkan saying that behind every hero stands a traitor is understandable considering the area's history. Today there are separate countries of Croatia, Slovenia, Republic of Macedonia, Bosnia and Herzegovina, Serbia, Montenegro, and Kosovo. Some conclude that the enmity between the different peoples during the 1990s was a strategy to establish independence (MacDonald 2002). Such claims only highlight the complexities involved in resolving this kind of problem.

Yet another area of historic conflict is in Rwanda, where the Tutsi and Hutu have fought each other for many years. In 1994 an estimated 800,000 Tutsis and moderate Hutus were killed by the Hutus in power, in what is now called *genocide* (BBC 2008). One version of this story was told in the movie *Hotel Rwanda*.

Ignorance

Sometimes problems develop because of *ignorance*. When severe acute respiratory syndrome (SARS) developed in Hong Kong at the end of 2003, it was a new disease. The means of transmission was unknown, and there was no known cure; the reported death rate was 10 percent (Ap 2003; Tam et al. 2004). The epidemic highlighted the importance of understanding health factors among the population (Loh et al. 2004).

Similarly, few people realized the cause of AIDS when it appeared, or its serious consequences. In the early 1980s, when the public and medical professionals were largely silent about the disease, an estimated 100,000 to 300,000 persons on five continents became infected (Mann 1990). The disease continues to spread in countries such as India, where up to 30 percent of those exposed have never heard of it (Chatterjee 1999). As U.S. medical professionals learned more about the disease, the information was disseminated throughout the population, giving individuals an opportunity to take precautions and reduce its spread.

In sum, common causes of social problems include development, natural disasters, inequality, self-interest, racism and discrimination, competing interests, history of enmity and conflict, and ignorance. Social problems are difficulties that need to be "taken care of," or irritations that need our attention, to be fixed as quickly as possible. Social problems also offer an opportunity to improve our collective social life. They highlight areas that need to be addressed, expanded, and developed. They point to areas that require new and imaginative thinking to create adequate structures, regulations, and governance for the well-being of everyone. They are frequently a sign of healthy growth rather than something to hide and be embarrassed about. They always lead to change, and because people frequently resist change, solutions are not always welcomed or sought out. But in the end, addressing social problems today can help shape the world that we live in tomorrow. The better the solutions, the better tomorrow's world.

LEVELS OF SOCIAL PROBLEMS

When analyzing social problems, we need to identify the level of the problem. This is determined primarily by the target group and the action group. Are the people in the target group from one place, or are they scattered across the country or the world? Is the action group (institution or government) local, state, national, or international? In general, widespread problems require more coordination among institutions, agencies, and governments.

A *local level* social problem will fall primarily to local authorities. Several communities may have similar problems, but each resolves its own situation. For instance, consider the problem that developed after the Fort Worth tornado in 2000. The Bank One building, a popular landmark, was effectively destroyed. This was a social problem because it occupied a complete city block in the middle of the downtown area and sat virtually empty for close to five years, raising concerns of safety, crime, and ambiance. Asbestos was discovered, which made rebuilding expensive. For two years, owners, developers, city and state officials argued. The only business that reoccupied the building was a popular restaurant on the top floor, which was forced to relocate when the building was to be imploded. Implosion was finally abandoned due to safety fears and associated costs. Three years after the tornado, concerned parties finally agreed to redevelop the building into residences, retail spaces, and public parking. Two years later the first residents moved in (Whiteley 2002; Metrocode 2009).

Other cities have faced similar problems after natural disasters. Local authorities assess the issues and resolve them—and perhaps consult others with similar issues.

State level problems fall under the jurisdiction of state authorities. States that have similar problems do not necessarily address them in the same way.

For example, the Amish live in religious communities separated from others. Because of their preference for horse-drawn buggies instead of cars, they present a special challenge. Their simple lifestyle puts them at risk of fatal accidents on the highways (NBC4i 2009). Since close to 80 percent of the Amish live in Ohio, Pennsylvania, and Indiana, this problem is addressed by those states but is not of concern elsewhere.

Sometimes it is not clear which authority should address a problem. Illegal immigration, for instance, is a federal issue (although a 1996 bill allowed Immigration and Customs Enforcement, or ICE, to certify state and local law enforcement officers; Carafano and Keith 2006). But people in border communities or states, or in the smaller communities where illegal immigrants settle, feel that the federal government isn't doing a good job.

For instance, in Farmers Branch, a small community in Texas, the Hispanic population has increased to 37 percent in recent years, with illegal immigrants making up a large portion of the increase. This has put a severe strain on public services in the city of only 30,000 residents. City officials passed an ordinance making it an offense to rent to undocumented persons. This was seen as a controversial action in the state and elsewhere in the country.

In 2010, after a local resident was murdered, Arizona farmers living along the Mexican border complained that the flow of illegal immigrants defaces their property and puts them at risk. Claiming that the federal government had neglected "its constitutional duty to secure the border" (CNN 2011), Governor Jan Brewer introduced a bill requiring Arizona police to verify the legal status of anyone they apprehend. The U.S. Justice Department sued, claiming that only it had that authority. The dispute has gained national attention.

At a *national level*, social problems concern all citizens in some way. Federal authorities are involved in attempts at resolution. National level issues include immigration, certain crimes, drugs, moral issues, cultural violence, and wars, such as the war in Iraq.

Sometimes actions taken by state or local level authorities are seen as part of a national identity. This is the case with the death penalty for non–U.S. citizens. Although people in the United States realize that the penalty varies from state to state, others do not. On the other hand, legalizing marijuana and euthanasia has given the Netherlands an interesting international reputation.

Last, there are problems that affect everyone on our planet. Many governments cooperate to resolve these kinds of *international level* problems. Pollution, protection of national resources, trade agreements, terrorism, extradition, and crime are some examples.

INFORMATION AND CLAIMS MAKING

Informed citizens, advocate groups, action groups, and social researchers are all interested in information about social problems. Some professional groups, such as doctors, lawyers, teachers, social workers, and police, address social problems as part of their job, so they regularly collect information about those they serve. Action groups look to these sources and collect their own information in order to carry out the mandate they are given. The data of the federal government, one of the largest action groups (or organization), is a major resource for everyone.

Collecting and analyzing data is a topic in and of itself. There are established procedures to ensure accuracy and reliability.[6] Since most advocate groups use data that has already been collected and analyzed, it is important for us to understand how to evaluate presentations of data by claims makers.

Claims making is the process by which a person (or persons) tries to convince others of the truth and importance of an issue. In terms of social problems, it is an advocate group's efforts to convince the public and government officials (or other action groups, organizations or institutions) that there is a problem and that it needs attention. Advocate groups are the main claims makers, but action groups, social researchers, and, in fact, everyone engages in claims making at some time or another.[7] The researcher needs to know what goes into a claim.

---

6. The main ways that sociologists and other social researchers collect data are surveys, interviews and field research, case studies, and experimentation. Sociologists also use secondary data sources, including government or other known organizations such as GSS, or others, and of course the U.S. Census.

7. Because of the focus of this book, most of the discussion centers on the claims making of advocate groups. Everything that is said about claims making and claims makers can apply to all other claims-making groups or individuals.

Social Construction and Bracketing

The first step in evaluating a claim is to understand the advocate group's reality or worldview. Everyone sees things differently, and consequently one group's solution can be another group's problem (the KKK example above). Different worldviews are possible because we, together with our friends, determine what is important and real. This is what sociologists call *social construction*—arranging the factors of one's experience into a coherent worldview. If we can understand what members of an advocate group have experienced, we will better understand their worldview. But to truly understand another worldview, researchers must set aside their own beliefs and political views and examine values, beliefs, and threats without judgment.

Setting aside one's own ideas does not mean embracing another view. Nor does it imply carelessness with details. But it does allow enough space to look carefully at the implicit and underlying motivations without dismissing them as silly, irrelevant, or wrong. Judgment is reserved for a later time. This method of setting aside one's own ideas of reality to study another reality is called "bracketing."

Once the researcher understands the group's worldview, he or she will be able to appreciate its proposed action. In some ways, the W. I. Thomas theorem is relevant here: if you think that something is real, it will be real in its consequences. The social researcher does not have to believe in the same reality as the advocate group in order to study and understand it.

A UFO study illustrates the usefulness of this approach. The researcher was not interested in whether UFOs are real or not. But he was very interested in how a belief in UFOs affects someone's actions and attitudes. The social researcher "bracketed" his own beliefs so that he could understand, without judgment, the worldview of someone who does believe in UFOs.

Approaching scientific studies in this way has become more common in recent years. Even the most objective scientists have come to accept that it is not possible to be completely objective, since everyone is influenced by his or her own worldview.

If the issue is one that the social researchers feel strongly about, it may be appropriate at a certain point for them to inform others that they are switching from the role of a social researcher to that of a claims maker. Researchers should realize that by taking on the role of a claims maker, they forfeit some authority and their claims will be evaluated along with all the others.

Author Bias

The second step in evaluating a claim is to look for *author bias*—a distorted or misleading interpretation of the information of which the author may or may not be aware. Many advocate groups have well-known positions or political affiliations, which are reflected in the language and arguments of their claims. But knowing they have a position doesn't necessarily mean that their claim is distorted or misleading.

If the position of an advocate group is not known, the researcher should ask a series of questions about the presentation of information. Has the situation been overstated? Can known positions be recognized in the argument? What experiences in the author's background led to this view? What does the author hope to achieve from presenting this information? How does this view compare to what others think on this subject? Sometimes the author wants nothing more than to inform the reader. But at other times the author clearly wants to motivate the reader to act in a particular way. Perhaps the author wants to persuade the reader to his own worldview. Or perhaps the author wants the reader to be more sympathetic to an unpopular cause.

There is nothing wrong with listening to all sides of an issue. The conscientious researcher should understand the reasons why people have different worldviews and their interpretation of the facts. In some respects, no truly "objective" viewpoint exists. Each person looks at the world from his or her own perspective and will present facts and arguments accordingly or risk being viewed as insincere or incoherent. The researcher might even find it valuable to "walk in the shoes" of the other person—look at the situation from that perspective, in order to better understand the viewpoint being presented. ("Walking in the shoes of the other" is an opportunity to understand what the social construction process is about.)

The researcher needs to be wary of the author who, in an attempt to win over the reader, is guilty of distorting the facts or presenting the arguments in a misleading way.

If the information appears evenhanded, the researcher might want to look for other signs of a claims maker's intentions. Are there any indications of affiliation to a group or category that has a known position? Certain organizations that are referred to repeatedly may offer a clue. An article on evolution that refers to a fundamentalist Christian organization would be suspect, since most fundamentalist Christians oppose Darwinian evolution.

Identifying who published the article might give another clue. An article on science in the public school system published by the American Association for the Advancement of Science (AAAS) is likely to promote a different view than one published by the American Baptist Association (ABA). Ideally, the two sources would agree on essential points. Failing that, the researcher should weigh the data and arguments of the respective organizations while being alert to potential bias.

The social researcher should not be fooled by reputation. Just because a group has a well-known position doesn't mean it is always unreliable. For instance, one might expect a certain bias when a religious organization reports the news. But despite its religious affiliation, the *Christian Science Monitor* has been highly respected for a hundred years.

On the other hand, advocate group members who are well respected may be biased. Persons with a reputation for accuracy may nonetheless mistake their point of view for objectivity. This is apparently the case with the respected scientists Isaac Asimov, Carl Sagan, and Paul Kurtz, who cofounded the Committee for the Scientific Investigation of Claims of the Paranormal.[8] The group claims to "promote scientific inquiry" when "examining controversial and extraordinary claims." But an examination of these men's views reveals they discount the reality of spiritual phenomena.[9] Hence anyone reading articles in their publication, the *Skeptical Inquirer*, should beware of an antispiritual bias.

8. Changed to Committee for Skeptical Inquiry, or CSI in 2006. www.csicop.org.
9. Paul Kurtz is professor emeritus of both the CSI organization and the Council for Secular Humanism. A statement from the latter organization reads: "We are generally skeptical about supernatural claims. We recognize the importance of religious experience; we deny, however, that such experiences have anything to do with the supernatural. We have found no convincing evidence that there is a separable 'soul' or that it exists before birth or survives death. We must therefore conclude that the ethical life can be lived without the illusions of immortality or reincarnation."

It is not uncommon for scientists to have a bias against religion or spiritual affairs. After all, there has been a "war" between science and religion for approximately five hundred years (Turrell 2004).

Another example of scientists who are biased against spiritual phenomena occurred more than a century ago. In the mid-1800s, the British Association for the Advancement of Science refused to hear papers on hypnotism or mesmerism, on the basis they were insignificant to scientific research. A few years later the British Royal Society of Science refused to hear a paper on spiritualism by physicist Sir William Crookes on similar grounds (Palfreman 1979; Doyle 1975). These incidents do not reflect the image that most people have of scientists objectively examining the data. Thus we can say that even scientists claiming objectivity are subject to bias. But again, the researcher must be careful not to assume that all scientists have a similar bias.

Last, the researcher should ask if the author has something to gain from the action he or she proposes. If a ketchup manufacturer advertised that its product helped prevent cancer, it obviously stands to benefit from all the people who believe the claim and rush out to buy ketchup to prevent cancer. The claim may be completely false or only partially true (more likely in a sophisticated world). The ketchup company may be using a study that found cooked tomatoes had a particularly healthful effect on participants. But it would be difficult to consume enough ketchup to approximate the required results. Thus the statement that ketchup can help reduce cancer is not technically false, but it is misleading.

Argument Bias

The third step in evaluating a claim is to look for *argument bias*—an attempt to convince by means other than use of data or information. Any argument made by an advocate group publication needs to be examined carefully. The researcher should be on the lookout for arguments that are intended to convince by means other than a careful weighing of the data. How specific is the argument? Does the author give details of the incidents, actions, or persons? Are the details left for the reader to figure out? Look for coherence and appropriateness. Are the claims that the author is making relevant to the question? Does the author stick to the point, going from one aspect to the next? Or does the author throw in a lot of unrelated points to stir the reader's emotions or give the impression of being knowledgeable?

An argument that uses glittering generalities will sound convincing until it is applied to a specific situation. Then the components of the argument break down. Other known tactics that are commonly used to sway someone include name-calling, plain Jane ("I'm just a simple boy"), testimonial, card stacking, bandwagon ("everyone knows"), and lies about the dead ("Before he died . . .").

Data Bias

Evaluating *data bias* in a claim can be difficult, and the researcher should ask the following questions: What data is used to substantiate the claim? Is it verifiable? Do the facts that are presented agree with reports from other reputable sources? Are the statistics exaggerated to make the claim more dramatic? Is there too much data included? Is it up-to-date?

The researcher is like a detective, sorting through all the available evidence, deciding which is credible and which is not, who to believe, and what arguments to take with a grain of salt. The social problems expert should never dismiss a source of information as invalid because the source does not seem reliable. On the other hand, giving an unreliable source undue weight could cause the conclusions to be biased.

It is impossible for sociologists and researchers to personally verify all the data and other information presented by advocate groups, action groups, or anyone making a claim. Most of the time a quick look at the way in which data is presented will reveal a lot about any misuse of data. Beyond that, to check specific claims, the social researcher can compare the advocate group claims with other claims about the same topic. If there is general agreement among the different claims, the data is probably correct.

Think tanks are advocate groups that study social situations and provide the public with reliable information.[10] Some of these groups have a better rep-

---

10. To name just a few: the Brookings Institution, American Enterprise Institute, Urban Institute, Cato Institute, Tellus Institute, Heritage Foundation, American Civil Liberties Union, and Pew Research Center.

utation for accuracy than others and most have a political leaning. It is important to know which sources are reliable. A researcher needs to know where to go for data, and how to verify its accuracy. There are large areas of agreement about data among the best think tanks, regardless of their worldview. If there is a discrepancy that the researcher feels needs to be checked, the most authoritative sources of information are the Census Bureau, or known national survey organizations such as General Social Survey, the Gallup Organization, and the Inter-university Consortium for Political and Social Research (ICPSR). Other government agencies sometimes provide reliable data.

Government agencies are generally careful to collect accurate data, but occasionally there are errors. Other organizations vary in the accuracy of their data and its availability to public inquiry. Sociological studies published in peer-reviewed journals can be taken as authoritative, unless there is a particular reason for questioning the way that the study was done.

Delineating all the ways to check for data bias is beyond the scope of this chapter. But we will consider, briefly, some things to watch for. In general, bias in the data means that a conclusion is not supported as claimed.

Wording

Look for exact meanings of the words and their implications. Scientific presentation of data is as precise as possible. A common mistake, for instance, is mixing up percentages. For instance, "The majority of the students taking the exam scored 80 percent or better" is easily misconstrued as "The majority scored above 80 percent." The word "majority," in this case, refers to the students taking the exam, not the majority of the whole class (or "population"). It is possible that only a small percentage took the exam. In that case, those who scored above 80 percent would be less than half.

Numbers Versus Percentages

Another way statistics are used inappropriately (some say, to "lie" with statistics) is to confuse numbers and percentages. For instance, the percentage of African Americans who live in poverty is higher than the percentage of white Americans who live in poverty, yet by far the majority (in terms of numbers) of those living in poverty are white.

Graphs

Exaggeration in graphic representation is not uncommon. A line going from 15 to 20 will appear more dramatic on a graph with a range of 10 to 25 than on a graph with a range of 0 to 50, particularly if the x axis markers are compressed. Someone reporting on the number of rapes in the United States could claim a dramatic increase using the first graph, while opponents could claim a slight increase using the second graph.

Errors in Conducting Studies

Usually evaluation of data bias will not include examining how a study was done. But occasionally nonscientific studies are given as evidence to support an advocate group claim. It is helpful to be able to recognize this when it happens.

Advocate group reports that cite data from specific studies should include enough information for the reader to find the study or the data. Census data should include the appropriate year and other pertinent information. Journal articles should include the author's name, the publication, and a date. If this information is missing, the data becomes suspect, and the researcher should not rely on it too heavily without verification.

Data that is public knowledge needs no reference. Election of U.S. presidents is a matter of public record, as are notable events such as that of September 11, 2001. At other times the datum is not public record but agrees with known facts; hence, it is believable. If it seems correct, and there is no reason not to trust the data, the researcher may decide to do so until it is discredited.

Additional Things to Watch For

Conceptualization: Did the authors of the study conceptualize the study correctly? Is the concept they claim to have studied really captured in their data? For many years church attendance was used as a measure of religiosity, whereas a person could be very religious and not go to church.

Sample and Generalization: To make generalizations about a larger population, the sample studied must be drawn statistically (randomly). If a researcher uses a convenience sample—stopping the first ten people he sees, for instance—the results tell you nothing beyond those ten people.

Significance: When statistics are used, significance tells the researcher if the results are by chance. The smaller the number, the less likely the results are by chance. However, results can be statistically significant but not substantively significant, meaning the difference is not important. A study comparing grades may find that a difference between 3.15 and 3.14 is highly significant. But how much difference does .01 make? Not much.

Cause Versus Correlation: Most social research only points to correlation. However, correlation is often interpreted as cause. If being hungry and eating is correlated, one is tempted to say feeling hungry causes eating. But what about the times when you visit someone's home and you eat the piece of cake your host offers? In other words, the cause and correlation are not so straightforward as they seemed at first.

CONCLUSION

The concepts in this chapter help clarify what is meant by social problems. Six ingredients help us know what to look for. By identifying the *advocate group* as a minimal public to recognize a social problem, we can track the ebb and flow of particular social problems. Identifying the *action group* and the *will to act* gives us insight into the inner dynamics of the situation. Examining the way in which the advocate group makes its claims and its proposed *ameliorating action* helps us spot other aspects of the problem that are not being addressed.

In the next chapter we will examine patterns of growth and development of advocate groups. Why do people organize themselves? How do they organize? What stages of development lead to successful advocating? What kind of action will a group think is appropriate? What kind of change is the advocate group seeking? To whom will it turn to take action? What motivates the group, and what will motivate others to go along with its proposed action? What are the likely consequences of the proposed action? There are no ready-made answers to these questions. Instead, conclusions will be drawn about each advocate group based on the information presented.

In the following chapters, we will consider specific solutions to particular social problems. Some problems are very complex, with many diverse advocate groups. In each case a summary is included to help sort these out.

Government action is not the only solution, although it is important. Some problems can be addressed with government programs or legislation. Other problems are addressed successfully by nongovernmental programs and actions. There are also educational campaigns and apologies—on the part of government officials or others. And of course there are actions of individuals. It is also important to look at how people react to advocate groups, and the consequences of actions that are taken. Not all consequences are positive or intended.

Later chapters discuss several models of change, drawn from the different assumptions that people have of human nature. In addition to the well-known models of human interaction, there are models having to do with structure, and models that emphasize resources.

It is always good to take a step back and look at the situation from a broader perspective. The social researcher who examines a social problem using these analytical concepts will surely have something worthwhile to contribute to any discussion.

The Social Construction of Social Problems

The Social Construction
of Social Problems

Darin Weinberg

This chapter moves on from the social construction of our external and internal, material and immaterial worlds to consider in depth the contribution social constructionism might make to critical theory—that is, those forms of social thought directly concerned not only with understanding the social world but also with critiquing it in the interest of progressive social change. It does so through an examination of the social construction of social problems. As is well known, John Kitsuse played a prominent and indispensable role in both founding and advancing the social constructionist approach to social problems. He did so in explicit opposition to structural functionalist approaches to theorizing social problems (Schneider 1985b; Spector and Kitsuse 2001). Whereas functionalist theorists have tended to regard social problems more or less as Durkheimian social facts that occur independently of the ways in which they are perceived by members of society, Kitsuse insisted that social problems cannot be separated from the perceptions and practical activities undertaken by members of the social worlds menaced by those problems. In observing that the very reality of social problems depends on how they are perceived and managed by members of historically and culturally specific constituencies, Kitsuse brought social problems research to an unprecedented level of epistemological depth and subtlety. Furthermore, through the use of constructionist insights, he and his social constructionist students and colleagues have illuminated an extensive domain of hitherto unexplored directions for sociological research. For example, constructionist theory has enabled social problems researchers to examine more effectively the social processes through which phenomena are construed as problematic, through which they are constituted as public rather than private problems, and through which prospective remedies for them are socially produced, implemented, evaluated, revised, combined, replaced, forgotten, and so on.

In each of these ways, constructionists have taken important theoretical strides beyond the limitations that had attended prior approaches to theorizing social problems. Attention to what Spector and Kitsuse (2001) once called the "subjective component" of social problems production and amelioration has indeed yielded a vast catalogue of empirical studies that demonstrate how social problems as various as AIDS (Epstein 1996), alcoholism (Schneider 1978; Wiener 1981), battered women (Loseke 1992), child abuse (Pfohl 1977), hate crimes (Jenness 1995), infertility (Scritchfield 1995), and stalking (Lowney and Best 1995), to name just a handful, acquired their characteristic features as problematic phenomena and as problematic phenomena worthy of particular types of public consideration and concern. But beyond demonstrating that by their very existence social problems entail the exercise and promotion of historically and culturally specific judgments that are themselves appropriate topics of empirical research, Kitsuse also proffered a still more radical claim, an ontological claim, regarding the relationship between the practices through which people construct social problems as meaningful phenomena and the worldly reality and repercussions of the problems so constructed.

In their classic formulation of the constructionist position, Spector and Kitsuse (2001, 76) admonished social problems researchers to studiously disattend whatever objective conditions claims makers presumed their activities to concern in favor of attending exclusively to the claims-making activities of those who propound or contest the nature of alleged social problems. This methodological advice deflected analytic attention away from how putatively problematic conditions, once assembled as meaningful objects of discourse and practice, might become dialectically related to the discursive claims made about them (Weinberg 1997, 2005). It thereby inaugurated a tradition in constructionist analysis of rendering the ostensive objects of claims-making activities *entirely* epiphenomenal to claims-making activities. Since the 1970s, a good deal of ink has been spilled in efforts to resolve the proper relationship of putatively objective conditions to constructionist analyses. While some argue for a "strict" constructionism that attends exclusively to claims-making activities and insists on their "symbol and language bound character" (Ibarra and Kitsuse 1993, 31), others advise a more tempered, "contextual" constructionism wherein the analyst might go beyond our research subjects' discursive claims to address the worldly practical circumstances that occasion those claims (Best 1993; Gubrium 1993; Holstein and Miller 1993). Advocates of both positions emphasize the importance of studying the activities by which people construct social problems, but a stable consensus has not yet been achieved as to whether putatively objective conditions might be legitimately invoked to understand and explain those activities.

In this chapter, I trace a brief genealogy of the debate Kitsuse inaugurated over objectivism in constructionist social problems theorizing and propose a solution to the dilemmas to which this debate has given rise. The proposed solution draws from post-foundationalist philosophers, sociologists, and historians of science who have radically reformulated the nature of empirical research such that the antinomy between subjectivism and objectivism is largely dissolved and the conceptual chasm between interpretive understanding and causal explanation is all but eliminated. Building on this literature, I describe and defend a middle road between Kitsusian constructionists' principled denials of any causal relationship between claims-making activities and the conditions those activities presumably concern and the theoretically moribund brands of objectivism that Kitsuse and his constructionist colleagues have been properly concerned to overcome.

On the Irrelevance of Putative Conditions

Building on Kitsuse's earlier work in the sociology of deviance (see Holstein 2009), Spector and Kitsuse (2001) galvanized a movement among social problems theorists to develop a thoroughly constructionist approach to the study of social problems. While acknowledging their debt to the earlier work of Fuller and Myers (1941a, 1941b), Blumer (1971), Becker (1966) and others affiliated with the value-conflict and labeling schools, Spector and Kitsuse (2001) were concerned that these researchers had not yet fully abandoned what they viewed as a problematic tendency to privilege certain accounts of social reality over others. This privileging took place when some accounts of a putatively problematic social condition were consecrated as objective while others were regarded as merely subjective. Schneider (1985b, 211) has written in this regard, "Kitsuse and Spector . . . argue that these authors compromised a distinct theory of social problems by their continued attention to objective conditions as a necessary part of the conceptualization." And Spector and Kitsuse (2001, 76) wrote: "We are interested in constructing a theory of claims-making activities, not a theory of conditions. Thus the significance of objective conditions for us is the assertions made about them, not the validity of those assertions as judged from some independent standpoint, as for example that of a scientist. To guard against the tendency to slip back into an analysis of the condition, we assert that even the condition itself is irrelevant to and outside of our analysis."

In place of attention to the conditions claims-making activities are ostensibly about, Spector and Kitsuse (2001) advised attending exclusively to the manner in which claims are formulated, promoted, contested, amended, defeated, or otherwise socially engaged. Social problems analysts were counseled to completely disregard any causal effect objective conditions might be held to exert on claims-making activities in favor of looking to a putative realm of purely symbolic interaction within which all claims making was held to be contained, confined, and, apparently, sealed off from so-called objective causal forces. This recommendation was quite clearly made in the interest of highlighting the enormous amount of strategic work and politicking that is involved in promoting and contesting claims about social problems. It was also intended to remedy what Spector and Kitsuse incisively noted was the disturbingly pervasive tendency of social scientists to uncritically endorse, legitimate, and indeed reify, the verity of accounts proffered of social problems by plainly interested parties. By radically dissociating their own research program from the agendas of those with obvious political, economic, and moral stakes in the outcomes of social problems debates, Spector and Kitsuse seemed to be offering a more scientific tack. Social problems researchers were to forsake the role of intellectual mercenary and stake out a disinterested, purely analytic ground of their own from which to scientifically assess the play of social forces that give rise to the symbolic identities of social problems (Gusfield 1984).

In the wake of Spector and Kitsuse's (2001) seminal contribution, most constructionist social problems theorists came to agree that, in principle, a very wide variety of social actors and actions might influence the symbolic identities of social problems and thus were proper subjects of social problems research. Most also insisted that, as a matter of theoretical principle, no one symbolic rendering of a putative social problem was to be given greater legitimacy than any other. In this way, the ascendance and demise of social problems claims came to be understood solely as products of people's symbolic interactions and perceptions. In other words, the empirical field of constructionist social problems research was strictly circumscribed as follows: *only the symbolic interactions of human individuals or human collectives were given credence as either causes or constitutive features of social problems.* For the purposes of constructionist analysis, the putatively nonsymbolic conditions people claim as problematic were to be understood as nonexistent, wholly irrelevant to, or mere epiphenomena of claims-making practices that are caused and constituted *only* by symbolic interaction.

On Formulating Radically Constructionist Empirical Analyses of Social Problems

For several years before Spector and Kitsuse published *Constructing Social Problems*, they, and a group of like-minded social problems researchers, had already been busy working out the methodological details of rendering radically constructionist empirical analyses of social problems (Conrad 1975; Gusfield 1975; Pfohl 1977; Schneider 1978). Specifically what kinds of data might be used to empirically demonstrate the total irrelevance of putative conditions to claims-making activities regarding them? Specifically how might those data be used to accomplish such empirical demonstrations? These questions posed challenging analytic puzzles for would be constructionists. As David Bloor (1976) famously noted, demonstrations of distance between descriptive activities and the things those descriptions are presumed to describe are usually intended to discredit those descriptive activities. Kitsusian constructionists, though, were not interested in simply debunking certain claims makers they did not find to their liking. They were concerned with devising analytic techniques that might be applied with equal vigor to the analysis of meritorious as well as erroneous claims-making activities. Ultimately, something of a working consensus was, in fact, forged regarding the proper conduct of radically constructionist empirical analyses.

One particular technique emerged during the 1970s to become the preeminent exemplar for radically constructionist empirical analyses of social problems. This analytic technique entailed empirically demonstrating that a condition had remained invariant while claims-making activities regarding it had changed. Thus, for example, in his classic study of the discovery of hyperkinesis, Peter Conrad (1975, 16) writes: "We assume that before the discovery of hyperkinesis this type of deviance was seen as disruptive, disobedient, rebellious, anti-social or deviant behavior. Perhaps the label 'emotionally disturbed' was sometimes used, when it was in vogue in the early sixties, and the child was usually managed in the context of the family or the school or in extreme cases, the child guidance clinic. How then did this constellation of deviant behaviors become a medical disorder?"

In this passage, Conrad refers to a "type of deviance" that earlier was regarded in one way and then, later, came to be regarded otherwise. By textually demonstrating that conditions remained invariant, radically constructionist social problems analysts also rendered them causally inert with respect to their explanations of changing claims-making activities. They thereby justified placing their explanatory focus on other matters (e.g., the clashing and confluence of rhetorical idioms, the practical interests of claims makers and their adversaries, power differentials between claims makers, or the historical and cultural circumstances under which claims are produced and promoted). Thus, as a matter of empirical analysis, it came to appear that if one was willing and able to demonstrate such a schism between claims-making activities and the putative conditions they concerned, even *changes* in the putative conditions that are the topic of claims-making activities could be construed as totally unrelated to changes in claims making regarding them. Spector and Kitsuse's classic theoretical assertion that such changes (if and when they might occur) are "irrelevant to, and outside of" constructionist analyses of claims-making activities thus appeared amenable to effective empirical defense.

Demonstrations that claims-making activities regarding a putatively problematic condition are unrelated to the objective status of that condition have been, and continue to be, invoked throughout the constructionist social problems literature. Thus, for example, in their study of the widespread alarm regarding crack use in the United States, Craig Reinarman and Harry Levine (1997) contrast various public claims made by politicians and news media personnel regarding the gravity of the American crack problem with official statistics regarding the prevalence of crack use and crack related problems in the United States. They show that while public claims making regarding crack is filled with hyperbole and doom saying, official government statistics provide evidence that the American crack problem is far less serious than public claims suggest. By way of this contrast, Reinarman and Levine (1997) make a strong case for finding the causes of public claims primarily in the political interests of claims makers, secondarily in the mass media's appetite for spectacle, and finally (and least significantly) in the objective prevalence of crack-related problems.

Properly accomplished, this type of empirical demonstration is powerful and no doubt will continue as a robust and significant resource in constructionist social problems research. Nonetheless, a nagging theoretical problem hovers over this analytic practice in constructionist studies. In an article that is now justly famous, Steve Woolgar and Dorothy Pawluch (1985) suggested there is an analytic difficulty in empirically demonstrating difference between changes in claims-making activities regarding a putatively problematic condition and changes (or stasis) in the objective status of that condition. If such demonstrations are held up as exemplars for radically social constructionist social problems theory, then they seem to entail espousing both a universal agnosticism regarding the objective existence of any putative conditions and, at the same time, telling how in specific cases the invariance of their manner of objective existence demonstrates their causal irrelevance to the dynamics of claims-making activities. Woolgar and Pawluch (1985) dubbed this analytic technique "ontological gerrymandering" because it appears to employ a strategically selective commitment to both radical constructionism and orthodox objectivism. By ontologically gerrymandering, one privileges one symbolic rendering of a particular condition as objectively superior to other renderings to first distinguish the condition from people's symbolic renderings and activities regarding it and then, ultimately, defend a systematically anti-objectivist theoretical program. Woolgar and Pawluch (1985) argued that such an analytic move is somewhat disingenuous because it requires that one trade on orthodox objectivist claims in particular empirical studies to defend a universal rejection of the legitimacy of objectivism in general social problems theorizing.

Woolgar and Pawluch (1985) sparked a great deal of debate in social problems theory. Disputants, by and large, either have accepted their critique and endeavored to formulate ways to banish ontological gerrymandering from constructionist analysis (Ibarra and Kitsuse 1993) or have argued against Woolgar and Pawluch's assessment of constructionist theorizing and insisted either that the best constructionists are not guilty of ontological gerrymandering (Schneider 1985a) or that ontological gerrymandering does not violate the principles of sound sociological theorizing (Best 1995; Gusfield 1985). For my part, I would like to suggest that despite the enlivened character of debate in constructionist social problems theorizing, we have not yet fully succeeded in emancipating ourselves from the hopelessly untenable forms of naïve objectivism that were the original impetus for constructionist theorizing. While it is surely inadequate to blithely presume the objective characteristics of putative conditions in our accounts of claims-making processes, there remain serious analytic difficulties that continue to attend our efforts as constructionists to ensure that putative conditions remain, in Spector and Kitsuse's (2001) words, "irrelevant to, and outside of" our analyses.

Beyond Ontological Gerrymandering

In probably the best known, and certainly the most theoretically sophisticated, effort to banish ontological gerrymandering from constructionist theorizing regarding the nature of social problems, Peter Ibarra and John Kitsuse (1993) proposed that constructionists make references to their research subjects' *condition categories* in place of the older constructionist convention of referring to the *putative conditions* their discourse and practice are presumed to concern. References to people's condition categories, they argue, highlight more emphatically than did references to putative conditions the fact that it is "they" (as members of the settings we are studying) and not "us" (as analysts) who do the work of realizing the characteristics of the worlds in which they live. This terminology is also meant to underscore another aspect of Ibarra and Kitsuse's (1993) argument. It is meant "to highlight the symbol- and language-bound character of claims-making," and, further, that "the strict constructionist never leaves language" (Ibarra and Kitsuse 1993, 31).

After proposing several revisions to the classic formulations, Ibarra and Kitsuse (1993) go on to advocate a program of constructionist research that includes greater attention to the rhetorical assemblages through which social problems processes occur and the dialogical processes through which claims and counterclaims, rhetoric and counter-rhetoric are played off each other in the social construction of social problems. Theirs is a formulation that grants causal influence over the social problems process to human claimants and counterclaimants, as when they note, "The 'war on drugs' *initiated* under the Reagan and Bush administrations was itself rendered problematic when civil libertarians *cited* the intrusiveness of such measures as drug testing in the work place" (Ibarra and Kitsuse 1993, 42; emphasis added); to rhetorical idioms and counter-rhetoric, as when they note, "Each rhetorical idiom *encourages* participants to structure their claims along particular lines and not others" (Ibarra and Kitsuse 1993, 36; emphasis added); and to social settings, as when they ask, "How do the formal qualities of particular settings *structure* the ways in which claims can be formulated, delivered, and received?" (Ibarra and Kitsuse 1993, 53; emphasis added). In a deliberate effort to avoid ontological gerrymandering, however, they stop short of granting causal influence to the objective sociohistorical conditions under which claims are made. Apparently, Ibarra and Kitsuse are not averse to characterizing agents, assemblages of resources, and social environments or their specific causal influences on the manner in which social problems are constructed. Their effort, however, is to do so without invoking privileged renderings of either social problems themselves or the sociohistorical conditions that influence how people's claims-making activities take place. Although their effort to attend to how people's claims-making activities constitute the meaningful substance of social problems for them—and, above all, to do so without irony—is certainly a laudable one (and one that will surely continue to yield sociological benefits), their effort to do so without objectivist invocations of the sociohistorical contexts of claims-making processes is, in my view, less promising. My difficulty is that I cannot imagine how we might speak to the "agents," "assemblages of resources," and "social environments" in and through which claims-making activities take place such that (at least provisionally) objectivist construals of specific sociohistorical contexts are not inevitably implicated in our accounts.

I therefore cannot help but agree with Joel Best's (1995) suggestion of a more tempered approach to social problems theorizing, one that allows the constructionist to leave language and not only attend to research subjects' communicative action but also to interpret their various other practical activities, how they do them, even why they do them—and to do so by the lights provided by our own social scientific knowledge of their interactional, cultural, and historical contexts. As Best (1993, 141) writes, "The language of claims does not exist independently of the social world; it is a product of—and influence on—that world." James Holstein and Gale Miller (1993, 152) have similarly noted that what they call "social problems work" is intrinsically embedded in the routines of practice constitutive of the organizational settings in which that work is accomplished (see also Holstein and Gubrium 1994). These theorists contend that all activities concerning putatively problematic conditions are embedded in historical, cultural, and interactional contexts that are themselves empirically discoverable, available, and, I would argue, absolutely indispensable for use both by our research subjects and by ourselves (in our own distinctly social scientific efforts) to better understand those activities. But what, if anything, might distinguish our own efforts from the efforts of those who are not social scientists to interpret the link between social contexts and claims making?

How to Think Sociologically

People have always tried to make sense of the world around them. Myths, fables, and religion provided traditional ways of making sense. More recently, science has provided additional ways of understanding the world. Sociology is part of the rise of science as a means of making sense of the world.

As we know in our own time, there can be tension between religious and scientific views. Contemporary disputes over evolution, sexuality, marriage, and even the age of our planet often pit religious values against scientific interpretations. More broadly speaking, both at home and abroad, religious fundamentalisms rest uneasily alongside modern, secular worldviews. These familiar tensions have a history that takes us back to the origins of sociology itself.

SOCIOLOGY AND MODERNITY

The rise of sociology is part of a much larger story about the emergence of the modern world itself. Modernity emerged in European societies through a long process of social change that unfolded from the sixteenth to the nineteenth centuries. During this time, virtually everything about organized social life in Europe was fundamentally transformed. In our day, we speak of globalization as a force that is changing the world in the most basic ways. But current patterns of globalization can be traced back to the rise of modernity itself; in many respects, they are a continuation of the changes that ushered in the modern world.

Economically, modernity transformed most people from peasants to workers in a complex division of labor. Politically, modernity created distinct nation-states with clear boundaries. Technologically, modernity applied scientific knowledge to producing everything from consumer goods to lethal weapons. Demographically, modernity triggered population growth and massive migration from small, familiar, rural communities to large, urban, anonymous cities.

When social worlds change like this, some people benefit while others are harmed. In addition, most people find rapid change and its inevitable conflict to be unsettling, and they seek to understand what is happening. It was this moment that gave rise to sociology. Explaining modernity became sociology's task at the same time that modernity was making sociology possible in the first place.

The link between modernity and sociology was the Enlightenment. This intellectual revolution accompanied other revolutionary changes occurring throughout Europe. In the broadest terms, the Enlightenment challenged religious belief, dogma, and authority. It sought to replace them with scientific reason, logic, and knowledge.

Four basic themes pervaded Enlightenment thought (Zeitlin 1987). First, human reason was the best guide to knowledge, even if it meant that scientific skepticism displaced religious certainty. Second, reason must be paired with careful, scientific observation. Third, Enlightenment thought insisted that social arrangements be rationally justified; if not, they must be changed until they could be rationally defended. Finally, Enlightenment thought assumed that with the systematic application of reason, the perfectibility of people and the progress of society were all but inevitable.

Enlightenment thought contained some potentially fatal flaws. It was a Eurocentric worldview, created by privileged white men, that made universal pronouncements about all people in all times and places. While applauding Europe's progress, it ignored the colonial domination of the rest of the world that provided the labor, goods, and wealth that underwrote that progress. Generalizations about "humanity" meant "males," to the exclusion of women, and pronouncements on the "human race" meant white Europeans, to the exclusion of darker people, who were viewed as subhuman.

The Enlightenment was much more than a justification of imperialism, sexism, and racism, but it could become that as well. More than two centuries later, the jury is still out on whether Enlightenment biases can be overcome and its promises be fulfilled. Some postmodernists see little hope for this to happen. Others, myself included, think that the critical spirit of the Enlightenment can help uproot its biases. The project is already under way as feminists, people of color, and postcolonial writers find their way into contemporary sociological discourses (Lemert 2013).

In its own day, the Enlightenment provoked a "romantic conservative reaction" (Zeitlin 1987) that rejected the elevation of reason and science over faith and tradition. It defended traditional customs, institutions, and ways of life from the new standard of critical reason. The debate between Enlightenment progress and conservative reaction set the agenda for sociology as the social science of modernity. Progress or order? Change or stability? Reason or tradition? Science or religion? Individual or group? Innovation or authority? Such dichotomies framed the subject matter of the new science of sociology.

The classical era of sociology refers to European thinkers whose ideas brought this new discipline to maturity from the late eighteenth to the early twentieth centuries. The very different sociologies of Auguste Comte, Herbert Spencer, Ferdinand Toennies, Karl Marx, Max Weber, Georg Simmel, Emile Durkheim, and others are variations on sociology's main theme: How do we understand modern society? Given these efforts, we might think of sociology as the ongoing effort of human beings to understand the worlds they are simultaneously inheriting from earlier generations and maintaining and transforming for future generations.

This approach has been described as the "sociological imagination." It arises when people realize that they can only know themselves by understanding their historical period and by examining others in the same situation as themselves. We think sociologically when we grasp how our historical moment differs from previous ones and how the situations of various groups of people differ from each other (Mills 1959).

The sociological imagination is guided by three related questions. The first concerns the social structure of society. How is it organized, what are its major institutions, and how are they linked together? The second concerns the historical location of society. How has it emerged from past social forms, what mechanisms promote change, and what futures are possible based on this historical path? The third concerns individual biography within society. What kinds of character traits are called forth by this society, and what kinds of people come to prevail? The sociological imagination is thus about grasping the relations between history and biography within society.

The sociological imagination sensitizes us to the difference between "personal troubles" and "public issues." A personal trouble is a difficulty in someone's life that is largely a result of individual circumstances. A public issue is a difficulty that is largely owing to social arrangements beyond the individual's control. The distinction is crucial because common sense often interprets events as personal troubles; we explain someone's difficulties as springing from individual shortcomings. The sociological imagination recognizes that such difficulties are rarely unique to one person; they rather happen to many people in similar situations. The underlying causes derive more from social structures and historical developments than the individual alone. If our goal is "diagnosis," the sociological imagination locates problems in a larger social context. If our goal is "treatment," it implies changing the structure of society rather than the behavior of individuals.

This applies to success as well. Common sense often attributes success to individual qualities. The sociological imagination asks what social and historical preconditions were necessary for an individual to become a success. Many successful people, in Jim Hightower's memorable phrase, "were born on third base but thought they hit a triple." The point is that whereas common sense sees the world in individual terms, sociological thinking sees it in structural terms. Only by seeing the connections between structure, history, and biography can we understand the world in a sociological way.

This discussion implies that professional sociologists and ordinary people see the world differently. This is often true, but the issue is more complicated. Modernity has also led ordinary people to develop a practical sociology in their everyday lives.

Think about it this way. Sociology sees the world as a social construction that could follow various blueprints. Indeed, social worlds *are* constructed in very different ways in different times and places.

In our time, an awareness of the socially constructed nature of social worlds is no longer the privileged insight of scholars, but has become part of everyday understanding. Whether owing to rapid change, frequent travel, cultural diffusion, or media images, many people understand that we live in socially constructed worlds. Some people are distressed by this fact, and others rejoice in it, but few can escape it. Thus, an idea that was initially associated with professional sociology has become part of the everyday consciousness of ordinary people today.

The result is that many people without formal sociological training understand social processes quite well. Put differently, the objects of sociological analysis are people who are quite capable of becoming the subjects of the sociological knowledge created by that analysis. Although few people can explain how quantum mechanics governs the physical world, many can describe sociological processes that shape the social world.

Certain circumstances prompt people to think sociologically. Perhaps the key stimulant is when familiar ways of doing and thinking no longer work. It is when people are surprised, puzzled, challenged, or damaged that they are most likely to think sociologically (Lemert 2008). People then develop sociological competence as they try to make sense out of specific, individual circumstances by linking them to broader social patterns. In this way, sociological awareness begins to understand bigger things as a by-product of wrestling with the practical challenges of everyday life.

Circumstances do not inevitably provoke sociological consciousness. Some people redouble their faith or retreat into ritualism. So perhaps we can conclude this way. Societies confront people with problems. These problems have always had the potential to promote a sociological awareness. In our times, there is a greater awareness of the socially constructed nature of the world. This makes it even more likely that when people in this society are confronted with practical challenges, they will develop sociological competence as a practical life skill. In late modernity, everyone can become a practical sociologist.

THINKING SOCIOLOGICALLY

The sociological perspective involves several themes. They overlap with one another, and some may be found in other social sciences as well as everyday consciousness. Taken together, they comprise a distinctive lens for viewing the social world. Here are some of those themes.

Society Is a Social Construction

People construct social order. Sociology does not see society as God-given, as biologically determined, or as following any predetermined plan beyond human intervention. At the same time, this does not mean that everyone plays an equal role in the process or that the final product looks like what people intended.

Social construction begins with intentions that motivate people to act in certain ways. When many people have similar goals and act in concert, larger social patterns or institutions are created. Goal-driven action is essential to the creation of institutions, and it remains equally important to their maintenance and transformation over time. Put succinctly, society is a human product (Berger and Luckmann 1966).

Basic human needs ensure some similarities in the goals that people pursue in all times and places. But these pursuits also unfold in specific historical circumstances and cultural contexts that have led to a dazzling variety of social worlds. This variety is itself the best evidence of the socially constructed nature of social worlds. If biology or genetics were the determining force behind social worlds, wouldn't they look a lot more similar than what we actually see around the globe?

Social constructionists thus insist that society arises from the goal-driven action of people. But they also recognize that the institutions created by such actions take on a life of their own. They appear to exist independently of the people who create and sustain them. They are experienced by people as a powerful external force that weighs down on them. When this external force becomes severe enough, people are likely to lose sight of the fact that society is a social product in the first place.

The value of the social constructionist premise is this dual recognition. On one hand, society is a subjective reality originating in the intentions of social actors. On the other hand, it becomes an objective reality that confronts subsequent generations as a social fact that inevitably shapes *their* intentional actions—and so it goes. Understood this way, the idea that society is a social construction is at the heart of the sociological perspective.

Society Is an Emergent Reality

Another premise of sociology is emergentism. This reveals sociology's distinctive level of analysis. For psychology, the level of analysis is the individual, even if it is acknowledged that individuals belong to groups. For sociology, the level of analysis is social ties rather than individual elements. Emergentism recognizes that certain realities only appear when individual elements are combined in particular ways. When they are, qualitatively new realities emerge through these combinations.

Take a simple example. Imagine a random pile of ten paper clips. Now imagine linking these paper clips together to form a chain. There are still ten paper clips, but a new emergent reality has appeared that is qualitatively different from the random pile because of how the elements are related to one another. Or consider human reproduction. Neither sperm nor egg is capable of producing human life on its own; in combination, qualitatively new life begins to emerge from a particular combination of elements.

Sociology specializes in the social level of analysis that emerges when elements are combined to create new, larger realities. Emergentism also implies that when we try to understand elements outside of their context, it is at best

The Social Construction of Class Problems

...[T]here is one thing that *will* get our current crop of politicians—be they presidents or prime ministers, board chairs or secretaries-general —all singing together: the catchall term "security". Where previous generations lived with constant (and useful) chatter about the need for full employment versus the threat of inflation or were encouraged to engage in the War on Poverty, our generation—the generation of the "risk society"—is encouraged to preoccupy itself with being secure, something that is rarely an incentive to generosity and is frequently an existential dead-end to boot.

The US Republican Tom Ridge— presumably choosing his words carefully on being charged with running "homeland security" in the months when America slipped from being a nation to a homeland in official public discourse— said that the new grand task of the nation was the protection of "essential liberty".[24] This was a task for which all Americans were now responsible. And to achieve it, security would become the new national mission, likened, he said, to the Transcontinental Railroad and putting a man on the moon. Really? In any case, this was not the sort of security envisaged by Franklin Roosevelt in the 1930s, at the beginning of a period when national interest and the general welfare of society merged.[25] It was not what Roosevelt envisaged in 1944 either, when in speaking of a "family of Nations" he sought to extend the vision of the New Deal—the belief that "freedom from fear is eternally linked with freedom from want"—to the rest of the world.[26]

Today's understanding of security is quite different to this. Sustained by the tireless efforts of what the French sociologist Didier Bigo calls "the managers of unease", it has become the wealthy world's "master narrative", directing citizens this way and that, telling them to mind not just their own business but other people's too—all in the name of policies which are themselves, as one insightful critic puts it, "predisposed towards the exercise of violence in defense of the established order".[27]

Security policy has thus become exactly the constellation of force arraigned on behalf of privilege that was predicted long ago, and not by Karl Marx, but by Adam Smith: "Civil government," Smith wrote in *The Wealth of Nations*, "so far as it is instituted for the security of property, is in reality instituted for the defense of the rich against the poor, or of those who have some property against those who have none at all."[28] Security, make no mistake, is about class. And in its post–Cold War guise consumes the money we might otherwise spend on things like preventive health care and channels it instead to the interests of private military contractors and the purveyors of zero-tolerance policing. We are told to be afraid, in short, because it makes some people richer when we are.

But it also undermines our democracies. While many aspects of the state have been in retreat over the past thirty-five years, for example, the corrections industry has consistently been the fastest-growing sector across all three levels of the US political system (county, state, and federal). White-collar crime today costs the United States several hundred billion dollars each year, with scandals like those that rocked Enron in 2001, WorldCom in 2002, and Bernie Madoff in 2008. But it is overwhelmingly blacks, Latinos, and unemployed whites who have been sucked into the country's growing prison-industrial complex.

A more punitive form of government in the name of security is also increasingly deployed internationally (in the age of Roosevelt the preference was for welfare). Before all of our eyes the global war on terror has become a "planetary security effort", in the words of one critic: a source of constant intrusion, disruption, and ultimately violence for those labouring to get on with their lives in countries that come on to the Pentagon's or MI6's radar.[29] At the same time, reducing *their* problems to prior questions of *our* security has become an ever more powerful means for the rich world to distance itself from the realities of poverty and its discontents. To make the world more just we have to act with greater justice, which means we have to open ourselves up to others. This is the very opposite of security.

The West is increasingly losing whatever moral grounds it might once have had to question the nature and causes of conflicts elsewhere in the world: be it China's bullying in Nepal or the current ethnic imbroglio that is Syria. Knowing this, is it any surprise that some countries pursue domestic military conflicts today with greater disregard to international opinion—with the literal expectation of getting away with murder? When Israel targeted 450 sites and individuals in Gaza in mid-November 2012, for example, of the first five BBC headlines on the event, two presented the attacks as "Israel's Gaza rocket problem". When BBC Radio 4 then reported that Israel would suspend "military operations" for the Egyptian prime minister's visit, it did not once use the word "violence" or "attacks", but merely "operations".

Amidst all this double-speak it is no surprise that Western leaders struggle to cling to the moral high ground. Yet they are reluctant to abandon the position altogether, since it serves them far too well in times of crisis—times we are hardly short of these days. NATO acted with increasing entrepreneurial verve under its former secretary-general Anders Fogh Rasmussen to loosen the definition of violence (the better to allow greater room for manoeuvre when deciding whether and how to intervene in countries like Libya). These are moves met in the opposite direction by humanitarian organisations seeking to expand their definition of violence, if not their market share of the world's suffering with it, and the effect has been to undermine the clarity of international law at just the historical moment when it has been needed most of all.

The associated blurring of the boundary between humanitarian and military interventions has, inevitably enough, carried Western nations into the fraught waters of the responsibility-to-protect doctrine. Enshrined as permissible international practice by NATO in Kosovo and under UN Security Council authorisation in East Timor in the late 1990s, interventions by multilateral coalitions of the willing are now "just"—in the words of Tony Blair, and he should know—to the extent that they are based not on military or political objectives in the first instance but on "values".

Little wonder, then, that by the mid-2000s development agencies and humanitarian organisations were crying foul that the military was simply using them as "force multipliers". They were right, of course. But to some extent they had only themselves to blame: for they had themselves plunged with eager hands into peace-building and protection for people who apparently could not be trusted to govern themselves. Imperialism now rides the coattails of the humanitarians; it once was the other way around—yet for those on the receiving end, it is far from clear that the change in roles makes all that much difference at all.

What is all too often overlooked today, amidst all the hand-wringing over our duty to intervene in crises elsewhere—to do *something*—is any consideration of the fact that we might bear some of the responsibility for what has brought events to such a sorry state in the first place. In the way we then *do* go about "protecting" the world's poor—with the current mantra of "protection of civilians", for example—we frequently open things up for more, not less, violence. There is more than a little irony in this. For as my colleague Ole Jacob Sending has observed, if it is true that in the current vogue for "ethical consumerism" the obligation to care and the desire to consume are collapsed into each other (help the poor by buying a cup of coffee or by purchasing a Louis Vuitton bag), the same is no less true in the political domain, as internationally, our promises of "protection" are collapsed into a simultaneous effort to order the world's societies, and its failed states especially, in a manner that is to our liking.

It is here that the logic of security proves its greatest worth for wealthy and powerful states, precisely because it encourages us not to notice connections such as this. But the logic of security also lies behind the revived fortunes of development. For much of the 1990s development had languished somewhat in the absence of superpower sponsorship. Official development assistance dropped off substantially: US contributions halved, in fact, from $16.2 billion to $8.4 billion between 1990 and 1997.[30] Its fortunes revived after 9/11, however, albeit by responding to a rather different tune. Development today is less about human flourishing than it once was, and more about the maintenance of a fragile—and culturally specific—vision of global order, for all that a great many people work in good faith to achieve rather more than this.

Development, as an adjunct to security—a holy grail that goes by the name of "human security"—is one way in which well-intentioned people have sought to square this circle in recent years. But the concept has itself now become a means to reshape poorer societies in light of the rich world's own particular needs and so in many ways it has merely reinforced the problem. High up on the list of those needs, of course, is the desire to calm our anxieties about the flux and flows of an interdependent world. Development and humanitarian actors must now accordingly address themselves not to people in need but to "situations of crisis" and "complex emergencies", and of course to the donors who are paying for all of this. The recent restructuring of the UK aid budget to focus primarily on only those countries that are deemed to be security risks to the United Kingdom says it all, really.

The old Cold War policy of containment—fencing in the Soviets and waiting them out in the hope that they would croak first—has in today's world been transformed into one of selective engagement. To some extent, this is inevitable and sensible. The footprint of our own societies is too large to avoid engaging with the places where the rare-earth metals we require in our laptops are mined and where our food is increasingly grown. But the terms on which we do so are so myopic that we frequently create more of the problems that we purport to solve.

Such realities ought to raise doubts as to the counsel, in this respect at least, of Michael Ignatieff, who in channelling none less than King Lear, proposes that we "'dig up the heath', put [it] under the sovereignty of a nation armed and capable of protecting its own people". This is mixed advice indeed. For we are already digging up the heath, and for our own gain. We are already putting it under the sovereignty of the international community and its coalition of leading states. And we are doing so in accordance with an increasingly corporate jargon that has so permeated national and international political discourse that we can today find it within ourselves to speak of government only as a matter of "efficiency" and "choice", as if the prior questions—efficiency and choice of "what" exactly—were nothing worth troubling ourselves about. It isn't clear that any of this is protecting the people on the heath at all.

THE GROUND BENEATH THEIR FEET

The law is of course a special sort of institution, and developing fair and effective laws should be a priority of any world that aspires not to be mired in inequality. Yet the law is presently failing the world's poor by affording them far too little protection when it comes to matters of trade policy or the economic relations between nations. Where the law is considered to have a central, public role to play today is in the context of human rights, which activists raise as a defence to exploitation in the hope that either marginalised people will claim the rights they are offered, or others will find the goodwill to do this for them. But individual rights without wider social and economic protections are little more than "paper parapets", as James Madison famously put it. Moreover, the law is as easily exploited as enforced by the powerful, perhaps because too many of our leaders trained as lawyers and they therefore feel they know better.

The failings of international law today are a reminder that it is not just the heath, as Ignatieff would have it, but the rule book of precedent and procedure that has been torn up of late. As Britain's Lord Rooker, then UK Home Office minister, put it in November 2001: "The terrorists rewrote the rule book, and we have to do the same."[31] And for the past decade that is precisely what we have done: a process that reached its present high-water mark with the spectacle of a sitting American president outlining a doctrine of war in his Nobel Peace Prize acceptance speech. Such rhetoric as Obama saw fit to deploy in Oslo—"the full force of our justice"—belies the bellicosity that *inflames* global tensions. It is not just the law but also the spirit of the law that matters. In this case, Obama the lawyer really should have known better.

But the law is demeaned in more mundane ways too, such as by the operations of the Orwellian-titled distressed debt investors, more popularly, and accurately, known as vulture funds. Vulture funds, run from regent offices in Kensington and Mayfair, tap into poor countries' wealth by exploiting rich countries' laws and courts. The "accepted" practice here is for funds to buy up bad debt in poor countries, which they sit on while the debt rises. Later, when market conditions are favourable, they take the indebted country to court for the full sum, plus fees. A British court, for example, awarded the American investor Michael "Goldfinger" Sheehan $20 billion in repayment costs against Zambia in 2009. In light of the attitude that British courts seemingly take to what is by any definition a demand for ransom, one is reminded of just such *conscience juridique* as was displayed by the international lawyers flocking about the Berlin Conference of 1883–1884, pardoning in advance their masters' thirst for territory.[32]

There remains, unfortunately, substantial opposition to the idea of an international law that is anything more than a rich man's club, and not just in the panelled offices of Mayfair. Even before 9/11, John Bolton, who would later become US undersecretary of state, said that international legal agreements and binding contractual duties—the Kyoto Protocol, for example—were nothing less than a "worldwide cartelization of governments and interest groups".[33] He could not have better channelled the spirit of Moynihan if he had tried.

Where the real cartels are at work, however, is in the almost invisible fabric of international standards and norms that set the terms of engagement in the global economy. Promoted via everything from ISO standards to trademark practices and intellectual property law, these silent normalisers do an essential job in enabling international harmonisation. But they also tend to hardwire into the international system a set of norms and rules that favours the rich. They create a world in which poorer countries that want to have a stake in the global marketplace must conform to the practices established by those who got there first, whether or not those practices actually work for them.

When it comes to things like producing generic and affordable medicines for consumption by the poor, the costs of a Western-dominated international intellectual property rights regime is measured in actual human lives. But again, the solutions we require here are political and not economic in the first instance. The International Labour Organisation, for example, does a hugely important job in promoting standards of "decent work" around the world. But compliance with its conventions is, at the end of the day, down to national political debate and international pressure.

"A RIGHT DISPOSITION"

Despite what we might hear on the news, we in fact live in a more peaceful world than ever before. Armed conflict within countries—by far the greatest cause of deaths globally—increased steadily over the past fifty years, peaking in 1992. Ever since then, the figure has more or less been on the decline.[34] But what does this formal status of peace really mean in light of the fact that, "universal and lasting peace can be established only if it is based upon social justice", as the preamble to the ILOs constitution reminds us?[35] In the years since 1989, democracy and human rights have come to define what has been referred to as the post–Cold War peace. But for all that America and Europe like to harp on about democracy, it is becoming increasingly less clear what they actually mean by this.

What is clear is that, like the lawyers, they do not consider social and economic rights to be anything like as important as they once were. Mozambique's first Action Plan to Reduce Absolute Poverty (2001–2005), to take just one country, was almost entirely in hock to foreign donor strategies, and foreign consultants largely decided on its replacement (2006–2010): donors were again invited to comment, but not the Mozambican parliament.[36] Really this was nothing unusual. The Millennium Development Goals and the Sustainable Development Goals have been organised in a not-dissimilar way. The underlying problem here is that democracy is rarely understood to mean democratic decision-making over the way that our economics, be they national or global, are run—even though the prioritisation of social and economic rights is supposed to be a core part of the UN's mandate. Instead, the West prefers to deploy the vernacular of human rights as a way to constrain the power of (other) states: though as at least one study has shown, across the twentieth century and all political systems, it is democracies that are most likely to target civilians, and it is in the name of other peoples' human rights, of course, that we today launch humanitarian interventions and the no-fly zones required to support them.[37]

Yet none of this is any longer just about the West. As a proliferating thicket of acronyms suggests, new constellations of political power, economic growth, and demographic influence now cut across the old North-South divide: be it the BRICS (Brazil, Russia, India, China, and South Africa) or the PINCIs (Pakistan, India, Nigeria, China, and Indonesia). Between them the BRICS nations now account for 40% of the world's population and produce 25% of its output. Europe, by contrast, which has been accustomed to having a growing share of world population, now sees both its share of GDP and its population declining, and the influx of immigrants through which it seeks, against its own instincts, to address these demographic disadvantages creates only further tensions.

But for all that BRICS have shaken up the international donor landscape and the *economics* of global order, it is actually far from clear that they represent very much of a change from the Western approach to international *politics*. China has been even more active than Western agribusiness in land-grabbing across Africa, enclosing the African commons for its own extra-territorial gain just as surely as Britain enclosed its own commons in the past. China is also currently seeking to build another Panama Canal (this time across Nicaragua), and for largely the same reasons the United States took over the building of the first one. The BRICS more generally are increasingly prominent contributors to Western-style peacekeeping too, Brazil having led the UN Stabilisation Mission in Haiti. And, as Russia has made clear with respect to the crisis in Syria, it is clear that the BRICS also expect to exert an increasingly decisive political influence over countries in which they have strategic interests. Perhaps the greatest problem with today's preoccupation with "emerging nations", therefore, is that if we concern ourselves only with the relative motions of rise and fall, then we blind ourselves to the more fundamental continuities of a world within which the lives of rich and poor are constantly made in relation to one another.

What, then, in the context of all this, is global poverty today? A product of market failure? A global injustice? A curse of nature and environment?[38] And what, in turn, are any of these things to us? Of course, global poverty is in reality many things to many people, and if you listen to the moral philosophers, it is also nothing to far too many of us. But in truth there is no such thing as "global" poverty beyond what it is made to be in relation to the interests of the privileged and the powerful. There *is* great poverty in our world, but that poverty derives from the way that structural forms of injustice are made, over and again, through specifiable policies and traceable political decisions. Poverty takes its place as one of those critical things whose "right disposition" is insisted upon because doing so enables the whole modern complex of power that revolves around the interests of the rich to be overlooked.[39]

Power is everywhere, and we must be attentive to where and how it is used. But for all that many would have us believe otherwise, we live in a world of actually rather shambolic power and distinctly unruly leviathans. The "heath" has at best been only partially turned into a commons; worse, it has been pre-emptively and unevenly enclosed. We have a patchwork of international regulations and laws and authorities that abet power at least as often as they constrain it. We have a world of nation-states not so much jealously competing with one another as working out their position on the food chain: for while the power of some nations' authority is a matter of their own executive decision, other sovereigns cower deep within their war-torn shells, abdicating all reasonable public duties.

The solution to this is neither to embrace the wishful cosmopolitan hope of an ideal-type of "global democracy" nor to keep fretting about the state of isolated sovereign crises. The solution is to build up state capacity wherever global public challenges require this. The re-democratisation of the national state and the democratisation of the international must go hand in hand. We must recognise that the demons that confront us internationally (the mantra of security, for example) are not impediments to this task, nor reasons to run the other way, so much as they are the shadows of petty spectres we have ourselves created. We must look to the international domain not with fear or loathing but with a caring yet dispassionate eye, rejecting the salve of a philanthropy that seeks only to secure the conditions of its own comfortable existence, but in a disciplined manner, which is to say to the extent that we replace it with something that is better.

And the best way of doing this will be to devise new "strategies of equality", as Tawney once put it. These will not be strategies that seek the greatest quantitative equality in the shortest possible time; we cannot avoid the need to keep asking "equality of what?"[40] But we do need to develop a series of concrete and comprehensive solutions to the myriad political forms of inequality that confront us. And it is to a brief sketch of this task that we now turn.

NOTES

24 A transcript of Tom Ridge's swearing-in ceremony is available at "America Strikes Back: Tom Ridge Worn in as New Director of Homeland Security," CNN, October 8, 2001, http://transcripts.cnn.com/TRANSCRIPTS/0110/08/se.09.html.

25 Mark Neocleous, "From Social to National Security: On the Fabrication of Economic Order," *Security Dialogue* 37 (2006): 363–84, 367.

26 Ibid., 376.

27 Ibid.

28 Cited in Esping-Andersen, *The Three Worlds of Welfare Capitalism* (Cambridge: Polity Press, 1989), 33.

29 Brad Evans, "Terror in All Eventuality," *Theory & Event* 13, no. 3 (2010): 1.

30 Jean Michel Severino and Olivier Ray, "The End of ODA: Death and Rebirth of a Global Public Policy" (Working Paper No. 167, Center for Global Development, Washington, DC, March 2009), 3n4.

31 Patrick Wintour, "Peers Warn of Terror Bill Cuts," *The Guardian*, November 28, 2001, http://www.theguardian.com/politics/2001/nov/28/uk.september11.

32 Rein Mullerson, "Book Review of Koskenniemi: *The Gentle Civiliser of Nations,*" *European Journal of International Law* 13 (2002): 725–35.

33 Martti Koskenniemi, "International Law and Hegemony: A Reconfiguration," *Cambridge Review of International Affairs* 17, no. 2 (2004): 197–218.

34 See Håvard Hegre, "Peace on Earth: The Future of Internal Armed Conflict," *Significance, Journal of the Royal Statistical Society* 4 (2013): 4–8.

35 The full text of the ILO's constitution is available at http://www.ilo.org/dyn/normlex/en/f?p=1000:62:0::NO:62:P62_LIST_ENTRIE_ID:2453907:NO.

36 Jonathan Glennie, "Is It Time for Mali to Plan an Exit Strategy from Aid?" (speech to the Annual Retreat of Technical Partners and Financiers, Bamako, February 8, 2011), http://www.odi.org/sites/odi.org.uk/files/odi-assets/publications-opinion-files/7149.pdf. He is here citing the work of Paolo de Renzio and Joseph Hanlon, "Contested Sovereignty in Mozambique: The Dilemmas of Aid Dependence" (Global Economic Governance Programme Working Paper No. 2007/25, Managing Aid Dependency Project, University College, Oxford, 2007).

37 Alexander Downes, cited in Patricia Owens, "Accidents Don't Just Happen: The Liberal Politics of High-Technology 'Humanitarian' War," *Millennium: Journal of International Studies* 32, no. 3 (2003): 595–616.

38 Patrick Hayden, "Superfluous Humanity: An Arendtian Perspective on the Political Evil of Global Poverty," *Millennium—Journal of International Studies* 35 (2007): 279–300.

39 The phrase is Foucault's (channelling La Perrière): See Graham Burchell, Colin Gordon, and Peter Miller, eds., *The Foucault Effect: Studies in Governmentality* (Chicago: University of Chicago Press, 1991), 93.

40 Amartya Sen, "Equality of What?" (Tanner Lectures on Human Values, Stanford University, May 22, 1979), http://tannerlectures.utah.edu/_documents/a-to-z/s/sen80.pdf.

Income and Wealth

How can it be that it is not a news item when an elderly homeless person dies of exposure, but it is news when the stock market loses two points?
  —Pope Francis, Evangelii Gaudium, November 26, 2013[1]

Today, after four years of economic growth, corporate profits and stock prices have rarely been higher, and those at the top have never done better. But average wages have barely budged. Inequality has deepened. Upward mobility has stalled. The cold, hard fact is that even in the midst of recovery, too many Americans are working more than ever just to get by; let alone to get ahead. And too many still aren't working at all. So our job is to reverse these trends.
  —President Barack Obama, State of the Union Address,
    January 28, 2014[2]

St. John's University education professor Allan Ornstein argues that "no country has taken the idea of equality more seriously than the United States," though he notes that "we are witnessing the rise of a new aristocratic class, based on wealth and power, far worse than the European model our Founding Fathers sought to curtail."[3] Americans largely accept the notion that capitalism will produce unequal outcomes with respect to income and wealth, but we prefer a more equal distribution than currently exists. Recently, a nationally representative sample of Americans was asked to (1) estimate the actual level of wealth inequality in the United States and (2) indicate preferences for ideal distribution of wealth. The researchers found that:

Respondents vastly underestimated the actual level of wealth inequality in the United States, believing that the wealthiest quintile[4] held about 59% of the wealth when the actual number is closer to 84%. More interesting, respondents constructed ideal wealth distributions that were far more equitable than even their erroneously low estimates of actual distributions, reporting a desire for the top quintile to own just 32% of the wealth.[5]

The researchers also found that this preference existed across demographic groups (including expressed presidential vote choice from 2004): "All groups—even the wealthiest respondents—desired a more equal distribution of wealth than what they estimated the current United States level to be, and all groups also desired some inequality—even the poorest respondents."[6] Finally, and perhaps most interesting, all groups agreed that the way to move toward this ideal is through redistributing wealth from the top to the bottom three quintiles.

The disconnect between what Americans of all ideological backgrounds desire and the reality of inequality is striking and calls into question the effectiveness of our representative system. So why is this happening? One answer could be that our elected officials wish to make changes to bring the wealth gap more in line with what Americans want but are constrained by systemic forces that make such meaningful change possible. Another answer is that our elected officials, most of whom (at the federal level at least) are wealthier than the average American,[7] are trying to protect themselves and their elite friends and family members. More likely, though, as the researchers suggest, we generally are not aware that the gap is so large; we are optimistic about our chances of getting into higher quintiles; we are not clear about the causes of inequality; and we often do not make a connection between these beliefs and our public policy preferences.[8] In this chapter, we explore the statistical realities of income and wealth inequality, as well as the relationship between that inequality and race. We will focus on the various elements in American society that perpetuate economic inequality in an attempt to understand how the current gap has not only persisted but has been greatly expanded over the past generation or so.

Income

Economic inequality is customarily discussed in terms of two distinct but related concepts: income and wealth. Wealth is a person's (or household's) total worth (assets minus debt), while income is simply the amount of money a person (or household) earns in a year. We will explore wealth disparities below, but in this section we consider the differences in annual household income and the ability to provide for oneself or one's family as a result.

Income and Employment

For most Americans, income is tied to employment; we only get paid when we work. Of course, there are exceptions. Disabled and retired individuals can collect Social Security from the federal government. Unemployed workers can receive benefits for a limited period after losing a job. Some wealthy individuals have invested money and earn from dividends and interest. For the most part, though, income is related to work.

Most recently, though, attention has been focused on the sluggish economy and the degree to which it has affected Americans in the workforce. With respect to recessions, it has been said that when America catches a cold, African Americans get the flu. That sentiment was clearly reflected in the recession that began with the housing crisis in 2008. Unemployment rates for October 2012 indicated a nationwide level of 7.9 percent (12.3 million persons), but a closer look reveals that the rate for whites (7.0 percent) was lower than for Hispanics (10.0 percent) or African Americans (14.3 percent, or double the rate for whites).[9] The gap has been even more pronounced among those with a college education. White unemployment among the college educated rose from 1.8 percent in 2007 to 3.9 percent in 2011, while black unemployment among the col-lege educated spiked from 2.7 percent in 2007 to 7.0 percent in 2011.[10]

Unemployment naturally has an effect on earnings. Data from 2011 demonstrate a notable income gap between white, black, and Hispanic families. In that year, the median household income for whites was $52,214, while the median income for African Americans was $32,229, and for Hispanics, $38,624.[11] Those numbers reflect a fairly stable gap over the past two decades.[12]

The income gap is most pronounced among Hispanics and African Americans, but its growth is notable among all segments of the popula-tion. In 2009, the highest quintile of earners collected 50 percent of the total income in the United States. In contrast, the bottom three quintiles combined brought in just 26.7 percent of the total income that year (with the second-highest quintile earning 23.3 percent).[13] There has been a steady increase in this trend over the past forty years, such that the top 5 percent of earners in 1970 pulled in 16.6 percent. That number was stable a decade later but rose to 18.5 percent in 1990 and to 22.1 percent in 2000. In 2011, the top 5 percent of households earned 21.5 percent of the total income.[14]

This shift can be analyzed in a variety of ways. One notable trend is that incomes in all ranges rose steadily (and relatively evenly) between the end of World War II and 1979. However, the top 20 percent of earners saw a 49 percent increase (including a 73 percent increase among the top 5 percent and a 224 percent increase among the top 1 percent) since the early 1980s while the bottom, second, middle, and fourth quintiles saw changes of 7 percent, 6 percent, 11 percent, and 23 percent, respectively.[15]

Gender is also related to income disparity. Much attention has been given to the wage gap in recent years, which stands today at about 23 percent. Put another way, women make an average of seventy-seven cents for every dollar a man makes in the United States.[16] The gap is largest for Latinas (39 percent compared to white men) and smallest for Asian American women (88 percent compared to white men). The gap for African American women is 70 percent.[17] About one-third of working women are heads of household in terms of earnings;[18] black women are most likely to be single heads of household (27.5 percent), compared to 9 percent of white women and 17.7 percent of Hispanic women,[19] and this responsibility is related to the decrease in African American women's labor force participation as compared to white women.[20]

On the opposite end of the spectrum, evidence of racial disparity is illustrated by an examination of the board members of America's top corporations. In 2010, white men comprised 72.9 percent of the board members at the largest one hundred companies and 77.6 percent of the largest five hundred companies in the United States. Nonwhite men held 10 percent of those seats, and white women held 13 percent.[21] It was not until 1999 that an African American became CEO of a Fortune 500 company, and there have been only thirteen; in July 2012, there were only six African American CEOs in such positions.[22] Women headed eighteen Fortune 500 companies in 2012,[23] the highest number in history.[24]

Further, there has been a tremendous shift in the ratio of CEO pay to the income of an average worker. Though the ratios found on bumper stickers and pro-union literature vary from 500 to 1 to 431 to 1 to 364 to 1 to 253 to 1,[25] the reality is complicated by the various types of compensation (besides monetary income) that CEOs receive. By one count, however, the ratio grew from 42 to 1 in 1980 to 107 to 1 in 1990 before spiking to its current levels in the last two decades.[26] In 2012, the median overall compensation of the top one hundred CEOs was $15.1 million, which represented a 16 percent rise from the previous year.[27] The monetary portion of these figures relates to gross income (before taxes). Since the United States has a progressive income tax structure (higher annual incomes relate to higher tax brackets), some of this income inequality will ostensibly be resolved once taxes are collected. As we see in the next section, though, it is not that simple.

Taxes

There is no denying that the US income tax code is tremendously complicated. It is full of complex rules and regulations that are designed to add fairness to the system. But "fair" is in the eye of the beholder and open to interpretation by Americans with differing ideological leanings. Those who earn a lot often complain that the so-called progressive tax structure punishes (and, more importantly, de-incentivizes) financial success, while those who earn less sometimes wish that a higher percentage of the nation's revenue would be paid by those who can most afford it. In sum, our tax code is a collection of deals and compromises between representatives who have different preferences (and who represent constituencies that have different preferences).

On the surface, the United States income tax system is progressive in that it appears to tax those who earn more at a higher rate than those who earn less. In 2012, the rate began with a base of 10 percent, with a married couple earning more than $17,400 paying a increasingly higher rate on the money they make over the first 10 percent—from 15 percent to 35 percent (for those earning more than $388,350).[28] The effective tax rates (which includes all forms of income tax, not just taxes on wages) for the highest earners have been reduced over the past forty years, from 66.4 percent after World War II to 47.7 percent in 1982 to 36.4 percent in the 1990s. The Bush tax cuts further reduced the top bracket to 32.4 percent.[29] However, before the tax rate is applied, the taxable income amount can be reduced by a host of deductions that are disproportionately available to higher earners. A recent study found that more than half of all tax benefits went to the wealthiest 5 percent of taxpayers and that "the top 1 percent of taxpayers, those making more than $1 million, received an average $95,000 in assistance. . . . By contrast, the poorest taxpayers, including families making $50,000, received less than $500 in benefits."[30] The most widespread of these policies is the mortgage interest deduction, which allows for a reduction in taxable income related to money paid toward interest on a home mortgage. The more expensive the home, the larger the deduction. There are also deductions for contributions to retirement plans, and a flat 15 percent tax on income made from the sale of capital assets held for more than a year.[31] Mitt Romney, 2012 Republican candidate for president, revealed that he paid 14 percent in 2010 and 2011 (the only years for which he released returns during the campaign), even though he earned $13.7 million and $21.7 million in those years, respectively, because most of the income was from investments.[32] Warren Buffett, the multibillionaire, has famously quipped that his secretary pays a higher percentage of her annual income than he does as a result of these complicated regulations.[33] Figure 2.1 reveals that the growth in after-tax income from 1979 to 2007 advantaged the wealthiest Americans; clearly, the income tax structure is disproportionately benefiting those with the most income.

At the same time, other taxes that disproportionately affect those who are not wealthy have increased. These are called regressive taxes. For example, Social Security is funded by a flat payroll tax (12.9 percent in 2013), with half paid by the employee and the other half by the employer. Individuals pay only on the first $113,700 earned.[34] Those who earn more make no further contributions. That means that higher earners pay a smaller percentage of their overall income to help fund the program than lower earners. Sales taxes are applied by state and local governments to products and services. Everyone needs to buy food and necessities, so everyone, rich and poor, is subject to these taxes. But a 3 percent tax on milk or an 18 percent excise tax on gasoline (in addition to local gas taxes) will have a more significant impact on a working family's budget than on a millionaire's. So increases in regressive taxes to make up for revenue lost from providing income tax breaks to the wealthy can cause a significant burden for those who are already economically vulnerable.

FIGURE 2.1. Growth in Real After-Tax Income, 1979–2007

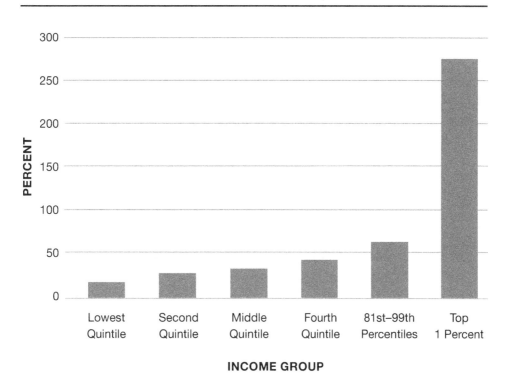

Source: United States Congressional Budget Oce, " Trends in the Distribution of Income," 2011. http://www.cbo.gov/publication/42537.

On the other hand, a number of provisions in the US tax code provide tax breaks that benefit low earners disproportionately (such as the deductions for children, tuition, and government-backed low-interest student loans) or solely (such as the low-income housing tax credit and credit for rent paid). One such program, the Earned Income Tax Credit (EITC), was expanded between 1984 and 1996 to provide an incentive for single mothers to work.[35] The EITC benefits working families (particularly those with children) by providing a reduction in taxable earnings for families earning less than $50,000 (married with three children or more).[36] The mortgage interest deduction program also benefits Americans in a variety of income ranges. So, while it is not the case that the high earners are the sole beneficiaries of US tax policy, they benefit disproportionately, even though they represent a distinct numerical minority of citizens.

Minimum Wage and the Poverty Line

In 1938, Congress set a federal minimum wage (at twenty-five cents per hour),[37] but it was not indexed to increase with inflation. As a result, there have been significant lags in the buying power of the dollar for minimum wage workers. The current federal minimum wage, set in 2009, is $7.25 per hour, though the highest level (in real dollars) was in 1968 ($10.04 in 2010 dollars).[38] Eighteen states and the District of Columbia have minimum wages higher than the federal level.[39] Individuals in occupations where tips are expected are not protected by minimum wage laws.

A full-time worker at the federal minimum wage will fall below the poverty line for a family of four. In 1968, a full-time minimum wage worker earned about 90 percent of the poverty level, but from the mid-1980s until Congress raised the minimum wage in 2006, full-time minimum wage

BOX 2.1. Representing: Steve Forbes and the Flat Tax (Continued)

society."[d] Nonetheless, it is an idea that has some intrinsic appeal to anyone who has filed a federal tax return. Because most of the wealthiest individuals pay others to compute their taxes, Forbes's proposal would likely generate significant mass appeal if elected officials ever took it seriously. Whether the result would be an increase in economic equality is unclear, but some scholars[e] have argued that it ought to be adopted in order to eliminate the complicated (often nearly invisible) benefits that the current system provides to those who need it least.

---

[a]Steve Forbes, *Flat Tax Revolution: Using a Postcard to Abolish the IRS* (Washington DC: Regnery, 2005).

[b]Ibid., 73. Other versions of the plan do not include the additional deductions for children under 16 or the EITC. See Daniel Mitchell, "A Brief Guide to the Flat Tax," The Heritage Foundation, July 7, 2005. http://www.heritage.org/research/reports/2005/07/a-brief-guide-to-the-flat-tax.

[c]Mitchell, "A Brief Guide to the Flat Tax."

[d]Michael Kinsley, "Steve Forbes's Flat Tire," *Washington Post*, August 7, 2005, http://www.washingtonpost.com/wp-dyn/content/article/2005/08/05/AR2005080501490.html.

[e]Dorothy Brown, "Let's Kill the Progressive Tax Rate System," CNN.com, April 17, 2012, http://www.cnn.com/2012/04/17/opinion/brown-progressive-tax-rates/index.html.

workers with a family of four only earned between 50 percent and 60 percent of the federal poverty level.[40]

The poverty line (technically "poverty threshold") is not without its critics (those who think it is too low and those who think it is too high). The poverty threshold was developed in the 1960s and is based on the cost of food, under the assumption that a family of three or more spends about one-third of its income on food.[41] In 2012, the poverty threshold for an individual was $11,170; the threshold for a family of four was $23,050.[42] In 2010, the poverty rate in the United States was the highest since 1993, with 15.1 percent of individuals living in poverty. Twenty-seven percent of African Americans and 26.6 percent of Hispanics lived below the poverty threshold in 2010; less than 10 percent of non-Hispanic whites and 12.1 percent of Asians lived in poverty that year.[43] Once again, gender matters:

Poverty rates are highest for families headed by single women, particularly if they are black or Hispanic. In 2010, 31.6 percent of households headed by single women were poor, while 15.8 percent of households headed by single men and 6.2 percent of married-couple households lived in poverty.[44]

Poverty rates are even higher for single women of color. In 2010, the rate for Hispanic single mothers was 50.3 percent and the rate for African American single mothers was 47.1 percent, compared with a 32.7 percent rate for white single mothers. Three-fifths of poor single mothers were black or Latino.[45] Because women earn less than men, and because women of color are more likely to be heads of household, a portion of the racial gap in income is related to gender.

Children are also disproportionately affected by poverty. Though they are 24 percent of the population, they represent 36 percent of the poor.[46] Twenty-two percent of all American children live below the poverty threshold: 12.4 percent of white children, 38.2 percent of African American children, 35 percent of Hispanic children, and 13.6 percent of Asian children.[47]

As is always the case with statistics and classifications, there is disagreement about how to appropriately operationalize poverty. Those who argue that the existing formula sets the level too low point to the fact that income from federal programs (often referred to as welfare; see below) is not counted in this calculation.[48] Those who argue that the level is too high note that while the rationale for calculating based on food as one-third of a family budget might have been appropriate a half century ago, housing prices in particular (not to mention transportation and utility costs) have increased at a rate disproportionate to food.[49]

Similarly, there are competing ideas about whether raising the minimum wage would help relieve income inequality. By one calculation, if the minimum wage had risen proportionately with CEO compensation, it would be more than $23 per hour.[50] The wisdom of raising the minimum wage can be considered in terms of our shared American values (*should* the minimum wage rise at the same level as CEO compensation?), as well as in terms of more practical considerations. A *New York Times* editorial in March 2011 argued for a raise, noting that even with the 2009 increase, in real dollars, the minimum wage is still lower than it was thirty years ago.[51] In his 2014 State of the Union Address, President Obama called on Congress to raise the federal minimum wage to

$10.10 per hour.[52] Business groups who oppose raising the minimum wage argue that doing so would harm job creation, force layoffs, or lead to hours being cut back for those earning the minimum wage.[53] They note, for instance, that many minimum wage workers are not trying to support families—they have a second earner, have supplemental income (such as Social Security retirement for seniors working part-time), or are students. In combination with other government programs, advocates of this position feel as if there is enough of a safety net in place to protect low-wage workers and that the government should not meddle with the invisible hand of the economy.

Welfare

Many advanced democracies have expansive welfare states that are designed to provide a safety net so that no citizen falls into economic despair. Such societies are generally characterized by high tax rates and active central governments that are involved in many segments of the economy.[54] The United States has sponsored a number of programs over the years that are designed to provide such protections, but the scope and duration of those programs was dramatically reduced in the 1990s.

"Welfare" is a catchall term for government-funded and operated programs that provide different forms of financial assistance to those who need it. While various levels of assistance have been in place since colonial times, New Deal programs established during the Great Depression were more expansive than their predecessors. Many of these programs, such as unemployment compensation, Aid to Families with Dependent Children, and the program that we now know as Social Security are still in place.[55] Though not income per se, health care programs such as Medicare (for senior citizens) and Medicaid (for needy persons who are not seniors) provide additional assistance to offset costs associated with taking care of oneself and one's family.

There has been great debate in the United States about how much assistance should be provided to the needy and under what circumstances. These debates involve conflict of several core values to which Americans subscribe.[56] While Americans have a commitment to equality in a broad sense, we also have a commitment to individualism that has roots deep into our history. Further, the language used to discuss welfare in the 1980s was highly racialized, causing persistent inaccuracies in perceptions about whom these programs benefit and how much money is spent in this area.

Ronald Reagan's reference to a "welfare queen" in Chicago with "80 names, 30 addresses, 12 Social Security cards and is collecting veterans' benefits on four nonexisting deceased husbands" to the tune of $150,000 per year[57] created an enduring image of poverty in America that is characterized by undeserving African Americans who are cheating the system to get rich on the backs of hard-working (white) taxpayers. The story he told on the campaign trail in 1976 about Linda Taylor was likely an exaggeration,[58] but the retelling of the story suggested that she was typical. As a result, the welfare queen script came to dominate the imaginations of white Americans who were asked to consider reforms to the welfare system in the following decade.[59] As political scientist Martin Gilens notes:

> The connection between "poor" and "black" exists simply because African Americans account for a disproportionate number of poor people in the United States. Only one in ten white Americans falls below the official government poverty line, but three out of ten blacks are poor. Still, blacks are a small segment of the American population, and even though they are disproportionately poor, they comprise only a minority (currently about 27 percent) of all poor people.[60]

Gilens's study reveals that white respondents who viewed blacks as hard-working were much less willing to decrease welfare spending than those who viewed blacks as lazy.[61] In this way, it is very difficult to disentangle Americans' views of the poor generally with their perceptions of poor persons of color. Deservedness lies at the heart of welfare policy debates. In a political culture that values individualism and has a history that is deeply rooted in racial animosity toward African Americans in particular (and more recently Latinos), support for benefits to veterans, retired persons, and the physically disabled is more plentiful than support for the working poor, the homeless, or the mentally ill. Further, we must consider that Reagan chose to focus on a welfare queen, not a welfare king. The public disdain for the poor that is reflected in Gilens's study and that led to reforms in the 1990s is rooted in patriarchal views of personhood that marginalize women's voices and delegitimize their lived experiences.[62] In other words, Reagan's simplistic and atypical story resonated with Americans because of preexisting sexist and racist narratives that we hold in our subconscious.

The reality, of course, is much more complicated. Government "handouts" do not only go to the needy. So-called corporate welfare refers to tax incentives and subsidies for businesses.[63] Most Americans may not be aware of these policies, and even if they are, programs such as these are generally not lumped into the category of welfare. Though subsidies and tax breaks to corporations (even if they are profitable) are not income in the individual sense of the word, they help to make businesses successful, which sometimes translates into job creation (and thus income for workers) and often results in increases in wealth for top executives and major stockholders.

Wealth

While income is the amount of money a person or household earns in a year, wealth is the value of that person or household overall. Wealth is calculated by subtracting debt from assets, and in many ways it is a more accurate window into economic and racial inequality in America. While it is important to understand income gaps as part of the cycle of disadvantage (and advantage) in the United States,

> wealth signifies the command over financial resources that a family has accumulated over its lifetime along with resources that have been inherited across generations. Such resources, when combined with income, can create the opportunity to secure the "good life" in whatever form is needed—education, business, training, justice, health, comfort, and so on.[64]

Some Americans (both rich and poor) earn no income on an annual basis. In that respect, they are equal in terms of income even though their opportunities may be quite different. Further, wealth and income are not highly correlated, and there is great variation in wealth within income categories.[65] In this section, we will briefly consider some markers of wealth inequality before turning our attention to the systemic factors that reflect and perpetuate the growing gap between the wealthy and the poor in the United States.

Wealth Gap

While the income gap is large (and growing), the wealth gap is even more dramatic.[66] Median household wealth in the United States grew from $79,100 in 1989 to $126,400 in 2007 before falling dramatically to $77,300 in 2010.[67] Rather than accumulating wealth throughout a lifetime, a sizable percentage of Americans struggle through their senior years, living primarily on Social Security. Nearly half of Americans die with less than $10,000 in assets.[68] The Pew Research Center produced a report based on data from the US Census Bureau[69] that found an increasing gap between the rich and poor in America that is more exaggerated when race is factored in. Specifically, the top 10 percent of US households now control 56 percent of the nation's wealth (up from 49 percent in 2005).[70] That increase, however, somewhat masks the reality that is faced by persons of color:

> The median wealth of white U.S. households in 2009 was $113,149, compared with $6,325 for Hispanics and $5,677 for blacks. . . . Those ratios, roughly 20 to 1 for blacks and 18 to 1 for Hispanics, far exceeded the low mark of 7 to 1 for both groups reached in 1995, when the nation's economic expansion lifted many low-income groups into the middle class. The white-black wealth gap is also the widest since the census began tracking such data in 1984, when the ratio was roughly 12 to 1.[71]

A similar report in 2010 found that nonhousing assets for white families are typically around $100,000 while African American families' assets averaged about $5,000, with 25 percent of black families having no assets at all.[72] Between 1984 and 2007, white families increased their median value from $22,000 to $100,000 (real dollars) while African American households had nearly imperceptible gains.[73, 74] That has resulted in a near tripling of the black-white wealth gap over the past twenty-five years (from a gap of $85,070 in 1984 to $235,500 in 2009).[75]

At this point, it should come as no surprise that gender is also relevant with respect to wealth, though it is much more difficult to measure since wealth is most often reported at the household, rather than individual, level. The data that are available center on nonmarried households and tend to show that

> women are less likely than men to own almost every type of asset. The median value of assets held by women is almost always lower than that of their male counterparts. A smaller percent of women own stocks, bonds, and other financial assets compared to men. Women are also less likely to hold retirement accounts and a woman's pension is typically smaller than a man's.[76]

When married couples divorce or when a spouse dies, women often face a disproportionate financial burden. If they were not in the labor force during marriage, they are disadvantaged when competing for positions with more experienced candidates. Children most often live with their mother after a separation or divorce, and men are not always willing or able to pay child support.[77] Women are also more likely than men to lose health insurance after a divorce,[78] which, as we will see later, can result in significant, even debilitating, financial strain. A woman whose husband dies tends to own only fifty-nine cents for every dollar of wealth that men have when a wife dies.[79] As we saw with income, because women of color are more likely to be heads of households, there is an interactive effect between race and gender, as well.

The very wealthiest Americans lost a lot during the Great Recession: "The 10 richest Americans lost a combined $39.2 billion" between September 2008 and September 2009 (which represents a 14 percent reduction).[80] One way to look at this, then, is to consider that the wealthiest were hit hardest by the housing crisis and resulting economic troubles. We must ask, though, how the day-to-day lives of those Americans were affected compared to the lives of the poorest Americans. Put another way, if given the choice, would we rather be one of those individuals who lost the most money, or an American living in poverty who either lost a low-wage job or had a harder time finding one as a result of the recession?[81]

Gifts and Inheritance

Some individuals get a head start on the road to financial security by having parents or other relatives with money. Whether gifts are made early in one's adult life or assets are left after a relative dies, being able to count on money that one has not personally earned can be a tremendous help. While many people who are wealthy have parents who were not as wealthy, most poorer Americans come from poor families and thus do not have the opportunity to get a head start in this way.[82, 83]

The racial gap with respect to inheritance is significant. While slavery and legal racial segregation seem to be in the distant past, when we consider the passing of wealth through generations, it becomes clear that African Americans who are alive today who trace their heritage to slaves have been systemically disadvantaged because accumulation of wealth was illegal or nearly impossible given the conditions in which their ancestors lived. Researchers Gittelman and Wolff conclude that "African Americans would have gained significant ground relative to whites [between 1984 and 1994] if they had inherited similar amounts."[84] Similarly, Menchik and Jianakoplos estimate that white households are at least twice as likely to receive an inheritance and that "racial differences in inheritances can explain between 10 percent and 20 percent of the average racial difference in household wealth (in 1989)."[85] A windfall inheritance—even if it is modest—can help to offset existing debt, be invested in a major purchase (such as a home), or be put aside for an emergency or to plan for retirement. Because whites are, on average, able to count on inheritance or financial help from family members more than persons of color, their starting line is closer to the finish line (economic security).

Savings and Investments

Children are often encouraged to save their money for a rainy day. As adults, we are generally expected to have some sort of reserve in the event of a job loss, an illness, or some other unforeseen event that affects our earning. But savings and investment can only occur after basic needs (housing, food, utilities, school supplies, etc.) are satisfied. Savings of disposable income (money available after basic needs are met) dropped to just over 1 percent in 2001, which is much lower than the average rate of nearly 8 percent between 1959 and 2001.[86] In 2009 (during the Great Recession), savings increased to between 3 and 6 percent, but those rates were much lower for poorer Americans, as one might expect.[87]

As noted above, only one in four African Americans have any non–real estate assets (such as stocks, bonds, or mutual funds); only one in six Hispanics hold any of these types of assets. Less than half of black Americans and less than a third of Hispanic Americans reported having an individual retirement account in 2011. Further, 18 percent of African Americans and nearly one-third of Hispanics reported having no checking or savings account. Half of whites reported having some form of non–real estate assets, two-thirds have a retirement account (such as an IRA or 401[k]), and 95 percent had a checking or savings account.[88] As will become clear in Chapter 3, home ownership is a significant asset for many white Americans, but far fewer African Americans and Latinos own homes (and those who do have less equity than whites).[89]

BOX 2.2. *What Can I Do?:* COMMUNITY EDUCATION

Understanding personal finance is difficult for everyone, irrespective of educational background. Even those of us with advanced degrees have trouble making sense of tax forms, understanding the difference between an IRA and a 401(k), knowing what mutual fund to consider, and choosing a savings account or certificate of deposit. If you have a good grasp of these matters, you can be helpful to people in your local community. See if your college (or another local college) has a community program related to finance, or check with the library to see if it has programs designed to educate the public (often these pop up around tax time in March and April).

There are also a number of not-for-profit groups that offer this sort of assistance. Foundation Communities[a] in the Austin, Texas, area, for instance, sponsors a program, Community Tax Centers, that provides free income tax preparation help to low-income families in the area. Participants work with volunteers who have a detailed understanding of tax law and who, in turn, educate additional volunteers to give hands-on assistance. The Community Financial Education Foundation (CFEF) is a nationwide group whose mission is "to educate the American public and reach underserved communities by teaching meaningful financial life skills, encouraging positive financial behaviors, and providing access to outcome-based, educational resources over the long-term."[b] It works with volunteers and community partners to provide these services in a number of communities, as well as through online educational tools.

---

[a]www.foundcom.org

[b]www.communityfef.org

Credit and Debt

The ability to get credit—borrow money—both reflects wealth and determines one's ability to accumulate it. Automobile commercials frequently promise low (or no) finance charges for "well qualified" buyers—those whose high credit score and income are deemed sufficient by the lender. Of course, someone who fits that categorization will certainly *appreciate* a better deal on the car, but he or she probably does not *need* the better deal nearly as much as someone who is not "well qualified" by those criteria. The person with less income or worse credit thus pays more for the car, which only contributes to his or her unsteady economic circumstances. Banks often charge fees on checking accounts that fail to maintain a minimum balance throughout the billing cycle, give stiff fines for overdrafts, and place restrictions on savings account withdrawals if there is not a minimum balance. While all of these practices can be justified from the perspective of the banks in terms of their ability to conduct business, there is a potential for very adverse effects on those with limited funds in their accounts.

Missing a payment or making a late payment can trigger a higher interest rate, which only exacerbates the problem for borrowers with financial uncertainty. (As detailed in Chapter 3, adjustable-rate mortgages can leave families in financial trouble even if bills are paid on time.) Missing payments or paying late, with the accumulation of late fees and interest, can harm credit scores or lead to bankruptcy.

Calculations of creditworthiness are complicated (sometimes including up to 100 variables),[90] but are essentially based on factors such as income, available existing credit, and history of repayment. Other factors such as zip code, marital status, and length of time at the present address may also be considered.[91] It is not difficult to understand how poorer Americans—those who live in less desirable zip codes, rent their homes, earn relatively low income, and so on—are disadvantaged by a system that is used by middle-class folks to increase their wealth. Credit scores do not affect only consumer financing or credit card applications. They are often used in determining whether a person is granted a lease for an apartment, rates for automobile and homeowner's insurance, and sometimes for evaluating candidates for employment.

Ability to secure conventional loans or access to credit, like other measures of economic inequality, are not unrelated to race. Because African Americans and Latinos are poorer on average than whites, there is a disproportionate tendency for persons of color to be victimized by predatory lending with respect to all aspects of consumerism.[92] Those who cannot secure traditional forms of credit often turn to riskier (and more costly) alternatives to stay afloat.[93]

Predatory Practices and Gambling

While gambling (betting on sporting events, at a casino, or through state-sanctioned lotteries) is available to and enjoyed by Americans from all social and ethnic groups, there is a tendency for those who are the most needy to turn to these potentially quick sources of revenue. Problem gambling can be so debilitating because the more desperate people are, the more likely they are to gamble.

Type of gambling is related to income. For instance, while only 6 percent of individuals living in households with incomes under $30,000 per year gamble on sports, 17 percent of those living in households with incomes between $30,000 and $75,000 do.[94] In general, gambling is much more common among higher-income than lower-income Americans.[95] However, individuals who play the lottery and have household incomes of under $10,000 per year bet nearly three times as much on lotteries as those with incomes over $50,000 per year.[96]

More systematic than gaming, however, is the existence and persistence of predatory loan businesses that are disproportionately located in communities that are most likely to use them (i.e., poorer communities). Payday loan shops offer quick access to cash in exchange for a commitment to have the amount (and an interest fee) deducted from the customer's next paycheck. There is no credit check or lengthy application. One must generally produce a valid form of identification and proof of employment (with wages and pay date). Payday loans are mostly for small amounts (less than $300), but the fees range from $15 to $30 for each $100 borrowed,[97] an interest rate that exceeds that of most credit cards. Researcher Michael A. Stegman describes the market for such services:

> The core demand for payday loans originates from households with a poor credit history, but who also have checking accounts, steady employment, and an annual income under $50,000. . . . A 2001 survey of low-income families in Charlotte [North Carolina] . . . estimated that African Americans were about twice as likely to have borrowed from a payday lender in a two-year period as whites . . . , and that, after controlling for a wide range of socioeconomic characteristics, blacks were five times more likely than whites to take out multiple payday loans.[98]

Americans who lack access to traditional forms of credit may also turn to rent-to-own (RTO) establishments to furnish their homes and buy appliances or items such as televisions. RTO programs allow customers to pay a small amount on a regular basis (rent) and then have a chance to buy (own) the item at the end of the contract. The majority of RTO customers earn less than $25,000 per year,[99] and those customers understand that they are going to end up paying more for the item than they would if they were able to pay cash outright.[100] *Consumer Reports* explains that customers are generally unaware, however, that they are paying what amounts to a 250 percent annual interest rate on some RTO transactions.[101]

Not everyone sees such systemic disadvantage as victimizing the poor, however. Historian Thomas Woods Jr. asks why poor Americans are not more responsible with money.[102] He suggests that Americans who cannot afford such luxuries as television sets should not purchase them or should save money so that they can purchase them later. He argues that consumers who pay RTO prices have "character flaws" that cause them to spend irresponsibly. Woods raises a valid point in terms of the wisdom of such purchases, but he is inattentive to the tremendous psychological pressure placed on all consumers—not just those who are economically disadvantaged—to appear to be in the middle class by, well, *consuming*. Each of us should practice frugality, spend wisely, and not live beyond our financial means. Those who have significant amounts of disposable income, however, can be financially irresponsible without life-altering consequences; those who do not, cannot. If we all had the same income, it would be difficult to argue with commentators such as Woods, who make reasonable points without considering the inherently unreasonable nature of the circumstances.

Such a position fits neatly within the myth of American meritocracy explained in the previous chapter: those who are able to access traditional methods of credit (and secure reasonable interest rates to borrow) are considered to be in such a position because of their wisdom, hard work, and perhaps some good luck. In exchange, they deserve to have beneficial terms for borrowing and spending, while poorer Americans do not, ostensibly because they have contributed to their own poverty. This individualistic view of inequality is convenient for those who have privilege because it removes any concerns about either the legitimacy of their own financial comfort or the responsibility to take action against a system that is flawed. As this chapter demonstrates, however, the convenient response is too simplistic to capture the reality of contemporary economic and racial inequality in the United States.

Representing the Poor

Thomas Woods's position is closest to that of most Americans: empathy for the poor does not run particularly high. In the abstract, most Americans believe that poverty is an important problem that is facing government,[103] but studies have also found

> that Americans believe there are multiple determinants of poverty but that individualistic or "internal" causes (e.g., lack of effort, being lazy, low in intelligence, being on drugs) tend to be more important than societal or "external" ones (e.g., being a victim of discrimination, low wages, being forced to attend bad schools).[104]

Further, polls have shown that an overwhelming majority of those who are doing well financially claim responsibility for their success, while less than half of those who believe they are doing poorly economically take responsibility for that condition.[105] Consider, then, the position of elected officials, who are responsible for responding to public opinion on policy issues as they seek to represent their constituents. If most Americans do not think that the system needs to be adjusted, then there will be little pressure on policymakers to make adjustments. Consequently, the belief that poorer Americans are largely responsible for their own financial condition has led to an unwillingness to address systemic barriers to greater equality. After all, if we do not believe it is broken, we will not try to fix it.

How race is related to wealth and poverty is a central theme of this book. Because of the way hegemonic power systems operate, the word "race" generally invokes images of persons of color in the minds of white Americans. When most people speak of "poverty and race," they assume that the conversation is about racial minorities. But poverty is widespread in the United States, and while it disproportionately affects communities of color, there are millions of poor whites, primarily living in rural areas, who are disadvantaged by systemic forces. Because our system of representation in the United States is primarily based on geography, and because housing patterns are influenced by economic circumstances, there are some dramatic differences in the constituencies of some representatives as opposed to others. While many elected officials represent diverse economic areas (US senators, for example, represent entire states, most of which have both rich and poor families, and big city mayors often have very economically diverse constituencies), many others represent areas that are overwhelmingly wealthy or overwhelmingly poor. In the strictest sense, these representatives are responsible for giving voice to the poorest Americans in national and state legislatures, even (and especially) if other elected officials fail to do so. In attempting to understand the relationship between representation and inequality, we will consider the demographics of some of the poorest areas in the United States and the officials who are charged with representing them.

The poorest counties in the United States are in rural regions. In terms of median income, the three poorest counties (as well as four of the top ten and twenty-two of the top one hundred) are in Kentucky.[106] In terms of percentage of residents living below the poverty line, the poorest county in the United States is Ziebach County in South Dakota (more than 54 percent of households are below the poverty line).[107] The number of residents within a county vary greatly, so perhaps a more appropriate way to examine the representation of the economically disadvantaged in America is to consider congressional districts (each of which contain approximately 710,000 people).[108] Congressional districts contain more people than most counties but fewer than large cities, which results in members of the US House of Representatives representing relatively, but not entirely, homogeneous geographical areas.

The poorest congressional district in the contiguous United States is New York's Fifteenth, which has 38 percent of its residents (and 49 percent of children) living below the poverty line.[109] José Serrano, who is a Democrat (see Box 2.3), represents this district.[110] Kentucky's Fifth District, represented by Harold "Hal" Rogers, who is a Republican, is also among most impoverished congressional districts in the nation with 28.9 percent of its residents living below the poverty line.[111] While Serrano's district is distinctly urban (covering the South Bronx), Rogers's is rural. Serrano's district is 63 percent Hispanic and 36 percent African American; Rogers's district is 98 percent white. Of the ten poorest congressional districts, only Rogers's is majority white. Four are majority Hispanic (Arizona 4, California 30, New York 16, and Texas 28), three are majority black (Michigan 13, Michigan 14, and Mississippi 2), one is plurality Hispanic (Texas 30), and one is plurality black (Pennsylvania 1).[112] Nine of the districts are represented by Democrats. Four of the representatives of America's poorest congressional districts are Hispanic, four are African

American, and two are white. Nine of the representatives are men (Rep. Eddie Bernice Johnson of Texas's Thirtieth District is the exception to this current trend).

BOX 2.3. Representing: JOSÉ SERRANO and HAL ROGERS

US Representatives José Serrano (D-NY) and Hal Rogers (R-KY) have been elected to Congress from the two most impoverished districts in the United States. Serrano, who is Latino, represents the South Bronx, while Rogers, who is white, represents a rural area in southeastern Kentucky.

On his website,[a] Congressman Serrano offers a lengthy, detailed explanation about how his district fell into economic despair. According to Serrano, the current conditions are attributable to several factors: changes in rental policy beginning in the 1960s, regional economic downturns, the installation of the cross-Bronx expressway, cutting through the borough, and the resulting exodus of those residents who were able to move. Serrano responds to the interests of his Latino constituents by sponsoring legislation relevant to their needs, such as a bill that would allow judges to take children with citizenship into consideration when considering deportation against undocumented parents.[b]

Since 1981, Congressman Rogers has advocated for his constituents by attempting to attract jobs to his district and encouraging the community to work together. Through a number of initiatives, he encourages residents of southeastern Kentucky to resist drugs, support small businesses, and attract tourism to what he calls "one of the most beautiful regions of the country."[c] As chairman of the powerful Appropriations Committee, Congressman Rogers has helped oversee the use of taxpayer funds, which is consistent with his conservative philosophy.

Though they represent vastly different areas with respect to race, political orientation, and geography, Serrano and Rogers both serve as a voice for poorer Americans and use their influence to advocate for the issues that disproportionately affect those with minimal political influence.

---

[a]http://serrano.house.gov/our-district.

[b]Albor Ruiz, "Immigration Reform Needed to Stop Heartbreaking Separations,"*New York Daily News*, July 6, 2011. http://articles.nydailynews.com/2011-07-06/local/29759431_1_citizen-children-immigration-status-immigration-laws.

[c]http://halrogers.house.gov/Biography/.

Leaving aside questions about voting behavior of constituents,[113] it is important to consider what this means at a policy level. All ten of these House members have constituents who are very poor but differ from one another in many ways. How might these representatives work together to consider policies that could help their citizens? Should they? If inequality is a result of individual shortcomings and behavioral elements, it is difficult to argue that there should be any governmental solutions to alleviate it. If, however, systemic factors contribute to and perpetuate economic and racial inequality, then it would seem that these officials, as well as others who represent large numbers of poor families, would have their sights set on advocating for meaningful change that will result in more opportunities for Americans who are suffering the most.

Summary

It is tempting to think of income as fluid (relating to securing a job, losing a job, getting a raise or a promotion, etc.) while wealth is more or less stable, growing over time (where possible). This characterization is inappropriate, though, as losses in income or an unexpected rise in expenses (due to an illness, a death in the family, etc.) can lead to a sudden and dramatic drop in wealth. According to sociologist Dalton Conley, "a significant proportion of individuals in the U.S. experience at least one drop in wealth."[114] Whites and African Americans have approximately the same number of drops (on average), but African Americans are more likely to have a greater drop.[115]

Researchers Shapiro, Meschede, and Sullivan argue that while America's racist past is certainly a driving factor behind the existence of the racial wealth gap,

> the four-fold increase in such a short time reflects policies, such as tax cuts on investment income and inheritances which benefit the wealthiest, and redistribute wealth and opportunities. Tax deductions for home mortgages, retirement accounts, and college savings all disproportionately benefit higher income families. At the same time, evidence from multiple sources demonstrates the powerful role of persistent discrimination in housing, credit, and labor markets.[116]

They note that persons of color pay more to access credit and are particularly susceptible to predatory lending in the mortgage industry. In short, while there may be overt, individualized bigotry involved in shaping income and wealth inequality, such incidents cannot come close to explaining these larger trends. First, while income and wealth inequality are pronounced between whites and persons of color, there is a tremendous gap between the highest earning whites and all other whites, as well. Second, the policies that perpetuate and exacerbate these trends are ostensibly colorblind. That is, they are not infused with explicit advantages for whites or disadvantages for persons of color.

Taking a colorblind approach to policy within a racist systemic context cannot lead to increased equality. As Figure 2.2 indicates, there is a cycle of advantage and disadvantage that centers on three major elements of American life: jobs, education, and housing. To earn access to the middle class in the twenty-first century, a college degree is increasingly necessary. Gaining admission into and succeeding in college is more difficult if one does not have a rigorous education in high school (which begins in elementary school). Because most areas fund the local public school districts disproportionately through property tax revenues, the neighborhood in which one lives is strongly related to the quality of education that is available. Of course, most people live in the neighborhood they can afford, so having money in the first place is important. This can be thought of as a

FIGURE 2.2. **Cycle of Advantage and Disadvantage**

cycle of disadvantage, but it is also a cycle of advantage. That is, if one is disadvantaged, it is quite difficult to break the cycle and gain access to economic security (let alone prosperity). Conversely, those who are privileged to be in an advantageous position have numerous opportunities to avoid falling into economic despair.

The cycle is not a guarantee of success or failure. There are many Americans who started in poverty and became financially comfortable and even wealthy, and there are wealthy individuals who fall on hard times and are unable to recover. The idea, however, is that the starting line is not the same for everyone, and that far from simply being behind (as the foot race metaphor suggests), there are systemic obstacles that are difficult to overcome. Many ideas and programs have been designed to interrupt this cycle at various points. As will become clear in the following chapters, the reasons for its persistence are complicated and affected by other related elements (such as disparities in health and in the criminal justice system). Solutions are multifaceted and present opportunities and challenges for ordinary Americans to become involved and make a difference.

Notes

1. Laurie Goodstein and Elisabetta Povoledo, "Pope Sets Down Goals for an Inclusive Church, Reaching Out 'on the Streets,'" *New York Times*, November 26, 2013, http://www.nytimes.com/2013/11/27/world/europe/in-major -document-pope-francis-present-his-vision.html.

2. Federal News Service, "Full Transcript: Obama's 2014 State of the Union Address," *Washington Post*, January 28, 2014, http://www.washingtonpost.com/ politics/full-text-of-obamas-2014-state-of-the-union-address/2014/01/28 /e0c93358-887f-11e3-a5bd-844629433ba3_story.html.

3. Allan Ornstein, *Class Counts: Education, Inequality, and the Shrinking Middle Class* (Lanham, MD: Rowman & Littlefield, 2007), 117, 150.

4. A quintile represents 20 percent of the population. In this case, if all households in the United States were listed from the wealthiest to the poorest and then divided equally into five groups, the top quintile would be the group that includes the wealthiest 20 percent of households.

5. Michael I. Norton and Dan Ariely, "Building a Better America—One Wealth Quintile at a Time," *Perspectives on Psychological Science,* 6, no. 1 (2011): 9–12.

6. Ibid., 10.

7. In 2009, nearly half of all members of the US Congress (261) were millionaires, with fifty of them having an average wealth of $10 million or more. Eight members were worth over $100 million. Median wealth in the US House of Representatives was $765,010; median wealth in the US Senate was nearly $2.38 million. Both numbers represent increases from the previous year. Center for Responsive Politics, "Congressional Members' Personal Wealth Expands Despite Sour National Economy," OpenSecrets.org, November 17, 2010, http://www .opensecrets.org/news/2010/11/congressional-members-personal-weal .html. In contrast, the median household income in the United States in 2009 was $49,777, which was virtually unchanged from the previous year. US Census Bureau, "Income, Poverty, and Health Insurance Coverage in the United States: 2009," September 16, 2010, http://www.census.gov/newsroom/releases/archives /income_wealth/cb10-144.html.

8. Ibid., 12.

9. US Bureau of Labor Statistics, "Employment Situation Summary," November 2, 2012, http://www.bls.gov/news.release/pdf/empsit.pdf.

10. Jesse Washington, "The Disappearing Black Middle Class," *Chicago Sun-Times*, July 10, 2011, http://www.suntimes.com/6397110-417/the-disappearing-black-middle-class.html.

11. Carmen DeNavas-Walt, Bernadette D. Proctor, and Jessica C. Smith, "Income, Poverty, and Health Insurance Coverage in the United States: 2011," US Census Bureau, September 2012, http://www.census.gov/prod/2012pubs/p60-243.pdf.

12. In 2008 dollars, the white-black-Hispanic medians were $58,952, $34,212, and $37,419, respectively, in 1990. US Census Bureau, Table 696, Money and Income of Families—Median Income by Race and Hispanic Origin and Constant (2008) Dollars: 1990 to 2008, *Statistical Abstract: Income, Expenditures, Poverty, and Wealth,* 2011, http://www.census.gov/compendia/statab/2011/tables/11s0696.pdf.

13. US Census Bureau, "Income, Poverty and Health Insurance Coverage in the United States: 2009," September 16, 2010, http://www.census.gov/newsroom/releases/archives/income_wealth/cb10-144.html.

14. US Census Bureau, Table 693, Share of Aggregate Income Received by Each Fifth and Top 5 Percent of Households: 1970 to 2008, *Statistical Abstract: Income, Expenditures, Poverty, and Wealth,* 2011, http://www.census.gov/compendia/statab/2011/tables/11s0693.pdf.

15. MoveOn.org, "Something Big Happened to America in 1979," June 7, 2011, http://front.moveon.org/something-big-happened-to-america-in-1979/?rc=fb.fan; Martha Hamilton, "Is It True the Rich Are Getting Richer?" Politifact.com, July 6, 2011, http://www.politifact.com/truth-o-meter/article/2011/jul/06/it-true-rich-are-getting-richer/; William Julius Wilson, "The Great Disparity," *The Nation*, July 10, 2012, http://www.thenation.com/article/168822/great-disparity. Wilson reviews two books on growing economic inequality: Timothy Noah, *The Great Divergence: America's Growing Inequality Crisis and What We Can Do About It* (New York: Bloombury Press, 2013) and Charles Murray, *Coming Apart: The State of White Amerca, 1960–2010* (New York: Crown Forum, 2013).

16. Marina Villeneuve, "Study Shows How Broad Pay Disparities Are Between Sexes," *USA Today*, April 20, 2012, http://www.usatoday.com/money/workplace/story/2012-04-17/gender-pay-gap-study/54368152/1.

17. Ibid.

18. Ibid.

19. Maternal and Child Health Information Resource Center, "Women's Health USA, 2011," http://www.mchb.hrsa.gov/whusa11/popchar/pages/104hc.html.

20. Irene Browne, "Explaining the Black-White Gap in Labor Force Participation Among Women Heading Households," *American Sociological Review* 62, no. 2 (1997): 236–252.

21. Allison Linn, "Minorities Lose Ground in Big Corporate Boardrooms," LifeInc, May 3, 2011, http://thegrio.com/2011/05/04/minorities-lose-ground-in-big-corporate-boardrooms; see also Alliance for Board Diversity, "Missing Pieces: Women and Minorities on Fortune 500 Boards," May 1, 2011, http://the-abd.org/Missing_Pieces_Women_and_Minorities_on _Fortune_500_Boards.pdf.

22. Chris Isidore, "African-American CEOs Still Rare," CNN Money, March 22, 2012, http://money.cnn.com/2012/03/22/news/companies/black-ceo /index.htm.

23. Two of the eighteen women CEOs in 2012 were of color: Ursula Burns (Xerox), who is African American, and Indra Nooyi (PepsiCO), who is Indian.

24. Bianca Bosker, "Fortune 500 List Boasts More Female CEOs Than Ever Before," Huffington Post, May 7, 2012, http://www.huffingtonpost.com/2012 /05/07/fortune-500-female-ceos_n_1495734.html.

25. CNN Money, "GDP Growth Not Reaching Paychecks," CNN.com, September 5, 2007, http://money.cnn.com/2007/09/03/news/economy/epi_report /index.htm; Huck Gutman, "Economic Inequality in the US," CommonDreams .org, July 1, 2002, http://www.commondreams.org/views02/0701-05.htm; MoveOn.org, "Something Big Happened to America in 1979."

26. Gutman, "Economic Inequality in the US"; Derrick Z. Jackson, "Income Gap Mentality," *Boston Globe*, April 19, 2006, http://www.boston.com/news /globe/editorial_opinion/oped/articles/2006/04/19/income_gap_mentality.

27. Gretchen Morgenson, "An Unstoppable Climb in C.E.O. Pay," *New York Times*, June 29, 2013, http://mobile.nytimes.com/2013/06/30/business/an -unstoppable-climb-in-ceo-pay.html. An interactive chart is available at http:// www.nytimes.com/interactive/2013/06/30/business/executive-compensation -tables.html.

28. "2012 Federal Income Tax Brackets and Marginal Rates," Consumerism Commentary, September 28, 2012, http://www.consumerismcommentary .com/2012-federal-income-tax-brackets-and-marginal-rates/.

29. Dave Gilson and Carolyn Perot, "It's the Inequality, Stupid," *Mother Jones*, March-April, 2011, http://www.motherjones.com/politics/2011/02 /income-inequality-in-america-chart-graph.

30. Ben Rooney and Julianne Pepitone, "$400 Billion in Tax Breaks Seen Favoring Wealthy," CNN Money, September 22, 2010, http://money.cnn.com/ 2010/09/21/news/economy/wealth_building_tax_policy/index.htm.

31. Dan Froomkin, "The Top 10 Tax Breaks—And How They Help the Wealthy the Most," Huffington Post, April 18, 2011, http://www.huffingtonpost .com/2011/04/18/the-top-10-tax-breaks-_n_850534.html.

32. Michael D. Shear, "Romney Releases 2011 Tax Returns," *New York Times*, September 21, 2012, http://thecaucus.blogs.nytimes.com/2012/09/21/romney-to-release-2011-tax-returns/; Brody Mullins, Patrick O'Connor, and John McKinnon, "Romney's Taxes: $3 million," *Wall Street Journal*, January 24, 2012, http://online.wsj.com/article/SB10001424052970204624204577179740171772850.html.

33. "Buffett Slams Dividend Tax Cut," CNN Money, May 20, 2003, http://money.cnn.com/2003/05/20/news/buffett_tax/; Steve Wamhoff, "How to Implement the Buffet Rule," Citizens for Tax Justice, October 19, 2011, http://www.ctj.org/pdf/buffettruleremedies.pdf.

34. US Internal Revenue Service. "Topic 751. Social Security and Medicare Withholding Rates." March 20, 2014. http://www.irs.gov/taxtopics/tc751.html. Medicare contributions were similarly regressive until 2013, but now there is now no wage cap. All income is taxed at 2.9 percent (also split evenly between employer and employee), and higher earners pay one-half of a 3.8 percent contribution for income over $250,000 (for married individuals in 2013). (US Internal Revenue Service. "Topic 751. Social Security and Medicare Withholding Rates." March 20, 2014. http://www.irs.gov/taxtopics/tc751.html).

35. Bruce D. Meyer and Dan T. Rosenbaum, "Welfare, the Earned Income Tax Credit, and the Labor Supply of Single Mothers," *Quarterly Journal of Economics* 116, no. 3 (2001): 1063–1114.

36. In 2011, a family of five (two adults and three children) could receive a tax benefit of $12,780. An estimated 26 million households received the benefit in 2010. Elaine Maag and Adam Carasso, "Taxation and the Family: What is the Earned Income Tax Credit?" Tax Policy Center, June 22, 2011, http://www.taxpolicycenter.org/briefing-book/key-elements/family/eitc.cfm.

37. Court Smith, "Minimum Wage History," 2011, http://oregonstate.edu/instruct/anth484/minwage.html.

38. Ibid.

39. US Department of Labor, "Wage and Hour Division: Minimum Wage Laws in the States, January 1, 2012," 2012, http://www.dol.gov/whd/minwage/america.htm.

40. Smith, "Minimum Wage History."

41. Jessie Willis, "How We Measure Poverty: A History and Brief Overview," Oregon Center for Public Policy, February 2000, http://www.ocpp.org/poverty/how.htm.

42. US Department of Health and Human Services, *The 2011 HHS Poverty Guidelines,* 2011, http://aspe.hhs.gov/poverty/11poverty.shtml.

43. National Poverty Center, "Poverty in the United States: Frequently Asked Questions," 2012, http://www.npc.umich.edu/poverty/.

44. Ibid.

45. Legal Momentum, "Single Mother Poverty in the United States in 2010," 2011, http://www.legalmomentum.org/our-work/women-and-poverty/resources–publications/single-mother-poverty-2010.pdf.

46. National Poverty Center, "Poverty in the United States."

47. Ibid.

48. Willis, "How We Measure Poverty."

49. Ibid.

50. Jackson, "Income Gap Mentality."

51. "A Minimum Wage Increase," *New York Times*, March 26, 2011, http://www.nytimes.com/2011/03/27/opinion/27sun2.html.

52. *Washington Post*, January 28, 2014, http://www.washingtonpost.com /politics/full-text-of-obamas-2014-state-of-the-union-address/2014/01/28 /e0c93358-887f-11e3-a5bd-844629433ba3_story.html.

53. Marilyn Geewax, "Does a Higher Minimum Wage Kill Jobs?" National Public Radio, April 24, 2011, http://www.npr.org/2011/04/24/135638370 /does-a-higher-minimum-wage-kill-jobs.

54. Raymond A. Smith, *The American Anomaly: U.S. Politics and Government in Comparative Perspective* (New York: Routledge, 2011), 165–169.

55. Social Security Administration, "Historical Background and Development of Social Security," 2011, http://www.ssa.gov/history/briefhistory3.html.

56. For example, see Stanley Feldman and John Zaller, "The Political Culture of Ambivalence: Ideological Responses to the Welfare State," *American Journal of Political Science* 36, no. 1 (1992): 268–307.

57. "'Welfare Queen' Becomes Issue in Reagan Campaign," *New York Times*, February 15, 1976, http://picofarad.info/misc/welfarequeen.pdf.

58. Though prosecutors argued that the characterization of her crimes was accurate, she was only indicted for theft of $8,000 from public welfare and for perjury. Dan Miller, "The Chutzpa Queen: Favorite Reagan Target as Welfare Cheat Remains Unflappable at Trial in Chicago, *Washington Post*, March 13, 1977, A3.

59. See Frank Gilliam Jr., "The 'Welfare Queen' Experiment: How Voters React to Images of African-American Mothers on Welfare," UCLA Center for Communications and Community, 1999, http://escholarship.org/uc/item /17m7r1rq; Ange-Marie Hancock, *The Politics of Disgust: The Public Identity of the Welfare Queen* (New York: New York University Press, 2004). Reagan did not mention the woman's race explicitly. Rather, he made references to Chicago or to the South Side of Chicago or to the inner city, which served as code for "African American." Paul Krugman, "Republicans and Race," *New York Times*, November 19, 2007, http://www.nytimes.com/2007/11/19/opinion/19krugman .html. As Gilliam explains, "The implicit racial coding is readily apparent. The woman Reagan was talking about was African-American. Veiled references to African-American women, and African-Americans in general, were equally transparent. In other words, while poor women of all races get blamed for their impoverished condition, African-American women commit the most egregious violations of American values. This story line tips into stereotypes about both women (uncontrolled sexuality) and African-Americans (laziness)."

60. Martin Gilens, *Why Americans Hate Welfare: Race, Media, and the Politics of Antipoverty Policy* (Chicago: University of Chicago Press, 1999), 68.

61. Ibid., 68–69.

62. Hancock, *Politics of Disgust.*

63. Stephen Slivinsky, "The Corporate Welfare State: How the Federal Government Subsidizes U.S. Businesses," *Policy Analysis* 592 (2007): 1–21.

64. Melvin L. Oliver and Thomas M. Shapiro, *Black Wealth/White Wealth: A New Perspective on Racial Inequality,* 10th ed. (New York: Routledge, 2006).

65. Lisa A. Keister, *Wealth in America: Trends in Wealth Inequality* (New York: Cambridge University Press, 2000), 10.

66. Ibid.; Joseph E. Stiglitz, *The Price of Inequality: How Today's Divided Society Endangers Our Future* (New York: Norton, 2012).

67. Figures are expressed in 2010 dollars. Linda Levine, "An Analysis of the Distribution of Wealth Across Households, 1989–2010," Congressional Research Service, July 17, 2012, http://www.fas.org/sgp/crs/misc/RL33433.pdf. Household wealth grew faster than median wealth over that period, suggesting concentration at the upper end of the wealth distribution. As Levine notes, while both declined by 2012, the greater decline in the median reflects that the recession "affected those in the lower half of the wealth distribution more than those higher up in the distribution" (p. 3).

68. Bonnie Kavoussi, "Nearly Half of Americans Die Without Money, Study Finds," Huffington Post, August 6, 2012, http://www.huffingtonpost.com/2012/08/06/americans-die-without-money_n_1746862.html.

69. Paul Taylor et al., "Wealth Gaps Rise to Record Highs Between Whites, Blacks and Hispanics: Twenty-to-One," Pew Research Center, July 26, 2011, http://www.pewsocialtrends.org/2011/07/26/wealth-gaps-rise-to-record-highs-between-whites-blacks-hispanics/.

70. "Census: Wealth Gap Widens Between whites and Minorities," *USA Today,* July 26, 2011, http://www.usatoday.com/news/washington/2011-07-26-census-wealth-data_n.htm.

71. Ibid.

72. Thomas M. Shapiro, Tatjana Meschede, and Laura Sullivan, "The Racial Wealth Gap Increases Fourfold," Brandeis University, May 2010, http://iasp.brandeis.edu/pdfs/Racial-Wealth-Gap-Brief.pdf; Chris McGreal, "A $95,000 Question: Why Are Whites Five Times Richer Than Blacks in the U.S.?" *Guardian,* May 17, 2010, http://www.guardian.co.uk/world/2010/may/17/white-people-95000-richer-black.

73. Shapiro, Meschede, and Sullivan, "Racial Wealth Gap Increases Fourfold."

74. This chapter focuses disproportionately on the black-white income and wealth gaps because most research on the question of race and economic inequality has been focused here. For a broader view, including discussion of Asian Americans and Native Americans, see Jessica Gordon Nembhard and Ngina

Chiteji, eds., *Wealth Accumulation and Communities of Color in the United States* (Ann Arbor: University of Michigan Press, 2006).

75. "Study Shows Racial Wealth Gap Continues to Widen," *USA Today,* February 27, 2013, http://www.usatoday.com/story/money/personalfinance/2013/02/27/racial-wealth-gap-growing/1948899/. This report from Brandeis University attributed the widening gap primarily to the housing crisis but also noted the effect of unemployment during the Great Recession, as well as the education gap and the cost of education.

76. Karuna Jaggar, "The Race and Gender Wealth Gap," *Race and Regionalism* 15, no. 1 (2008), http://urbanhabitat.org/node/2815.

77. Megan Thibos, Danielle Lavin-Loucks, and Marcus Martin, "The Feminization of Poverty," YWCA Dallas, 2007, http://www.ywcadallas.org/PDF/womens-health/FeminizationofPoverty.pdf.

78. Bridget Lavelle and Pamela Smock, "Divorce and Women's Risk of Health Insurance Loss in the U.S.," *Population Studies Center Research Report no. 11-734,* Institute for Social Research, University of Michigan, March, 2011, http://www.psc.isr.umich.edu/pubs/pdf/rr11-734.pdf.

79. Jaggar, "Race and Gender Wealth Gap." For more information on gender and race in wealth disparity, especially with respect to homeownership, see Beverlyn Lundy Allen, "Race and Gender Inequality in Homeownership: Does Place Make a Difference?" *Rural Sociology* 67, no. 4 (2002): 603–621.

80. Matthew Miller and Duncan Greenberg, "The Forbes 400: Almost All of America's Wealthiest Citizens Are Poorer This Year," Forbes.com, September 30, 2009, http://www.forbes.com/2009/09/29/forbes-400-buffett-gates-ellison-rich-list-09-intro.html.

81. For a video representation of the US wealth gap, see http://mashable.com/2013/03/02/wealth-inequality/. For a video representation of the racial wealth gap in the United States, see this video from the Urban Institute: http://urban.org/changing-wealth-americans/video/.

82. During the Republican nominating contests in 2012, Mitt Romney offered that the way to achieve economic success in America is to "take a shot, go for it. Take a risk. Get the education. Borrow money if you have to from your parents. Start a business." Sarah Huisenga, "Romney Suggests Young Adults Get Loans . . . From Their Parents," *National Journal,* April 27, 2012, http://www.nationaljournal.com/2012-presidential-campaign/romney-suggests-young-adults-get-loans-from-their-parents-20120427. Opponents seized on the statement as a reflection of some Republicans' willingness to reduce student loan benefits, but the Romney campaign insisted that the "borrow" comment was meant to relate to starting a business. Either way, the prospects are slim for most young Americans. The United States has one of the strongest links between individual and parent earnings in the industrialized world. Organisation for Economic Cooperation and Development, *Economic Policy Reforms: Going for Growth 2010,* chap. 5, "A Family Affair:

Intergenerational Social Mobility across OECD Countries," http://www.oecd.org/tax/public-finance/chapter%205%20gfg%202010.pdf.

83. For an in-depth examination and analysis of the transfer of wealth in various forms and from a number of perspectives, see Yuval Elmelech, *Transmitting Inequality: Wealth and the American Family* (Lanham, MD: Rowman & Littlefield, 2008).

84. Maury Gittleman and Edward N. Wolff, "Racial Differences in Patterns of Wealth Accumulation," *Journal of Human Resources* 39 (2004): 193–227.

85. Paul L. Menchik and Nancy Ammon Jianakoplos, "Black-White Wealth Inequality: Is Inheritance the Reason?" *Economic Inquiry* 35 (2007): 428–442, at 441.

86. Federal Reserve Bank of San Francisco, "What Steps Can Be Taken to Increase Savings in the United States Economy?" February 2002, http://www.frbsf.org/education/activities/doctor-econ/2002/February/savings-disposable-personal-income.html.

87. New America Foundation, *Savings in American Households,* November 16, 2009, http://assets.newamerica.net/files/1109SavingsFacts.pdf.

88. Michael A. Fletcher, "Blacks, Hispanics Hold Few Investments, Poll Shows," *Washington Post,* February 21, 2011, http://www.washingtonpost.com/wp-dyn/content/article/2011/02/21/AR2011022104350.html.

89. Matt Fellowes, *From Poverty, Opportunity: Putting the Market to Work for Lower Income Families*, Brookings Institution, 2006, http://www.brookings.edu/reports/2006/07poverty_fellowes.aspx.

90. See David J. Hand and William E. Henley, "Statistical Classification Methods in Consumer Credit Scoring: A Review," *Journal of the Royal Statistical Society* 160, no. 3 (1997): 523–541.

91. Ibid.

92. Statistical and qualitative studies of black business owners, for example, identify unique and persistent challenges in securing loans, intrusion of larger companies into traditionally black markets, and lack of experience. See Timothy Bates, *Banking on Black Enterprise: The Potential of Emerging Firms for Revitalizing Urban Economics* (Washington DC: Joint Center for Political and Economic Studies, 1993); Michael Bonds, "Looking Beyond the Numbers: The Struggles of Black Businesses to Survive: A Qualitative Approach," *Journal of Black Studies* 37, no. 5 (1997): 581–601; Jan E. Christopher, "Minority Business Formation and Survival: Evidence on Business Performance and Visibility," *Review of Black Political Economy* 26, no. 7 (1998): 37–72; Robert W. Fairlie and Alicia M. Robb, "Why Are Black-Owned Businesses Less Successful Than White-Owned Businesses? The Role of Families, Inheritances, and Business Human Capital," University of California–Santa Cruz, 2005, http://repositories.cdlib.org/ucsc econ/618; Robert Mark Silverman, "Black Business, Group Resources, and the Economic Detour: Contemporary Black Manufacturers in Chicago's Ethnic Beauty Aids Industry," *Journal of Black Studies* 30, no. 2 (1999): 232–258; Joe

William Trotter Jr., *Black Milwaukee: The Making of an Industrial Proletariat, 1915–1948* (Urbana: University of Illinois Press, 1985).

93. There is a rich literature in economics regarding conditions under which individuals tend to be risk averse as opposed to risk seeking. See, for instance, Daniel Kahneman and Amos Tversky, "Choices, Values, and Frames," *American Psychologist* 39, no. 4 (1984): 341–350.

94. Jeffrey M. Jones, "One in Six Americans Gamble on Sports," Gallup, July 30, 2008, http://www.gallup.com/poll/104086/One-Six-Americans-Gamble -Sports.aspx.

95. Ibid.

96. "Gambling Facts and Statistics," OvercomingGambling.com, http://www .overcominggambling.com/facts.html; see also H. Roy Kaplan, "The Social and Economic Impact of State Lotteries," *Annals of the American Academy of Political and Social Science* 474 (1984): 91–106.

97. Michael A. Stegman, "Payday Lending," *Journal of Economic Perspectives* 21, no. 1 (2007): 169–190.

98. Michael A. Stegman and Robert Faris, *Welfare, Work, and Banking: The North Carolina Financial Services Survey* (Chapel Hill, NC: Center for Community Capitalism, 2001); Stegman and Faris, "Welfare, Work, and Banking: The Use of Consumer Credit by Current and Former TANF Recipients in Charlotte, North Carolina," *Journal of Urban Affairs* 27, no. 4 (2005): 379–402, cited in Stegman, "Payday Lending," 173–174.

99. Matt Fellowes, "From Poverty, Opportunity: Putting the Market to Work for Lower Income Families," Brookings Institution, 2006, http://www.brookings .edu/reports/2006/07poverty_fellowes.aspx.

100. Ronald Paul Hill, David L. Ramp, and Linda Silver, "The Rent-to-Own Industry and Pricing Disclosure Tactics," *Journal of Public Policy and Marketing* 17, no. 1 (1998): 3–10.

101. "Consumer Protection: Reforming the 'RTO' Rip-Off," *Consumer Reports,* August 1995, 507, cited in Hill, Ramp, and Silver, "Rent-to-Own Industry and Pricing Disclosure Tactics."

Thomas E. Woods Jr., "Do Rent-to-Own Stores Hurt the Poor?" Ludwig von Mises Institute, August 3, 2006, http://mises.org/daily/2261.

102. Woods, Jr. "Do Rent-to-Own Stores Hurt the Poor?"

103. Elizabeth T. Powers and Emilie Bagby, "Poverty and Inequality in Illinois," Institute of Government and Public Affairs, University of Illinois, 2008, http://igpa.uillinois.edu/system/files/08-ILRept08-Pov-IneqPg49-60.pdf.

104. Catherine Cozzarelli, Anna V. Wilkinson, and Michael J. Tagler, "Attitudes Toward the Poor and Attributions for Poverty," *Journal of Social Issues* 57, no. 1 (2001): 207–227, 209.

105. Powers and Bagby, "Poverty and Inequality in Illinois"; see also Matthew

O. Hunt, "Race/Ethnicity and Beliefs About Wealth and Poverty," *Social Science Quarterly* 85, no. 3 (2004): 827–853.

106. Dean Preatorius, "2010 Census: Poorest Counties in America," Huffington Post, December 21, 2010, http://www.huffingtonpost.com/2010/12/21/2010-census-the-poorest-c_n_799526.html; Kenneth Stepp, "Twenty-two of the One Hundred Poorest Counties in the U.S. Are Here," *Economic Journal*, February 28, 2009, http://steppforcongress.blogspot.com/2009/02/twenty-two-of-one-hundred-poorest.html.

107. "The Poorest Counties of America," *New York Times*, November 18, 2009, http://economix.blogs.nytimes.com/2009/11/18/the-poorest-counties-of-america/.

108. This figure, calculated after the 2010 census and reapportionment of House seats, represents an increase of approximately 60,000 persons over the average after the 2000 census.

109. Data in this paragraph are assembled from US Census data reported by Half in Ten, "Interactive Map: Poverty Data by Congressional District," September 30, 2010, http://halfinten.org/issues/articles/poverty-data-by-congressional-district/; "Election 08 Results by District: Presidential Results," *Congressional Quarterly*, 2010, http://innovation.cq.com/atlas/district_08; and available from the US Census Bureau, "Fast Facts for Congress," 2011, http://fastfacts.census.gov/home/cws/main.html. What was New York's Sixteenth District when this report was written is largely composed of what is now the Fifteenth District after the 2012 congressional map was adopted.

110. Richard Sisk, "South Bronx Is Poorest District in Nation, U.S. Census Bureau Finds: 38% Live Below Poverty Line," *New York Daily News*, September 29, 2010, http://www.nydailynews.com/new-york/south-bronx-poorest-disrict-nation-u-s-census-bureau-finds-38-live-poverty-line-article-1.438344.

111. Puerto Rico is the poorest congressional district with 45 percent of its residents living in poverty. While Puerto Rico has a delegate in the US House of Representatives, Pedro Pierluisi, he does not vote; because Puerto Rico is not a state, it has no representation in the US Senate.

112. Half in Ten, "Interactive Map: Poverty Data by Congressional District"; US Census Bureau, *Fast Facts for Congress*, 2011, http://fastfacts.census.gov/home/cws/main.html.

113. For a detailed analysis of voting behavior and representation in minority communities, see John D. Griffin and Brian Newman, *Minority Report: Evaluating Political Equality in America* (Chicago: University of Chicago Press, 2008), especially pt. 2.

114. Dalton Conley, *Being Black, Living in the Red: Race, Wealth, and Social Policy in America,* 10th ed. (Berkeley: University of California Press, 2010), 157.

115. Ibid.

116. Shapiro, Meschede, and Sullivan, "Racial Wealth Gap Increases Fourfold," 2.

For the children in our study, it was clear that they were aware of social class differences and inequality. Further, they expressed an understanding that some kids' parents give them money (either for allowance or for college or for private elementary school or for toys). They understood that some kids go to better schools than other kids, and that schools are linked directly to the amount of money that parents have. It is also clear that for these children, while they were aware of inequality and differences in the amount of money one's parent has or the educational opportunities provided for that child, they still held on tightly to their belief in the American Dream.

Wealth Privilege as a Private, Public Power

Within a structure of wealth inequality, family wealth or lack of it grants unearned advantages to some individuals and disadvantages to others, depending on the families to which they were born. This was acknowledged by the parents interviewed as they expressed their beliefs that wealth gives families who have it advantages that they did not merit through individual achievement. In examining one site where this can potentially play out—school decision making—parents believed wealth made a significant difference in a family's capacity to choose the schools that they thought would most benefit their children. And their direct experiences made plain that this was, indeed, the case. Their collective action was patterned. Families with wealth privilege used it to actively choose good schools (schools that were the most reputable, and also that tended to be populated by children from predominantly white, relatively wealthy families), while families with histories of relative wealth poverty, who were disproportionately black, were constrained from acting on what they believed in and wanted for their children—good schools. Wealth was a very private power that was used in a very public domain to access advantageous education for children.

Given the landscape of vastly disparate schools, a structure of wealth inequality is a powerful way in which opportunity for children is unequally distributed. Wealth can enable a family to access resources and advantages for the next generation that they would not be able to provide otherwise. And family wealth is usually, at least to some extent, unearned. There are always exceptions—individuals who truly start from nothing and manage to create fortunes in a lifetime; people who win the lottery and are suddenly millionaires; families who save pennies and amass assets without any assistance whatsoever. Most of us know at least one such example. However, as we have seen, even in the only two hundred families we interviewed, the patterns were very clear—most families do not amass wealth from nothing; most families do not strike it rich by sheer luck; and most families do not accumulate their wealth from savings alone. These interviews provide a rare glimpse into the inner workings of wealth within families, and into those families' perspectives on wealth inequality—rare because wealth, like most aspects of money and social class, is not something we usually talk about, especially not in the United States.

We learn from an early age that it is inappropriate, improper, even rude to ask questions about other people's money. We may talk around it, complain about it, or flaunt it, but social class and specifics of money wrapped up in it most often go ignored—at least overtly, at least publicly. Social class is, as bell hooks writes, "a taboo topic" in our society.[3] Wealth is part of the taboo. *The fact that wealth is not talked about is important because it means that how families acquire wealth, the intergenerational transmission of it, and the purposeful use of it are normally hidden from public view.* In this way, wealth remains a "taboo"—or, what Katherine Newman refers to as a "hidden dimension"—of our society.[4]

There is a code of secrecy that surrounds wealth in our society. We normally do not ask such things as how much someone has saved in the bank; what was inherited when a relative died; how much cash was received on a wedding day; what portion of a down payment was contributed by family; how much of children's education is financed by grandparents; what value a family's furniture or jewelry holds; or how much interest was accrued on this quarter's investments. Family wealth might be discussed with financial advisors, but usually not with neighbors or coworkers, and often not even with close friends or family. The story of family wealth is almost never told, and when it is, the details are often vague. A family's wealth portfolio, let alone how much of it originated from family sources and how it is used to propel advantage, can easily fly under the radar despite its power in shaping that family's experiences and worldviews. But surely if the two hundred families interviewed here are any indicator at all, among middle- and upper-class families, and disproportionately white families, intergenerational transfers are significant and occurring regularly. In these families, wealth was being passed along, amassed, and used in a myriad of ways throughout the life course. The power of wealth is *private*. But it creates opportunities, provides experiences, and opens doors that very often are in the *public* domain.

The private, public power of wealth has big implications, especially when the undercurrent of the American Dream runs so strong. Wealth can easily go unnoticed, and we are often left to assume that it is not an important variable in a life trajectory or that only a very small group of people benefit from family wealth in any significant way. Meanwhile, as we have seen, it was an important variable in a life trajectory, and many more families than we might have imagined were benefiting from it. Wealth privilege is like a buoy, helping to keep those who have it ahead and afloat, pushing them upward, and there to rely upon if the waters get choppy.

Most of the white families interviewed had experienced—to some extent—the privileges, or the buoying effects, of family wealth. In comparison to black parents of all socioeconomic backgrounds, white parents much *less* often were supporting their own parents and extended families and had much *more* often reaped the benefits of the financial assistance and support associated with family wealth over time: intergenerational transfers and inheritances passed down to them in small or large amounts; the "push" and the "safety net" of their families' relative class positioning; their college educations at least partially paid for by their own parents; help with first-home down payments and other major purchases; gifts; loans; assistance in funding investments and business ventures; new or used furniture, appliances, cars, and the like passed along—a steady stream of "big" or "tiny" things that made a difference. These were sometimes passed along at major milestones during the life of a family, or they might have been given routinely, perhaps even daily.

Others studying wealth have implicitly and explicitly argued that while income is received and used from day to day to support daily living, wealth is received and used in families at important milestones in life to create opportunities and leverage advantages for the next generation.[5] While wealth was certainly received at major milestones in the wealth-holding families interviewed here, its accumulated receipt in the more mundane experiences of these families was just as important to its acquisition, development, use, and far-reaching impact. Not only did wealth appear to take on a "cumulative effect" as it was passed along at major milestones and continued to amass,[6] but the interviews also brought to light the more day-to-day, commonplace receipt and privileges of family wealth—the *accumulative advantage* of family wealth over time, the relatively minor, "invisible," taken-for-granted privileges for people from wealthy backgrounds that together add up, that matter. The transfer of wealth within families can happen in momentous moments, but it can also be more fluid: buoying, securing, and orienting those individuals who have it in thousands of subtle ways.

Others have discussed the accumulation of advantage and disadvantage as small differences in daily lives that amount to significant disadvantage or advantage over time.[7] In sociology, this idea is probably best established in work on gender. Virginia Valian, for example, draws attention to the ramifications of the accumulation of advantage and disadvantage in individuals' occupational careers over time, pointing to how "the long-term consequences of small differences in the evaluation and treatment of men and women also hold up the glass ceiling."[8] What the interviews here point to is something similar—specifically, the trickle-down effect of how seemingly little things can add up to translate into big differences, both material and sociopsychological, for individuals who benefit from family wealth. Over time, accumulative advantages are, as one parent said, "paving the way" for individuals with family wealth, and allowing them "to live worry free," as another said. Previous research on wealth has alluded to this—for instance, referring to the way that wealth "feeds heads," or orients people's future aspirations[9]—but much more work in this area is required to further our understanding.

One way to conceptualize the use of wealth in wealth-holding families is as providing the next generation with *foothold steps of advantage*. Conceptualizing family wealth this way, in the families we interviewed, foothold steps of advantage were created both by small, subtle transfers of wealth (those more day-to-day) and by more massive, obvious transfers (at milestone events); but, over time, these all added up to enable a firmer grip on children's future chances for success, however defined. A good analogy for this legacy of foothold steps of advantage in wealth-holding families is the rock-climbing wall. On the rock-climbing wall, parents use their own family wealth to nail extra foothold steps for their children's climbs. These may be material or nonmaterial, but these footholds are advantageous because they are additional steps that are not provided for other climbers. We all want to secure footholds for our children; we all want to make the path less slippery, less steep, less difficult to climb. Wealth gives some families the ability to provide footholds for their children while other families cannot; this leads to very different climbs, very different experiences, and very different mobility patterns.

Foothold steps of advantage materialized in how wealth-holding families were able to buy in and opt out more easily than the other families, but they also took shape in the tutoring, piano lessons, cultural and social capital, higher-quality housing, better health care, financial guidance, home computers, and all sorts of other things that were more easily acquired—and in operation—within the families with wealth to rely upon. As previously mentioned, in her books, *Home Advantage* and *Unequal Childhoods*, sociologist Annette Lareau discusses how these sorts of things contribute to what she refers to as a "concerted cultivation" of childhood in middle-class families.[10] As she also found, the middle- and upper-middle-class families we interviewed were conscientiously "cultivating" their children's growth by providing family vacations, professional college-admissions preparation, cultural activities, and a myriad of other activities, opportunities, and experiences to their children. Any of these things taken alone would not necessarily impact the life of a child. However, taken together they add up over the course of a childhood, and in the case of the families interviewed here, family wealth was often being relied upon to help facilitate such things.

The families were forthcoming on the subject of wealth privilege; they understood and acknowledged a structure of wealth inequality and the ways that inequality plays out for the next generation in terms of educational trajectories and children's life chances. Taken together and comparing those with and without backgrounds of family wealth, the parents' perspectives, beliefs, and experiences brought to light a sort of "glass floor" connected to wealth privilege. In conjunction with the concept of a "glass ceiling" invisibly keeping disadvantaged individuals from rising, a *glass floor* seemed to keep individuals with family wealth from falling very far. And people were aware of it. Essentially, in families who had access to wealth, parents consciously used it to access advantageous opportunities for their children in their attempts to ensure that the next generation would not only rise from the relatively privileged position in which they already stood, but also not fall very far either. Wealth privilege—the glass floor—was there to stand upon; it served as an invisible safety net, buoying up the families who had it and granting them a sense of security that felt to them like "peace of mind."

Given their acknowledgment of wealth privilege and a structure of wealth inequality, it might be hard to imagine that these same parents truly believed that all Americans have an equal shot at whatever they aspire to, and that people who "make it" do so entirely on their own. The most provocative aspect of the interviews, however, was just that—the families discussed their beliefs in meritocracy with the same forthrightness with which they had discussed wealth privilege.

Notes

3 For an in-depth analysis of the subject of social class as taboo in the contemporary United States, see hooks 2000.
4 Newman 1988.
5 For some of the most important work related to this see Conley 1999; Oliver and Shapiro 2006; Shapiro 2004; Sherraden 1991. See also policy work, such as Friedman 2003a and 2003b; Miller-Adams 2002.
6 See Oliver and Shapiro 2006, pp. 5 and 51, for examples regarding their use of the notion of wealth's "cumulative effect."
7 Sociologist Robert Merton coined this sort of phenomenon the "Matthew effect." See Merton 1968.
8 Valian 1998, p. 3.
9 See, for example, Sherraden 1991.
10 See Lareau 2000, 2011.

NORTH AMERICAN GHETTOS AND BARRIOS

In the United States, the practice of social segregation was historically related to the different social and legal rights of slaves and free individuals. Although there were both black and white slaves and indentured servants in the colonial years, after some decades a racial system had come into use as a way to categorize and reproduce inequality (Massey 2007; Tilly 1998). Despite the legality of slavery, in the South black and white quarters were often next to each other, showing the close interdependence and interaction between masters and slaves. As black Americans became emancipated from their slave condition, many migrated north in search of supposedly greater tolerance and work opportunities in industrializing urban areas. There they became concentrated in certain neighborhoods, not only because of social networks and affinity but also because of employer and public policies and the racism and exclusionary practices of northern whites who moved out of neighborhoods after a certain racial tipping point was reached (Massey and Denton 1993). Yet the ghettos of Harlem and the Bronx (areas where this author lived for years) are far more heterogeneous than the stereotype of them, as well as more heterogeneous than Chicago, a city that, with a large African American population, has often and wrongly stood as a representative city for all of the United States (Small 2008).

Puerto Rican migrants followed a pattern similar to blacks moving north. As citizens from a U.S. territory, they moved into the continental U.S. landmass in search of opportunities and often ended up in areas that bordered African American enclaves in cities like Chicago and New York.

The work of anthropologist Oscar Lewis (1966) on the poor *vecindades* of *El Barrio de Tepito* in Mexico City, extended later to working-class neighborhoods in Puerto Rico and New York, was important in documenting the daily lives of poor people in these neighborhoods. A misreading of what he termed "the culture of poverty" would contribute to a stereotype that blames the victim and questions the morality of the so-called "undeserving poor" (Katz 1996). The realities on which Lewis's "culture of poverty" was based only got worse following the large migration into central cities of blacks and Puerto Ricans and the loss of many jobs in urban areas due to offshoring and deindustrialization (Marwell 2007; Wilson 1997). The state provided subsides to white ethnics to build and inhabit suburban areas, but blacks and Latinos were left behind (Gans 1982; Katznelson 2005).

This resulted in ethnic and class concentrations in certain neighborhoods. Poverty became spatially concentrated in these neighborhoods, at first because of the struggles associated with first-generation migration and subsequent poverty, and then because of unemployment and lack of opportunities for social mobility. To this argument must be added the rise of neoliberal moral discourses and the socio-scientific literature and simplistic policies that criminalized and pathologized poverty and created symbolic boundaries between whites and blacks and between poor and successful blacks and Latinos (Lamont 2000). In the imaginations of the American public and policymakers, "the ghetto" became black and "el barrio" brown. In this view of these areas as dangerous, immoral, and undeserving places in need of drastic policy (and police) intervention, the effects of poverty were misunderstood as causes and justified what Wacquant (2008) calls a "malign neglect" that allowed these areas to fall into increasing disrepair. This response was answered by an increase in the language and action of "law and order," following the "broken windows" theories, and by an increase in the penalization of poverty, drug-dealing, and incarceration, mainly of minorities living in these neighborhoods.

New York has witnessed the arrival of many groups from Latin America and the Caribbean (Aranda 2008; Bourgois 2003; Dávila 2004; Fuentes 2007; Grasmuck and Pessar 1991; Jones-Correa 1998; Kasinitz, Mollenkopf, and Waters 2004; Kasinitz, Mollenkopf, Waters, and Holdaway 2008; Loveman and Muniz 2007; Marwell 2007). If we take a close look at the realities of Latino neighborhoods in the New York City metropolitan area, a more complex image of changing composition emerges—one that is relevant here because in many ways Latinos in New York City offer a closer comparison than African Americans to North Africans in Paris (Castañeda 2010; Wacquant 2008).

A neighborhood just north of the Upper East Side of Manhattan is known as Spanish Harlem, or El Barrio. This area has served as an arrival gate for multiple waves of significant numbers of immigrants (Bourgois 2003; Orsi 2002); the last such waves were Puerto Ricans in the 1940s and Mexicans in the last couple of decades (Smith 2006). Lexington and East 116th Streets may feel to a visitor like a small version of Chicago's Little Mexico, yet research by the author has shown that, despite the storefronts, the neighborhood is very heterogeneous and most Mexicans in New York have never lived in this area

(Castañeda 2010). Furthermore, although this place has offered a home and a sense of community to many ethnic groups, many socially mobile immigrants and their children have left the stigmatized East Harlem, even if they now remember it with nostalgia (Dávila 2004).

CONCLUSION

This chapter has shown that boundary-making processes and historical legacies are at play in the formation of banlieues, barrios, immigrant enclaves, and Jewish and African American ghettos. Most of these spatial boundaries disappear or dissipate over time. Place of residency matters because of its differential effect on life chances, yet scholarship and folk understandings tend to overstate spatial concentration—to a point of assuming that all members of a certain social group live in a particular neighborhood.

The built environment matters as well, because it displays social characteristics and embodies a particular cultural presence. The existence of a number of storefronts with foreign goods and symbols immediately marks a place as other, exotic, communal, ghettoized, premodern, or gentrified. The conclusions drawn from a superficial reading of streets and buildings are then applied to the inhabitants of that area. When this happens, spatial, symbolic, and social boundaries coincide and become anchored in place and reinforced in the public imagination.

Black Harlem, Spanish Harlem, and the Parisian banlieues are empirically more diverse in terms of social class and ethnicity than their popular representations would have us believe. Yet the mental maps, framing, and stereotypes—the *idées reçus* ("received ideas")—create social boundaries that pair stigmatized people with stigmatized places. In this sense, the ideal-type coming from the historical European Jewish ghetto is useful in describing contemporary inequalities, social boundaries, and limited mobility of labor across space. Unauthorized immigrants sell their labor, but they cannot move freely through space because of fear of deportation (Núñez and Heyman 2007); they may be as entrapped as Jews were in Venice. Banlieusards can legally move throughout France, yet some of them rarely do so.

For educated members of the second and later generations, the boundaries of "el barrio" and the banlieue may have been more permeable than for the inhabitants of the black ghetto after the great migration from the American

South, since, as with white ethnics, many middle-class Latinos and banlieue-dwellers who experienced social mobility moved out. Sometimes success means leaving the neighborhood where one was born. Yet in the American case, race trumped class mobility and blacks had a harder time moving far from the poor ghettos—Chicago's Hyde Park being the most common example (Pattillo 1999). Today, even as some blacks are better able to choose their neighborhood based only on income, urban ghettos, just like the barrio and some parts of the banlieue, continue to house the poorest members of a stigmatized group (poor in terms of economic, social, political, and symbolic capital). The residents of these areas suffer the scorn not only of the majority group but also of the members of their own group who have moved out, succeeded, assimilated, or "passed." They remain behind what is not only a symbolic boundary but a social boundary, since an undesirable address on a résumé often results in fewer employment opportunities—and thus fewer opportunities for social mobility.

As social scientists, we reify and "ghettoize" neighborhoods if we study them in isolation. World systems theory reminds us that we cannot fully understand the periphery without including its unequal relations with the core. The same applies to wealthy urban centers and stigmatized neighborhoods—they have to be understood relationally. The chic neighborhoods are so only in relation to stigmatized neighborhoods.

To conclude, despite somewhat enviable objective conditions for some of the "poor" population in the banlieue and in some public housing in New York City, relative deprivation is what matters the most for those who live in these areas. In the media and the popular mind, the banlieues now play an equivalent role to the U.S. ghetto. As in the United States, the French state has a very direct role in producing and limiting ethnic concentrations in public space—for example, through its colonial policies and the subsequent building of housing for migrant workers in particular areas of *metropole*. Long-lasting ethnic segregation is not voluntary but imposed from the outside. Objectively, material conditions in the American barrio and immigrant enclave tend to be very low (historical slums and present-day *colonias* in the Southwest being the most extreme examples), yet confinement to these areas tends to decrease over time, and with access to citizenship and work. Immigrant enclaves, including Chinatowns, tend to experience ethnic succession when their inhabitants are replaced by people from another country or region. In contrast, present-day banlieues have become problematic because, in the popular imagination, they house and contain immigrants and minorities. If the concept of the ghetto cannot be applied to France, it is only because France lacks the historical equivalent of an African American population. This does not mean, however, that contemporary social boundaries against stigmatized groups are not also inscribed in space, in minds, and in speech in the word *banlieue*. The term *ghetto* is a concept that classically represents stigmatization and spatial and social boundaries. But because of its long history and changing composition, it can sometimes create more polemic misunderstandings rather than provide clarity. Thus this chapter proposes the term *places of stigma* to designate the different spaces that result from the same categorical processes of creation and reproduction of social inequality (stigmatization, constraint, confinement, marginalization, underemployment) that become inscribed in flesh and stone.

Notes

1. Kevin Beck, Lesley Buck, and Natalie Schwarz helped in the preparation of the text. The NYLON research network, Gil Eyal, Emmanuelle Saada, Robert Smith, Craig Calhoun, Richard Sennett, Ray Hutchison, and Bruce Haynes provided feedback on earlier versions of this chapter. All errors remain my own.

2. To a large extent, this class segregation continues to this day and indeed has only been exacerbated by de-industrialization and the declining support for the welfare state.

3. These observations may be further biased when one observes the women covered head to toe who accompany oil millionaires from Saudi Arabia and the Emirates during the day but who stay home at night while the men, dressed in conservative religious clothing, go to bars, discos, and strip clubs and enjoy what they could not be seen consuming at home. This reality has little to do with the conclusions that a casual observer could draw from strolling down les Champs a couple of times.

4. I started filming this incident of unprovoked and unwarranted police brutality with my digital camera, until another bystander informed me that it was illegal to do so; I stopped filming before the police realized what I was doing and seized the camera. The footage of part of this incident is available on YouTube at: http://www.youtube.com/watch?v=mh8VXMPmkAU. Minutes later, ambulances arrived to take away the bleeding person, and everyone dispersed. I went next door to get a crêpe, and when I came back, the scene on the street was back to normal, as if nothing had happened, but I could still see the young man's blood on the pavement.

5. This is similar to the situation that Cecilia Menjívar (2000) documents among Salvadorans in San Francisco.

6. The second immigrant generation and subsequent generations tend to be more integrated into diverse social networks and to have more capital, depending on the social segment to which they have assimilated.

7. *"La cité est une cage de verre. Les frontières sont la. Tellement inscrites sur le bitume que tu as l'impression que c'est un message implicite: vous ne faites pas partie de la société. Ici, s'arrête la civilisation."*

8. Rohff was born on the African island of Comoros, a country that is 98 percent Muslim. Kéry James was born in the West Indies to Haitian parents. Both were former members of the influential Mafia K'1 Fry, a group of rappers from the banlieue of Val-de-Marne.

References

Aranda, Elizabeth M. 2008. "Class Backgrounds, Modes of Incorporation, and Puerto Ricans' Pathways into the Transnational Professional Workforce." *American Behavioral Scientist* 52: 426–456.

Blokland, Talja V. 2008. "From the Outside Looking In: A European Perspective on the Ghetto." *City & Community* 7, no. 4: 372–377.

Boltanski, Luc, and Laurent Thévenot. 2006. *On Justification: Economies of Worth*. Princeton, N.J.: Princeton University Press.

Blokland, Talja. 2008. "From the Outside Looking In: A 'European' Perspective on the Ghetto." *City & Community* 7, no. 4 (December): 372–377.

Bourdieu, Pierre. 1991. *Language and Symbolic Power*. Cambridge, Mass.: Harvard University Press.

———. 1998. *Practical Reason: On the Theory of Action*. Stanford, Calif.: Stanford University Press.

Bourgois, Philippe I. 2003. *In Search of Respect: Selling Crack in El Barrio*. Cambridge: Cambridge University Press.

Bowen, John R. 2007. *Why the French Don't Like Headscarves: Islam, the State, and Public Space*. Princeton, N.J.: Princeton University Press.

Caldwell, Christopher. 2009. *Reflections on the Revolution in Europe: Immigration, Islam, and the West*. New York: Doubleday.

Carr, Patrick J., and Maria Kefalas. 2009. *Hollowing Out the Middle: The Rural Brain Drain and What It Means for America*. Boston: Beacon Press.

Castañeda, Ernesto. 2009a. "Banlieue." In *Encyclopedia of Urban Studies*, edited by Ray Hutchison. Thousand Oaks, Calif.: Sage Publications.

———. 2009b. "The Great Sleep-In: Demonstrating for Public Housing in Paris." *Progressive Planning* 178: 31–33.

———. 2010. "The Political Voice of Migrants in a Comparative Perspective." PhD diss., Columbia University, Department of Sociology.

———. Forthcoming. "Exclusion and Everyday Citizenship in New York, Paris, and Barcelona: Immigrant Organizations and the Right to Inhabit the City." In *Remaking Urban Citizenship: Organizations, Institutions, and the Right to the City*, vol. 10, *Comparative Urban and Community Research*, edited by Michael Peter Smith and Michael McQuarrie. New Brunswick, N.J.: Transaction Publishers.

Dangschat, Jens S. 2009. "Space Matters—Marginalization and Its Places." *International Journal of Urban and Regional Research* 33, no. 3: 835–840.

Daniels, Cora. 2007. *Ghettonation: A Journey into the Land of Bling and the Home of the Shameless*. New York: Doubleday.

Dávila, Arlene M. 2004. *Barrio Dreams: Puerto Ricans, Latinos, and the Neoliberal City*. Berkeley and Los Angeles: University of California Press.

Dendoune, Nadir. 2007. *Lettre ouvert à un fils d'immigre: Cher Sarko* (*Open letter to the son of an immigrant: Dear Sarko*). Paris: Danger Public.

Doytcheva, Milena. 2007. *Une Discrimination positive à la française: Ethnicité et territoire dans les politiques de la ville* (*Positive discrimination the French way: Ethnicity and territory in urban policy*). Paris: La Découverte.

Fassin, Didier, and Eric Fassin. 2006. "De la question sociale à la question raciale? Représenter la société française" ("From the social question to the racial question: Representing the French society"). In *Cahiers Libres*. Paris: La Découverte.

Fourcaut, Annie, Emmanuel Bellanger, and Mathieu Flonneau. 2007. *Paris/Banlieues: Conflits et solidarités* (*Paris/Banlieues: Conflicts and solidarities*). Paris: Creaphis.

Frank, Thomas. 2004. *What's the Matter with Kansas? How Conservatives Won the Heart of America*. New York: Metropolitan Books.

Fry, Richard. 2009. "The Rapid Growth and Changing Complexion of the Suburban Public Schools." Washington, D.C.: Pew Hispanic Center.

Fuentes, Norma. 2007. "The Immigrant Experiences of Dominican and Mexican Women in the 1990s: Crossing Boundaries or Temporary Work Spaces?" In *Crossing Borders and Constructing Boundaries: Immigration, Race, and Ethnicity*, edited by Caroline B. Brettell. New York: Lexington Books Press.

Gans, Herbert J. 1982. *The Levittowners: Ways of Life and Politics in a New Suburban Community*. New York: Columbia University Press.

———. 2008. "Involuntary Segregation and the Ghetto: Disconnecting Process and Place." *City & Community* 7, no. 4: 353–357.

Goris, Indira, Fabien Jobard, and René Lévy. 2009. "Profiling Minorities: A Study of Stop-and-Search Practices in Paris." New York: Open Society Institute.

Grasmuck, Sherri, and Patricia R. Pessar. 1991. *Between Two Islands: Dominican International Migration*. Berkeley and Los Angeles: University of California Press.

Gravier, Jean-François. 1947. *Paris et le désert français: Décentralisation, équipement, population* (*Paris and the French desert: Decentralization, equipment, and population*). Paris: Le Portulan.

Grinberg, León, and Rebeca Grinberg. 1989. *Psychoanalytic Perspectives on Migration and Exile*. New Haven, Conn.: Yale University Press.

Harvey, David. 2008. "The Right to the City." *New Left Review* 53 (September-October).

Haynes, Bruce, and Ray Hutchison. 2008. "The Ghetto: Origins, History, Discourse." *City & Community* 7, no. 4 (December): 347–398.

Jones-Correa, Michael. 1998. *Between Two Nations: The Political Predicament of Latinos in New York City*. Ithaca, N.Y.: Cornell University Press.

Kasinitz, Philip, John H. Mollenkopf, and Mary C. Waters. 2004. *Becoming New Yorkers: Ethnographies of the New Second Generation*. New York: Russell Sage Foundation.

Kasinitz, Philip, John H. Mollenkopf, Mary C. Waters, and Jennifer Holdaway. 2008. *Inheriting the City: The Children of Immigrants Come of Age*. New York and Cambridge, Mass.: Russell Sage Foundation and Harvard University Press.

Katz, Michael B. 1996. *In the Shadow of the Poorhouse: A Social History of Welfare in America.* New York: Basic Books.

Katznelson, Ira. 2005. *When Affirmative Action Was White: An Untold History of Racial Inequality in Twentieth-Century America.* New York: W. W. Norton.

Lacorne, Denis. 2003. *La Crise de l'identité américaine: Du melting-pot au multiculturalisme (The crisis of American identity: From the melting pot to multiculturalism).* Paris: Gallimard.

Lamont, Michèle. 2000. *The Dignity of Working Men: Morality and the Boundaries of Race, Class, and Immigration.* New York and Cambridge, Mass.: Russell Sage Foundation and Harvard University Press.

Lamont, Michèle, and Virag Molnar. 2002. "The Study of Boundaries in the Social Sciences." *Annual Review of Sociology* 28 (August): 167–195.

Le Corbusier. 1927. *Towards a New Architecture.* New York: Payson & Clarke. (Originally published in French in 1923.)

———. 1967. *The Radiant City: Elements of a Doctrine of Urbanism to Be Used as the Basis of Our Machine-Age Civilization.* London: Faber. (Originally published in French in 1935.)

Lewis, Oscar. 1966. *La Vida: A Puerto Rican Family in the Culture of Poverty—San Juan and New York.* New York: Random House.

Loveman, Mara, and Jeronimo O. Muniz. 2007. "How Puerto Rico Became White: Boundary Dynamics and Intercensus Racial Reclassification." *American Sociological Review* 72, no. 6: 915–939.

Mahler, Sarah J. 1995. *American Dreaming: Immigrant Life on the Margins.* Princeton, N.J.: Princeton University Press.

Marwell, Nicole P. 2007. *Bargaining for Brooklyn: Community Organizations in the Entrepreneurial City.* Chicago: University of Chicago Press.

Massey, Douglas S. 2007. *Categorically Unequal: The American Stratification System.* New York: Russell Sage Foundation.

Massey, Douglas S., and Nancy A. Denton. 1993. *American Apartheid: Segregation and the Making of the Underclass.* Cambridge, Mass.: Harvard University Press.

Menjívar, Cecilia. 2000. *Fragmented Ties: Salvadoran Immigrant Networks in America.* Berkeley and Los Angeles: University of California Press.

Núñez, Guillermina Gina, and Josiah M. Heyman. 2007. "Entrapment Processes and Immigrant Communities in a Time of Heightened Border Vigilance." *Human Organization* 66, no. 4: 354–365.

Orsi, Robert Anthony. 2002. *The Madonna of 115th Street: Faith and Community in Italian Harlem, 1880-1950.* New Haven, Conn.: Yale University Press.

Pattillo, Mary E. 1999. *Black Picket Fences: Privilege and Peril Among the Black Middle Class.* Chicago: University of Chicago Press.

Pinçon, Michel, and Monique Pinçon-Charlot. 2004. *Sociologie de Paris (The Sociology of Paris).* Paris: Découverte.

———. 2007. *Les Ghettos du Gotha: Comment la bourgeoisie défend ses espaces (Ghettos of the Gotha: How the bourgeoisie defends its spaces).* Paris: Seuil.

———. 2009. *Paris: Quinze promenades sociologiques (Paris: Fifteen sociological walking tours).* Paris: Payot.

Portes, Alejandro, and Rubén G. Rumbaut. 2001. *Legacies: The Story of the Immigrant Second Generation.* Berkeley and Los Angeles: University of California Press.

Price, Gordon. 2008. "Périphérique." *Price Tags* 102 (April 7, 2008. Available at: http://www.price tags.ca/pricetags/pricetags102.pdf.

Roy, Beth. 1994. *Some Trouble with Cows: Making Sense of Social Conflict.* Berkeley and Los Angeles: University of California Press.

Sassen, Saskia. 2001. *The Global City: New York, London, Tokyo.* Princeton, N.J.: Princeton University Press.

Schneider, Cathy Lisa. 2008. "Police Power and Race Riots in Paris." *Politics and Society* 36, no. 1: 133–159.

Sennett, Richard. 1994. *Flesh and Stones: The Body and the City in Western Civilization.* New York: W. W. Norton.

———. 2008. "The Public Realm." Available at: http://www.richardsennett.com/site/SENN/ Templates/General2.aspx?pageid=16.

Silberman, Roxane, Richard Alba, and Irène Fournier. 2007. "Segmented Assimilation in France? Discrimination in the Labor Market Against the Second Generation." *Ethnic and Racial Studies* 30, no. 1: 1–27.

Simmel, Georg. 1964. *Conflict and the Web of Group Affiliations.* New York: Free Press.

———. 1971. "The Metropolis and Mental Life." In *Georg Simmel on Individuality and Social Forms*, edited by Donald N. Levine. Chicago: University of Chicago Press.

Small, Mario Luis. 2008. "Four Reasons to Abandon the Idea of 'the Ghetto.'" *City & Community* 7, no. 4: 389–398.

Smith, Robert C. 2006. *Mexican New York: Transnational Lives of New Immigrants.* Berkeley and Los Angeles: University of California Press.

Stovall, Tyler Edward. 1990. *The Rise of the Paris Red Belt.* Berkeley and Los Angeles: University of California Press.

Taylor, Sally Adamson. 2005. *Culture Shock! France: A Survival Guide to Customs and Etiquette.* Tarrytown, N.Y.: Marshall Cavendish/Graphic Arts Center Publishing Co.

Thorne, Barrie. 1993. *Gender Play: Girls and Boys in School.* New Brunswick, N.J.: Rutgers University Press.

Tilly, Charles. 1998. *Durable Inequality.* Berkeley and Los Angeles: University of California Press.

———. 2004. "Social Boundary Mechanisms." *Philosophy of the Social Sciences* 34, no. 2: 211– 236.

———. 2005. *Identities, Boundaries, and Social Ties.* Boulder, Colo.: Paradigm Publishers.

———. 2008. *Credit and Blame.* Princeton, N.J.: Princeton University Press.

Tilly, Charles, and Harold C. Brown. 1967. "On Uprooting, Kinship, and the Auspices of Migration." *International Journal of Comparative Sociology* 8 (September): 139–164.

Venkatesh, Sudhir Alladi. 2001. "Chicago's Pragmatic Planners: American Sociology and the Myth of Community." *Social Science History* 25, no. 2: 275–317.

———. 2002. *American Project: The Rise and Fall of a Modern Ghetto.* Cambridge, Mass.: Harvard University Press.

———. 2006. *Off the Books: The Underground Economy of the Urban Poor.* Cambridge, Mass.: Harvard University Press.

Wacquant, Loïc J. D. 2008. *Urban Outcasts: A Comparative Sociology of Advanced Marginality.* Cambridge: Polity Press.

———. 2010a. "Class, Race, and Hyperincarceration in Revanchist America." *Daedalus* 139, no. 3: 74–90.

———. 2010b. "Designing Urban Seclusion in the Twenty-First Century." *Perspecta: The Yale Architectural Journal* 43: 165–178.

Wilson, Kenneth L., and Alejandro Portes. 1980. "Immigrant Enclaves: An Analysis of the Labor Market Experiences of Cubans in Miami." *American Journal of Sociology* 86 (September): 295–319.

Wilson, William Julius. 1997. *When Work Disappears: The World of the New Urban Poor*. New York: Vintage Books.

Wimmer, Andreas. 2008. "The Making and Unmaking of Ethnic Boundaries." *American Journal of Sociology* 13, no. 4 (January): 970–1022.

Zelizer, Viviana A., and Charles Tilly. 2006. "Relations and Categories." In *The Psychology of Learning and Motivation*, vol. 47, *Categories in Use*, edited by Arthur Markman and Brian H. Ross. San Diego: Elsevier.

How Civil Society Can Help
Sweatshop Workers as Globalization's Consequence

JEFF BALLINGER

Italy's idyllic region of Tuscany is known as a top-tier tourist destination. Less well known is that it is also one of Europe's frontiers of human trafficking and a case-study in the effects of globalization. The garment and textile factories of Prato figured prominently in Italy's "miracle" economic performance of the 1950s and 1960s, with more than 4,500 small shops producing many of the world's most sought-after brands. Garment production is buoyant there again, but "economia sommersa" (submerged economy) sweatshops account for more than a third of the goods produced, and many of the Chinese workers are working long hours for little or no pay, due to huge debts to trafficking gangs. Now that the new anti-immigration mayor is closing illegal operators, hundreds of workers without legal working papers are in limbo as the Chinese government has refused the Italian government's attempts at repatriation.

Immigrant-bashing media in Italy decry the rise of sweatshops, but NYU's Andrew Ross points out that they had their place in Prato decades ago, when there was a high-wage "core" fed by peripheral sweatshops. Hence, the current situation is not a "Chinese import." This

JEFF BALLINGER is Director of Press for Change, a human rights organization with a focus on worker rights in the developing world. He has just finished three years as a Research Associate at the Harvard Kennedy School.

mobile workforce has been a hallmark of globalization, spawning a hugely contentious debate and ugly—if understandable—resentment.

Aside from the worker migration topic, there are other key globalization questions as well. Has globalization turned good companies bad? Has the outsource model forced the buyers to accept the often brutal practices of supplier-factory managers in some of the world's most corrupt and lawless environments? Is the current wage allocation truly fair and efficient? Several myths occlude helpful discussion of these questions and the solutions to their larger underlying issues.

There is one myth that has served the most vulnerable industries (electronics, toys, garments, and footwear) well over the last decade: a global brand will meticulously monitor its supply chain because conscientious consumers, informed by the latest technologies, will punish the company at the retail level for any transgression. Rather, according to Jeffrey Swartz, the CEO of Timberland, consumers do not think too much about workers' rights in the supplier factories. "Don't do anything horrible or despicable" and the company will be safe, he opined in late-2009. His remarks are supported by a striking example:

Sethi, has addressed what is perhaps the most pernicious myth: Northern-based "buyers" have an arm's-length relationship with their Korean, Taiwanese, or Chinese suppliers and therefore are not responsible for their well-documented records of contumacy. For years he was the architect of Mattel's efforts to track compliance with supplier "codes of conduct"—pushing outsource factories to observe local laws, prohibit child labor, etc.—and he has done consulting work in this field for several other Fortune

---

"Has the outsource model forced the buyers to accept the often brutal practices of supplier-factory managers in some of the world's most corrupt and lawless environments?"

---

the complete lack of media attention when the toy-maker Mattel scrapped all factory monitoring in 2010.

Another misperception—shared by "free trade" critics and proponents alike—is the race-to-the-bottom discourse, which posits that any improvement in wages or conditions will send factory managers off in search of more vulnerable workers. In 2000, shortly after the anti-WTO protests in Seattle, over 200 economists sent an open letter to college presidents in the United States that chastised them for too easily acceding to the students' demand to clean sweatshop-stained apparel out of university bookstores. The message was simple: they will hurt the very workers that they are trying to help because of this outsourcing imperative to seek lower standards.

In practice, there appears to be much room for wage improvement. Indonesia's "real" wage nearly tripled in the early 1990s, while foreign investment continued to flow. China and Vietnam have pushed up minimum wages several times in the last five years while maintaining double-digit growth rates. The incontrovertible and simplest proof that there is ample room for wage growth may be seen in the cost breakdown for a typical university-logo "hoodie"—the labor cost of the US$38 garment is less than 20 cents, while the university's licensing fee is over two dollars.

One of the most refreshingly honest voices in the global workers-rights field, Dr. Prakash

500 firms. He says that the major global players, including the World Bank, the OECD countries, and the International Labor Organization, have failed to apply pressure on low-cost producing countries that do not protect workers' health, safety, or human rights. Boldly, he has also called on corporations to pay restitution to developing-world workers for "years of expropriation" enabled by corrupt, repressive regimes. Particularly poignant is his brusque assertion that "bigotry" was at the root of most companies'

Tracking Trafficking

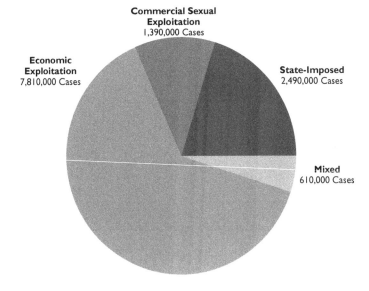

Forced Labor Worldwide
Considering Categories of Trafficking

Commercial Sexual Exploitation
1,390,000 Cases

Economic Exploitation
7,810,000 Cases

State-Imposed
2,490,000 Cases

Mixed
610,000 Cases

International Labor Organization; 2005

refusal even to try to grapple with some of these issues. Lending weight to Sethi's call for restitution is a pair of recent capitulations by Nike in claims against contract factories in Honduras and Malaysia, wherein Nike paid several millions of dollars to harmed workers.

For almost two decades, policy-makers have suffered the deleterious effects of these myths, resulting in inefficient allocations of time and effort. The child labor controversy offers a concise example. Although there were never more than a negligible percentage of 10- to 13-year-olds in factories, hundreds of millions of dollars have been directed at this perceived problem since the early 1990s. A focus on raising adult wages and thereby eliminating the need for the children to help support the family, by contrast, might have resulted in hundreds of thousands of poor families being able to keep those same children in school. What then is the current situation? How has globalization affected the production sector, wages, and working conditions?

Globalization and Supply-chains

Before globalization, most consumer-product companies were vertically-integrated—design, production, and marketing all occurred in one country. Then, a boom in out-sourcing created the global "supply-chain," an interesting twist to the familiar sweat-shop narrative.

The result may be seen in sub-Saharan Africa, Southeast Asia, and the Middle East. In the last, for example, a reader unfamiliar with the current practices of global garment producers may well ask why Jordanian factories are filled with Asians, when Jordan's unemployment rate lies between 13.4 percent to 30 percent (official/unofficial figures). The answer, of course, is that the supplier factories can pay foreign workers less and being "guests" they are less likely to make trouble.

An observer with more knowledge about global supply chains and garment production after the formation of the World Trade Organization would perhaps point to the remedy in the 2001 US-Jordan Free Trade Agreement, which contains "labor rights" requirements. Unsurprisingly, Jordanian officials aver that all workplaces are inspected and workers, of every nationality, in the 100+ factories are protected. In an altogether too common oversight, the reporters who noted this pledge presented no enforcement statistics to support the claim, and one can only conclude that the agreement's requirements remain empty promises.

New Abuse, Intriguing Opportunity

Sending workers abroad to the newly-rich Gulf countries in the 1970s was perhaps the first meaningful benefit of globalization for states such as Egypt, the Philippines, Bangladesh, Pakistan, and India, since workers' remittances meant billions of dollars. After the outsourcing boom of the 1980s, filling factories with foreign workers became a familiar practice in Taiwan and South Korea, where shoe and apparel brands "nudged" long-time suppliers towards cheaper labor in China and Indonesia. As democratization in the late-1980s began to push up wages in the factories that have churned out millions of pairs of sneakers each month since the mid-1970s, they were soon filled with cheaper immigrant workers from the Philippines, Thailand, and later, Vietnam.

The issue remained below the radar for over a decade, despite Fortune magazine's searing portrayal of factories in Taiwan in 2003, which dubbed it "indentured servitude." With the lack of attention, brands

Work Without Consent

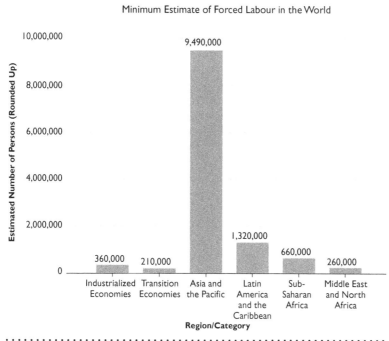

Minimum Estimate of Forced Labour in the World

International Labour Organization; 2005

sourcing from the factories suffered no sustained criticism for their contractors' abusive practices, nor for those of labor suppliers or "brokers," who often become prone to corruption on both ends: supply and delivery. Over the last decade, a "perfect storm" has developed: lucrative contract-labor fees (often triple what laws allow); growing demand for workers, coupled with relative impunity for brokers; bigger profits; malleable "host" governments for contract-factories; and finally, complacence on the part of buyers. Most striking about the last is the surprising ease with which Corporate Social Responsibility (CSR) tactics such as simple codes of conduct for supplier factories with cheap (and easily manipulated) "social audits" refuted "sweatshop" allegations.

The Role of Civil Society

There is, however, hope for consumer power: globalization's fallen barriers have made it possible for small civil society organizations to punch above their weight in trans-border solidarity campaigns. One such group is the Committee to Protect Viet Workers (CPVW) which, as the name makes clear, has a narrow focus, with a global reach and membership, as it draws volunteers from Europe, North America, and Australia. One of the clear positives of globalization is the access to news media outlets enabled by hundreds of these new citizen-watchdog nongovernmental organizations, who are joining the more-established legal aid and independent trade union movements.

Being based outside of Vietnam, the CPVW is free to advocate on behalf of several independent union activists now jailed in Vietnam. Although many grievances had come to the fore since foreign investment began to transform the country in the mid-1990s, the powerful 2006-7 wave of wildcat strikes—protests generally spontaneous in nature with ad-hoc leaders preferring anonymity—focused on wages. Inflation had hit double digits in 2006, but Vietnamese workers' wages in exports-factories had been fixed at US$42 per month for over a decade. An assessment of the protests yields some interesting findings: more than 70 percent of the 580 strikes took place at foreign-investment factories, with Nike—the country's largest "buyer" with over 200,000 contract-factory employees—suffering wage-related protests in more than a third of its 35 source factories. These huge shoe and apparel factories are also plagued by extraordinarily high turnover rates, mainly due to forced overtime and pressures to boost production.

The CPVW began observing "destination" countries when Vietnamese authorities dramatically increased the number of workers sent abroad in the period from 2006 to 2008. Workers returning from Malaysia informed CPVW's correspondents about cheating and horrendous living conditions at a t-shirt factory producing for Nike. The nongovernmental organization then turned the controversy into a minor scandal in Australia, and Nike immediately put the issue on the "fast track" for settlement, which contrasts sharply with the contemporaneous

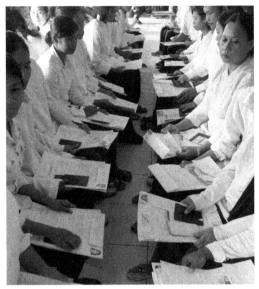

Migrant workers wait to receive passports at an immigration office in Indonesia. In 2010, over 300,000 Indonesians migrated to the Middle East in hopes of finding a job.

case in Honduras, which dragged on for two years. One possible explanation for the disparate treatment is the media, since the Vietnamese migrants' story was presented as a case of "human trafficking on a massive scale." Nike's contract-workforce in Malaysia numbered around 10,000 at the time; 1,100 foreign workers at the t-shirt factory are receiving about $2,000 each as restitution (paid in installments over nearly three years). The company will not reveal settlement deals at the other workplaces. The investigation itself earned the Best TV award at 2009's Every Human Has Rights ceremony in Paris.

Forcing a Re-examination of CSR?

A CPVW activist recently expressed frustration that Nike has for years had "independent" inspectors inspect its contract factories in Malaysia. How could it be, then, that workers worked under "indentured servitude" conditions which were clear for all to see, but inspections never disclosed this fact? The CPVW merely brought to public view what inspectors should have brought to the fore years ago. Perhaps the answer lay in the circumstance of Nike's "independent" inspectors, which number over 70, in an in-house CSR team of 215. The methodology deployed by most of these "responsibility" operations places great emphasis on the cultivation and maintenance of "stakeholder" relationships—predominantly, civil society organizations in both producer- and consumer-nations. Standard-setting and analysis of supplier-factory performance is certainly a part of their work, but the company's buyers operate with a wholly different set of metrics.

To return to the beginnings of CSR in the mid-1990s

would show a very strong link to the sweatshop controversy. In other words, the current proliferation of CSR artifice and funding started with anti-sweatshop activism, as illustrated in the huge jump in mentions of "Corporate Social Responsibility" or "CSR" in major news sources, from 28 articles in the decade 1988-98, to 561 from 1998-2003, to 2,643 between 2003-2008. The means of gathering this data, a simple Lexis-Nexis search, points to another issue. Given that this explosion was driven by worker mistreatment and below-subsistence wages, it would be reasonable to assume that much CSR "action" would be concentrated in this area. As it turns out, the vast majority of CSR press

ment made little practical sense when China, pre-reform Indonesia, and Vietnam were experiencing growth rates which were the envy of most poor nations. The off-the-charts venality of these states mocked the World Bank's decade-long focus on fighting corruption. Now is the time and climate to change and strengthen the US signals.

At an appropriate venue—such as a gathering of trade unionists and labor rights activists in Mexico or Thailand—Obama should outline the ways in which workers are disadvantaged in the global economy. Activists across the globe would be thrilled to hear an American president calling into question such neoliberal tenets

---

"If workers are deceived, distracted or dispirited by buyer-driven self-regulation schemes, it is possible that the traditional strategies available to workers wishing to form independent unions are similarly affected."

---

releases deal with environment-related issues and less than 1 percent concern workplace issues.

Just to reiterate, CSR had an incredible growth spurt because of workers' exploitation related to outsourcing, but the industry relies almost exclusively on environmental initiatives to demonstrate some kind of "responsibility" progress. Recently, in recognition of this fact, more CSR officers have simply replaced "responsibility" with "sustainability" in their titles and work-product.

Refreshing the Anti-Sweatshop Struggle

The corporate self-regulation "solution" which consisted of codes of conduct for supplier factories and spot-checking by social auditors has been a chimera. Since the early Clinton years, global labor rights received scattershot support; grants would go abroad through the Department of Labor or the State Department's Bureau for Democracy, Labor, and Human Rights. Many of these focused on "capacity-building" for workplace inspectors, but paid little attention to the lack of political will to actually do the enforcement work in any given country. Several millions more are funded more effectively each year through the AFL-CIO, though this has declined precipitously since the 1980s.

Addressing the rule of law as applied to the workplace ought to be a key priority for President Obama's State Department, even given the chance that such a worker-advocacy platform may discomfit countries such as China (a big holder of US Treasury bonds), Turkey (where the Pentagon's needs often drive U.S. policy), and Bangladesh (which has a host of stability concerns), to name a few. For far too long, autocratic regimes have received conflicting advice from American policy makers. The boiler-plate nostrums involving multiparty democracy and clean govern-

as the "flexible" workforce and the necessary "reform" (often downward-leveling of worker protections), which together have opened the door to a noxious insecurity of employment. As an exercise in public diplomacy, a clear and forceful statement would bring hope to opposition movements fighting entrenched economic elites allied with autocratic regimes.

Policy and program energies simply need to be redirected. If workers are deceived, distracted, or dispirited by buyer-driven self-regulation schemes, it is possible that the traditional strategies available to workers wishing to form independent unions are similarly affected. Numerous national and international trade union organizations and individual leaders have been drawn into dialogues, partnerships, conferences, and pilot programs with "multi-stakeholder" groups or the corporations directly. Many of these activities lent an undeserved patina of respectability to corporate self-regulation, often under the rubric of CSR. In addition, the long tweaking, critiquing, and field assessing of code-of-conduct "social audits," sometimes undertaken directly by unions and labor rights NGOs, diverted precious resources from the challenging task of devising realistic worker-empowerment strategies.

Further research is desperately needed on the actual labor law enforcement performance in countries where most low-skill assembly takes place. While living in Indonesia twenty years ago, I asked the US Embassy's labor attaché to get labor law enforcement numbers from the Ministry of Manpower in Jakarta. We learned that there were over 700 inspectors who found a total of 12,640 violations that year, but only 60 cases made it to the first adjudicative step; of these, only nine verdicts were reported. Ten years later, the Ministry again provided enforcement statistics: This time 700 inspectors only managed to do

243 factory visits for the entire year. Presumably, government officials—pressured by foreign investors to reduce the amount of bribe-seeking from various departments—restrained inspectors from making factory visits.

It is clear that a new architecture of rights must be erected, beginning with a no-nonsense survey of current practices. Every labor attaché or labor reporting officer at an American embassy should compile the following facts: Has the country signed International Labor Organization Convention 81 (Labor Inspection)? If so, when is the last time a report was sent to Geneva? How many labor inspectors are there? How many factory inspections were done last year? What is the number of violations found? How many prosecutions started? How many back pay awards were made? Our attachés should also map out the bureaucratic chain of command, with names of responsible local officials and an account of who-reports-to-whom—beginning in huge export-processing zones. This is information about dysfunctional governance unavailable to local journalists, legal aid, and worker-assistance organizations. US-based companies importing more than US$50 million worth of goods should have to post these findings on their corporate websites—in both English and the local language—for every country in which they have more than three contract factories.

This data should be folded into a matrix maintained by a nongovernmental organization working under a several-year grant from the State Department's Bureau of Human Rights, Democracy, and Labor. Alongside the raw numbers, wiki-style narratives should be included on such issues as freedom for non-governmental organization operating in the labor sector, labor history, recent strikes, opinions on the adequacy of the minimum wage, academic papers on all these issues, and contact information for unions and activist groups. Such an interactive website would make possible a global dialogue about key issues.

The world's workers need this dialogue both to build resilient movements and to challenge globalized production practices now ruled by top-down declamations, such as those issued in the World Bank's "competitive index," which ranks countries higher for ease of hiring and firing, reduced severance benefits,

and other employer-friendly policies, or its recent study which concludes that workers have to sacrifice even more than they have already, in the name of economic growth. These overweening influences—that are keeping the workers' share of a US$38 hoodie frozen at 20 cents—are being challenged by brave activists every day. The Hoover Institution's Larry Diamond sums up the tool-kit succinctly as "struggle, personal risk-taking, mobilization, and sustained imaginative organization." The path to meaningful change may debut some attention-grabbing tactics (perhaps young workers in Vietnam will tweet-up wages using their incredibly cheap mobile phones), but the "struggle" piece of this is age-old.

Leaders in rich countries need to rethink policies that have been foisted upon them by free-market fundamentalists over the past three decades of globalization. Enforcement need not be a cudgel used by politicians pandering to the fearful; lovely Prato should be a model of fair governance over a diverse landscape of small shops, where consumers need not pay more and the bel paese receives tax revenue. It is possible with some of the steps outlined above. Countries wishing to attract foreign investment would feel pressure from rich-nation governments to protect their workers. This modest push may not offset the global business community's antipathy toward regulation, but it may begin to redress the balance. ▣

Assessing the Abused

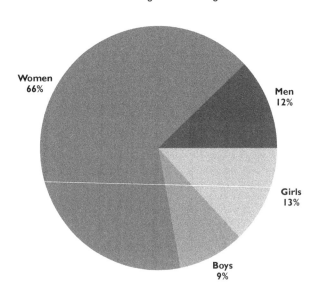

Profiling the Victims*
Considering Gender and Age

Women 66%

Men 12%

Girls 13%

Boys 9%

* Profile of victims identified by State authorities in 61 countries where was collected, aggregated for 2006.

International Labour Organization; 2005

The Social Construction of Race and Ethnic Problems

Racial and Ethnic Inequality

Racism has a long history in the United States. The country's Founding Fathers were deeply ambivalent about the institution of slavery. On the one hand, slavery stood in opposition to the ideals famously expressed in the Declaration of Independence: "We hold these truths to be self-evident, that all men are created equal, that they are endowed by their Creator with certain unalienable Rights, that among these are Life, Liberty and the pursuit of Happiness." On the other hand, the founders did not advocate for immediate emancipation of slaves for at least three reasons: their need to compromise with pro-slavery advocates to maintain the American republic, their view of slavery as a form of property protected by the Constitution, and their own attitudes about the racial superiority of whites.[1]

The founders themselves had varying views of slavery. George Washington owned hundreds of slaves but generally opposed the institution of slavery and provided for the freeing of his slaves upon the death of his widow. John Adams (the nation's second president) never owned slaves and was against slavery but generally did not take a strong political stand on the divisive issue. Notably, his son, John Quincy Adams, the sixth president, became a strong anti-slavery advocate during his postpresidency congressional career in the 1830s and 1840s. He accused slaveholders of immorality and stridently called for slavery's abolition.

Thomas Jefferson is perhaps the best personification of the nation's ambivalence on the issue. On the one hand, he was the primary author of the lofty language in the Declaration of Independence, and he believed that slavery was an evil stain on the nation's character. As president in 1807, he signed into law a bill that banned the importation of slaves into the United States. In an 1814 letter to Thomas Cooper, he wrote, "There is nothing I would not sacrifice to a practicable plan of abolishing every vestige of this moral and political depravity."[2] On the other hand, he remained a slave owner to his death (at which time his 130 slaves were auctioned off to cover his family's debts), and he believed in the biological inferiority of African Americans. He also believed that freed slaves and their former masters could never live in harmony and that racial mixing would be degrading to whites and to the country. As historian Stephen Ambrose writes, "Jefferson, like all slaveholders and many others, regarded Negroes as inferior, childlike, untrustworthy and, of course, as property."[3] For these reasons, he preferred to gradually free slaves but then deport them to Africa or the West Indies.[4]

Disagreements about slavery festered for decades after the founding of the country, at times threatening to break it apart. The tenuous compromise between slaveholding states of the South and free states of the North finally buckled with the election of Abraham Lincoln, who was feared by many for his anti-slavery convictions. The military victory by the North in the Civil War and the passage of the Thirteenth Amendment to the Constitution that outlawed involuntary servitude settled the issue once and for all. However, despite the abolition of slavery, black subjugation continued for another century in the South in the form of Jim Crow segregation. Northern blacks often fared only a little better, increasingly crowded into ghettos as the twentieth century progressed and facing strong discriminatory barriers in the labor market. Legal barriers to equality final fell during the civil rights movement, which culminated with the passage of a number of laws in the 1950s and 1960s forbidding racial discrimination in many walks of life. Americans attitudes toward race have also continued to liberalize steadily since then.

Many argue that race therefore has a different meaning and significance for the generation coming of age today than for previous ones. For example, National Public Radio (NPR) conducted a series of conversations about race (The Race Card Project), for which thousands of people submitted their thoughts on race and cultural identity today in six words. One respondent that NPR highlighted, George Washington III, an African American married to a white woman in North Carolina, submitted the following entry: "My mixed kids have it differently." By this, he meant that unlike in the past when anyone with any African American ancestry was considered black (the "one drop" rule), his children now have the freedom to identify as mixed race and can celebrate both sides of their family.[5]

With the election of Barack Obama as president in 2008 (and his reelection in 2012), some have argued that the United States is now postracial—that race no longer plays a very meaningful role in people's lives. Others scoff at this notion, arguing that race still plays a central role in determining people's life chances. The goal of this chapter is to examine the role of race in contemporary American society. I describe differences in socioeconomic outcomes across racial and ethnic groups, discuss the factors that contribute to these differences, and reflect on the trajectory of the American color line today.

WHAT IS RACE AND ETHNICITY?

Race commonly has been thought of as a biological concept that distinguishes groups by physical, mental, and genetic traits. While some research activity continues today exploring genetic differences between races, most contemporary social and biological scientists do not believe any evidence exists indicating that racial differences have a deep biological or genetic origin. Instead, most accept the notion that race is a social construction, and as such, meaningful social distinctions between racial groups vary across time and place. During the Enlightenment in the 1700s, many European scholars became interested in understanding racial differences and created all sorts of classification schemes that included anywhere from three to thirty categories of race. Some of these scholars, for example, divided Europeans themselves into four races:

Nordic or northern, Alpine or central, Mediterranean or southern, and Slavic or eastern.[6]

Many southern and eastern European immigrants to the United States in the late nineteenth century and the early twentieth were initially viewed as racially distinct, stoking the fears of nativists and public officials, as previously discussed. Theodore Roosevelt warned of "race suicide" and bemoaned the higher fertility rate among inferior immigrant women compared with that of Anglo-Saxon women. Notions of race were legitimized by scientists who developed theories of eugenics and the role of genes in explaining broad social differences across populations.[7] One of the earliest applications of IQ testing was to show that southern and eastern European immigrants were not as smart as the native stock—a hypothesis that was believed to have been confirmed.[8]

The sociologist Mary Waters notes, "At the peak of immigration from southern and central Europe there was widespread discrimination and hostility against the newcomers by established Americans. Italians, Poles, Greeks, and Jews were called derogatory names, attacked by nativist mobs, and derided in the press. Intermarriage across ethnic lines was very uncommon. . . . The immigrants and their children were residentially segregated, occupationally specialized, and generally poor."[9] Assimilation occurred only gradually through the twentieth century as immigration ebbed, the country's attention turned to two world wars and a depression, and social and economic changes in the post–World War II period further facilitated the upward mobility of the descendants of these immigrants.[10]

Illustrating differences in views about the meaning of race across places, conceptions of race have been more fluid in Latin American societies, where skin color is seen along a continuum, than in the United States, where the division between black and white racial identities has long been sharply defined (perhaps at least until recently). The Brazilian census, for example, has the following categories: white, brown, black, yellow, indigenous, and undeclared. More generally, different societies use different physical attributes to construct racial categories.[11] Skin color seems like an easily observable way to divide people, but is it any more important than eye color, curliness of hair, or any other physical characteristic? Thus, social scientists today see race as representing social relations embedded in a society's specific historical context.[12] Racial distinctions are real and meaningful in a given place to the extent that people are treated differently and have different kinds of life experiences and outcomes.

There is often some confusion about the distinction between "race" and "ethnicity." *Race* typically refers to a group of people who are perceived, by both themselves and others, as possessing distinctive hereditary traits. In the U.S. context, phenotypical difference (skin color) has been the most salient marker of racial difference. In contrast, *ethnicity* refers to a group of people who are differentiated by culture rather than by perceived physical or genetic differences. Nevertheless, the terms *race* and *ethnicity* are often used interchangeably in public conversations today, especially given the growing diversity of the U.S. population, increasing intermarriage, and the changing meaning and importance of group differences. There is also some ambiguity about whether some groups, such as Hispanics or Middle Easterners, are distinct races or ethnicities.[13]

The U.S. Census Bureau has collected data on race/ethnicity in a variety of ways over the years, reflecting changing notions of salient social divisions. It currently collects such information with two questions. The first question asks, "Is this person Spanish/Hispanic/Latino?" There is an answer box for "no" and additional "yes" boxes for people to indicate if they are Mexican, Puerto Rican, or Cuban. There is also a write-in box where respondents can identify other origins. The next question on the form asks, "What is this person's race?" There are answer boxes for White, Black, American Indian, or Alaska Native, and a series of boxes for various Asian groups and Native Hawaiians. People can also mark "some other race," as well as (beginning in the year 2000) two or more races. When disseminating data on race and ethnicity, the Census Bureau essentially uses five race categories (White, Black, American Indian and Alaska Native, Asian, and Native Hawaiian and other Pacific Islander) and one ethnicity (Hispanic origin). A number of respondents are confused by these questions and wonder why Hispanic origin is asked separately.[14] Some advocate using a single combined question that asks more simply about ethnic origins, with the view that "race" has little or no objective basis.[15] Given the fuzziness in the use of these concepts, I often use the terms *race* and *ethnicity* either together (as in the title of this chapter) or interchangeably.

U.S. society has become increasingly racially and ethnically diverse. The proportion of the population that was non-Hispanic white decreased substantially from 83 percent in 1970 to 63 percent in 2011. Meanwhile, the relative size of the black population stayed fairly steady (12 percent in 2011), and the representation of Hispanics (5 to 17 percent) and Asians (1 to 5 percent) increased significantly over the period. In this section we examine changes in the educational attainment, income, poverty, and wealth of different groups to shed light on the extent of racial and ethnic socioeconomic inequality in American society.

Figure 37 shows that college completion has increased markedly for all racial/ethnic groups over time, but significant disparities remain. In 2012, only about 1 in 7 Hispanics who were 25 years old and over had completed college, compared with over a fifth of blacks, over a third of non-Hispanic whites, and over half of Asians. In 1940, only 5 percent of the total population age 25 years and older had a college degree, including 5 percent of whites and just 1 percent of blacks. As one would expect, educational attainment disparities show up in high school graduation rates as well, though the white-black gap is narrower, with 93 percent of non-Hispanic whites and 85 percent of blacks graduating from high school among those age 25 and older in 2012. Hispanics have the lowest levels of high school completion at 65 percent. About 89 percent of Asians had completed high school in 2012.[16]

Racial and ethnic differences persist when looking at median household income (see figure 38). All groups experienced real increases in income over time, with all groups also taking a tumble during the Great Recession. Consistent with the educational differences described above, the median household income was highest among Asians at $65,129, followed by non-Hispanic whites ($55,412). However, even though African Americans had higher levels of education than Hispanics, median household income was higher among Hispanics ($38,624) than blacks ($32,229).

Unsurprisingly, racial and ethnic differences also show up in poverty statistics (figure 39). In 2011, 10 percent of non-Hispanic whites and 12

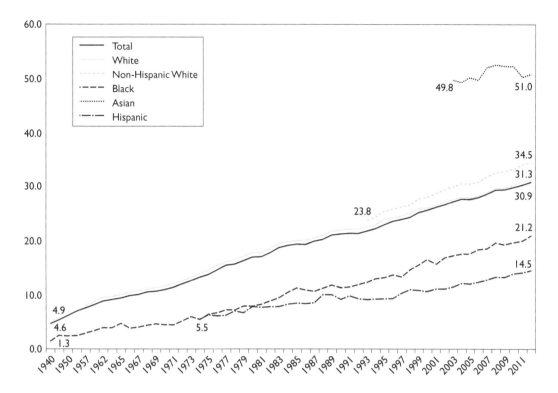

Figure 37. Percentage of people age 25 years and older who have completed college, by race and ethnicity, 1940–2012. Note: Data were collected for different groups at different points in time, which accounts for the various gaps in the graph, including that for whites between ca. 1947 and 1957. Please refer to U.S. Census Bureau 2013d for more information. Source: U.S. Census Bureau 2013d.

percent of Asians were poor, compared with 25 percent Hispanics and 28 percent of African Americans. Notably, the black poverty rate declined significantly over time, from a high of 55 percent in 1959. Nevertheless, the 2000s were a difficult decade for low-income Americans, with blacks experiencing the largest absolute increase in poverty. Finally, racial and ethnic inequality in wealth is even larger than in education, income, or poverty. The mean net worth of white households was $593,000 in 2010, whereas the mean net worth of African American and Hispanic households was only $85,000 and $90,000, respectively. Part of this reflects the fact that non-Hispanic whites are much more likely to be homeowners (75 percent) than African Americans (48 percent) and Hispanics (47 percent), and the value of one's home is most often a household's greatest single asset.[17]

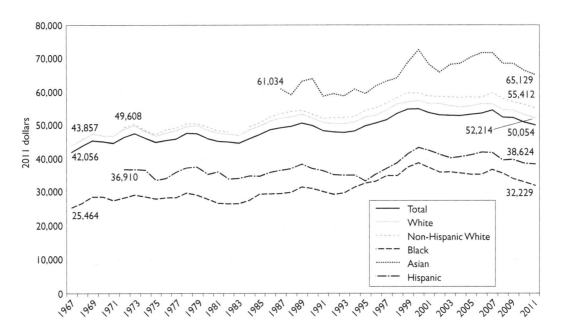

Figure 38. Median household income, by race and ethnicity, 1967–2011 (in constant 2011 dollars). Note: No published data are available for non-Hispanic whites in 1984. Source: U.S. Census Bureau 2012k.

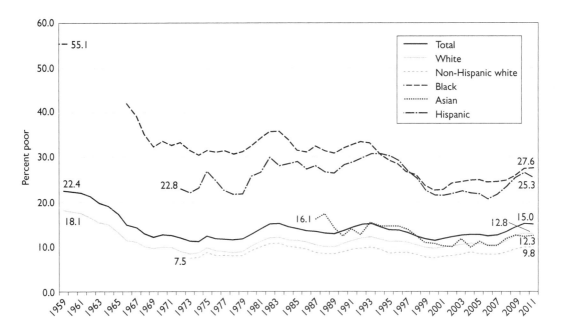

Figure 39. Poverty rates, by race and ethnicity, 1959–2011. Note: No published data are available for blacks between 1959 and 1966. Source: U.S. Census Bureau 2012g.

What factors help explain these disparities? Broad social inequalities in multicultural societies are often a function of what sociologists refer to as "social stratification," which involves members of one group in power seeking to maximize their position by restricting others' access to resources such as jobs, education, health services, and political power. Max Weber noted that usually a social group "takes some externally identifiable characteristic of another group—[such as] race, language, religion, local or social origin, descent, residence, etc.—as a pretext for attempting their exclusion."[18] In this way, broad social boundaries are drawn and maintained.[19] African Americans, Asian Americans, Hispanics, Native Americans, and even many white ethnic and national groups, such as Jews and the Irish, have all at times had to cope with limited opportunities, though their experiences have differed in very important ways. Below I discuss the experiences of contemporary racial and ethnic minority groups in more detail.

African Americans

African Americans have long struggled against racial oppression. They first arrived in the United States in large numbers as involuntary immigrants during the slave trade and were heavily concentrated in southern states. The Civil War and accompanying constitutional amendments ended slavery and conferred citizenship upon African Americans. Nevertheless, after some hope of equality during Reconstruction, from about 1865 to 1877, when blacks gained the right to vote and a number were elected to state legislatures, the U.S. House of Representatives, and even the U.S. Senate, they were relegated to second-class citizenship by the late 1870s, with southern whites reestablishing their own supremacy. Through violence and intimidation, southern whites denied blacks the power to vote. As many as two thousand to three thousand lynchings were perpetrated in the last decade and a half of the nineteenth century.[20] In the economic sphere, blacks in the South often worked as sharecroppers, mainly because they were barred by law or custom from most other full-time jobs outside the black community. Jim Crow laws mandated segregation in all public facilities, ensuring inferior services, including education, for the black community.[21]

Gunnar Myrdal, in his book *An American Dilemma: The Negro Problem and Modern Democracy*, published in 1944, described the nature and extent of black subjugation in the South:

> Violence, terror, and intimidation have been, and still are, effectively used to disfranchise Negroes in the South. Physical coercion is not so often practiced against the Negro, but the mere fact that it can be used with impunity and that it is devastating in its consequences creates a psychic coercion that exists nearly everywhere in the South. A Negro can seldom claim the protection of the police and the courts if a white man knocks him down, or if a mob burns his house or inflicts bodily injuries on him or on members of his family. If he defends himself against a minor violence, he may expect a major violence. If he once "gets in wrong" he may expect the loss of his job or other economic injury, and constant insult and loss of whatever legal rights he may have had.[22]

During the twentieth century many blacks left the oppressive conditions in the South to look for opportunity in the North, especially in booming industries in many northeastern and midwestern cities such as Chicago, Detroit, and New York. This Great Migration resulted in a striking regional redistribution of the black population in the United States. In 1900, about three-quarters of all African Americans lived in rural southern areas; a century later, that figure had declined to about 12 percent. By 1950, more than 2.5 million southern-born African Americans were living outside the region, a number that increased to more than 4 million by 1980.[23] While economic opportunities were better in the North, and the racial climate was not as oppressive (northern blacks, for example, could for the most part vote), blacks still faced a wide range of discriminatory barriers in the labor and housing market and were segregated in congested northern ghettos.

The civil rights movement in the 1950s and 1960s overturned the legal framework that supported the unequal treatment of blacks. In 1954, for example, in the case *Brown v. Board of Education of Topeka,* the Supreme Court ruled that the separate-but-equal doctrine underlying the Jim Crow system was invalid. In the 1960s several laws were passed in Congress (including the far-reaching Civil Rights Act of 1964) that prohibited racial discrimination in employment practices, public accommodations, and housing market transactions. The civil rights movement itself was propelled mainly by nonviolent protest and civil disobedience. The Montgomery Bus Boycott in Alabama in 1955–56, for example, protested racial segregation in the city's public transit system, which relegated blacks to seats in the back of the bus. The campaign began when Rosa Parks, an African American woman active in the movement, refused to give up her seat to a white person. The boycott was a success, and the Supreme Court eventually declared segregation laws to be unconstitutional.

Legal changes have also been accompanied by gradual changes in public opinion. The proportion of whites holding blatantly racist attitudes has dropped considerably over the decades according to national polls. For example, in the 1940s and 1950s, fewer than half of whites surveyed believed that white and black students should attend the same schools or that black and white job applicants should have an equal chance of getting a job. By the 1990s, however, over 90 percent of whites said they believed that schools and employers should treat whites and blacks equally.[24]

The removal of legal barriers and the slowly changing social norms, however, did not translate into immediate social and economic equality. Civil rights legislation was being passed during a time of deindustrialization—when the share of people employed in manufacturing was declining—and when many northeastern and midwestern cities were losing jobs and people through outmigration to the Sun Belt. (Many jobs also went abroad.) For example, in the twenty-year period between 1967 and 1987, Philadelphia lost 64 percent of its manufacturing jobs, Chicago lost 60 percent, New York City lost 58 percent, and Detroit 51 percent. This hurt blacks as well as whites living in those cities and contributed to the increasing poverty of blacks concentrated in inner cities.[25]

Some commentators, such as William Julius Wilson, have argued that race has become less important in determining the labor market success of African Americans and that class position has become more important.[26] From colonial times through the first half of the twentieth century, racial oppression was deliberate and overt. By the latter half of the twentieth century, many traditional barriers were dismantled as a result of political, social, and economic changes of the civil rights era. Wilson emphasizes that although discrimination has become less common though not eliminated, economic conditions have come to play an increasingly important role in shaping opportunities available to African Americans.

He argues that deindustrialization and class segregation in particular have hampered the economic mobility of less-skilled blacks.[27]

Studies show that the economic "penalty" of being African American has declined since the 1960s, in that occupational mobility has increased, as has wage parity.[28] Racial differences in economic outcomes are significantly reduced when one accounts for educational achievement.[29] Measuring the direct effects of discrimination is difficult, because it is not always clear when a discriminatory action has occurred or if general observed differences between whites and blacks are a result of unmeasured differences (e.g., quality of schooling received) or of discrimination itself. Careful examinations of this issue tend to indicate that discrimination still occurs in labor markets and in other areas. For example, "paired-test studies," in which minority job applicants were paired with white applicants with similar backgrounds and trained to be as similar as possible in behavior, have shown that minorities, particularly African Americans and foreign-sounding Latinos, were less likely to be given job interviews and offers, at least in the low-wage labor market.[30] Economists have estimated that perhaps one-quarter of the black-white wage gap is due to prejudice, suggesting that racism continues to contribute to African American economic disadvantage.[31]

Other factors have also contributed to relatively low levels of socioeconomic attainment among African Americans, some related to race and others more nonracial in origin. One race-related factor is residential and social segregation. Because African Americans often live in segregated and disadvantaged communities, they may have fewer economically useful contacts ("social capital") on which to draw to help achieve success. Many people, for example, find a job via word of mouth through friends and neighbors. Those with affluent friends and neighbors typically have access to more and better opportunities.[32] Residential segregation also affects educational disparities because a significant portion of school funding comes from local taxes. Schools in poor neighborhoods often have inferior resources and fewer enrichment programs. High neighborhood poverty rates are strongly correlated with lower student test scores.[33] Declining levels of black segregation in recent decades, along with rapid black suburbanization, has likely reduced the effects of segregation in contributing to racial inequalities over the past couple of decades. However, many cities—particularly some in the Northeast and Midwest such as Chicago, New York, Detroit, and Milwaukee—still have very high levels of black segregation.[34]

Another factor that contributes to higher poverty rates among African Americans is differentials in human-capital skills. Human capital refers to education attainment and subsequent work experience and skills. The gap in average levels of education has declined over the past few decades. Nevertheless, the quality of schooling received by children in the United States still varies widely, and, as mentioned above, African Americans are more likely to attend inferior schools with fewer resources and have lower test scores. Lower employment levels among young African Americans subsequently contribute to earnings differentials. High black incarceration rates (black men are eight times more likely to be incarcerated than white men) translate to a relatively high proportion of young black men entering the labor force with a criminal record, which further dampens their employability. The rapid growth in the prison population from the late 1970s through the mid-2000s exacerbated this problem. Many contend that high black incarceration rates are in part due to racial profiling by law enforcement and racial biases in the sentencing process.[35]

Differences in family structure affect ethnic socioeconomic differentials as well. While 36 percent of white births were to unmarried women, the figure was double (72 percent) among African Americans.[36] This contributes to socioeconomic inequalities because single-parent families are considerably more likely to be poor: about 4 in 10 (41 percent) female-headed families with children were poor in 2011, compared with fewer than 1 in 10 (9 percent) of married-couple families with children.[37] Single parents often struggle to earn sufficient income for their family while also providing an attentive, nurturing environment for their children.

Thus, some have emphasized that an African American disadvantage has persisted across generations because of *cumulative disadvantages*. Racial gaps show up early in childhood and widen through the life course. As author Michael Wenger puts it:

> On average, African Americans begin life's journey several miles behind their white counterparts as a result of the legacy of our history of racial oppression. This disadvantage is compounded by institutional hurdles they encounter at every stage of the journey: the socioeconomic conditions into

which they're born, the system of public education through which they pass, the type of employment they are able to secure, the legacy they are able to leave behind. These hurdles, arduous, relentless, and often withering to the soul, do not confront many white people as they pursue their hopes and dreams.[38]

The importance of cumulative disadvantages suggests that ending inequality has no single easy solution and helps explain why progress has been slow—though some suggest that early childhood interventions revolving around schooling could be the most effective approach to reducing racial disparities.[39] Even as race has become less important in American society, economic inequality and class background have become more important. For example, while the black-white reading gap used to be substantially larger than the rich-poor reading gap in the 1940s, by the 2000s the reverse was true.[40] As a result, while we have seen considerable growth in the black middle class in recent decades, the economic challenges faced by poor African Americans remain daunting.[41]

Hispanics, Asians, and the Role of Immigration

The many racial and ethnic dividing lines in American society have historically reserved privilege for whites. Through much of the twentieth century, some of the factors that impeded African American mobility—discrimination and segregation—also affected Hispanics and Asian Americans. Some of the traditional racial dividing lines have eased, however, mainly since the civil rights era, enabling many members of these groups to achieve socioeconomic mobility and broader incorporation into mainstream society, though people still debate the extent to which racial dividing lines continue to inhibit opportunity.

Hispanics have a long history in the United States, dating at least as far back as the annexation of territory in Florida in the early 1800s. At the request of a growing number of U.S. settlers in what had been Mexican territory, the United States annexed Texas in 1845, precipitating the Mexican-American War. After defeating the Mexican army in 1848, the United States annexed California, New Mexico, Nevada, Arizona, Utah, and Colorado as well. The Mexican-origin population in the American Southwest in 1848 was likely about 80,000 people—roughly one-fifth of the total population of that area.[42] Mexican Americans living in these territories were often treated as second-class citizens. In subsequent decades Mexicans were used as cheap labor in the building of railroads, in mining, and in agriculture. During labor shortages they were often recruited, but at other times they were encouraged to return to Mexico, often with force. Between 1930 and 1960, almost 4 million Mexicans were deported.[43]

The presence of other Hispanic groups is more recent. Puerto Ricans migrated to the U.S. mainland in large numbers in the 1950s and 1960s. Reflecting Puerto Rico's status as a U.S. territory (Spain ceded Puerto Rico to the United States in 1898 as a result of its defeat in the Spanish-American War), Puerto Ricans are U.S. citizens at birth. The Puerto Rican population is generally very mixed, and in the past the darker-skinned Puerto Ricans in particular encountered significant racial barriers.[44] Cubans entered the United States in significant numbers after the Cuban Revolution in 1959. Many of these immigrants were highly educated professionals who had been supporters of the deposed president and dictator, Fulgencio Batista. Another wave entered in 1980 as part of the Mariel Boatlift; this group was decidedly more socioeconomically mixed. Cubans overwhelmingly settled in Miami, and many found success as entrepreneurs and small business owners.[45]

As of 2010, there were 31.8 million Mexican-origin people in the United States (63 percent of the Hispanic population), up from 8.7 million in 1980. The next two traditionally largest groups—Puerto Ricans and Cubans—have been falling as a fraction of the total Hispanic population, from 14 percent and 6 percent, respectively, in 1980 to 9 percent and 4 percent in 2010. In the meantime, the number of Salvadorans, Dominicans, and Guatemalans in the United States has grown rapidly in recent years, though each of these groups still made up no more than about 2 to 3 percent of the Hispanic population nationally in 2010.

Among Asian groups, the Chinese were the first to immigrate in significant numbers around the time of the California gold rush in 1848. In the 1860s, an estimated 12,000 to 16,000 Chinese laborers were employed to build the western leg of the Central Pacific Railroad. Some Chinese also worked in agriculture, and others were entrepreneurs in San Francisco.[46] The Chinese experienced a good deal of discrimination and violence as the community grew; they were viewed as economic competitors who would drive down the wages of native-born Americans. The Naturalization Act of 1870 limited naturalization in the United States to "white persons and persons of African descent"; this meant that the Chinese were aliens ineligible for citizenship and remained so until 1943. The 1882 Chinese Exclusion Act went further, barring the immigration of all Chinese laborers. Because Chinese immigration was so heavily male, the Chinese population in the United States began to gradually decline until about 1920, after which it slowly rebounded as a result of natural increase.[47]

The first group of Japanese arrived in California around 1869 but began to increase more markedly in the 1890s. Initially, most Japanese worked in agriculture, filling a large demand for labor, though many went on to live in larger cities, including San Francisco and Los Angeles, and others became successful farm owners and entrepreneurs. However, white California workingmen and others eventually lobbied for their exclusion. Cognizant of the military might of Japan, which was a considerably more powerful country than China at the time, and not wishing to offend it, the Gentleman's Agreement of 1907 was negotiated between the United States and Japan, ending most kinds of immigration from Japan to the United States, except for family-reunification purposes. In 1913 and 1920 California enacted anti-alien land laws aimed at Japanese farmers, barring "aliens ineligible for citizenship" from purchasing and leasing agricultural land. The resident Japanese population, however, found ways to get around some of these obstacles, and many continued to prosper. Japanese immigration was later completely halted in 1924.[48] Many Japanese on the West Coast were infamously interned in camps during World War II—a fate not suffered by the German American and Italian American communities—indicative of the racism of the time.

Initial migration of Filipinos to the United States came shortly after the American annexation of the Philippines in 1898. In the 1920s and 1930s larger numbers came as farmworkers, filling in the kinds of jobs held by the Chinese and Japanese immigrants in previous years. As Asians, Filipinos were aliens ineligible for citizenship until the 1940s. Filipinos faced a significant amount of prejudice and discrimination. As writer Carlos Bulosan wrote in 1946, "Do you know what a Filipino feels in America? . . . He is the loneliest thing on earth. There is much to be appreciated . . . beauty, wealth, power, grandeur. But is he part of these luxuries? He looks, poor man, through the fingers of his eyes. He's enchained, damnably to his race, his heritage. His is betrayed, my friend."[49] Another time he wrote, "I feel like a criminal running away from a crime that I did not commit. And that crime is that I am a Filipino in America."[50] Filipinos, like other Asians and other minorities, were excluded from a broad array of economic opportunities and were viewed as unwelcome aliens by the native white majority population.

The second wave of immigration after the elimination of discriminatory national-origin quotas in 1965 included Asians from a variety of other countries, including India, Vietnam, and Korea. In 2010, the largest Asian subgroup was Chinese (24 percent of the Asian population), followed by Asian Indians (19 percent) and Filipinos (17 percent). The fraction of the Asian population that is Chinese has stayed roughly the same over the past three decades, with the percentage of Asian Indians growing substantially (they were 10 percent of the Asian population in 1980) and the percentage of Filipinos declining, but slowly (they were 22 percent of the Asian population in 1980). The percentage of Japanese as a share of the Asian population has fallen considerably, from 20 percent in 1980 to 5 percent in 2010, and Korean and Vietnamese each made up 10 percent of Asians in 2010.[51]

In some respects Latinos and Asian Americans share certain experiences, because both groups have been historically discriminated against, both have experienced substantial increases in their population resulting from immigration since the 1960s, and both are heterogeneous in terms of their national origins (though Mexicans are by far the largest group among Latinos and overall). Nevertheless, as figures 37 through 39 indicate, socioeconomic outcomes of Hispanics and Asians differ substantially. For the most part Asians are on equal socioeconomic footing with native-born whites, and in fact their outcomes exceed those of whites in some respects. Because nearly two-thirds of Asians and about 2 in 5 Hispanics are foreign born and many more of both groups are of just the second generation, we need to investigate the characteristics of immigrants from Latin America and Asia to understand their disparate outcomes.[52]

Chapter 5 described patterns of assimilation among Asians and Hispanics and noted important differences in characteristics of the immigrants from different origins, especially in levels of education. Specifically, immigrants from Asia tend to constitute a more "select" group than immigrants from Latin America. Immigrants from Korea, India, and the Philippines achieve higher average levels of education than both Latinos and native-born whites. For example, about 80 percent of immigrants from India have a bachelor's degree or more, compared with 6 percent from Mexico.[53] One factor explaining these differences is that while many immigrants from Asia become eligible to migrate to the United States because of their work-related skills, a larger proportion of immigrants from Latin America immigrate because they have relatives who are U.S. citizens.[54]

It is important to note of course that poverty among immigrants also varies considerably by country of origin; not all subgroups among Asians and Hispanics are similarly advantaged or disadvantaged. Among foreign-born Hispanics, for example, poverty rates in 2007 were high among Dominicans (28 percent) and Mexicans (22 percent) but more moderate among Cubans (16 percent) and Colombians (11 percent).[55] South Americans have nearly reached parity with non-Hispanic whites in terms of both the proportion having a college education and median household income.[56] Among Asian immigrant groups, poverty rates were a little higher for Koreans (17 percent) than for immigrants from Japan (9 percent), India (7 percent), and the Philippines (4 percent).[57] Many of these differences are explained by the average characteristics of the immigrants themselves (especially educational attainment), though as noted above each group has a unique history of immigration to the United States.

Initial disadvantages tend to persist over time and across generations. Native-born Hispanics obtain on average higher levels of education than immigrant Hispanics, but their educational levels still lag behind those of native-born whites, largely because of the lower initial level of family resources of Hispanics.[58] In contrast, native-born Asian Americans tend to achieve high levels of education, which translate into better jobs, higher incomes, and less poverty. Once family characteristics are taken into account, there is little difference in the poverty rates between native-born Asians and native-born non-Hispanic whites.[59] While Latinos are less likely to have a college degree and tend to work in lower-skill, lower-wage jobs, once human capital differences are accounted for (especially education and English-language proficiency), there is not that much difference between whites and Hispanics in terms of occupational status and earnings.[60]

The research literature does not offer a definitive answer as to the extent of racial/ethnic discrimination faced by Asians and Latinos in the labor market. For Asians, it is probably safe to say that discrimination is not widespread enough to significantly affect average levels of socioeconomic achievement. For Latinos, family background characteristics (such as education and income) are likely to play the most prominent role and ethnicity a more minor one. Race appears to continue to play a significant role in explaining lower wages and higher poverty among blacks and darker-skinned Latinos.[61]

Native Americans

The experience of Native Americans, as the original inhabitants of the North American continent, differs from that of all the other groups. At the time when Jamestown was established in 1607, estimates of the number of Native Americans living in what is now the United States is estimated to have varied from about 1 million to 10 million.[62] The population declined substantially over the course of the seventeenth through the nineteenth century, reaching an estimated low of 250,000 in 1890. The most important factor contributing to the decline in population was the diseases brought by American colonists to which Native Americans had little immunity or resistance, including scarlet fever, whooping cough, bubonic plague, cholera, and typhoid. Other causes for population decline include warfare, displacement, the slaughter of buffalo on which some tribes depended, and alcoholism.[63] The Native American population has grown rapidly since the 1970s, not just from natural increase but also in part because a greater number of Americans have asserted some Indian heritage. The civil rights movement and the decline in negative stereotyping of Native Americans—as well as the increase in positive representations of Native Americans in popular culture, such as the movie *Dances with Wolves*—help explain the increase in self-reported Native American identity.[64] As of 2010, 2.9 million Americans identified as solely Native American (0.9 percent of the total U.S. population), and another 2.3 million (0.7 percent) said they were at least part Native American.[65]

Despite this demographic growth, Native Americans tend to have low levels of educational attainment and income and high levels of poverty. In 2010, among the Native American population age 25 years and older, 13 percent had a college degree or more (compared with 30 percent among the population as a whole). Median household income was $35,000 (the national average was $50,000), and their poverty rate was 28 percent (the national average was 15 percent), placing their level of disadvantage near that of African Americans.[66] Native Americans have long had to overcome a dearth of job opportunities in and around reservations and also poor schooling. Although some evidence indicates a decline in the net negative effect of being Native American on wages over the last half of the twentieth century, Native Americans still have lower levels of educational attainment and earnings than otherwise comparable whites.[67] It is not clear whether these differences are explained by discrimination or by other difficult-to-observe factors correlated with being Native American.[68] Research on Native Americans tends to be more limited than that of other groups, in part because of the relatively small Native American population. Additional research on Native Americans, not to mention the other groups, would help shed further light on the complex interrelationship between race and socioeconomic disparities.

MULTIRACIAL AMERICA: ARE WE POSTRACIAL?

The number of mixed-race marriages and multiracial individuals has grown considerably in recent years. The multiracial population grew by 50 percent between 2000 and 2010, from 1.8 million to 4.2 million, making it the fastest growing group of children in the country. Despite this growth, the overall proportion of Americans who report two or more races is still small, at 2.9 percent, according to the 2010 census (the races consist of white, black, American Indian, Asian, and Native Hawaiian). The most common multiracial combination is black and white. Nevertheless, only 2.5 percent of non-Hispanic whites reported more than one race (i.e., among those who reported being white either alone or in combination with another racial group), compared with 6.1 percent of blacks, 13.5 percent of Asians, and 44 percent of Native Americans.[69]

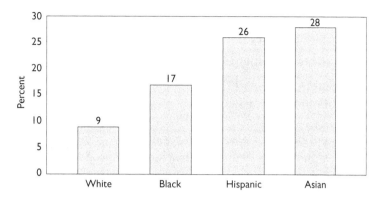

Figure 40. Percentage of newlyweds married to someone of a different race/ethnicity, 2010. Source: Wang 2012, 8.

The number of Americans identifying as multiracial will likely grow rapidly in the coming years because of recent increases in intermarriage. According to one study, about 15 percent of all new marriages in the 2008–10 period involved spouses of different races or ethnicities—more than double the percentage (6.7 percent) in 1980. (In this same study Hispanic origin was considered as a separate race/ethnicity from white.) The percentage of marriages involving a mix of differing races/ethnicities varies across groups, with a low of 9 percent of newlywed whites who married someone of a different race/ethnicity, compared with 17 percent of blacks, 26 percent of Hispanics, and 28 percent of foreign-born and U.S.-born Asians (see figure 40). In fact, nearly half of all U.S.-born Asians marry whites.[70] Overall, about 7 in 10 of mixed-race/ethnicity marriages still involve a white spouse, reflecting the fact that whites constitute the largest racial/ethnic group in the United States. The median household income of mixed-race newlywed couples tends to fall somewhere between the median incomes of couples in the same-race groups.[71]

Americans have become more accepting of intermarriage. In 2011, nearly two-thirds of Americans (63 percent) said they "would be fine" if a family member married someone of a different race. In contrast, in 1986 (when the question was asked differently), about a third of the public viewed intermarriage as acceptable for everyone, 37 percent said it was acceptable for others but not themselves, and 28 percent said different races marrying one another was not acceptable for anyone. Younger respondents were more accepting of intermarriage than older ones, suggesting differences in views about race over time and across age cohorts.[72]

One news story reporting on the rise in intermarriage told the story of seventeen-year-old Kayci Baldwin of Middletown, New Jersey, who was the daughter of a mixed-race couple:

> She remembers how her black father and white mother often worried whether she would fit in with the other kids. While she at first struggled with her identity, Baldwin now actively embraces it, sponsoring support groups and a nationwide multiracial teen club of 1,000 that includes both Democrats and Republicans.
>
> "I went to my high school prom last week with my date who is Ecuadoran-Nigerian, a friend who is Chinese-white and another friend who is part Dominican," she said. "While we are a group that was previously ignored in many ways, we now have an opportunity to fully identify and express ourselves."[73]

One blogger, Leighton Woodhouse, describes broader social changes and his own experiences in a similar way:

> My girlfriend and I are both of mixed racial heritage. I'm half Japanese and half Anglo. She's half Salvadoran and half Jewish. If and when we have children, they'll be a quarter Asian, a quarter Latino and half white, with the white side split WASP/Jewish. When our kids become 18 and fill out their first voter registration forms, the only ethnic category that will make any sense for them to check off is "Multiracial." Today, checking off that box feels pretty close to checking off "Other" or "None of the above" on a questionnaire on any given topic; it's a throwaway category for misfits that has little if any analytical value to the researchers who review the data, but that has to be in there to get the respondent to the next section. When enough Americans start checking off that box, however, it's going to be impossible to ignore.[74]

So are we postracial? The short answer is no. Changes in American society since the 1950s and 1960s have been momentous. The fall of legal barriers and changes in attitudes have opened up many opportunities that were previously closed, if not unimaginable. African Americans, Hispanics, and Asians hold more high-level jobs in government and in the private sector than they used to, and this pattern is more pronounced among younger cohorts.[75]

However, as long as the socioeconomic disparities highlighted in figures 37 through 39 persist, it will be hard to claim that we are "beyond race." The disparities are caused in part by factors directly related to race (especially in the case of African Americans), such as discrimination. As Woodhouse goes on to say in his blog about the growing multiracial population and its consequences, "That's not to suggest that the age of the generation that follows the Millennials will be some sort of post-racial paradise. Countries like Brazil have had broad racially mixed populations for generations; that hasn't lessened their citizens' propensity for bigotry."[76]

Racial inequality is also exacerbated by factors that are not specifically racial, and they have disparate impacts. Of note, growing economic inequality in American society is serving to hamper the opportunities of low-income Americans and their children. The soaring cost of college has made it more difficult for poor families to utilize a traditionally important avenue to upward mobility. The overrepresentation of blacks and Hispanics among the poor exacerbates racial inequalities and will serve to lengthen the time until racial and ethnic parity is achieved.

Notes

1. Diggins 1976, 216.
2. Lipscomb and Bergh 1903–4, 14: 183–84.
3. Ambrose 2003, 4.
4. Peterson 1984, 1343–46.
5. National Public Radio 2013.
6. Arthur 2007, 3731–32.
7. Brodkin 2009, 58.
8. Alba 2009, 30.

9. Waters 2009, 31.

10. Alba 2009, 81–89.

11. Dulitzky 2001, 85; Marger 2011, 282.

12. Omi and Winant 2009, 21.

13. Hirschman, Alba, and Farely 2000, 381–93.

14. Compton et al. 2012.

15. Hirschman, Alba, and Farley 2000, 390–91.

16. U.S. Census Bureau 2013d.

17. Wolff 2013, 15.

18. Weber 1994, 128.

19. See Alba 2009.

20. Gill, Glazer, and Thernstrom 1992, 221.

21. See Foner 1988.

22. Myrdal 1996, 485.

23. Tolnay 2003.

24. Pager 2008, 24–25, from Schuman et al. 2001.

25. W. J. Wilson 1996, 29–30.

26. W. J. Wilson 1978.

27. W. J. Wilson 1987.

28. Hout 1994, 531–42; Sakamoto, Wu, and Tzeng 2000; Farkas and Vicknair 1996.

29. Fryer 2011, 856.

30. See Pager 2009; Cross et al. 1990; Turner, Fix, and Struyk 1991.

31. Charles and Guryan 2008.

32. Loury 2000, 60.

33. Massey and Denton 1993, 141–42.

34. Iceland 2009; Iceland, Sharp, and Timberlake 2013.

35. Western and Wildeman 2009, 221–42; Wakefield and Uggen 2010.

36. Ventura and Bachrach 2000; J. A. Martin et al. 2011; see also Wildsmith, Steward-Streng, and Manlove 2011; and DeParle and Tavernise 2012.

37. U.S. Census Bureau 2012h.

38. Wenger 2013, 1.

39. Lin and Harris 2008, 1–17; Fryer 2011.

40. Reardon 2011.

41. Landry and Marsh 2011.

42. Gill, Glazer, and Thernstrom 1992, 349.

43. Marger 2011, 293.

44. Rodriguez 1989.

45. Portes and Rumbaut 2006.

46. Daniels 2002, 239–43; Gill, Glazer, and Thernstrom 1992, 33.

47. Daniels 2002, 245.

48. Daniels 2002, 250–55; Gill, Glazer, and Thernstrom 1992, 333–34.

49. Bulosan 1946, as quoted in Daniels 2002, 357.

50. San Juan 1995, 9.

51. Iceland, Weinberg, and Hughes 2013 (from decennial censuses).

52. Grieco 2010, 6–8.

53. Camarota 2007, 23.

54. Chiswick and Sullivan 1995, 211–70.

55. Camarota 2007, 18.

56. Logan and Turner 2013, 11.

57. Camarota 2007, 18.

58. White and Glick 2009, 111; see also Bean and Stevens 2003.

59. Takei and Sakamoto 2011.

60. Duncan, Hotz, and Trejo 2006.

61. White and Glick 2009, 148.

62. Healey 2012, 123; Gill, Glazer, and Thernstrom 1992, 30.

63. Gill, Glazer, and Thernstrom 1992, 31.

64. Shoemaker 1999.

65. Norris, Vines, and Hoeffel 2012, 4.

66. U.S. Census Bureau 2010c. Note that the statistics cited here for Native Americans and those cited for other groups come from different surveys (the American Community Survey for Native Americans; and for the other groups see U.S. Census Bureau 2012k). The CPS is too small a survey to provide reliable annual data on Native Americans. Since the data come from different sources, the two sets are not perfectly comparable, but they still provide an accurate general picture of Native American socioeconomic disadvantage in American society.

67. Sakamoto, Wu, and Tzeng 2000; Sandefur and Scott 1983.

68. Huyser, Sakamoto, and Takei 2010.

69. Saulny 2011; see also Humes, Jones, and Ramirez 2011.

70. Qian and Licther 2007.

71. Wang 2012, 8 and 19.

72. Wang 2012, 7.

73. Yen 2009.

74. Woodhouse 2012.

75. Alba 2009, 90–135.

76. Woodhouse 2012.

Sociology as Worldview

Where White Privilege Came From

Allan Johnson

Where White Privilege Came From

The history of white privilege is a long and complicated story, too long and too complicated for me to tell completely here,[1] but what I can do is identify major aspects of the story as a way to show how the sociological model works.

We begin with the long history of the British struggle to conquer Ireland and subjugate its people. This structural relation of domination along with British frustration in the face of stubborn resistance gave rise to a cultural belief that the Irish were an inferior and savage people, not merely in the organization of their societies but in their nature as human beings. The British came to see the Irish as something like a separate species altogether, possessing inferior traits that were biologically passed from one generation to the next.

In perceiving the Irish in this way, the British were changing their worldview by creating a concept of race that encouraged them to see other peoples as subhuman if not inhuman. By not seeing them as members of their own kind, they saw them instead as objects to be controlled through any means necessary, not as human beings whose suffering might be an occasion for empathy and restraint. Using such a worldview, it would seem to the British both reasonable and right that they would assert control through the use of force, much as they would over the land or nonhuman animals.

When the British came to North America in the seventeenth century, they brought with them a worldview that included the idea of race and a view of themselves as a people destined to dominate any land in which they might choose to establish themselves. To this was added the explosive growth of industrial capitalism as an economic system in the eighteenth and nineteenth centuries, whose structure is organized around capitalists' ability to control the conditions and resources on which profit depends.

In the early stages of capitalism, for example, markets were the object of control, as capitalists bought goods in one place and took them to another where they were in scarce supply and could command a higher price than the one they originally paid. Later, as capitalists became involved in the production of goods, profit depended more on the ability to control workers and natural resources than on markets—the less the capitalist pays for labor and materials, the more is left over for the capitalist to keep.

The ecology of North America lent itself to agriculture on a massive scale, and the capitalist demand for land and cheap labor far outstripped the available supply. Most of the land that was to become the United States was gained through a system of military and political dominance over Native Americans, a campaign of deceit, broken treaties, and military conquest that included the use of forced migration (now known as ethnic cleansing) and genocide, practices that today would be considered crimes against humanity.[2]

Most of the labor was drawn from the population of indentured European servants, Native Americans, and Africans, none of whom was initially held in a state of perpetual slavery. The structure of the capitalist system, however, and the British worldview in which they saw themselves as an inherently and distinctly superior race of people combined to lay down a path of least resistance leading in that direction.

Attempts to convert indentured white servants to permanent slaves failed because most were from England and had too strong a sense of their rights as individuals to allow it. It proved equally impractical to enslave Native Americans, because they could easily escape and disappear among native populations. This left black Africans, who were not among their own people in their own land and whose physical features made them stand out among the rest of the population, leaving them with no place to hide should they manage to run away. They alone were selected for the status of permanent slavery.

Complicating the process, however, was the existence of sacred cultural beliefs and values on which the fledgling democracy was founded. The Declaration of Independence and the Constitution with its Bill of Rights clearly contradict such practices as genocide, conquest, forced migration, slavery, the buying and selling of human beings, and the denial of basic rights to dignity, self-determination, and freedom.

To resolve the contradiction, the concept of race was invoked to create cultural categories of 'white' and 'nonwhite' human beings. Native Americans, whose societies Thomas Jefferson had regarded as equal to those of Europeans—and in some ways superior—were increasingly regarded as biologically and socially inferior and doomed either to be absorbed into the English way of life or made to disappear altogether.

Unlike Native Americans, however, Africans were held in a state of perpetual bondage that extended to their biological descendants. Because of this, the concept of race was carried to an extreme by defining white people as a separate and biologically superior species and black people as innately inferior and therefore incapable of learning or advancing themselves. This view, in turn, was used to justify holding black people in a permanent status of subordination to white people, on whom they supposedly were to depend for guidance and discipline. It was a common belief among white people that they were doing Africans a favor by bringing them to live in service as a kind of deliverance from what they assumed was an inferior and savage existence in Africa.

It is important to emphasize that prior to the British experience with the Irish and the enslavement of Africans in North America, the cultural concept of race, including such categories as 'white' and 'color' as social markers of inferiority and superiority, did not exist.[3] Notice, then, how cultural ideas can come into being as a way to justify structural arrangements and how those same ideas can go on to play a role in shaping other systems in various ways, such as the subordination of Africans and Native Americans when English migrants came to North America to make new lives for themselves. This kind of interaction among the various characteristics of social systems is basic to understanding how social life happens—everything is connected to and has the potential to affect everything else.

Structural patterns of dominance also operate among whites, of course, and the concept of race has played a role in this as well. In the nineteenth century, for example, white people in dominant classes carried out a campaign to encourage lower- and working-class white people to think of themselves as white—to make the ascribed status of 'white' an important part of their social identity and worldview. This was offered as a form of compensation for their miserable situation as workers, as in 'I may be poor, but at least I'm white.'[4]

Since then, racial identity has played an important role in distracting white workers from the realities of capitalism by encouraging them to focus on race instead of class. At the turn of the twentieth century, for example, when the labor movement was at its peak, unions routinely excluded workers of color. When white unions went on strike to enforce demands for better working conditions, employers often brought in people of color as strikebreakers, hoping white workers would channel their energy and anger into issues of race and away from the reasons that caused them to go on strike in the first place. Today, similar dynamics operate around issues related to affirmative action and immigration policy.

This history happened through the participation of individual people in social systems of various kinds, but it is important to note that none of it *had* to happen as it did. The characteristics of systems produce paths of least resistance for people to follow, but nothing in the nature of those paths precludes the possibility of people choosing otherwise.

There was, for example, overwhelming support for the doctrine of Manifest Destiny as part of the American worldview that was used to justify the conquest of new territory and the practice of slavery, but there was also opposition. The abolitionist movement, for example, was based on a radically different worldview when it came to the subject of race and slavery. And protesters like Henry David Thoreau were willing to go to prison rather than pay taxes to fund a war against Mexico instigated solely to enlarge the United States by taking Mexican land. People who participate in social systems, in short, are not robots or puppets in relation to them and their dominant worldview. A system's characteristics can load the odds in ways that create paths of least resistance, but the rest depends on what people choose to do from one moment to the next.

Most of the choices we make are unconscious, it being in the nature of paths of least resistance to make our choices appear to be the logical, normal things to do without our having to think about them. This means, of course, that we can participate in systems in ways we are not aware of, help produce consequences without knowing it, and be involved in other people's lives, historically and in the present, without any intention to do so. I came to this awareness for myself through tracing my own family's connection to the history of the United States, including white privilege and racism.

On the face of it, the path of least resistance is for me to jump to the conclusion that since, as far as I know, I do not behave in overtly racist ways and since my ancestors are not from the South and did not own slaves, this troubling history has nothing to do with me. But the history of race in this country and how it plays out today show that things are more complicated than that.

My mother's grandfather, for example, migrated from Connecticut to Wisconsin, where he bought land and started what became a prosperous dairy farm. As it turns out, the land he purchased had been taken from the Ho-Chunk Native American tribe several decades earlier, even though the federal government had promised to protect forever their rights to their ancestral homeland. That promise was honored only until white miners showed an interest in rich deposits of lead on Ho-Chunk land, and so the United States reneged on its promise and called in its army to force the Ho-Chunk from their land in spite of the treaty.

From the Ho-Chunk point of view, my great-grandfather had purchased stolen property, but since white people had the power to make and enforce the law, they could also decide what was stolen and what was not, and so he was allowed to purchase the land without a second thought. He went on to be a successful farmer in the midst of the booming U.S. economy that, as the saying goes, was a rising tide that lifted all boats, including his. For people of color, however, who were systematically denied the opportunity to own their own 'boats,' the rising industrial capitalist tide brought little benefit.

When my great-grandfather died, the farm was inherited by my grand-father, and when my grandparents died, it was sold, and my mother and her four siblings each received a share of the proceeds. And when my parents bought their first house in 1954, they used her modest inheritance for the down payment. They also obtained an affordable mortgage from the Federal Housing Administration (FHA), which was set up after World War II to help returning veterans buy their own homes. Being ordinary citizens, they may well have been unaware of the fact that federal regulations and guidelines governing FHA loans overwhelmingly favored whites over veterans of color, putting them on the receiving end of white privilege in one of the biggest transfers of wealth in U.S. history. Regardless of whether my parents knew it, however, the effect was the same.[5]

My parents now had a 'boat' of their own that was lifted by the rising tide of an expanding economy in the 1950s and 1960s, and when my wife and I wanted to buy our first house in the 1980s and didn't have enough money for the down payment, we borrowed it from my mother. Now we had a boat that we were able to sell some years later so that we could then build the house that we are living in now—a house that, I recently learned, is sitting on land that was once part of the homeland of the Massacoe tribe, from whom it was taken by white people in the seventeenth century. The method by which it was taken was illegal under colonial law, but when those who took the land offered to share it with the colony, the officials decided not to interfere.

I could say this history has nothing personally to do with me, that it was all a long time ago and caused by someone else, that my ancestors were all good, moral, and decent people who never killed or enslaved anyone or drove anyone from their land. Even if that were true (I'll never know for sure), the only way to let it go at that is to ignore the fact that if someone were willing to take the time to follow the money, they would find that some portion of the house and land that we now call home can be traced directly back through my family history to the laws and practices that white people have collectively imposed through their government and other institutions, back to the capitalist Industrial Revolution and the exploitation of people of color that made it possible, and back to the conquest, forced expulsion, and genocide through which the land that is now the United States was first acquired by Europeans. In other words, some portion of this house is our share of the benefits of white privilege passed on and accumulated from one generation to the next.

For some white people, the share of benefits is greater or less than for others, depending on, among other things, the dynamics of social class. But one thing is certain: collectively, the white population of the United States now holds an enormous unearned advantage of wealth and power. Regardless of what kind of people we are as individuals or what we have or have not done ourselves, that advantage cannot be uncoupled from the history of race and racism in this country. The past is more than history. It is also present in structural distributions of wealth and power and cultural ideologies, laws, practices, beliefs, and attitudes whose effect is to justify, defend, and perpetuate the system of white privilege. And the past is present in the huge moral dilemmas that arise from such a history and the question of what to do about the unnecessary suffering and injustice that continue to result from it.

The path of least resistance in any system is to adhere to a worldview in which none of these considerations are acknowledged and to accept the organization of social life as just the way things are and were always meant to be. This is especially true of dominant groups in systems of privilege, who can indulge in the luxury of obliviousness, the freedom to live unaware of the system they participate in and how and with what effect.

By contrast, there is no moment of greater awareness for anyone than when they step off the path of least resistance and both the path and the system of which it is a part become visible. There is also no moment of greater potential to make a difference. In 1960, for example, most public accommodations were racially segregated throughout the American South. One day, in Greensboro, North Carolina, four young African American college students walked into a Woolworth's and bought school supplies for their first term in college and then sat down at the lunch counter and asked for menus. The waitress, however, refused to serve them—"We don't serve your kind here"—and told them to leave.[6]

They were furious at being treated this way, being from Northern cities where racism and segregation were certainly alive and well but not in such a blatant form. For weeks, they argued among themselves about what to do, until finally they decided to return to the lunch counter and refuse to leave until they were served like everyone else. As they sat on the stools that day, they were threatened, verbally abused, and physically manhandled and had food and drink thrown on them, and yet they refused to leave. Finally, the manager announced that the lunch counter was closed. As the students rose to leave, they said they would return the next day. And they did, along with others who had heard of their actions, and then still more the day after that, until every seat was occupied by a person of color openly defying the overt racial segregation that had been a hallmark of the South for hundreds of years.

Within a matter of weeks, news of what happened in Greensboro spread and prompted similar sit-ins across North Carolina and then, within a few months, throughout the South in all kinds of public accommodations. The eventual result was an end to this form of segregation.

Notice what these young men did and did not do. They did not try to change anyone's mind. They did not speak, much less argue, with anyone or hand out written statements. Instead, they made use of the fact that every social system happens only through the participation of individuals, any one of whom has the potential to change how the system happens by stepping off the path of least resistance. By changing the way the system happened, they changed that thing larger than themselves that shapes people's experience, behavior, and expectations about what is *supposed* to happen from one moment to the next. In other words, they discovered that changing the way a system happens is a far more powerful—and potentially more dangerous—strategy than trying to change individuals one at a time.

Notice also how their choices fit into the sociological model. By stepping off the path of least resistance, they changed the ecology and the structure of that small system known as a lunch counter. They altered patterns of interaction and the arrangement of people in physical space, which is the essence of segregation. Their actions challenged not only the distribution of power that had kept these arrangements in place as cornerstones of white privilege but also the worldview of race that had made it seem the natural order of things. This, in turn, produced all kinds of consequences, including tension and conflict and the manager closing the lunch counter and more people showing up the next day and so on, all of which continued to affect how the system happened from one moment to the next. Those consequences reverberated from that small place to much larger systems, and on and on from there, including my retelling of the story in these pages and whatever effect this might have on the people who read it and the people whose lives they will affect.

This is how social life happens and how it may change. But notice that for all the years of struggle over civil rights, white privilege is still alive and well in the United States. Why? In part, it is because white elites have the power to slow the pace of change by controlling social institutions. But a deeper answer lies in the dominant worldview that makes the reality of race either appear as normal and acceptable or not appear at all, to be invisible. To understand change, then, and how it is resisted, we must also understand something more about worldviews that makes us reluctant to give them up.

A Worldview Is Hard to Change

The history of white privilege depended on the cultural invention of the ideas of race in general and whiteness in particular as part of a radical shift in the European worldview. It helped create a taken-for-granted reality in which an institution like slavery might appear not only to 'make sense' but also to be morally acceptable, if not an act of virtue in the fulfillment of God's intention.

So, too, does our understanding of that history depend on a sociological worldview that is itself at odds with the prevailing worldview in our society. In part, this conflict is due to the tendency of many sociologists to focus on issues of social justice and inequality, a perspective that has always been a minority point of view. But the main reason for the sociological worldview's not taking hold in the United States is that it directly conflicts with the individualistic model that is the bedrock of our culture.

If we were to adopt the view that social life happens through a dynamic relation between people and social systems, it would upend the American fixation on the individual, a core part of our worldview that endures in spite of the fact that it is not based in reality. This would also challenge the use of individualism as a way to rationalize inequality and oppression so as to protect privilege in all its forms. It is no surprise, then, that sociology is often viewed as a somewhat alien way of thinking: in the context of the dominant American worldview, it is.

Worldviews are resistant to change because we depend on them as the sum total of what we know or think we know or just assume, consciously or not, a vast collection of interconnected beliefs, values, attitudes, images, and memories. Most of the time a worldview provides the deep unconscious background that enables us to navigate reality from one moment to the next. It shapes how we see everything, from the cosmos and what happens when we die to why people do what they do. It provides the material out of which we construct a taken-for-granted reality that we do not have to question or even think about. It shapes not only what we perceive as real but also how we make sense of it, how we explain what happens and what is and is not, and how we justify what we do in any given situation. Even more powerful is that we tend not to be aware that worldviews even exist or of how complex they are. Expose one part to scrutiny and doubt and you cannot help but bring others into question.

When I consider why it is so hard to change a worldview—whether someone else's or my own—I find that it depends on how it came to be there, what authority is behind it, and how 'centrally located' or interconnected it is in relation to the rest. My worldview, for example, includes the belief that the Earth is roughly 4.5 billion years old. That bit of reality was added when I read about it somewhere. I do not remember where or when it was, but I do know I adopted this piece of information because the source was identified as science, and my worldview includes a general trust in what scientists claim as true, knowing all the while that it can change as new evidence comes to light. Adding this belief to my worldview happened in a particular moment in a particular way and from a particular source, and I could have decided against it or withheld judgment for one reason or another, as I sometimes do.

What I take to be real about the age of the Earth is a simple and isolated piece of my and many other people's worldview. It is not connected to other beliefs that matter to me and has little effect on my life, so I don't really care whether it's true and would not hesitate to give it up if scientists came out and said the age of the Earth was, say, 3.3 billion years.

It is a very different matter to believe in race or capitalism, ideas that we acquired without our knowing it, being almost literally in the air we breathe from the moment we are born and then repeated and affirmed over the years in stories and images and what people say and do. As they become embedded in an expanding web of beliefs, values, experience, and feeling, they acquire so many connections to other parts of our worldview that they can seem to originate from everywhere at once, to have no origin at all but instead to have been for all time, giving them an authority far wider and deeper than that of any particular source. Instead of being the belief of a person, a group, or even a society, they appear as something beyond the reach of mere evidence, opinion, time, or place, not beliefs at all but intuitively true, undeniable, obvious, the way things are, what everybody knows, ordained by God, immutable facts.

So it is that the core principles of white dominance, white identification, and white centeredness have come to be embedded in and indispensable to the mainstream American worldview, along with an almost religious belief in capitalism. This has provided generation after generation of Americans with a lens through which to perceive, interpret, and shape both what is seen to be real and what is imagined to be possible.

Unlike adopting an idea about the age of the Earth, however, we do not decide one day that from now on we are going to believe in race and capitalism. To the extent that we do believe, it is because we grew up with an unquestioned sense of *knowing* it to be so, as something that is second nature and taken for granted as undoubtedly true.

It is an awareness of this kind of 'knowing' that is perhaps the most important thing I have acquired from sociology as a worldview, because it was through this that I came to realize that I even *had* a worldview that I might step back to examine and understand. It is in this way that sociology can provide both a mirror in which to see ourselves in ways we otherwise would not and a window into a larger world, both as it is and what it might become.

1. See Theodore W. Allen, *The Invention of the White Race*, vols. 1–2, 2nd ed. (New York: Verso, 2012), and Audrey Smedley and Brian Smedley, *Race in North America: Origin and Evolution of a Worldview*, 4th ed. (Boulder, CO: Westview Press, 2011).

2. See Smedley, *Race in North America*. See also Dee Brown, *Bury My Heart at Wounded Knee: An Indian History of the American West*, 30th anniv. ed. (New York: Owl Books, 2001).

3. For a history of this transition, see Basil Davidson, *The African Slave Trade* (Boston: Back Bay Books, 1988).

4. For more on this history, see James R. Barrett and David R. Roediger, "How White People Became White," in *Critical White Studies,* ed. Richard Delgado and Jean Stefancic (Philadelphia: Temple University Press, 1997), 402–406, and David R. Roediger, *The Wages of Whiteness: Race and the Making of the American Working Class,* rev. ed. (New York: Verso, 2007).

5. See George Lipsitz, *The Possessive Investment in Whiteness: How White People Profit from Identity Politics,* rev. and enl. ed. (Philadelphia: Temple University Press, 2006).

6. William H. Chafe, *Civilities and Civil Rights: Greensboro, North Carolina and the Black Struggle for Freedom* (New York: Oxford University Press, 1981).

Native Americans in Sports

Historically, Native American tribes have been physically active in games and athletics. Traditional Native American sports such as stickball, lacrosse, archery, running, and canoeing were often connected to spiritual, political, or economic worldviews (King 2004). They were important in training children, and the outcomes often held ritual significance. In the late 19th century, Native American boarding schools were developed with aims to "kill the Indian and save the man," taking Indian children out of their homes away from their families and indoctrinating them with European language, culture, religion, and sports (Churchill 2004: 14). While many Native Americans continued to participate in traditional games and sports, this forced **assimilation**, a form of ethnic genocide in boarding schools, produced a decline in traditional games.

Organized interscholastic sports were institutionalized by European Americans as a form of cultural control. Sports were used as a tool of domination in which Native American boys learned to see their traditional games as "inferior" and were taught that there were more "civilized" ways to compete. For example, according to Gems, football "taught Indians rules, discipline, and civilization" (1998: 146), which were considered European American virtues. The White headmasters perceived sports as an effective tool in channeling males into more acceptable European roles and behavior. As an unintended consequence, many boarding schools fielded successful athletic teams in football and baseball, taking on and winning against collegiate powerhouses such as Harvard and Syracuse between 1900 and 1932 (Haggard 2004).

The Carlisle Indian School and Haskell Institute produced exceptional athletes, such as Jim Thorpe, who is considered one of the most versatile athletes in American history. A Sac and Fox tribal member, Thorpe played professional baseball, football, and basketball and also won gold medals in the 1912 Olympics for the pentathlon and decathlon. He attended the Haskell Institute in Lawrence, Kansas as a youth (Wheeler 1979). As Gems (1998) notes, athletic participation at such schools allowed Native Americans in the early 1900s to assert their racial identity,

> by providing a collective memory of self-validation and the creation of kindred heroes as they successfully tested themselves against the beliefs of Social Darwinism and dispelled notions of white dominance … In that sense football proved to be not only an assimilative experience, but a resistive and liberating one as well.
>
> (Gems 1998: 148)

Nonetheless, there was an obvious absence of Native American athletes reaching national success between World War II and the 1964 victory of Billy Mills at the Olympic Games (King 2004). Mills began running at the Haskell Institute in Kansas as a youth and became the second Native American to win a gold medal at the Olympics (Jim Thorpe was the first). His win in the 10,000-meter run was unexpected as he competed against a world record holder from Australia, Ron Clarke (Mills 2009). Mills often discussed why many traditional Native Americans did not participate fully in organized sports. Mills believed that engaging in a sporting program that does not acknowledge cultural heritage creates a fear among Native American athletes, a fear of going too far into White society and losing one's "Indianness" while participating in mainstream sports (Simpson 2009: 291).

In 1968, the American Indian Movement (AIM) was launched in Minneapolis, Minnesota and soon thereafter spread across the country. The movement sought to address problems affecting the Native American community such as poverty, police harassment, and treaty violations. During its initial stages, the movement was known for its pan-Indian philosophy and protests. Perhaps the most famous protest occurred in 1973 at Wounded Knee, South Dakota at the Pine Ridge Indian Reservation. Armed members of the movement occupied the area in protest at Native American poverty and U.S. government treaty violations. The event culminated in a 71-day standoff with federal law enforcement and ended only after two Native Americans were killed (Banks and Erdoes 2004). Today, AIM continues to fight against the same problems of poverty and treaty violations and also actively protests the use of Native American mascots (American Indian Movement n.d.).

Other organizations such as the National Indian Athletic Association (NIAA), founded in 1973, and the Native American Sports Council (NASC), founded in1993, were created to promote athletic participation and excellence among Native American athletes throughout North America. Today, the NASC sponsors sports leagues and provides training and other forms of support to potential Olympians. These organizations support the development of Native Americans through fitness, community involvement, and boosting self-esteem (Kalambakal 2004). Formerly a colonial tool used to force Native American children of both sexes to reject their heritage and adopt European-American cultural norms, these athletic organizations employ sports to steer youngsters in a positive direction and reduce the high rates of suicide, drug and alcohol use, and gang activity on the reservations (Kalambakal 2004). Through both the NIAA and NASC, sports education, sports camps, and clinics have led to an increase in Native American participation in mainstream sports in the Olympics, college, and professional sports; however, this "trend has yet to produce the numbers experienced during the early twentieth century" (Haggard 2004: 226).

Native American athletes are hardly visible in contemporary sports. Aside from a few teams and individual athletes in segregated Indian schools, Native American sport participation has been limited by many factors. Poverty, poor health, lack of equipment and facilities, and a lack of cultural understanding by those who control sports, as well as academic unpreparedness and negative academic stereotypes of

Native American student-athletes, has limited the non-reservation sports opportunities of these athletes (Simpson 2009). This cultural group remains underrepresented as athletes at all levels despite the obvious talent and the popularity of basketball on Native American reservations. However, this talent garnered recent attention with the story of two sisters on the University of Louisville's women's basketball team, which finished as the national championship runner-up in 2013. Shone and Jude Schimmel were raised on the Umatilla Reservation in Oregon and were considered exceptional local talent. Playing a style they call "rez ball," the sisters captivated local audiences growing up. Their national success has led to an explosion of interest in basketball among the local reservation youth and a sense of pride among Native Americans in general (Block 2013).

Youth sports are associated with forms of capital including social capital that can advantage Native youth. For example, children and youth who participate in organized sports perform better academically, are less likely to drink or do drugs, have higher self-esteem, and lower rates of obesity and diabetes (Bailey 2006; Broh 2002; Eitle and Eitle 2002; Ewing et al. 2002; Pate et al. 2000). Native Americans are underrepresented in youth sport leagues and have higher rates of alcoholism, high school dropout, suicide, obesity, and diabetes than any other minority group (Bachman et al. 1991; Center for Native American Youth 2012; Gray and Smith 2003). Greater participation may be a valuable resource for Native American youth.

Native Americans also remain underrepresented at the elite levels. In NCAA Division I, II, and III sports, Native American men and women make up 0.4 percent of student-athletes (NCAA 2012b). As illustrated in Figure 2.1, White men and women make up the largest majority of NCAA Division I, II, and III student-athletes in most sports, while Native Americans are widely underrepresented in all sports. In fact, even in lacrosse, a sport thought to have roots in the Cherokee traditional game "stickball," Native American men and women make up less than 0.5 percent of collegiate players. The highest representation of Native American NCAA student-athletes is seen in softball, where Native American women make up 0.7 percent of all players.

While they are underrepresented as students on college campuses along with most minority groups, Native Americans are far less represented as collegiate athletes compared to Blacks and Hispanics. In fact, the most visible representation of Native American culture in popular commercialized sports is found among mascots. In addition to the many professional sports teams, hundreds of high schools and close to 100 universities have Native American images for mascots and nicknames—not to mention the countless little league and peewee teams that follow suit using these images to represent their teams. Along with class and access issues in youth sports, these disparaging mascots may be linked to the lack of participation of Natives in youth sports and the benefits that go along with participation.

	All sports (Division I)	Football	Basketball	Track and field	Soccer	Baseball	Softball	Lacrosse
White Men	62.5	55.1	43.5	64.9	68.5	84.7		88.2
White Women	70.6		55.7	66.2	80.7		81.1	88.2
Black Men	29.4	35.4	45.5	21.6	7.2	3.9		2.7
Black Women	16		32.7	20.4	3.7		5.8	2.8
Hispanic Men	4.2	3	2.8	4.6	9.9	5.6		1.5
Hispanic Women	4.2		3	4.1	5.6		6	2.1
Native American Men	0.4	0.5	0.2	0.4	0.2	0.4		0.3
Native American Women	0.4		0.4	0.4	0.3		0.7	0.2
Asian Men	2	0.7	0.5	1.4	1.6	0.9		0.9
Asian Women	2.4		0.8	1.4	1.5		1.2	1.2

Source: Lapchick 2011

Figure 2.1 NCAA Student-Athlete Racial Composition by Selected Sport 2010–2011

Contemporary Racism in Sports: Native American Symbols as Mascots

Native American mascots have remained a common fixture in the world of athletics at all levels from peewee leagues to professional teams. The Washington Redskin has been the mascot of one of the most popular NFL teams, located in our nation's capital, since 1932. The term is considered a disparaging reference to many Native American people. According to Stapleton (2001), "redskin" is a term with a 400-year history and first emerged in sport during a time when the American government actively sought to assimilate Native Americans. In his book *Skull Wars*, Thomas (2000) writes,

> There is today no single word more offensive to Indian people then the term "redskins," a racial epithet that conjures up the American legacy of bounty hunters bringing in wagon loads of Indian skulls and corpses—literally the bloody dead bodies were known as "redskins"—to collect their payments.

(p. 204)

Although many Native Americans are offended by the term, 88 percent of Americans surveyed oppose a name change for the team (Sigelman 2001).

In a survey of the top 10 most common team mascots, most were birds or beasts of prey, with the exception of two: "Warriors" and "Indians" (Franks 1982). The only two nickname categories that are not predatory animals refer to Native Americans. Many would ask, what's the problem? Are we not honoring indigenous people for being such fierce warriors?

To perceive Native Americans through the eyes of mascots and sports nicknames creates a myopic and inaccurate version of the rich traditions, culture, history, and contemporary existence of the population. Native American mascots are based on the stereotypical "Cowboy and Indian" Wild West images of America's indigenous peoples, with no regard for the diverse cultures and religious beliefs of tribal groups. This manner of stereotyping Native Americans began very early upon European contact. Colonizers portrayed "Indians" as "barbaric," "wild," "bestial," and most of all "savage" (Berkhofer 1978). In fact, Americans' view of "Indians" as predatory beasts has been ingrained from the inception of our nation. George Washington wrote that "Indians" were "wolves and beasts who deserve nothing from whites but total ruin," and President Andrew Jackson stated that troops should seek out "Indians" to "root them out of their dens and kill Indian women and their whelps" (Stannard 1992: 240–41). Racist and dehumanizing descriptions produced mass fear of Native Americans as an entire race or category of people. This fear negates the concept of "honoring" tribes as the basis for naming teams as fierce warriors or other Native American-derived images.

As America grew, these stereotypes were used to justify the systematic genocide of Native Americans, as they were seen as a threat to the safety of colonizers. These images remain a part of American culture, as many Americans continue to visualize the image of a "savage warrior" with feathers and war paint when thinking of Native Americans. One can go into any costume shop and find a Native American costume complete with tomahawk and a feathered headdress. These images have become embraced by **popular culture** and controlled by the **dominant group** instead of Native Americans themselves.

Activism around Native American Imagery

Native American mascots and the use of Native American imagery in advertising and branding (i.e., Land O'Lakes butter, Sue Bee honey, Jeep Cherokee, Crazy Horse Malt Liquor, Winnebagos) grew during the era of racial segregation and legalized discrimination in America (Meerskin 2012). The use of Native American peoples as mascots ranges from generic titles such as Indians, Braves, Warriors, or Savages to specific tribal designations such as Seminoles, Apaches, or Illini. These have been prevalent since the turn of the century, at a time when Little Black Sambo, Frito Bandito, and other racially insensitive branding was commonplace in "less enlightened times" (Graham 1993: 35). While Little Black Sambo and Uncle Rastus have long since been abandoned, the equally insensitive **Chief Wahoo** remains. These images exaggerate physical and cultural aspects of Native Americans and reduce them to one stereotypical representation: savage warrior.

The fight to remove the stereotypical images of Native American mascots and nicknames in sport has been active for nearly four decades. It occurred alongside the **civil rights movement** of the 1960s as the **National Congress of American Indians (NCAI)** began to challenge the use of stereotypical imagery in print and other forms of media (Staurowsky and Baca 2004). The use of Native American mascots also fell under attack when this campaign was launched in 1968. NCAI contended that the use of Native American imagery was not only racist but further reproduced the perception of Native American peoples as sub-human. By 1969 universities began to respond, as Dartmouth College changed its nickname from "the Indians" to "Big Green." Many followed suit, including the universities of Oklahoma, Marquette, and Syracuse, which all dropped Indian nicknames in the 1970s. Currently, an estimated 1,000 academic institutions have relinquished use of Native American mascots or nicknames.

Other institutions have resisted and remain invested in retaining their racist mascots. Close to 1,400 high schools and 70 colleges and universities have refused to cede to calls for change (Staurowsky and Baca 2004). Although Native Americans protest at every home opener with signs that read "We are human beings, not Mascots," MLB's Cleveland Indians maintain the use of the caricatured Chief Wahoo. The Washington Redskins have lost trademark protection, but continue to fight through litigation to maintain the use of the team's mascot. The University of Illinois Fighting Illini fought to maintain their mascot, **Chief Illiniwek**, amid major controversy for over a decade before finally retiring the chief in 2007. The Florida State Seminoles also maintain the use of their Native American imagery, citing an endorsement from the Seminole tribe as justification. All argue that they are honoring the history of Native Americans by using them as mascots. For example, the Cleveland Indians proclaim that the team's designation was chosen to honor the first Native American to play professional baseball, Louis Francis Sockalexis. The University of Illinois argued that their mascot was an honor to the extinct tribe that once inhabited the state. Although Florida State University has been given "permission" to maintain the use of its mascot and nickname by the Seminole tribe and its chief, "there are American Indians protesting outside every Florida State game, including some Seminole people. They say the mascot looks like a Lakota who got lost in an Apache dressing room riding a Nez Perce horse" (Spindel 2002: 16).

Many organizations using Native American designations argue that some Native American individuals and tribal groups have no issue with the use of the mascots and indeed feel a sense of pride. And many fans of these teams agree. In his study of local public opinion, Callais (2010) found that supporters of retaining Native American mascots base their position on maintaining tradition and promoting a color-blind society through a tribute to Native Americans.

While some individual tribes and persons may approve of this practice, all major Native American organizations have denounced it and called for a cessation of the use of their images as mascots, nicknames, and in the branding of products. Mascots are "manufactured images" of Native Americans, and their continued promotion results in a loss of power to control use of those images.

> Indigenous mascots exhibit either idealized or comical facial features and "native" dress, ranging from body-length feathered (usually turkey) headdresses to more subtle fake buckskin attire or skimpy loincloths. Some teams and supporters display counterfeit Indigenous paraphernalia, including tomahawks, feathers, face paints, and symbolic drums and pipes. They also use mock Indigenous behaviors such as the tomahawk chop, dances, chants, drumbeats, war-whooping, and symbolic scalping.
>
> (Pewewardy 1999: 2)

These images were manufactured by their respective schools, universities, and teams. They were created in the minds of those who established them during a time of racial hatred, stereotyping, and when Native Americans were seen as a threat (Callais 2010). The "costumes" of the mascots are derived from stereotypical and widely oversimplified views of a diverse group of people. In reality, each feather and bead, the facial paint, and especially the dances have a distinct, significant, deeply spiritual, and religious meaning to each tribal group. Particular dances mark "the passage of time, the changing of the seasons, a new status in a person's life" and "dancing expresses and consolidates a sense of belonging" (Spindel 2002: 189). In the eyes of many Native Americans, to put on the "costume" and perform a "war dance" at halftime is to mock their religion. How would it go over to have a team designated the "Black Warriors" with a mascot named Chief Watutsi dressed in a loincloth dancing around with a spear? While this mascot would not probably last a single day, Native Americans have been unable to have the use of their images stopped, despite a 40-year struggle to do so.

All in Fun?

Charlene Teters, the Native American activist who called national attention to the University of Illinois fighting Illini, describes how her children reacted when they first witnessed Chief Illiniwek in the documentary *In Whose Honor* (Rosenstein 1997). She describes her son sinking into his chair as he tried to become "invisible." One of the primary arguments against the use of Native American mascots is how it affects children of all races, but especially Native American children. The flippant and inaccurate depiction of Native American culture and identity "causes many young indigenous people to feel shame about who they are as human beings" (Pewewardy 1999: 342). These feelings become a part of the identity and self-image of Native American children, working together with the objective experiences of poverty and deprivation to create low self-esteem and high rates of depression (Pewewardy 1999). One in five Native American youth attempts suicide before the age of 20. In fact, suicide is the second leading cause of death for Native American youth between the ages of 15 and 24 (Center for Native American Youth 2012). This is two and a half times higher than the national average. While there are many factors that contribute to this statistic, such as poverty and drug and alcohol abuse, the use of Native American mascots further damages the self-image of Native American youth. Mascots dehumanize Native Americans and present images, sacred rituals, and other symbols in a way that negates the reverence instilled in Native children, thus negatively impacting their self-esteem. In fact, the American Psychological Association (2001) states emphatically that the use of Native American mascots perpetuates stigmatization of the group and has negative implications for perceptions of self among Native American children and adolescents.

For non-indigenous children, the use of Native American stereotypes as mascots perpetuates the mythical "Cowboys and Indians" view of the group. In a study conducted by Children Now, most of the children studied were found to perceive Native Americans as disconnected from their own way of life (Children Now 1999). Debbie Reese, a Nambe' Pueblo who travels across the country educating children and teachers concerning Native American stereotypes, recounts the many times that children described native people as "exotic," "mythical," or "extinct" and asked if she drove cars or rode horses (Spindel 2002: 224). Most Americans do not come into meaningful contact with traditional Native Americans very often, if at all. Thus, these stereotypical images of mascots and mythical beings are how we learn about Native American culture. Unfortunately, they disallow Americans from visualizing "Indians" as real people, but encourage viewing them as fierce warriors or even clowns dancing around with tomahawks, war paint, and feathered headdresses.

Children and adults alike are profoundly influenced by stereotypical images. The **stereotype threat** is a popular social psychological theory that has been researched empirically since introduced to the literature in 1995 (Steele and Aronson 1995). Claude Steele, a Stanford University professor of social psychology, defines a stereotype threat as "the pressure that a person can feel when she is at risk of confirming, or being seen to confirm a negative stereotype about her group" (Steele and Davies 2003: 311). For instance, when women are reminded that they are women, they perform poorly on math tests due to the stereotype that women are not good at math (Spencer, Steele, and Quinn 1999). Applied to the stereotypical images of Native Americans perpetuated through mascots, these violent and trivialized images may be associated with the lowered self-images of Native youth or the current statistic in which violence accounts for 75 percent of deaths among Native Americans between the ages of 12 and 20 (Center for Native American Youth 2012).

The use of Native American mascots is an example of institutional discrimination. Chief Wahoo and other such images have become as American as baseball itself. They are ingrained into the interworking of our society and its institutions. Major societal institutions such as the economy, sports, and education discriminate against Native Americans by continuing to denigrate living human beings through mascots and team designations. Perhaps if the elite levels of sport (professional and intercollegiate) terminated their use of Native American mascots and raised awareness on the issue, K–12 schools would follow suit. This could serve as an instructional piece for schools as they confront the issue of stereotyping, a process that begins early in one's childhood.

The U.S. Civil Rights Commission released a statement in 2001 condemning the use of Native American mascots. In fact, the National Congress of American Indians, American Indian Movement, National Education Association, National Association for the Advancement of Colored People (NAACP), countless state and local school boards, and the American Psychological Association have all issued similar resolutions. Such images and symbols have been found to perpetuate stereotypes and stigmatization, and negatively affect the mental health and behaviors of Native American people (American Psychological Association 2001). As stated by Native American activist Dennis Banks, "what part of ouch do they not understand?" (Rosenstein 1997).

Conclusion

The issues that Native Americans currently experience in sport—underrepresentation and stereotyping—bring us back to the image of sport as contested terrain. While many believe that the use of Native American mascots is a way of paying tribute, many Native Americans themselves battle to gain more control over the portrayal of their own identity. Athletes are often portrayed as "savages" and "animals," images that Native Americans have fought hard to be disassociated from. And while universities and professional teams generate millions of dollars from the sale of merchandise using Native American imagery, "real" Native Americans remain one of the most impoverished racial groups in society. With a group that experiences disproportionately high rates of dropout, obesity, and suicide, perhaps more effort should be spent on encouraging Native American youth athletics participation, which may help reduce these very problems. Furthermore, their heightened level of participation in sport could also result in society adopting a more positive outlook and understanding of Native Americans, an identification that goes beyond equating Native Americans and sports with mascots.

The Social Construction of Gender Problems

Gender Inequality

The last fifty years have been marked by profound changes in people's views on gender norms and patterns of gender inequality. The women's rights movement and accompanying social changes have significantly reduced women's disadvantage in the labor force and other arenas. The changes have been so deep that some commentators have questioned whether current trends portend a reversal in patterns of gender inequality, leaving men at a distinct disadvantage. Hanna Rosin argues: "For much of history, the mark of an enviable woman has been her ability to secure a superior match, through her beauty, cleverness, or artful deception. After civil rights, that expectation mellowed into something called 'homogamy,' meaning women marrying men of equal money and education. But that happy place of equilibrium seems to be fading as well. Instead, women have started doing something demographers thought they would never see: they are marrying down, not just in the United States but all over the world."[1]

The reason women are marrying down, according to Rosin, is that they are now often outearning their male peers and thus need to settle for spouses with lower salaries. However, others are not so sure that the evidence supporting the ascendancy of women and the decline of male power in society is that compelling. As Stephanie Coontz, a scholar of the family and gender, has argued: "How is it, then, that men still control the most important industries, especially technology, occupy most of the positions on the lists of the richest Americans, and continue to make more money than women who have similar skills and education? And why do women make up only 17 percent of Congress?"[2]

This chapter takes a look at the role of gender today from a sociological point of view. Sociology is the study of how social structure affects our everyday life. Some of these structures are so ingrained in us that we take them for granted. We often assume that things are the way they are simply because they are "natural." However, anthropologists have long noted that what is natural and commonplace in one society seems unnatural and positively puzzling in another. Gender is one such social construction that we often take for granted. As sociologist Judith Lorber has written:

> Gender is so pervasive that in our society we assume it is bred into our genes. Most people find it hard to believe that gender is constantly created and re-created out of human interaction, out of social life, and is the texture and order of that social life. . . . For the individual, gender construction starts with assignment to a sex category on the basis of what the genitalia look like at birth. Then babies are dressed or adorned in a way that displays the category because parents don't want to be constantly asked whether their baby is a girl or a boy. . . . Once a child's gender is evident, others treat those in one gender differently from those in the other, and the children respond to the different treatment by feeling different and behaving differently.[3]

Much of what we do is gendered. Boys and girls in school typically have same-sex friends and often role-play games following social norms. Toy stores reinforce this; they are full of toys that are distinctly for boys (action figures) and others that are clearly targeted at girls (dolls and accessories). Gender stereotypes are also perpetuated in the media, as male characters are more likely to act aggressively and be leaders, and females are more likely to be cast in the role of caregivers.[4] Parenting is gendered, with mothers usually playing the leading role in child raising. Housework is gendered, such as with "outdoor" work assigned to men (lawn mowing) and indoor work to women (cooking). Jobs and careers are gendered—construction jobs are still overwhelmingly filled by men, and receptionists are still much more likely to be women. Caregiving for sick family members is gendered, with women more typically caring for aged parents.

However, gender norms, at least in Western countries, are generally more fluid these days than they used to be. A generation ago, a husband taking care of the children while his wife worked would have been a striking oddity and perhaps an object of derision. Today, women can be soldiers, and men can be nurses. Many would argue that women can be smart and tough, and men can be expressive and emotional and still fall within the socially acceptable bounds of femininity and masculinity. The increasing emphasis on individualism and self-actualization discussed in chapter 2 has released people from the tyranny of very tightly bound gender norms. This has led to a withering of gender inequality in the United States and other wealthy, modern countries around the world.

Or has it? How much have gender norms and gender inequality in American society really changed? Are men and women now just about on equal footing? These are the central questions guiding the rest of this chapter. What follows is a review of the evidence on gender inequality in education, labor force attachment and occupations, and earnings. I explore patterns and trends in gender inequality in other countries as well. I evaluate arguments about the rise of women and the decline of men and discuss emerging patterns of gender inequality in American society today.

TRADITIONAL DIVISION OF LABOR IN THE HOUSEHOLD

Conventional wisdom used to hold that differences between men and women, including the division of labor between the two, were rooted in biological differences. For example, researchers writing in the 1960s documented how among some primates the male is dominant and aggressive, extrapolating that humans are much the same. However, others have shown that significant variation occurs in primate social systems, in which females of many species are "fiercely competitive, resourceful and independent, sexually assertive and promiscuous and, in some cases, more prone than males to wanderlust at puberty."[5]

While it would be wrong to say that there are no meaningful biological differences between men and women that can affect their behavior, biological predispositions are strongly affected by social influences and the culture in which individuals are embedded. The goal here is not to definitively determine to what extent biology affects the behavior of boys and girls and men and women, but rather to discuss the role of social constructions of gender in shaping normative behavior and in particular how such norms have changed over time.

Societies today vary considerably in their level of *patriarchy*, or the systematic dominance of males over females. In several countries in the Middle East and South Asia, women who have committed adultery or have had premarital sex are in some cases killed by their father, brothers, or husbands as a way to protect the family's honor.[6] The practice of purdah in many such societies, or the concealing of women from men, is viewed by many as an institutional method of subordinating women and signals their subjugation (though individual women sometimes choose to wear some kind of covering, such as a *hijab,* for varying personal, cultural, or political reasons).[7] Gender inequality is not confined to developing countries. In the United States into the 1960s and Japan into the 1970s (just to provide two examples), a woman could be legally fired from a job if she married or had children.[8] Thus, there is considerable variation in gender norms across countries that is not necessarily contingent on their level of development or wealth. The overall status of women in Thailand is fairly high; in most professions, in universities, and in the corporate sector, the occupational attainment of Thai women is higher than in most Western industrial nations, including the United States.[9]

Historically, patterns of gender inequality have been linked to changes in the family. As we've seen, in preindustrial America, men and women worked alongside each other in the home and around it, often specializing in particular activities. The husband was generally seen as the ultimate arbiter and decision maker. With industrialization and urbanization, men increasingly worked away from the home, and the home itself became the province of women, which created different economic spheres for the two. Many advocated for men to be paid a "family wage" that could support not only the husband but the wife and children as well. Henry Ford, for example, promoted paying a family wage to workers in his factories in the early 1900s in part as a way of keeping more women in the home with children.[10] Men's authority as head of the household was reinforced by the money they were responsible for earning to support the family. A significant amount of productive work in which women were engaged (e.g., taking care of the home, childrearing, caring for the sick and elderly, volunteer work) was at least implicitly not valued as highly as men's paid work.

It should be noted, however, that while this traditional family arrangement—the husband earning a family wage and the wife taking care of the home and children—was the cultural ideal, in lower-income families women still continued to work to help make ends meet. Single-parent families were not entirely anomalous either. For example, 9 percent of children lived in such families (mainly with a widowed mother) in 1900.[11] In the 1950s, before the women's rights movement, only about half of all families with children were in the traditional breadwinner/homemaker family model.[12]

Women's labor force participation increased through the twentieth century for several reasons. For one, as family sizes generally declined, less time and energy were needed to care for children and maintain a household. Technological changes, including the invention of time-saving household appliances such as vacuum cleaners, washing machines, refrigerators, dishwashers, and microwaves, all reduced the time needed for housekeeping and the need for a full-time homemaker. The availability of new consumer products and rising living standards may have also made earning money through paid labor more attractive to families.[13]

Changes in the economy, such as the increase in the number of white-collar versus blue-collar jobs, especially with the service sector generating more of the former, provided greater opportunity for women in the paid labor market. Similarly, the rise of women's earnings and the stagnation of men's earnings, especially in the second half of the twentieth century, provided greater impetus for women to work. Increasing divorce rates likewise led many women to gain job experience to prepare for the possibility of marital dissolution. In the social and cultural realm, changing ideas about gender norms made work for women more socially acceptable, including for mothers of young children. The feminist movement emphasized the importance of women having the ability to pursue independence and self-actualization on an equal footing with men, both in and outside the home.[14] The Civil Rights Act of 1964, along with other anti-discriminatory measures and affirmative action, expanded the opportunities open

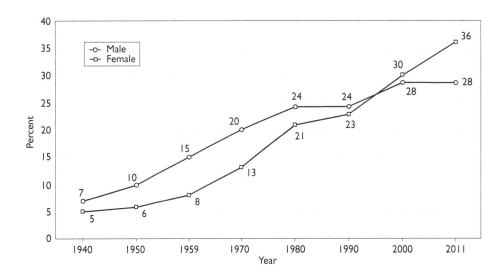

Figure 13. Percentage of 25- to 29-year-olds who completed four years of college or more, by gender, 1940–2011. Source: U.S. Census Bureau 2012f.

to women.[15] As a result, women today are better educated and are more likely to work, have higher-status jobs, and receive more in terms of wages than before.

EDUCATIONAL ATTAINMENT

An increasing number of Americans pursue a college degree. However, there are important differences in educational trends by gender. Figure 13 shows the percentage of 25- to 29-year-old men and women who have completed four or more years of college over the 1940 to 2011 period. Men were consistently more likely to be college graduates than women from 1940 to about 1990, when the two lines intersect. For example, in 1940, about 7 percent of young men had completed four or more years of college, compared with 5 percent of women. If anything, the male educational advantage grew larger, such that in 1959 the percentage of men (15 percent) who had completed four or more years of college was nearly double that of women (8 percent). By 1990, however, 24 percent of men and 23 percent of women had four or more years of college, after which women consistently achieved higher levels of educational attainment. In 2011, 36

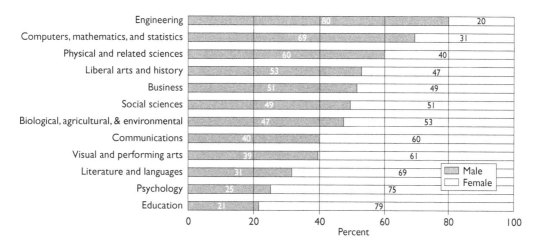

Figure 14. Gender distribution by field of study among 25- to 39-year-olds holding bachelor's degrees, 2009. Source: Siebens and Ryan 2012, table 2.

percent of young women, compared with just 28 percent of men, had finished four or more years of college.[16]

While more women are completing college than men, there are striking differences in the major fields of study chosen by gender (see figure 14). Among 25- to 39-year-olds surveyed in 2009, about 80 percent of engineering majors and 69 percent of majors in computers, mathematics, and statistics were men. In contrast, women were overwhelming concentrated in education (79 percent of education majors were women), psychology (75 percent), and literature and languages (69 percent). Although these differences are notable, the imbalances were even greater among respondents who were 65 years old and over (most of whom presumably finished their bachelor's degrees decades ago). Among this group, 97 percent of engineering majors were men, as were 83 percent of those majoring in physical and related sciences.[17] The choice of majors has implications for the types of jobs men and women have and hence gender differentials in earnings. For example, median annual earnings in 2011 for those with degrees in computers, mathematics, and statistics was $80,180, and for those in the physical sciences it was $80,037; in contrast, median earnings among those in education and psychology, both majors in which women are more highly represented, were $50,902 and $55,509, respectively.[18] Many argue that the "choice" of majors should not necessarily be

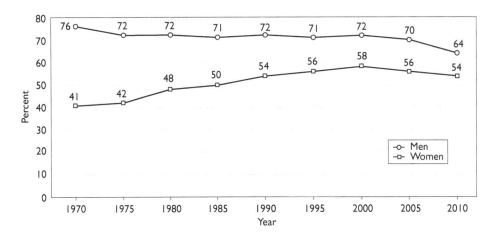

Figure 15. Percentage of the population age 16 years and older who are employed, by gender, 1970–2010. Source: U.S. Bureau of Labor Statistics 2011c, table 2.

viewed simply as an act of free will; choices are strongly influenced by others' expectations of what is socially acceptable for women and men and also by popular perceptions of their capabilities.[19]

Nevertheless, the increase in women's education has also translated into greater labor market participation. Whereas only 41 percent of women age 16 years and older were employed in 1970, by 2000 that figure had risen to 58 percent, before dipping somewhat to 54 percent in 2010 (see figure 15). Among women with children at home (which includes mainly women who are working age), the proportion who were in the labor force increased from just 47 percent in 1975 to 71 percent in 2007.[20] In contrast to the general upward trend in employment among women, the overall percentage of men age 16 and older who were employed declined slightly, from 76 percent in 1970 to 72 percent in 2000, before falling precipitously to 64 percent in 2010 in the wake of the 2007–9 Great Recession.[21] Thus, the gender employment gap has narrowed significantly in recent decades.

OCCUPATIONAL SEGREGATION

The gender employment gap has narrowed, but to what extent do men and women still have different kinds of jobs? Through most of the twentieth

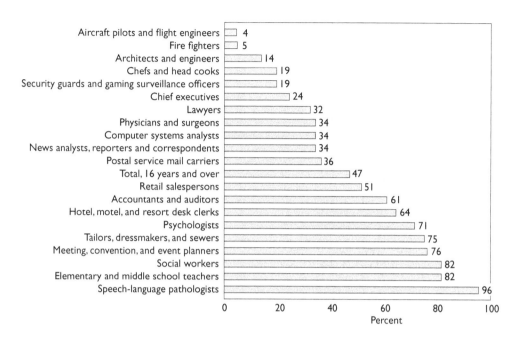

Figure 16. Women as a percentage of the total number employed in selected occupations, 2011. Source: U.S. Bureau of Labor Statistics 2012c.

century men and women were concentrated in very different occupations. At times, men actively resisted the entry of women into highly paid "male" jobs, and informal job networks reinforced the gender divide in the workplace. Differences in educational majors also contributed to occupational segregation, many of which persist today. Figure 16 shows that women constitute an overwhelming percentage (over 80 percent) of schoolteachers, social workers, and speech-language pathologists. They are also very highly represented among meeting and event planners and psychologists. At the other extreme, only 4 to 5 percent of firefighters and aircraft pilots and flight engineers are women, as are just 14 percent of architects and engineers. About three-quarters of chief executives are men. Thus, many of the jobs women occupy require a relatively high level of education (a BA or more) but are not known for paying all that well (such as social workers and teachers) for that level of education.

The extent to which men and women are clustered in different occupations has declined over time, though the pace of this decline has slowed in recent years. Figure 17 illustrates the slow of the downward trend using a

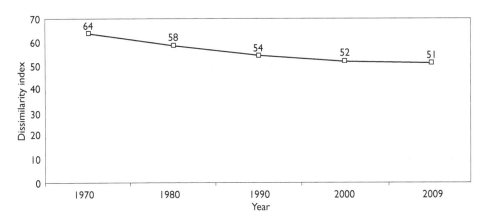

Figure 17. Occupational segregation, by gender, 1970–2009. Source: Blau, Brummund, and Yung-Hsu Liu 2012, table 3.

summary indicator called the segregation (or dissimilarity) index. This measures the proportion of women or men who would have to change occupations for the occupational distribution of the genders to be the same. The index stood at 64 in 1970, before declining to 54 in 1990. By 2009 it had inched down to 51. The decline was driven much more by women entering what had been male-dominated occupations—mainly white-collar and service jobs—than by men moving into predominantly female ones. More specifically, women have been increasingly likely over time to be employed as management, business, financial, and other professionals, including as lawyers, physicians, and veterinarians.[22] As a result, professional occupations have become less segregated over time, whereas working-class jobs have retained their higher levels of occupational segregation. White middle-class women have benefited most from these changes.[23]

It is not clear if, in the future, men will move into predominantly female occupations, particularly since such jobs continue to pay less than jobs in male-dominated occupations with similar educational requirements (though men in women's occupations typically are paid better than women).[24] Future changes in the labor market may help determine whether men will enter traditionally female occupations. For example, the extent to which manufacturing and other blue-collar jobs continue to disappear may determine if men will increasingly look for jobs in other sectors. Also of critical importance is the extent to which different choices become culturally less gendered, thus permitting both women and men to consider a broader range of opportunities with little social penalty and greater family and spousal support.[25]

EARNINGS INEQUALITY

As we've seen, gender inequality extends to differences in earnings. Figure 18 shows the change in the female-to-male ratio of earnings since 1960. It relies upon a common indicator of the gender wage gap—women's median annual earnings as a percentage of men's among full-time, year-round workers. While the ratio of earnings did not budge (remaining at close to 60 percent) over the 1960 to 1980 period, it finally began to increase thereafter. By 2011 women earned 77 percent of what men earned.[26] It is important to note that some of the narrowing of the wage gap was a function of the decline or stagnation in men's wages rather than just the increase in women's earnings.[27] Some of the earnings gap is explained by occupational segregation and the tendency for women's work, such as care work, to be devalued.[28] However, women tend to earn less than men even within the same occupational categories. For example, among elementary and middle school teachers, waiters, and chief executives, women earn, respectively, 91 percent, 77 percent, and 69 percent of what men earn, even when only full-time workers are considered.[29]

So why does the gap persist? In contrast to the gap caused by the blatant and broad-based gender discrimination that occurred in the past, the gap today is probably best explained by gender socialization and women's resulting weaker attachment to the labor market, as well as continued discrimination faced by mothers in particular. A greater percentage of women than men still tend to leave the labor force for childbirth, child care, and elder care. As of 2009, about a quarter of married-couple households with children still had a stay-at-home mother (down from 44 percent in 1969), though fewer than 10 percent of mothers stay at home until their oldest child hits the age of twelve.[30] Stay-at-home dads have until recently been viewed as oddities, and this arrangement is still relatively rare. Exiting the labor force or even working part-time, especially if it is for an extended period of time, leads to a lower accumulation of human

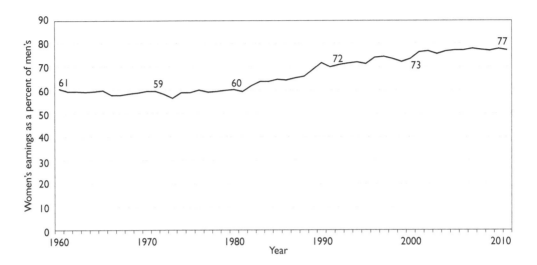

Figure 18. Women's median annual earnings as a percentage of men's earnings for full-time, year-round workers, 1960–2011. Source: U.S. Census Bureau 2012m.

capital (job-related skills) and hence lower pay, which affects women disproportionately. Similarly, working mothers tend to value workplaces that have "family-friendly" policies; many of these offer less pay, if perhaps better fringe benefits. One study estimated that once many of these factors (such as accumulated human capital and differences in occupations) are taken into account, the gender wage gap is reduced to between 4.8 and 7.1 percent, rather than about 20 percent.[31]

The wage penalty among low-income mothers in particular is not attributable to lost human capital alone; it is also strongly suggestive of continued discrimination and other barriers to work.[32] Some argue that women still have to strike a delicate balance between femininity and assertiveness in male-dominated environments. Women, for example, have had a notoriously difficult time making inroads into high-paying jobs on Wall Street.[33] Informal job networks and mentoring opportunities may still favor men, and women may be stereotyped as having a low commitment to work and be put on a "mommy track" that keeps them from moving into higher management positions as quickly as men.[34]

Sheryl Sandberg, who has served as the chief operating officer of Facebook, has attributed the gender gap in part to chauvinism and corporate obstacles and in part to socialization early in life that results in women not pursuing economic opportunities as aggressively as men. "We internalize the negative messages we get throughout our lives, the messages that say it's wrong to be outspoken, aggressive, more powerful than men. We lower our own expectations of what we can achieve. We continue to do the majority of the housework and child care. We compromise our career goals to make room for partners and children who may not even exist yet."[35] Others stress that in addition to women choosing to leave the workplace, they also feel pushed out by inflexible workplace environments that are inhospitable to working moms that seek some balance between work and home.[36]

It is important to note that the gender wage gap is smaller among younger workers. For example, one study found that women 16 to 34 years old make somewhere between 91 and 95 percent of what men make, even without taking into account the wide array of factors (e.g., differences in occupations) described above. In contrast, women above 35 years old earn between 75 and 80 percent of similarly aged men.[37] A growing number of women are remaining employed steadily throughout their young adulthood, and this contributes to wage parity. Some of the movement toward gender equality has thus been the result of a gradual process of "cohort replacement," in which younger women are taking on new roles and earning more in the labor market than their mothers. In recent years women have been more likely than in the past to find good jobs, with opportunities for advancement, and to experience social support from their spouses and significant others for their continued employment.[38]

The role of socialization and gendered behavior is also reflected in the differing amounts of housework men and women do. In 2009–10, married women ages 25 to 64 reported doing on average 18 hours of housework per week. This is considerably higher than the 10 hours reported by married men in the same age range (see figure 19). Notably, the gap in housework has narrowed over time, though it has changed little since the 1990s. In 1965, married women reported doing 34 hours of housework, compared with only 5 hours among men. The narrowing of the gap is partly accounted for by an increase in housework reported by men and, more important, a sharp decline in housework being done by women. This decline reflects mainly the increase in the number of hours women have come to spend in the paid labor force. Interestingly, both men and women

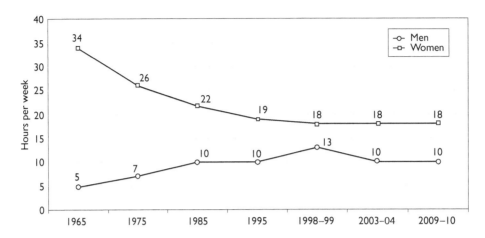

Figure 19. Trends in average weekly housework hours, by gender, among married women and men of ages 25 to 64, 1965–2010. Source: Bianchi et al. 2012, table 1.

spent more time caring for their children in 2009–10 than in 1975, indicating that childrearing has become more time intensive than it was a generation ago, especially among middle-class families who have adopted the "concerted cultivation" model of raising children.[39] More specifically, the time spent caring for children rose from 7 hours to 14 hours among women and from 2 to 7 hours among men over the 1975–2010 period. Because men are more likely to be in the paid labor force than women, overall work hours (those spent both inside and outside the home) of men and women are quite similar.[40]

INTERNATIONAL COMPARISONS

How do patterns of gender inequality in the United States compare with those in other countries? Figures 20 and 21 show female employment rates and gender earnings gaps across mainly wealthy countries of the OECD. Figure 20 shows that employment rates of women of ages 25 to 64 in the United States (72 percent) is very close to the OECD average (71 percent). There is considerable variability across countries, with the highest employment rate in Iceland (86 percent) and the lowest rate in Turkey (28 percent). In terms of gender gaps in earnings, figure 21 shows that the

United States fares a little worse than average, with a 20 percent gender gap among full-time workers, compared with the OECD average of 16 percent. Again, we see significant variation, with the gap as high as 39 percent in Korea and 28 percent in Japan to a low of 4 percent in Hungary and 8 percent in New Zealand.

The World Economic Forum created the Global Gender Gap Index a number of years ago to track the magnitude and scope of gender disparities across a larger number of countries and indicators. Specifically, it measures gender gaps in economic, political, educational, and health dimensions in 135 countries. It takes into account measures such as the ratio of women to men in earned income, the ratio of women to men with high levels of education, the ratio of women's to men's life expectancy, and the ratio of women to men in parliamentary positions, to name a few indicators. In 2012, Iceland ranked first among the 135 countries, indicating that it had the smallest gender gap. The Scandinavian countries of Finland, Norway, and Sweden (which have a reputation for being particularly egalitarian across many social and economic dimensions) occupied the second through fourth ranks. The United States ranked 22nd overall, slightly behind countries such as the United Kingdom and Canada and ahead of others such as Australia and Spain.[41]

The United States fared quite well on some specific indicators, such as women's estimated earned income (ranked 4th, in large part reflecting high overall standards of living in the United States) and numbers of legislators, senior officials, and managers (10th); rather moderate on others, such as female representation among professional and technical workers (30th), female labor force participation (43rd), and wage equality (61st); and poor on yet others, including women represented in Parliament/ Congress (78th) and number of years with a female head of state (the United States ranks last with dozens of other countries that have never had a female head of state).[42] The United States therefore has a moderate record on gender inequality overall when compared with other countries.

Honing in on one comparative aspect of gender inequality—employment—some scholars hold that in most Western countries the norm is that both women and men work. Married men with children in particular display nearly universally high employment rates. What varies more across these countries is the extent to which *women with children*

Figure 20. Percentage of women of ages 25 to 54 who are employed in selected OECD countries, 2009. Source: OECD 2012, table LMF1.2.

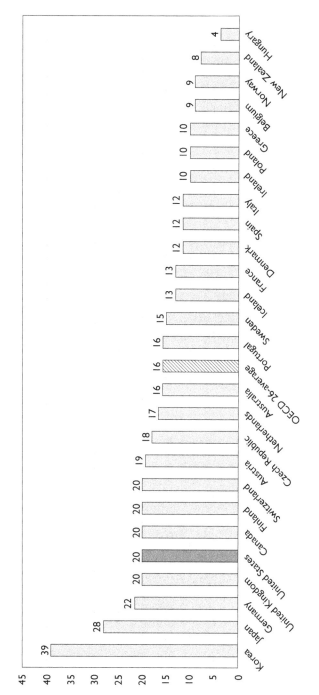

Figure 21. Percentage of difference in the median earnings of men and women among full-time employees in selected OECD countries, 2009. Source: OECD 2012, table LMF1.5.

work; this pattern is indicative of the extent to which raising children remains a gendered activity and the availability of resources that support work among parents with children. In some European countries, including Italy and Spain, a large percentage of women do not work at all; in others, such as Sweden, few mothers do not work, but a high percentage work part-time. The United States falls somewhere between these two models, as a significant percentage of mothers in the United States do not work, but a fairly high proportion work full-time.[43]

Researchers find that countries' governmental work-family policies play a role in shaping women's work patterns. Some policies seem to boost work among mothers, such as those that facilitate access to child care by subsidizing it. Parental leave policies can have a mixed effect on female employment: short- and moderate-length parental leaves can help parents remain attached to the labor force immediately after the birth of their children, whereas very long parental leaves may be used to ease women out of the labor market or perhaps to reinforce "mommy tracks." The United States is one of the very few countries in the world that does not provide paid time off for new parents. Current policy in the United States (as specified in the Family and Medical Leave Act of 1993) is that all public agencies and private companies with 50 or more employees must provide 12 weeks of unpaid leave to parents. In contrast, in the United Kingdom, for example, all female employees are entitled to 52 weeks of maternity leave, 39 weeks of which are paid. The relatively ungenerous policy in the United States may serve to strain parents and keep them attached to the labor market, but the difficulty that many parents continue to have in finding affordable child care is likely serving to depress parental employment.[44]

EMERGING TRENDS REVISITED: MEN IN DECLINE?

Many of the trends outlined above suggest that we will continue to see a narrowing of the gender gap in the labor market. In fact, some education, employment, and earnings trends among men in particular are alarming. For example, over the 1969 to 2009 period, the proportion of men of ages 25 to 64 who were not working increased by 11.8 percentage points (from approximately 6 percent to 18 percent), and most of this change is not a function of men staying at home and taking care of kids. Among high school dropouts, the increase in those not employed was 23 percentage points (from 11 to 34 percent).[45] In contrast to the trend among women, only college-educated men have seen their earnings rise over the past three decades. Among male high school dropouts, median weekly earnings plummeted by 38 percent.

Women now make up half the workforce. They also earn 58 percent of all bachelor's degrees awarded in the United States, as well as 59 percent of master's degrees and about half of the doctoral degrees. Women are likewise awarded about half of law and medical degrees. The general educational advantage among women occurs among all racial and ethnic groups but is largest among blacks, among whom, for example, women earn 66 percent of all bachelor's degrees awarded.[46] Whereas in 1987, 24 percent of wives of all ethnicities earned more than their husbands, by 2011 this figure had risen to 38 percent.[47] These trends strongly suggest that women's relative economic position will rise in the coming years.

Those who believe that the day is near when women will surpass men offer different arguments to explain this startling reversal. Columnist David Brooks argues, "To succeed today [given the kinds of jobs that are available], you have to be able to sit still and focus attention in school at an early age. You have to be emotionally sensitive and aware of context. You have to communicate smoothly. For genetic and cultural reasons, many men stink at these tasks."[48] Brooks also gives credence to Hanna Rosin's related theory on these trends, which emphasizes that women are facing changes in the labor markets with more adaptability, largely because of their historically disadvantaged position within it, while men are clinging to the old order. As she puts it:

> While millions of manufacturing jobs have been lost over the last decade, jobs in health, education and services have been added in about the same numbers. The job categories projected to grow over the next decade include nursing, home health care and child care. Of the 15 categories projected to grow the fastest by 2016—among them sales, teaching, accounting, custodial services and customer service—12 are dominated by women. These are not necessarily the most desirable or highest-paying jobs. But they do provide a reliable source of employment and a ladder up to the middle class.
>
> In Alexander City [Alabama], while the men were struggling, women either continued on with their work or found new jobs as teachers, secretaries

or nurses or in the service industry. . . . More important than the particular jobs available, which are always in flux, is a person's willingness to adapt to a changing economy. These days that usually requires going to college or getting some job retraining, which women are generally more willing to do. Two-thirds of the students at the local community college are women, which is fairly typical of the gender breakdown in community colleges throughout the country.[49]

Rosin tells the stories of several couples, including Charles and Sara Beth, now in their fifties, living in Alabama where many construction and manufacturing jobs have disappeared over the years. Charles had worked in a textile plant as a manager making a considerable salary before employment at the company withered; he left at one point to try to start his own business, though without much success. Meanwhile, Sara Beth, who started as a nurse, ended up becoming an executive at a large medical center. In Rosin's interview with Charles, he remarks on his wife's achievements: "I know what you're asking. How does it feel to go from being the major breadwinner to the secondary breadwinner? It used to bug me, but now I've gotten used to it"—in part because he wasn't the only person in town in that situation.[50]

Not everyone is so optimistic that gender equality is on the immediate horizon. After all, many of the jobs in growing, traditionally female sectors, such as care work, do not pay all that well.[51] In response to a number of books and articles that have predicted the rise of women and decline of men, Stephanie Coontz has argued:

> These books and the cultural anxiety they represent reflect, but exaggerate, a transformation in the distribution of power over the past half-century. Fifty years ago, every male American was entitled to what the sociologist R. W. Connell called a "patriarchal dividend"—a lifelong affirmative-action program for men. The size of that dividend varied according to race and class, but all men could count on women's being excluded from the most desirable jobs and promotions in their line of work, so the average male high school graduate earned more than the average female college graduate working the same hours. At home, the patriarchal dividend gave husbands the right to decide where the family would live and to make unilateral financial decisions. Male privilege even trumped female consent to sex, so marital rape was not a crime. The curtailment of such male entitlements and the expansion of women's legal and economic rights have transformed American life, but they have hardly produced a matriarchy.[52]

Coontz goes on to point out that women's wages have grown faster than men's, but mainly because discrimination had held them down for so long. What she argues, and my review of the evidence also indicates, is that we are seeing a convergence in economic fortunes and not necessarily the ascendancy of women. Young women are probably in no worse shape when entering the labor market than young men; one study, for example, showed that median full-time income for young, single, childless women is 107 percent of their male counterparts in the largest metropolitan areas.[53] However, once we take into account educational and other differences between men and women, men remain at an advantage within and across most occupations. Gender norms about who should care for children and the elderly still influence behavior and serve to weaken women's labor force attachment over the course of their lives. As researchers Joan C. Williams and Nancy Segal put it, "We all know about the glass ceiling. But many women never get near it; they are stopped long before by the maternal wall." Thus, while the wages of young women without children are close to young men's, the wages of mothers are roughly 60 percent of those of fathers, in part because some have observed a fatherhood "bump" in wages—fathers have higher earnings than seemingly similar men without children.[54] Women have many more choices than they used to, but cultural expectations still tend to funnel women into caregiving much more often than men. How much this will continue remains to be seen.

Some recent research suggests that fathers now report higher levels of work-family conflict than mothers do. Men still work more hours a week than women do, and with changing norms many feel that they should or would like to spend more time with their children. As Joan Williams, a researcher of these issues, put it, "Men face as many struggles when it comes to using flexible work policies—if not more—because child care, fairly or unfairly, is still seen as a feminine role."[55]

CONCLUSION

American society has traditionally been patriarchal. In the past this has manifested in a number of ways, such as unequal educational opportunities for women, lower rates of female participation in the paid labor force, and lower earnings for women than men. Men have historically excluded women from many kinds of jobs and limited women's social roles more generally. Labor market discrimination is a manifestation of unequal power. First, discrimination occurs when men are paid more than women for the same work. Second, discrimination contributes to occupational gender segregation, when men and women are highly concentrated in different types of jobs. The result is that women's work is typically accorded both lower status and lower earnings than occupations with high concentrations of men.[56] Inequality in the labor market may also result from common social practices or discrimination prior to a person's entrance into the labor market, such as in the education system or in the family. For example, girls have traditionally been socialized into family-oriented roles, while boys and young men have been expected to build careers that pay enough to support a family.[57]

Gender norms have changed, however. The women's rights movement, which took flight in the 1960s, pressed for more equal treatment in the workplace, such as in the form of equal pay for equal work, and for the easing of gender norms that limited women's opportunities in society at large. Until that time, women were rarely in positions of power—be it in private business or in politics—nor were they represented among a wide range of professionals, such as lawyers, judges, doctors, professors, and scientists. For a while, progress in reducing inequalities seemed slow. However, by the 1970s and 1980s there were clear indications that women's educational attainment was rising, women were entering new occupations, and the gender earning gap was beginning to narrow.

By some measures, progress has slowed in recent years. There have been relatively small changes in occupational segregation by gender, and there is a persistent earnings gap, even among full-time workers. By other measures, however, women continue to do very well, as they now handily surpass men in educational attainment. Job growth is greatest in jobs in which women are currently concentrated. However, women are still much more likely to be caregivers to both children and sick family members and aged parents. This has resulted in women's weaker attachment to the labor force, which in turn has translated into lower lifetime earnings. The extent to which gender norms continue to become more egalitarian in the coming years will likely determine the future level of gender inequality in the labor market.

Notes

1. Quote from Rosin 2012b; see also Rosin 2012a.

2. Coontz 2012.

3. Lorber 2009, 111–12.

4. Newman 2007, 90.

5. Blau, Ferber, and Winkler 1998, 16.

6. Marger 2011, 336.

7. Blau, Ferber, and Winkler 1998, 19; Nodi 2008, 268–69.

8. Kerbo 2009, 307.

9. Kerbo 2009, 308.

10. May 1982.

11. Blau, Ferber, and Winkler 1998, 20–25.

12. Coontz 1992.

13. Gill, Glazer, and Thernstrom 1992, 184–86.

14. Blau, Ferber, and Winkler 1998, 25; Reskin and Roos 1990.

15. Gill, Glazer, and Thernstrom 1992, 186–88.

16. U.S. Census Bureau 2012f.

17. Siebens and Ryan 2012, table 2.

18. Ryan 2012, 2.

19. Correll 2001; Jacobs 1989.

20. U.S. Bureau of Labor Statistics 2010a.

21. U.S. Bureau of Labor Statistics 2011c, table 2.

22. Blau, Brummund, and Yung-Hsu Liu 2012, 19–22.

23. England 2010; Reskin and Maroto 2011.

24. England 2010, 150; C. L. Williams 1995.

25. An extended discussion of these issues can be found in Damaske 2011; Gerson 2009; Stone 2007; and J. C. Williams 2000.

26. U.S. Census Bureau 2012m, table P-40.

27. Kerbo 2009, 313.

28. England 2005.

29. Institute for Women's Policy Research 2012, table 2.

30. Kreider and Elliott 2010; Frech and Damaske, 2012.

31. CONSAD Research Corp. 2009.

32. Budig and Hodges 2010.

33. Roth 2006.

34. Kerbo 2009, 317.

35. Sandberg quoted in Kristoff 2013.

36. P. Stone 2007.

37. U.S. Bureau of Labor Statistics 2011a, 62–76.

38. See Bianchi 1995, 107–54; Damaske 2011.

39. Lareau 2003.

40. Bianchi et al. 2012, 56–58.

41. Hausman, Tyson, and Zahidi 2012, table 3a.

42. Hausman, Tyson, and Zahidi 2012, appendix D.

43. Misra, Budig, and Bockmann 2010.

44. Misra, Budig, and Bockmann 2011, 139.

45. Looney and Greenstone 2011.

46. Buchmann, DiPrete, and McDaniel 2008.

47. U.S. Bureau of Labor Statistics 2012b.

48. Brooks 2012b.

49. Rosin 2012b.

50. Rosin 2012b.

51. Dwyer 2013.

52. Coontz 2012.

53. Rosin 2012b.

54. J.C. Williams and Segal 2003, 77–78; Glauber 2008.

55. J.C. Williams 2013; see also Galinsky, Aumann, and Bond 2011.

56. England 2010.

57. Polachek and Siebert 1994, 83–89.

"Joey Spit on Me"

How Gender Inequality and Sexual Violence Make Women Sick

We have an abundance of rape and violence against women in this country and on this Earth, though it's almost never treated as a civil rights or human rights issue, or a crisis, or even a pattern.

—Rebecca Solnit, "The Longest War Is the One against Women" (2013)

Men—they don't want to leave me . . . they want to control me.

—Robin

FRANCESCA

After the strip club gig ended, Francesca picked up a series of day jobs giving out free samples of juice "from an Amazonian rainforest fruit known since the dawn of time for its rejuvenating properties," selling beauty supplies from a table outside a tourist information center, and loading the truck for a one-man moving company run by a Christian pastor she dated for a few months. Homeless, Francesca couldn't provide a place to live for her kids (one in his late teens, the other in his early twenties), but she did her level best to help them network with potential employers and to arrange for them to stay with friends and pay for their cell phones so that they could stay in touch with her. When her younger son was arrested for assault and battery (with a great deal of pride she told us that he had beaten up a man who was trying to hurt a girl), she met him at the police station and put money in his canteen so that he could buy coffee and snacks in jail.

Within a year she met Chris. His blond hair, blue eyes, and wiry build made it easy for Francesca to fall in love with him. In a whirlwind of dress shopping and flower arranging, she married him in a small ceremony on the beach followed by a party at a local karaoke bar. In the first months of their life together, she was delighted with what seemed a Christmas-card home life: he lived with his extended family in a small town two hours away from the drugs and temptations of Boston. Francesca moved in, hoping that her children would join the household and that they could live like "a real family" again.

But things soon turned sour. Because their house was not within walking distance from any town, Francesca depended on Chris's family for rides to the store, to work, or to Boston to see her children. Chris wanted to be with her "every minute," carrying on if she went out without him for even a few minutes. As things deteriorated, Chris began insulting her, pushing her buttons by calling her "fat ass" and "ugly," and accusing her of cheating on him. One morning he broke her cell phone and removed the chip (SIM card) with her phone numbers, making it nearly impossible for her to call on friends for help in finding another place to live. Hitchhiking and begging rides, she returned to Boston and moved in with an acquaintance. That arrangement seemed to be working out until Chris called the police with a "tip" that there were drugs in that apartment. There were no drugs, but the police checked everyone's identification, and Francesca was locked up on an outstanding warrant—she had not been able to pay restitution on a breaking-and-entering conviction ten years earlier. While she was in prison, the friend she had been staying with was evicted, and all of Francesca's possessions, including her ID and her dentures, were thrown out.

After serving a brief jail sentence she tried to look for a job, but with no teeth or decent clothes she was unemployable. Out of desperation she reunited with Chris, who by that time had moved out of his family's house. The two stayed for a few days at a time with various relatives and then settled in for several weeks with her younger son's friend. That worked reasonably well until Chris tried to knock down the door of a neighbor. As had become our routine, Francesca called us and asked us to pick her up. With all of her earthly possessions in one small plastic bag, she next stayed for a few days each at the homes of various friends, moving on when Chris stalked and found her. During this time she contracted pneumonia and her hepatitis C began to flare up. Her stomach became visibly distended; she had pain in her side and several episodes of vomiting. By early winter her feet and legs had swollen up, and she was making frequent trips to her doctor and the hospital. At one visit she was told that she might have a blood clot in her heart, and an appointment was scheduled for her to see a cardiologist two weeks later. Francesca's posture changed—she no longer stood up straight. Even her hair lost its luster. With none of the bravado she had displayed when we first met her, Francesca sighed, "I'm just tired of everything."

———————

Frequent trips to doctors and hospitals became routine for Francesca. Her need for medical treatment was driven both by the violence and poverty in her life and by her sense that she needed a doctor's validation in order to receive recognition as well as medication for her pain. Over the next few months Francesca lost close to thirty pounds, her stomach became bloated, and she developed rectal bleeding. The doctor told her that she had "a mass the size of a small apple and probably colon cancer," and scheduled her for a colonoscopy. The afternoon of the colonoscopy Francesca called us from the hospital in a panic. She had spent the previous night trying to sleep on an air mattress on the floor of her son's girlfriend's parents' apartment, where she had carried out her colonoscopy preparation according to the instructions she received (instructions that did not take into account that she would be sharing a bathroom with six other adults and a baby). The apartment was located a good thirty minutes by car and ninety minutes by public transportation from the Boston hospital, so she had arranged with a friend of her son (one of the only people she knew who had a car) to drive her to and from the appointment. However, when it was time for her to be picked up at the hospital, he didn't show, and the hospital would not allow her to leave without an adult escort (which is the typical protocol for procedures that involve sedation). "Please," she asked us, "could you come pick me up?"

Knowing firsthand how miserable the whole colonoscopy experience is even in the best of circumstances, we drove posthaste to the hospital, where a forlorn Francesca was sitting on a bench waiting for us to pick her up and walk with her to her primary care doctor's office in another wing of the hospital complex. Earlier in the day she had spoken to a nurse in his office and had arranged for her doctor to leave a prescription for Percocet at the desk. The envelope with her name on it, however, contained only a form for blood tests, and no prescriptions for pain medication. We sat, and sat, and sat while the receptionist looked around the office for the prescription. After an hour during which Francesca looked as if she would melt in her chair (she had not yet eaten that day), the nurse came out and called us into an examining room. Francesca explained what had happened, the nurse went out to speak to the doctor, and after another hour of waiting, the doctor came in, barely glanced at Francesca, and told her that he was not comfortable giving her Percocet, that she should take 800 milligrams of Motrin instead. Half in tears with postcolonoscopy exhaustion, she reminded him that when she was in his office the week before, she had told him that she had been taking Motrin for her arthritis and that he had told her to stop because she had taken far too much. Barely listening to her recounting (his attention was on the computer screen), he wrote a prescription for Motrin and told her she would need to go to the pain clinic. He left the room, and we sat and waited for another half hour, thinking he would return with a referral. Deflated, Francesca (more sensible than I) realized he would not be coming back; the medical assistant soon confirmed that "he was finished" with us. Not only did Francesca not receive a referral that day, but six months later the doctor still had not met with her to go over the colonoscopy results. We still do not know why.

At the time, about two years into our project, we could not comprehend what happened at the doctor's office. In retrospect, we understand that the doctor assumed that Francesca was "pill-seeking." Though young, the doctor must have known that by turning her away, there were two possible outcomes: she'd go to an emergency room (at great cost to the health care system), or she'd buy pain pills illegally on the street, putting herself into the dangerous hands of drug dealers and setting herself up for another prison sentence.

Francesca prides herself on being a "survivor." Finished with Chris, she moved in with a friend whom she had met in prison. Known as "Mama Fran" to the women of MCI-Framingham, Francesca embraced the opportunity to help out a former associate who was suffering from debilitating depression. In return for a place to stay, Francesca took over care of her friend's household and children. Francesca's younger son, now twenty and the father of an infant, moved in with them as well. Delighted to be a grandmother, Francesca regained much of her old bravado, revamped her wardrobe, and cut down on her Percocet use during her grandchild's visits.

In the summer of 2011 she met Joey, and Francesca's old exuberant persona returned in full force. "Joey is the love of my life!" she gushed. "He knows how to treat women. He buys me things and kisses me on the forehead and tells me that I am beautiful and deserve good things." A short, bald ex-con who had been out of prison for almost three years, Joey had a steady job and lived in a two-bedroom apartment furnished with an air mattress, an enormous television, and little else. Within a month of their meeting she moved in with him. Joey was generous to Francesca's children, warmly welcoming them for weekend visits. In Francesca's words, Joey was "a family man," and from the start she looked forward to celebrating a "real Christmas"—her first in a long time—with "my man and my kids."

High on the list of Joey's good qualities was his promise to support her so that she could take care of her health problems. Within a few months of meeting Joey, she planned to have surgery to fix her teeth, nose, throat, back, and hip (all injuries caused by her ex-husband). Before she could get to these surgeries, however, she had to take care of an immediately pressing health issue: flying debris during a storm scratched her cornea. Once her eye healed, she had surgery to remove all of her teeth and grind down and fix the bones in her upper mouth.

Christmas 2011 was a big day for Francesca. The living room—still empty of furniture—had plenty of room for the elaborately decorated tree and the piles of Christmas gifts Francesca had obtained through a local charity. We arrived just in time to see her son charge into the living room to peer inside his Christmas stocking (Francesca had filled it with candy and cigarettes). Beaming with pride, Francesca unwrapped the Chanukah cookies she had bought especially for Susan. Her e-mail message on Christmas proclaimed: "♥ IM TRULY BLESSED AND I GET TO SPEND TIME WITH BOTH MY KIDS TONIGHT AND MY MAN. . . . FAMILY IS [WHERE] ITS @. . . . CANT PUT A PRICE TAG ON THAT . . . (PRICELESS) ♥"

Like nearly all of the other Boston women, Francesca craves a life that matches her idealized vision of middle-class gender normativity. When she and her friends speculate about what their lives will be like in five years or ten years, they offer one of only two scenarios: either things will stay as bad as they are now and they likely will be dead; or they will live with their children in a *Leave It to Beaver*–style, 1950s house with a white picket fence and a friendly family pet. Francesca on occasion allows herself to dream aloud: "I will own a house, have a dog and my two boys with me." As both of her boys became fathers over the study's five years, her dream home evolved to include cooking and baking for her grandchildren when they come for frequent and lengthy sleepovers.

Once her mouth, eye, and various other body parts healed, Francesca felt healthier than she had in a long time. She worked for a while at a diner owned by an Italian family. Thrilled to be serving up authentic Italian food, Francesca treated us to a platter of spaghetti and sauce. But the job was very part-time with no real schedule: the boss would call her in only when the restaurant needed her, and she was paid under the table. When that job petered out, she was hired at a Dunkin Donuts where she worked erratic, long shifts at the whim of the manager. Standing at work exacerbated bone spurs in her foot. Her doctor gave her an orthopedic boot to wear, but the boot caused her to trip at work. She was not called back in. Without a job she was dependent on Joey for food, shelter, and pocket money. While he sometimes spontaneously gave her twenty dollars for a "mani-pedi" (Francesca loves bright patterned nails), at other times he would "call me a fat cunt" or "say my cooking is bad and throw it out the window" and "throw it [the new pocketbook, manicure, shoes, etc.] back in my face." On one occasion, "Joey spit on me. He doesn't trust women."

Living with Joey did allow her to arrange surgery for her foot. But in late April 2012, when Joey kicked her out and we came to pick her up, she was standing on the curb with her possessions in a few bags and her foot still in a cast. After a few half-hearted declarations of "Joey doesn't deserve a woman like me," Francesca fell into an uncharacteristic silence. Per doctor's orders, she kept her foot elevated—propped up on the dashboard of the car as we drove her back to the apartment of the friend she had been staying with before she moved in with Joey.

VICTIMS, PERPETRATORS, AND THE SOCIAL FOUNDATIONS OF SEXUAL VIOLENCE

Why—despite our society's efforts to help victims of violence—do Francesca and so many other women continue to suffer assaults, abuse, sexual exploitation, and rape? The federal Violence Against Women Act, signed into law by President Bill Clinton on September 13, 1994, increased penalties for repeat sex offenders, trained law enforcement officers to deal with victims of sexual offenses, and established the National Domestic Violence Hotline. Most cities like Boston have police, social workers, psychologists, battered women's shelters, rape crisis hotlines, mandatory reporting requirements—surely these have solved the problem of violence against women. Yet notwithstanding public proclamations that raise awareness of childhood sexual abuse, date rape, and domestic battering, mainstream social responses to sexual violence have not been particularly helpful; they have not changed the culture of violence that endangers women, children, and many men; and rates of gender violence have not declined.

Despite strong evidence linking gender inequality to higher levels of violence, contemporary American law and culture continue to address gender violence as an individual tragedy rather than a product of inequalities or structural violence. During the years Francesca lived with her ex-husband, she was a "frequent flyer" at her local emergency room. "They [the hospital staff] knew what was going on," she told us. Often, they would admit her for a day or two "to give me a break." For the most part, the staff treated her well, but hospitals do not have the resources to provide financial independence or stable housing for the millions of American women who suffer abuse. When we asked Francesca if she had ever gone to a battered women's shelter during the years that her ex-husband regularly beat her, she shrugged, "What was the point? They couldn't do anything." Battered women's shelters provide a temporary escape from a battering man, but are not positioned to solve the underlying problems of poverty and violence.[2] "How about reporting him to the police?" we asked. That was not even a possibility, Francesca explained, because Child Welfare Services could have used domestic violence as a reason to take her children away.

The dominant American paradigm according to which sexual violence is understood to be the aberrant actions of a single perpetrator against one or more specific victims cannot eliminate violence against women. Indeed, certain public policies, inadvertently or not, exacerbate the potential for violence. In response to police inaction regarding domestic violence, many states have passed mandatory arrest laws that require the police to arrest abusers when a domestic violence incident is reported. While this is a good idea in principle, women who report abuse risk further harm when violent men get a day or two in jail and come out even angrier and more likely to batter the women or their children (Davis, Weisburd, & Hamilton 2010; Iyengar 2007). Pouring salt on the wound, women who report abuse may find that they themselves are evicted from their homes. Vanessa, for instance, lost her government-subsidized housing because her violent and psychopathic former boyfriend stalked her. In the private housing sector, "nuisance" ordinances that sanction landlords for their tenants' behavior have been used to punish women for reaching out to the police for assistance. In Milwaukee, over a two-year period, nearly one-third of all nuisance citations were generated by domestic violence, and "most property owners 'abated' this nuisance by evicting battered women" (Desmond and Valdez 2012, p. 117). At least some, and possibly many, of these women end up homeless and thus even more vulnerable to violence and abuse.

————

Glass Ceilings, Floors, Walls, and Cliffs

> It always happens at [conferences of business women]. I speak, I listen, I hear the same words over and over—"baffled," "angry," "lost," "trapped," "stuck," "overwhelmed"—as each woman tell me she feels that she's gotten only so far in business and can't get any further.[1]
>
> Gail Evans, *Play Like a Man, Win Like a Woman* (2000)

Feminists describe the glass ceiling as the transparent barrier "that allows women to see, but not to obtain, the most prestigious jobs" in Corporate America.[2] On her first day as Hewlett-Packard CEO, Carleton Fiorina proclaims that the glass ceiling no longer exists.[3] Mary Sammons, Rite Aid CEO, refuses interviews which might lead to an implication that she is in any way different because of her gender.[4] Three-fourths of male CEOs firmly state that the glass ceiling no longer exists.[5] Conservative economists go further: they maintain that in free markets corporations could not survive if they discriminated against women.[6] The Harvard Business School Press publishes *Through The Labyrinth*, by two women's rights scholars, which asserts that the glass ceiling concept no longer has validity.[7]

Does evidence exist as to whether the glass ceiling endures? Related concepts—glass floors, glass walls, glass cliffs—give support to the proposition that a glass ceiling does exist and begin the inquiry into why, blatant sexism aside, a glass ceiling remains in place.

Does the Glass Ceiling Exist?

The proof of something such as the glass ceiling at best turns on circumstantial evidence. It is not susceptible to direct proof. Yet the circumstantial proofs are persuasive. The first of these originate in corporations' selection of female directors.

Sixty-two percent of female directors "side step" onto corporate boards from positions in not-for-profits, government, academe, consulting, and law. They do not rise vertically, as it were, in corporate organizations, in the manner we would expect if the glass ceiling had shattered. In fact, attempting to rise vertically within the organization is the *worst* route a female executive can take in attempting to ascend to the boardroom: in 2001 only nine, and in 2006, only 11, of 460 and 568 women directors, respectively, had taken the inside route.[8] Corporations are forced to go outside of the organization because an insufficient number of women are rising into the pool of executives from which corporations might choose directors. Fifty percent of the middle managers are women while only eight percent of the executives are female. A cogent reason why is that in their ascension numbers of women bump into glass ceilings.

A second line of evidence is corporations' repeated selection of "serial," or "trophy," directors when it comes to women. Trophy directors serve on four or more corporate boards.[9] Of the women this book features, Brenda Barnes of Sara Lee Corp. had trophy director status while Ann Mulcahy, CEO of Xerox, Meg Whitman, ex-CEO at eBay, Paula Reynolds, ex-CEO at Safeco Insurance, and Pat Woertz, CEO at ADM, have had or come perilously close to trophy designation.[10] The number of women who have trophy director status is rapidly increasing while the number of male trophy directors is rapidly decreasing. Between 2001 and 2005, the number of women trophy directors in the *Fortune 500* increased from 29 to 80.[11] Simultaneously, many corporate boards forbade their CEOs (males) from serving on any outside board, or limited them to a single board engagement.[12] That among women large corporations choose the same people over and over again indicates that the pool from which corporations chose women executives, which is similar, is static. Again, the reason for such a trifling inflow is that numbers of women are bumping into the glass ceiling before they have risen high enough for corporations to consider them director or officer material.

Other Evidence

In her autobiography, an ardent public advocate that no glass ceiling exists, Carleton Fiorina reveals her private belief that she has had to confront a glass ceiling at every turn in her career. Early on a male district director called her a "token bimbo." Lower level managers at AT&T, of which she was one, described those the company was most likely to promote but who lacked substance as "42 longs" (male suit size). An aerospace executive with whom Fiorina dealt "could not talk to [a woman] without a constant leer on his face." A Boeing manager tells her that "some of you women can't take the pressure. . . . Don't you want to spend more time with your husband and have children?" Only one senior manager at AT&T Network Systems was female: "she was the head of Human Resources, an accepted position for a woman," recounts Fiorina. A manager told her after a promotion that she "was one of very few women and she would ruffle feathers." A fellow corporate officer tells Fiorina that "You're being emotional, not objective [because she was a woman]." Because she was a woman, men had tried to "pigeonhole me" for "my entire career."[13] In her book, Carleton Fiorina—the woman CEO celebrated for denying that the glass ceiling exists—gives as complete a picture as can be found of the attitudes and obstacles which make up a glass ceiling for women in business.[14]

But "[t]imes have changed and the glass ceiling metaphor is now more wrong than right. [T]here have been female chief executives, university presidents, state governors, and president of nations gives lie to the charge [that a glass ceiling exists]," reports a *Harvard Business Review* article.[15] That is the point: the very nub of the glass ceiling argument has been that women have not advanced in business while they have in academics, politics, and other spheres. Statistics give robust support to the argument: only 3 percent of corporate CEOs and 8 percent of the bylaw officers, are women, while 25 percent of university presidents, 17 percent of U.S. senators, 30 percent of parliament members, and so on, are female.

The *Harvard Business Review* depiction that the glass ceiling refers to "an absolute barrier at a specific high level in organizations" is not only overly literal, it is wrong. Women complain that they bump up against a barrier at various career stages, in various corporate organizations, and in few not at all. The glass ceiling is an abstract but representative idea, not an actual and uniform barrier, like the sneeze shield on a salad bar. All the better reasoned arguments, and the evidence, indicate that the glass ceiling exists in many business organizations and across the business sector generally.

The Glass Floor

A closely aligned concept is the "glass floor." When they fall out of favor, men in the ranks of higher management do not fall far. They rebound off the glass floor. Senior managers retain the under performing manager in some nook or cranny within the executive suite from which the fallen executive crawls back to respectability and another senior management position.

A glass floor also exist for, and protects, CEOs, at least male ones. Professor Rudiger Fahlenbrach at Ohio State University has studied 1,500 CEOs at large corporations during the period 1995–2002. He found that 65 of them are "boomerang CEOs," who had been CEO at the same or another publicly held corporation and returned to a second CEO tenure.[16] Needless to say, none of the boomerang CEOs has been a woman.

A common variant involves ex-CEOs who have caused themselves to be "kicked upstairs," relinquishing their CEO positions to become non-executive board chairs. When the corporation's share price falls, or revenue and profits lag, they take over the CEO suite once more. Examples include Michael Dell of Dell Computer and Howard Schultz at Starbucks.[17]

The boomerang CEO and glass floor are documented. Much like major league baseball managers who, no matter how badly they perform, seem always to re-surface as managers elsewhere, so, too, have male CEOs whose boards have forced them out found positions at other corporations. William Agree destroyed Bendix Corporation by making an ill-advised takeover bid for Martin Marietta. After the Bendix board deposed him, Agee found employment as CEO at Morrison Knudson, the international construction firm, which Agee proceeded to mismanage into bankruptcy. The labor unions and employee-owners of UAL, United Airlines' holding company, forced Stephen Wolf, formerly CEO of Flying Tiger, out as CEO. Wolf resurfaced as chairperson and CEO at U.S. Airways. Many other poorly performing CEOs rebound off the glass floor.

Pundits hypothesize that female CEOs who have lost their offices will bounce back up as well, but so far they have not. Although the numbers have been small, the deposed CEOs (Jill Barad at Mattel, Carleton Fiorina at Hewlett-Packard, Linda Wachner at Warnaco Group) have been high profile. They have yet to reappear in other organizations.

The group of deposed women senior executives is larger and perhaps more illustrative of what might be occurring. Women who fall from those lofty heights also seem to disappear, while many comparable male executives reappear in other senior positions, at the same or another public corporation. The difference may be that as she reaches toward the top, a woman is apt to be the only, or one of a very few, females, while a male surrounds himself with other male managers. When she falls from grace, then, a female senior executive does not have the same support group, or any support group at all, to retard or cushion her fall. When she falls from grace in a male-dominated management group, a deposed woman executive spirals into a black hole, never to be seen again.

The glass floor's existence, and the pronounced trend to replace CEOs with CEOs, of which it is a part, affects women in business if only because of the phenomenon of men rebounding within the clubby ranks of upper management results in fewer openings in which women could prove themselves.[18]

Glass Walls

According to Catalyst, 80 percent of the male CEOs they interviewed had an alternative explanation to the glass ceiling for why women have not advanced to the very top of their organizations, namely, women's lack of experience in line positions, that is, positions with profit-and-loss responsibility.[19] Of course, the CEOs themselves bear much of the responsibility for corporations not giving women line positions in which they could gain the requisite experience. Irene Rosenfeld, CEO of Kraft Foods (Chapter 9), is the opposite. She has spoken about how part of a CEO's responsibility is to ensure that promising subordinates, men as well as women, rotate through a number of worthwhile positions and experiences so that they are in positions for further advancement.

It can be worse for women in many businesses. Many CEOs and other male senior executives shunt women into staff positions, such as general counsel, head of human resources, public relations director, chief of the captive foundation, and the like. These positions are the antithesis of line positions, evoking a less than felicitous name ("pink collar jobs") in certain quarters, because women occupy a disproportionate number of them.

"Glass Walls" compound the problem. They "represent invisible barriers that prevent women from moving between functions and getting the experience of the variety of responsibilities that organizations require for upward movement."[20] Women who accept assignment to staff positions (many pink collar jobs) report that it becomes extremely difficult for them to "get back," resuming a mainline upward track. Similar to the imaginary barrier the glass ceiling represents, glass walls permit women in pink collar jobs to see, but not join, or re-join, their male counterparts as they scale the corporate ladder.

The Glass Cliff Phenomenon

The latest twist, which British theorists hypothesize, is the glass cliff theory.[21] They posit that corporations are more likely to turn to a female for an officer or CEO position when events magnify the risk of failure. Psychologists Michelle Ryan and Alexander Haslam found that businesses appoint women to corporate leadership positions "in problematic circumstances." Their appointments "[hence] were more precarious than men's appointments."[22] If she succeeds, of a woman CEO, directors and senior executive say "we expected nothing less." If she falls from grace, many will say "I told you so," leaving unstated that failure must have been due to gender.

The glass cliff theory seems to bear up under examination. Patricia Woertz became CEO after Archer Midland Daniels had reached a nadir, with the former CEO's son beginning a term in prison for price fixing on AMD's behalf. Susan Ivey became CEO at Reynolds American when the $346 billion settlement with 46 states and other adverse judicial outcomes had laid the tobacco industry low. Brenda Barnes got the reins at Sara Lee after over-diversification and lackluster returns had driven the company down. Ann Mulcahy got the top job at Xerox only after a sea of red ink flowed and the company's future was uncertain. Mary Sammons became the CEO of Rite Aid in the midst of deeply troubled times, with former CEO Martin Grass beginning a prison term and the share price reduced to a few dollars and cents. Patricia Russo became CEO of Lucent after it had laid off over 100,000 employees, while the shares price flirted with the $1.00 barrier. Carol Barz came to the CEIO suite at Yahoo! after a badly botched response to a takeover proposal, along with continuing losses, had caused previous management to resign. In fact, a near majority, 10 of 21, of the female CEOs this book portrays came to power only when the corporation faced very uncertain circumstances, or worse.[23] The glass cliff phenomenon has explanatory power in the United States as well as in Great Britain.

Why the Glass Ceiling?

The easiest approach, and one many militant feminists favor, is to ascribe the glass ceiling and its staying power to deep-seated sexism in our society and, most particularly, in business organizations. The evidence is persuasive that causes are much more subtle than deeply rooted sexism. Many males in business do detect a problem and have varying degrees of willingness to do something about it. Whether or not the militant view is accurate is also irrelevant in the sense that it does not lead to any proposal for a solution.

Many suspects exist, such as work–life, the price of motherhood, and opting out (Chapter 13), for the lack of women's ascension into the higher ranks of American business. The glass ceiling is only one. For this chapter's purposes, though, the glass walls and floors phenomenon indicate that the scarcity of women in senior management positions also is a critical mass problem. Women who do obtain promotions find that at their management level they are the token woman, or member of a skewed group (Chapter 15). They then find that they must walk a tightrope, as they have no support group, or a minimal one at best, should they falter. If they do falter, they fall completely from view. Conversely, they have little or no support group to push them up, helping them ascend through the glass ceiling, at whatever level it exists in that particular organization. Women writers urge women managers to "build networks," formal and informal, which will include male co-workers, advisers, and superiors, as an antidote to this lack of a support group. Most authors of advice books do not articulate that that is what they are doing, sensing it rather than spelling out an explanation for the advice they dispense.

Glass floors and glass walls have descriptive power. They tell us what goes on in many business organizations. They also have explanatory power. They give us insights into why the glass ceiling still exists and has such staying power.

Glass Ceilings, Floors, Walls, and Cliffs

1. Gail Evans, *Play Like a Man, Win Like a Woman* at 7 (New York, Broadway Books, 2000).
2. Martha Chamallas, *Introduction to Feminist Legal Theory* at 184 (New York, Aspen Law and Business, 2000). See also Anthony Stith, *Breaking the Glass Ceiling: Sexism and Racism in Corporate America: The Myths, the Realities, and the Solutions* (Toronto, Warwick Publishers, 1998); Pat Heim & Susan K. Golant, *Smashing the Glass Ceiling* (New York, Simon & Schuster, 1995); Ann Morrison, Ellen Van Velsor & Randall P. White, *Breaking the Glass Ceiling* (Cambridge, Perseus Publishing, 1992). See also Naomi Cahn & Michael Selmi, "The Glass Ceiling," *Maryland Law Review*, 65, 435 (2006) (the glass ceiling as viewed looking upward by women and minorities on the lowest rungs of the economic latter).
3. Maureen Dowd, "Victimized by Gender," *Pittsburgh Post-Gazette*, Oct. 12, 2006, at B-7; Carleton Fiorina, *Tough Choices* at 171 (New York, Penguin, 2006) ("When I said the 'glass ceiling does not exist,' it made headlines").
4. Email from Karen Ruger, senior vice-president, Corporate Communications, Rite Aid Corporation, to Douglas Branson, dated March 20, 2008 (Mary Sammons "declines interviews relating to being a 'female' CEO, believing that gender shouldn't matter").
5. Federal Glass Ceiling Commission, "Good for Business: Making Full Use of the Nation's Human Capital," *BNA Daily Labor Report*, March 17, 1995, at 634–37.
6. Leading works espousing these views include Richard Epstein, *Forbidden Grounds: The Case Against Employment Discrimination* (Cambridge, Harvard University Press, 1992), at 41–42, 102, and Richard Posner, "An Economic Analysis of Sex Discrimination Laws," *University of Chicago Law Review*, 56, 1311 (1989).
7. Alice H. Early & Lindi L. Carli, *Through the Labyrinth: How Women Become Leaders* (Cambridge, Massachusetts, Harvard Business School Press, 2007) (based upon advancement of women in not-for-profit and educational fields rather than in business).
8. Douglas M. Branson, *No Seat at the Table: How Corporate Governance and Law Keep Women Out of the Boardroom* at 87 (New York, NYU Press, 2007).
9. The expression seems to have originated with Judith H. Dobrzynski, "When Directors Play Musical Chairs," Money and Business, *New York Times*, Nov. 17, 1996, at 1.
10. See Chapters 7 (Woertz) and 8 (Barnes and Whitman) in this volume.
11. *No Seat at the Table* at 87, 97–98.
12. See Anna Raghhavan, "Many CEOs Say 'No Thanks' to Board Seats," *Wall Street Journal*, Jan. 25, 2005, at B-1.
13. *Tough Choices* at 39, 43, 68, 69, 89, 106, 109, 146.
14. See also idem at 52: "[G]ender alone could deny me the presumption of competence. [Many] people wouldn't give me the benefit of a doubt [because I was a woman]"; at 53 ("I could see [sex] bias in [co-workers'] faces and body language"); at 145 (There is "no Fifty Most Powerful Men in Business" but business periodicals feel compelled to issue one for women).
15. Alice H. Eagly & Linda L. Carli, "Women and the Labyrinth of Leadership,"

Harvard Business Review, Sept. 2007, 61, at 64, previewing Alice Eagly & Linda Carli, *Through the Labyrinth: The Truth About How Women Become Leaders, supra.*

16. Rudiger Fahlenbrack, Bernadette Morrison & Carrie H. Pan, "Former CEO Directors: Lingering CEOs or Valuable Resources as Comeback CEOs?" (2008) (on file with the author).

17. See Janet Adamy, "Schultz Takes Over to Try to Perk Up Starbucks," *Wall Street Journal*, Jan. 8, 2008, at B-1 ("Mr. Schultz's return to the CEO post at Starbucks is similar to the recent returns of company founders, such as Jerry Yang at Yahoo!, Inc., Michael Dell at Dell Computer, Inc., Steve Jobs at Apple, Inc., Charles Schwab at Charles Schwab Corp., Ted Waitt at Gateway Inc., and Thomas Frist. Jr., at HCA Inc.").

18. Joann Lublin, "The Serial CEO," *Wall Street Journal*, Sept. 19, 2005, at B-1 (sitting or former CEOs are often the safe choice but "highlight a shortage of in-house talent and weak succession planning at many companies").

19. Catalyst, Inc., "Women in Corporate Leadership: Progress and Prospects," at 136 (1996).

20. Sheila Wellington, *Be Your Own Mentor* at 185 (New York, Random House, 2002).

21. See, for example, Mark Henderson, "Women Who Break Through the Glass Ceiling Face a Cliffhanger," *The Times* (London), Sept. 7, 2004, at 3.

22. Michelle K. Ryan & Alexander Haslam, "The Glass Cliff: Evidence That Women Are Over-Represented in Precarious Leadership Positions," *British Journal of Management*, 16, 81 (2005). See also Jayne W. Barnard, "At the Top of the Pyramid: Lessons from the Alpha Woman and the Elite Eight," *Maryland Law Review*, 65, 315 (2006).

23. Those who came to power in precarious corporate settings (10) include: Jill Barad at Mattel; Andrea Jung at Avon; Ann Mulcahy at Xerox; Patricia Russo at Lucent; Susan Ivery at Reynolds; Patricia Woertz at AMD; Brenda Barnes at Sara Lee; Mary Sammons at Rite Aid America; Christina Gold at Western Union; and Carol Bartz at Yahoo!. Those female CEOs of whom the same thing cannot be said (11) include Carleton Fiorina at Hewlett-Packard; Marion Sandler at Golden West Financial; Paula Rosport Reynolds at Safeco; Angela Braly at Wellpoint; Indra Nooyi at Pepsico; Carol Meyrowitz at TJX; Meg Whitman at Ebay; Lynn Elsenahns at Sunoco; Ellen Kullman at DuPont; Irene Rosenfeld at Kraft; and Laura Sen at BJ's Wholesale Club.

Understanding Social Problems of Health

THE MENTAL HEALTH AND CRIMINAL JUSTICE SYSTEMS AS AGENTS OF SOCIAL CONTROL

MENTAL ILLNESS OR CRIME?

- In January 2008, a 37 year-old Asian American man threw his four children off of an Alabama bridge. According to news reports, Lam Luong was motivated by an argument with his wife, or perhaps by a crack cocaine habit.
- In October 2005, a 23 year-old African American woman threw her three children off of the Golden Gate Bridge. According to news reports, LaShaun Harris was influenced by voices in her head telling her to commit this offense.
- In June 2001, a 36 year-old white woman drowned her five children in a bathtub in Texas. According to news reports, Andrea Yates suffered from post-partum psychosis which, together with her extreme religious values, resulted in her belief that she was saving her children from hell by killing them.

In cases like these, the criminal justice system has the difficult task of determining whether potentially mentally ill offenders bear criminal responsibility for their actions. Because lawyers and judges cannot know with certainty the mindset of these individuals at the time of the offense, they must rely on various other factors, including the offender's self-report of his or her mental status. Beyond this, there are other clues that might be used to determine responsibility or sanity. For instance, some legal commentators have suggested that socially constructed factors—including gender and race—might be considered in these decisions. Since a mother killing her children elicits a very different social reaction than a father committing a similar offense, gender may be one clue used by criminal justice decision-makers to determine whether the offender is legally sane and therefore criminally responsible for his/her offense. Furthermore, because the media tends to suggest that people of color—particularly African Americans—are more "typical" criminals, the social reaction to a white offender versus an African American offender is also quite different. To test these expectations, this chapter seeks to provide evidence of the impact of gender, race, and social class on attributions of mental illness, and treatment for mental illness in the criminal justice system.

A staggering number of persons with mental illness are confined in U.S. prisons and jails, according to one estimate more than half of all prison and jail inmates have (or had in the past) a mental health problem (U.S. Department of Justice 2006). This means that approximately 705,600 state prison inmates, 78,800 Federal prisoners, and 479,900 inmates in local jails are mentally ill (U.S. Department of Justice 2006). When combined with an estimated 678,000 mentally ill individuals on probation (U.S. Department of Justice 1999; 2007), it is clear that the U.S. criminal justice system is the primary source of social control for almost two million mentally ill criminal offenders. Since the 1970s, the incarceration rate has grown by almost 600 percent (U.S. Department of Justice 2000; 2009); at the same time, the rate of persons in mental hospitals has significantly decreased. At its peak, the rate of hospitalized for a mental disorder was 339 persons hospitalized for every 100,000 persons in the population in 1955 (Mechanic and Rochefort 1990). Since then, the rate of mental hospital admissions has declined dramatically: from a rate of 283 admissions in 1990, down to 89 in 2004 (National Center for Health Statistics 2008). Furthermore, the number of available non-correctional mental health beds in the United States has significantly decreased, with a 1986 rate of 112 mental health beds per 100,000 persons in the U.S. reduced to 71 per 100,000 only 18 years later in 2004 (National Center for Health

Statistics 2008). Meanwhile, the number of prisons continues to grow. Regardless of the causes, the effect of these trends is a significant increase in the number and rate of individuals with mental illness being handled by the criminal justice system and a disproportionately high rate of mental illness in the U.S. correctional system compared to persons outside the justice system. What has been largely ignored to date is the role of social factors such as race, gender, and social class in affecting these numbers. Thus, this chapter asks: how do race, class and gender affect mental health treatment in the criminal justice system?

Mentally ill criminal offenders are in a unique position at the intersection of both the mental health and legal systems (Freeman and Roesch 1989), often resulting in debates over which system should control them. Consequently, involuntary civil commitment laws have changed dramatically, with patients' rights emphasized from the 1960s through approximately 1980; since then, the law has emphasized community security (LaFond 1994).

The analysis of the criminal justice system and the role of legal and extralegal factors in processing decisions is an important and well-established area of study in the sociology of law and criminology. This literature suggests that official responses of the criminal justice system to offenders are based on many intersecting factors, such as evidence, individual biographies, situational factors, cultural expectations, and prior legal events (Farrell and Swigert 1986; Reskin and Visher 1986; Steffensmeier and Allen 1986; Wooldredge 1998). The research in this area has also suggested that decision-makers' expectations about criminal defendants and their typical crimes affect criminal justice outcomes (Sudnow 1965; Bridges and Steen 1998). This set of expectations is developed through social interaction and results in at least two socially constructed sets of assumptions: one based on gender and another based on race.

The first set of expectations held by the criminal justice system is based on gender, where assumptions about normative male and female behavior may influence criminal justice decision-making. Stereotypes of feminine behavior include passivity, dependence, and submissiveness, whereas masculine stereotypes include dominance, assertiveness, and independence (Baskin et al. 1989; Chesney-Lind and Shelden 1998). Criminal behavior may be interpreted in light of these gendered expectations so that women who engage in non-normative criminal behavior—particularly violent crimes—are thought to violate these stereotypes (Baskin et al. 1989). Because of this, feminists have asserted that the criminal justice system is more likely to label female criminal offenders as mentally ill while treating male offenders as "rational" and therefore more responsible for their actions (Smart 1995); this process is termed "the medicalization of female deviance" (Offen 1986).

Supporters of the medicalization of female deviance hypothesis point out that 23 percent of female prisoners have been diagnosed as mentally ill compared to only 8 percent of the male prison population (U.S. Department of Justice 2006), suggesting that mental disorders are over-diagnosed in female prisoners. An alternative hypothesis, however, is that female offenders are labeled mentally ill at a higher rate due to greater levels of actual mental illness in the female inmate population (see U.S. Department of Justice 2006).

The second set of expectations criminal justice officials hold are related to the race of the defendant. While violent women might be considered incomprehensible or mentally ill, stereotypes of African Americans frequently focus on criminality and violence (Smith 1991; Sniderman and Piazza 1993; Emerson, Yancey, and Chai 2001; Quillian and Pager 2001). This stereotype of African Americans as criminal is deeply embedded in Americans' collective consciousness and may be used by decision-makers who must make choices based on incomplete information (Devine and Elliot 1995; Emerson et al. 2001; Quillian and Pager 2001; Pager 2004). This argument is postulated by economic theories of statistical discrimination. Statistical discrimination refers to the use of information concerning groups, rather than individuals, in decision-making. These uses of group norms in decision-making often occur in the absence of scientific data—and may in fact be contrary to these data—yet are used in the pursuit of expedience (Phelps 1972).

Sociologists have similarly argued that individuals use stereotypes about racial minorities in their perceptions of neighborhood crime rates and the stigma of incarceration (Emerson et al. 2001; Quillian and Pager 2001; Western 2002). Applying this perspective to the legal system, the use of group norms is efficient in screening cases to decide which types of punishment are fair and appropriate. Group variables such as race, age, or gender are therefore assumed to provide information regarding an individual's expected criminality or insanity[1] (Becker 1985; Kennedy 1997; Konrad and Cannings 1997). Therefore, it is expected that stereotypically "normal" offenders will be less likely than other defendants to be referred for a psychiatric evaluation to determine criminal responsibility. The average criminal defendant, who is young, African American, and male (Steffensmeier, Ulmer, and Kramer 1998; U.S. Department of Justice 2009), will be less likely to be psychiatrically evaluated since he is not viewed as an abnormal criminal defendant. In fact, some have argued that behavior indicating severe mental pathology in minority groups is often ignored or considered to reflect criminality rather than mental illness (Kutchins and Kirk 1997:225).

DEINSTITUTIONALIZATION OR TRANSINSTITUTIONALIZATION?

Since its peak in the 1950s, the rate of hospitalization for severely mentally ill individuals has dramatically declined. As Figure 1-1 shows, the rates of hospitalization (or beds available for hospitalization) have declined dramatically since the 1980s. At the same time, the rate of incarceration in prisons and jail has dramatically increased. Although we cannot know whether these individuals moved from the mental health system directly into the criminal justice system, there does appear to be a relationship between the criminal justice and mental health systems. This relationship is complex but essentially reciprocal, with increased hospital admissions in times of fewer jail admissions and decreased hospital admissions when jail populations increase (Rothman 1980; Hochstedler 1986; Cirincione et al. 1992; Torrey et al. 1992; Miller 1993; Cirincione, Steadman, and Monahan 1994; Teplin and Voit 1996; Hiday 1999; Liska et al. 1999; National

---

[1] The term "insanity" is used throughout this book to refer to the use of a defense of mental disease or defect. Although the actual term "insanity" is not typically used in the statutory language of mental illness defenses, this term is nevertheless used because of its ease of use—it is significantly simpler to refer to an insanity defense than to repeatedly say "defense of mental disease or defect" (which is the actual statutory language).

Center for Health Statistics 2008). As a general rule, if prison populations are large, the asylum populations are relatively small; the reverse also tends to be true (Steadman et al. 1984; U.S. Department of Justice 1997a; Kupers 1999; Liska et al. 1999).

Figure 1-1. Rate (per 100,000) of Imprisonment and Beds in State and County Mental Hospitals, with trendlines

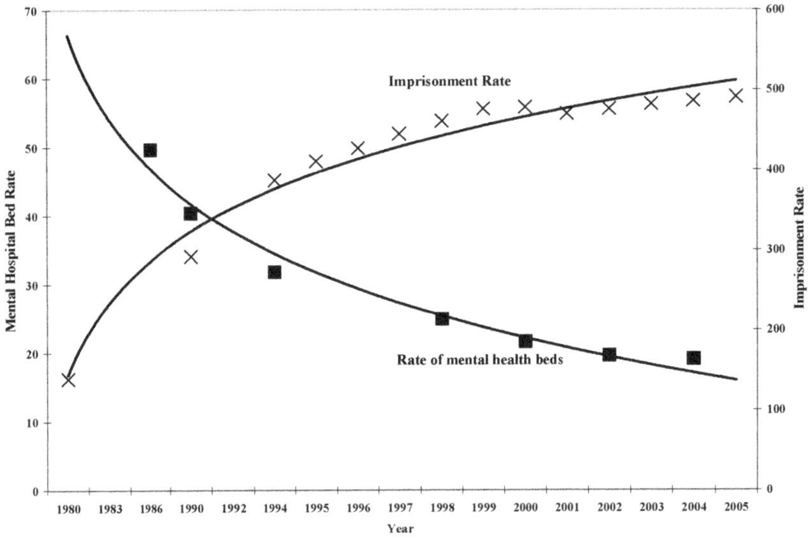

Note: Data from U.S. Department of Justice (2009) and National Center for Health Statistics (2008).

Today the majority of mental health care is on an outpatient basis, as opposed to inpatient services. This was not always the case; in the 1950s, emphasis was on inpatient care. Several factors in the U.S. led to this push toward the deinstitutionalization of mental hospitals, including the passage of the *National Mental Health Act of 1946*. This Act led to significant increases in community programs and in training mental health practitioners and workers. There was a corresponding increase in numbers of outpatient clinics, general hospital inpatient services, and nursing home beds for the mentally ill. The increasingly widespread use of psychoactive drugs to treat mental patients has widely been considered the primary factor leading to deinstitutionalization. In addition, the enactment of the *Mental Health Study Act in 1955*, establishing the Joint Commission on Mental Illness and Mental Health, whose purpose is to analyze and evaluate the needs of the mentally ill played an important role. The passage of the *Mental Retardation Facilities and Community Mental Health Centers Construction Act in 1963* stimulated programs designed to provide community mental health services (Mechanic and Rochefort 1990). Finally, the Supreme Court also entered the fray, with the "Willowbrook Consent Decree." In 1975 the Supreme Court decided that mental patients must be kept in the "least restrictive setting" necessary for their well-being. Despite these efforts at deinstitutionalization, critics have suggested that rather than deinstitutionalization, what currently exists is "transinstitutionalization" with mentally ill individuals who would have, in the past, been kept in a psychiatric hospital setting, instead being moved into other institutionalized settings, in particular the criminal justice system.

Concerns regarding transinstitutionalization and mental illness include the difficulties mentally ill prisoners face coping in prisons, due largely to inadequate mental health treatment. One issue that has been raised focuses on medication as the sole treatment for prisoners. There have also been concerns regarding a tendency to treat mental illness in segregation, which has a negative impact on the socialization and adjustment of the mentally ill. There are apparent race, class, and gender differences in the definition of and access to treatment in prison. With respect to gender, according to a 2006 Bureau of Justice Statistics report (the most recent year available), 55 percent of male inmates in state prisoners had suffered a mental health problem in the past as opposed to 73 percent of females. To some extent, these gender differences may reflect differences in labeling on the part of the criminal justice system. For example, Auerhahn and Leonard explain that, depending on the institution, female inmates are medicated at two to ten times the rate of their male counterparts (2000). Women who engage in violent offenses are also disproportionately medicated (Auerhahn and Leonard 2000). Luskin (2001) explains that part of the gender difference in receipt of psychiatric treatment has to do with perceptions of dangerousness. Luskin notes that due to the larger physical size and strength of men, they are often seen as more dangerous and thus are less likely to get diverted into mental health programs (2001).

Race can also affect whether or not one receives a mental health label and possible treatment. According to 2006 data from the Bureau of Justice Statistics, 62 percent of white inmates, 55 percent of black inmates, and 46 percent of Hispanic inmates had suffered a mental health problem in the past. Although inconsistent, there is some evidence that race might play a role in the diversion of convicts into the mental health system in lieu of prison (Luskin 2001).

In addition, social class may affect mental illness and the labeling and treatment of these disorders. According to 2006 data from the Bureau of Justice Statistics, in state prisons 13 percent of mentally ill inmates had been homeless in the past year compared to only 6 percent of non-mentally ill inmates. Furthermore, 70 percent of mentally ill inmates had been employed in the month before their arrest in comparison to 76 percent of non-mentally ill inmates. This book seeks to provide additional information regarding the impact of race, class, and gender on the diagnosis of mental illness and receipt of treatment.

THEORIES OF GENDER, RACE, MENTAL ILLNESS, AND CRIMINAL LABELING

Both gender and race affect criminal justice processing. Racial minorities are disproportionately represented in the criminal justice system (U.S. Department of Justice 2006). This has often been attributed to systematic discrimination in each stage of justice processing (Spohn and Holleran 2000; Steffensmeier and DeMuth 2000; Bushway and Piechl 2001; Chiricos, et al. 2004; Steen et al. 2005). Many researchers also argue that when decision-makers are free to exercise discretion, they systematically favor female offenders over similarly situated male offenders (Farrell and Swigert 1986; Simon and Landis 1991; Boritch 1992; Nagel and Johnson 1994; Daly and Bordt 1995; Katz and Spohn 1995; Kruttschnitt 1996; Steffensmeier et al. 1998).

While most gender roles are unwritten, Schur (1984) contends that gender norms work as a "mechanism for the social control of women" (p. 52). He explains that women are doubly stigmatized, since behavioral extremes are not tolerated, and instead are labeled. For example, women who show too little emotion are labeled "cold," "calculating," or "masculine." Conversely, if they demonstrate too much emotion, they are "hysterical" (Schur 1984:53). Therefore, women suffer from a double bind in which they are always labeled unless they act within narrowly defined limits. Thus, the response to different criminal women on the part of the criminal justice system may vary considerably, dependent on whether the woman's behavior is considered to be a violation of typical gendered expectations.

Many gendered explanations are based on the chivalry or paternalism thesis; while paternalism is considered more pejorative than chivalry, these terms tend to be used interchangeably. This concept is not always precisely defined, but generally refers to a protective attitude toward women that is linked to gender stereotypes of women as (1) weaker and more passive than men, and therefore not proper subjects for imprisonment, and (2) more submissive and dependent than men, and therefore less responsible for their crimes. Judges might also regard women as more easily manipulated than men, and therefore more receptive to rehabilitative efforts (Nagal and Johnson 1994).

A corollary to the chivalry/paternalism thesis: the "evil woman" thesis. This thesis hypothesizes that women whose criminal behavior violates gendered assumptions are treated more harshly than their male counterparts. In other words, not only do certain types of female offenders fail to benefit from paternalistic treatment, they are actually subject to heightened social control for their choice of an "unladylike" offense (Crew 1991; Boritch 1992; Nagel and Johnson 1994). Thus, the criminal justice system may punish women harshly only when they fail to live up to their expected role (Simpson 1989; Worrall 1990; Kruttschnitt 1996). When women are fulfilling their gender roles (by marrying and taking care of their children), they are treated in a paternalistic manner, with more lenient treatment. When women fail to fulfill prescribed gender roles, however, social control is increased— more so then for men—in an attempt to bring the behavior back into line with what is expected of women (see Schur 1984; Horwitz 1990:113-114).

While women might be expected to act in a "feminine" manner, expectations of African Americans include criminality and violence (Smith 1991; Sniderman and Piazza 1993; Quillian and Pager 2001). This stereotype of African Americans as criminal is deeply embedded in Americans' expectations (Devine and Elliot 1995; Emerson et al. 2001; Quillian and Pager 2001). For example, individuals have used stereotypes about racial minorities in their perceptions of neighborhood crime rates, in support for punitive crime policies, and the stigma of incarceration (Chiricos et al. 2001; Emerson et al. 2001; Quillian and

Pager 2001; Western 2002; Chiricos, Welch, and Gertz 2004). This perception of racial minorities as criminal is so strong and so deeply embedded that some have argued that behavior that actually reflects severe mental pathology in minority groups is often ignored or considered to be criminal behavior rather than mental illness (Kutchins and Kirk 1997:225).

Medical Tyranny

The 2010 documentary *Burzynski: The Movie* features a lengthy interview with Dr. Li-Chuan Chen, a medical scientist at the NCI during the 1990s whose research on alternative treatments of cancer roused the medical establishment and drove him from the profession. For Chen, native of an authoritarian Taiwanese society, the supreme irony was that the United States—a reputedly thriving model of political democracy—was the locale of a closed, intolerant, monolithic healthcare structure. He found that the open pursuit of truth in the service of optimum healing was surprisingly off-limits, obstructed by arrogant experts at the NIH and the NCI, where money, careers, and egos prevail over public-health interests supposedly central to the medical vocation. He found an ideological orthodoxy so tight it called to mind the far-reaching power of a ruling party in control of an entire country, nothing less than a "medical tyranny." When Chen complained that "the medical system in the U.S. is very undemocratic—to put it mildly," he was thinking mainly of the cancer industry and the place of Big Pharma within it.

In a different vein, and after many difficult years working within the medical system, Angell said she wrote her book to "show how the [drug] industry, corrupted by easy profits and greed, has deceived and exploited the American people."[89] Like Abramson, Davis, Moss, and Bartlett and Steele (the latter won a 2004 Pulitzer Prize for their book), Angell laid out careful arguments illustrating the bankruptcy of capitalist health care and the many fictions of "free-market" medicine.

Although these critics generally failed to articulate the full economic and political ramifications of their powerful attacks, they did frame a narrative as to how the early 1980s witnessed a shift toward unfettered corporate profit-making bolstered by deregulation, privatization, and freeing up of capital mobility. Matters have only worsened across the intervening years, exacerbated by the post-2008 economic downturn. Behind the ideological façade of market relations, the corporate edifice has grown steadily more globalized, expansionist, and oligopolistic, fueled by a gradual stripping away of Keynesian public agendas and the social contract inherited from the New Deal and the Great Society. By 2010, with the rapid ascendancy of the Tea Party, it seemed right-wing American politicians were prepared to commodify everything—government, public services, culture, social life, education—purportedly in opposition to "big government." Gorging on superprofits and driven by a medicalized culture tied to expensive quick fixes, the pharmaceutical industry managed to permeate all realms of American society, including the military, owing to its enormous financial power and institutional leverage. To maintain its hegemony, the industry created a public-relations, advertising, and marketing empire rivaled by none, spinning grand myths about the curative powers of the hundreds of potent but frequently harmful drugs, all within the fictional construct of "free enterprise."[90]

The corporate-medical system has corrupted democratic politics to a degree probably beyond any other sector, evident not only in the dismal character of health care but in the restrictive public discourse surrounding it. From this standpoint, the low level of "debates" at the time of Obama's 2009 healthcare reforms should come as no surprise. Prospects for significant changes within American medicine—the only system lacking universal coverage in the industrialized world—seem dismal, whatever the status of "Obamacare." The president's hope for overhaul of a crisis-ridden system is progressive enough on the surface, but daunting obstacles remain: aggressive lobbies, a media complicit with orthodox agendas, members of Congress dependent on medical-sector funding for their election campaigns, and Obama's own tepid liberalism and indebtedness to big business for his presidential campaigns. Big Pharma and insurance companies had invested tens of millions of dollars to protect their profit-making machines. Within months of Obama's ascent to the White House, only watered-down legislation (much of it preapproved by Big Pharma) was within reach and the "public option" (or extension of Medicare to everyone) had been jettisoned as too radical. Unyielding opposition to genuine reforms moved along four tiers—corporate lobbies, grassroots resistance (the Tea Party), continuous talk-radio blitzes, and Republican hostility to the long-feared "government takeover" of American medicine.[91]

In 2009 the Obama administration had cozied up to Big Pharma and insurance companies to win crucial backing for its measures; any legislation was destined to favor these interests—and that indeed was the outcome, still denounced as "socialist" by Republicans. While Obama as candidate blasted the drug and medical lobbies for their contribution to astronomical healthcare costs, as president he altered course, moving closer to the drug industry and its agents, including chief lobbyist Billy Tauzin, a frequent White House visitor during 2009. Working with Tauzin and leading CEOs from Merck, Abbott, Pfizer, and other drug companies, Obama arranged to block cheap imports, fight against price caps, and ensure continued government subsidies in return for Big Pharma support of the reforms. These deals, greased by tens of millions of dollars in campaign spending, narrowed the debate and helped shape the final outcome. James Lowe, speaking for nonprofit health care, remarked, "Since Obama came into office, the drug industry has received everything it wants, domestic and foreign."[92]

The drug giants spent $110 million lobbying Congress in 2009, as Democrats and Republicans alike catered to an industry pulling in more than $40 billion in profits yearly, while prices for brand-name drugs rose a record 9.3 percent.[93] Meanwhile, the White House welcomed lobbyists from insurance companies like WellPoint and Health Net, along with such operatives as America's Health Insurance Plans president Karen Ignani and American Medical Association president Dr. J. James Rohack, all hoping to sharply curtail the legislation.[94] In the end, the reform process was not so much "co-opted" as constrained by deeply embedded economic interests already at work. The result was predictable enough—a legislative package composed of a few important measures (such as ending limits tied to preexisting conditions and lifetime caps on coverage) but a boondoggle for corporate interests that would be awarded large government subsidies for tens of millions of new customers.

The medical-industrial complex remained fully intact as its supporters in Congress shepherded through reforms bereft of any public option, stricter controls over Big Pharma, binding insurance rules, and universal healthcare guarantees. Passed by Congress in 2010, the reforms would continue to meet conservative political and legal challenges, though the bulk of the Obama legislation was declared constitutional by the Supreme Court in 2012. In fact there was little in the reforms that would undermine the capacity of medical oligopolies to reap outrageous profits. And, of course, healthcare costs for the average consumer would continue to soar, as we have seen.[95]

As of late 2014 this tightly administered, costly, disabling medical complex remained a seemingly immovable fixture of American society. As for Big Pharma, pill consumption would continue to be the order of the day—with profits amounting to a staggering $711 billion worldwide in a decade spanning 2003 to 2012, as drugs became increasingly central to the healthcare regimen in the United States and elsewhere.[96] The more problems to treat medically, and for the longest periods of time, the more profitable for those who thrive on the great pill industry. Despite the supposedly controversial Obama reforms, therefore, this is a system that for tens of millions of people remains dysfunctional, bureaucratic, and costly. Three decades ago, Ivan Illich wrote prophetically about the perils of a "disabling profession" ruled by technocratic experts and corporate managers and driven by power, money, and status, with arrogant claims to specialized knowledge that legitimate a regime of domination.[97] Today the medical system is perhaps the most undemocratic realm of American public life. A self-proclaimed repository of truth, wisdom, and healing, the healthcare industry—Big Pharma at the forefront—resists every progressive alternative as it reproduces authoritarian politics and social relations across the entire public landscape.

Poverty and Economic Inequities Within Societies

Economic inequities *within* states are just as powerful a determinant of health outcomes as inequities between developed and developing countries. Low-income populations in developed countries face many of the same economic constraints that negatively impact their health that low-income populations in developing countries face. Likewise, high-income populations in developing countries share many of the same socioeconomic advantages as their counterparts in developed countries and achieve similar health outcomes.

Regardless of overall levels of national development or a country's position in the global economy, individuals living in poverty tend to have worse health outcomes in every country and region of the world. A variety of reasons help explain the strong relationship between poverty and relatively poor health. Individuals living in abject poverty often do not have access to adequate food and suffer the effects of malnutrition. If they do not have access to clean water, low-income populations are more likely to contract waterborne illnesses. Individuals living in poverty may live in substandard housing, which can lead to a

variety of health problems, including chronic respiratory illness due to indoor cooking without adequate ventilation (an illness with particularly high prevalence among women in poor communities) or communicable illnesses resulting from a lack of access to basic sanitation infrastructure.

The ways in which poverty contributes to and exacerbates the global burden of communicable diseases are illustrative. People living in poverty are more likely to reside in crowded conditions, putting them at increased risk for exposure to infectious agents, such as tuberculosis, that are transmitted via the respiratory route. Lack of access to clean drinking water and poor sanitation and hygiene increase the risk for the spread of waterborne agents that lead to diarrheal illnesses. In regions of high malaria risk, poor people have less access to insecticide-treated bed nets that serve to decrease the spread of disease by mosquitoes. Individuals living in poverty, particularly women, are less likely to use condoms to prevent the spread of HIV due to limited access to condoms, a lack of education about the efficacy of such practices, and cultural obstacles to condom use.[22] Once exposed to infectious agents, individuals living in poverty are more likely to develop disease, often with more severe clinical manifestations. The most notable reason for this increased susceptibility is that people who are poor are often malnourished, a condition that adversely impacts an individual's immune system and skin integrity, two of the most important barriers to infection. Notably, malnutrition is more prevalent in developing countries. More than four out of five children who are underweight for their age live in developing regions in Africa or South Asia.[23] This fact helps explain why communicable illnesses make up such a large proportion of the burden of disease in developing countries.

Additionally, individuals living in poverty are less likely to have access to adequate health care services. As a result, they are less likely than individuals in higher-income brackets to receive preventive care or appropriate treatment in the case of illness. For example,

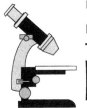

UNDER THE MICROSCOPE

Reflections on Global Health Aid to Developing Countries

I lived in Botswana for six months in 2009. Prior to my arrival, most of what I knew about public health in southern Africa involved the HIV/AIDS crisis. Because this crisis has had such devastating consequences throughout the region, discussion of HIV and AIDS dominates much of the news on southern Africa. Similarly, international aid efforts to the region have been largely directed to HIV/AIDS projects. My first weeks in Botswana confirmed the importance of HIV/AIDS—you could not travel a block in the capital city, Gaborone, without seeing an AIDS-related billboard or an HIV clinic, and the city is full of American medical students doing short rotations at Princess Marina Hospital, the primary public medical facility in the city.

Yet, it did not take me long to realize that the public health situation in Botswana is more complicated than the media, dominated by coverage of the AIDS crisis, suggest. Despite the fact that Botswana is a middle-income country, it is a highly inequitable society with enormous gaps between the wealthy and the poor in terms of income and health care access. AIDS has hit the poorest and most vulnerable people in the society especially hard, and international programs focused on dealing with the AIDS crisis address this reality. Although these contributions have obvious importance to individuals suffering from HIV/ AIDS, the international community has paid less attention to the poverty-related health challenges faced by the poor on a daily basis—lack of access to adequate nutrition, high rates of child and maternal mortality, and substandard housing and working conditions.

On a drive from Gaborone to the Khutse Game Reserve, we passed through the town of Molepolole. At the edge of town, we saw a state-of-the-art medical facility, one I presumed had been partially funded through global health aid. It was located in proximity to low-income neighborhoods with substandard housing. It was a stark visual reminder of the gap between the extremes of wealth and poverty in the developing world. My observations led me to question whether the international community has been providing the type of public health aid most needed by the populations it purports to serve. Certainly,

many children living in poverty do not receive appropriate oral rehydration therapy for diarrheal illness—a simple, inexpensive treatment shown to decrease morbidity and mortality due to diarrheal illnesses. In fact, in developing countries, less than 40 percent of children receive such therapy, with those in the lowest percentiles of household income being particularly vulnerable.[24] Many children living in poverty fail to receive care for other communicable diseases as well. One survey in rural Tanzania found that children from low-income families with malaria were less likely than their counterparts from higher-income families to be evaluated by a health care professional and less likely to receive antimalarial drugs even when being evaluated by a clinician.[25] Low-income populations often do not receive expensive, long-term treatments for chronic illnesses, such as diabetes, because the treatments are unaffordable and because these individuals do not have regular access to health care facilities. As a the government of Botswana welcomes global health aid, and international programs have helped to bring the HIV/AIDS crisis under control. However, general poverty-related public health challenges have not been adequately addressed by HIV/AIDS funding. Notably, international organizations and major aid donors (public and private) have dominated the process by which public health priorities have been determined in Botswana and elsewhere in the developing world.

A related criticism is that local health care workers and other individuals with skills to contribute to improving public health infrastructure get drawn into working for international programs directed toward the AIDS crisis rather than working on public health more generally. According to Laurie Garrett, this dynamic represents a sort of internal brain drain where well-intentioned international actors place a high demand on local financial and human resources in ways that may not be the best for long-term, sustainable solutions to public health problems in the developing world.[a] In short, Garrett's criticisms suggest that there may be a fundamental gap between the international community's assessment of public health priorities in the developing world and actual public health needs in these countries.

The global emphasis on the HIV/AIDS crisis has developed despite the fact that HIV/AIDS is not the leading cause of death in the developing world. Rather, a number of other risk factors, including high blood pressure, smoking, high cholesterol, and childhood underweight, cause a greater number of deaths throughout the developing world. Thus, a preliminary evidence-based assessment of the causes of death in the developing world lends some support to the argument that the overarching emphasis on HIV/AIDS in global health funding initiatives might be misplaced.

My own observations of daily life in Botswana certainly made me wonder whether the international community should be devoting more resources to sustainable development and general poverty alleviation measures rather than disease-specific funding.

—Debra L. DeLaet

---

[a] Laurie Garrett, *The Coming Plague: Newly Emerging Diseases in a World out of Balance* (New York: Penguin Books, 1994): 456.

result, people living in poverty are more likely to suffer greater morbidity and mortality from both communicable and noncommunicable illnesses.

Several factors contribute to this disparity in the receipt of appropriate medical treatment. Due to limited education, individuals living in poverty often fail to recognize the clinical severity of an illness, making it less likely that they will seek medical evaluation and treatment. For example, one survey in western Nepal demonstrated that poor education was associated with a greater likelihood of parental failure to recognize the severity of respiratory illness in their children and to seek medical care.[26] Across the globe, the working poor also may not have adequate health insurance and may not be able to take off work in order to get the care they need.

People living in poverty often forgo accessing medical care due to the considerable distance they must travel to receive such care.

Individuals and families living in poverty often do not have means of transportation to hospitals, doctors' offices, or other medical facilities. This problem is especially acute for more serious health issues that require care at medical facilities offering advanced care. For instance, hospital-based clinics are typically located in urban centers at some distance from rural populations living in poverty. Thus, the rural poor have difficulty accessing treatments that are available only in hospital-based settings.

Moreover, care is often perceived to be of higher quality in hospital-based facilities in urban centers.[27] One example of the lower quality of care offered by rural primary facilities is that they are less likely than urban hospital-based centers to stock vital medications, such as antibiotics.[28] Where available in rural areas, antimicrobials are often of lesser quality due to poor governmental regulation of handling and manufacturing of these products. Preventive services such as vaccinations are also less likely to be available to low-income populations. In many countries, this disparity in quality among health centers is a direct result of an allocation of national and regional budgetary resources that favors urban centers. Further, an underdeveloped private-sector health care system in these countries often results in many public-sector resources being utilized by wealthier individuals in that country, further limiting access for low-income populations who are unable to financially compete for these resources. Many families living in poverty are then left to prioritize spending for health care services, with adult males often receiving care at the expense of women and children.[29]

Health challenges may also create poverty traps for individuals and households, contributing to the likelihood that low-income populations will get stuck in poverty. Ill health undermines people's ability to be economically productive and to pursue education that would enable them to improve their economic opportunities. Also, catastrophic illness can result in the loss of employment and can bankrupt individuals who do not have adequate health care. Indeed, illnesses and injuries are among the most common reasons that individuals fall into poverty. People affected by disease are less likely to be able to work, with resultant loss of income. Additionally, they are often forced to sell assets to help pay medical expenses. Children who are sick also face negative socioeconomic consequences. For example, infectious illnesses during early childhood can have a negative impact on both physical and cognitive development. An appropriate level of iron in the blood is necessary for the cognitive development of a young child. Because certain intestinal parasites, such as hookworms, are associated with decreased iron absorption, infection with these parasites leads to cognitive delay in children.[30] In another example, infection due to malaria is a significant contributor to school absenteeism among low-income populations in many developing countries.[31] Illness also increases a person's risk for malnutrition (and vice versa), with an obvious effect on the ability to work or to attend school.

The types of inequities discussed here are not reflected in aggregate measures of national wealth and population health. In every country in the world, high-income populations have a high probability of good health outcomes because of socioeconomic advantages that give them access to preventive care, appropriate treatments in the event of illness, education, and good nutrition. Conversely, people living in poverty—in developed as well as developing countries—face numerous constraints in their efforts to stay healthy.

Racial and Ethnic Inequities in Global Health

Race refers to a classification of human beings into distinct population groups historically based on presumed biological and genetic differences. In contrast, **ethnicity** refers to a classification of human beings into distinct population groups based on the self-identification of people according to shared language, history, culture, or other social factors. Although these terms are often used interchangeably, they reflect a deep tension regarding the nature of differences among human populations. Historically, the concept of race has been used to suggest that innate physical variations among populations, most notably skin color, are at the root of social and cultural differences among groups of people. At one level, such categorization might be seen as a harmless way to describe real differences—cultural, linguistic, social—that appear to be associated with skin color. At another level, such categorization has had nefarious consequences. Historically, the concept of race has been used to rationalize slavery, colonialism, genocide, and a wide range of human rights abuses. Indeed, critics argue that the very idea that fundamental biological and genetic distinctions divide the human species is itself at the heart of racism. Critics of the concept of race also note that all human beings are members of the same species. As such, humans largely share the same genetic material across population groups. Indeed, some geneticists note that human beings are genetically more homogenous than other mammal species and that more genetic variation exists within specific populations than among these populations.[32] For these reasons, many social scientists prefer to use the term *ethnicity* rather than *race* when describing significant differences among human populations.

The controversy over the concept of race notwithstanding, it provides an important framework for discussing significant economic and social inequities in the world. Whether or not the concept of race itself captures real differences among human populations, racism and racial inequities are very much real phenomena. Accordingly, scholars and practitioners still rely on this category to investigate inequities faced by disadvantaged racial and ethnic groups. For our purposes, the category of race remains very important in the medical literature on disparities in health among population groups. Moreover, it should be noted that some scholars use the term *race* because they see it as interchangeable with *ethnicity*, not because they want to signify innate physical differences among populations. We will follow that convention by referring to both racial and ethnic inequities throughout this section.

Health Disparities Among Disadvantaged Racial/Ethnic Populations

Significant disparities in health have been demonstrated among disadvantaged racial and ethnic groups across the globe. Racial and ethnic populations experience inferior physical and mental health outcomes in terms of both morbidity and mortality in all geographic regions in which such comparative data are available. In most cases, such inequities are faced by racial and ethnic minorities within countries, but, in some cases, racial and ethnic populations that face health disadvantages actually constitute the majority of a population. Blacks in South Africa, where the legacy of apartheid fundamentally shapes population health outcomes, are a prominent case in point. The available data are particularly robust in developed countries, but evidence from developing regions supports similar conclusions.

While a comprehensive review of data from developed regions is beyond the scope of this section, several examples highlight these inequities. According to 2009 data, the life expectancy among whites in the United States was 76.2 years for males and 80.9 years for females, as compared to 70.9 years for males and 77.4 years for females among African-Americans.[33] The infant mortality rate was 5.32 per 1,000 live births for whites and 12.71 per 1,000 live births for African-Americans.[34] Similarly, African-Americans, Asian-Americans, Pacific Islanders, and Hispanics have a higher overall childhood mortality rate than their white counterparts.[35] Data from other developed

countries, such as Canada and Brazil, also demonstrate racial and ethnic inequities in infant and childhood mortality rates.[36]

Using health-related quality-of-life measures such as healthy days, defined as "the overall number of days during the previous 30 days during which a person reported good (or better) physical and mental health," it appears that racial and ethnic minorities in the United States also experience greater morbidity.[37] Similarly, with the exception of Asian-Americans, racial and ethnic minorities are much less likely than whites to report their health status as "excellent" or "very good," as is demonstrated in Figure 6.1. These self-reported measures of disparities in health status are consistent with the extensive body of evidence demonstrating racial and ethnic inequities in health outcomes for specific medical conditions. To cite only a few examples, studies have shown that racial minorities in the United States experience poorer outcomes for cardiovascular disease, asthma, and cancer.[38] This is

FIGURE 6.1 Self-reported Health Status by Race, 2005

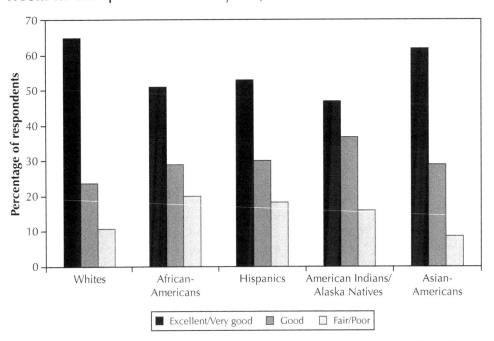

Source: Adapted from Holly Mead, Lara Cartwright-Smith, Karen Jones, Christal Ramos, and Bruce Siegel, "Racial and Ethnic Disparities in U.S. Health Care: A Chartbook" (The Commonwealth Fund, 2008). Available online at: http://www.commonwealthfund.org/usr_doc/mead_racialethnicdisparities_chartbook_1111.pdf.

particularly true for African-Americans, who are significantly more likely than other racial and ethnic groups to suffer a chronic medical condition or disability, even after adjusting for income.[39] These findings have been replicated in other developed countries. For example, racial and ethnic minorities in the United Kingdom, Australia, South Africa, and Brazil are more likely to develop end-stage kidney disease as a result of an increased incidence of hypertension and diabetes mellitus.[40] As a final example, among both children and adults, racial and ethnic minorities have been found to experience an increased burden of mental health disease, including depression and anxiety, in countries such as the United States, Canada, and the United Kingdom, to name just a few.[41]

Though considerably sparser, data from developing countries across global regions also demonstrate similarly increased morbidity and mortality for disadvantaged racial and ethnic populations. For example, studies in sub-Saharan Africa reveal that, consistent across all countries studied, ethnic inequalities exist in the infant and under-five mortality rates. In Asia, a recent study from Vietnam found that ethnicity was the main socioeconomic determinant for neonatal mortality.[42] In lower-income countries in Central and Latin America, overall health inequities have been demonstrated among indigenous and black people in comparable geographic and social locations.[43] Just as in the case of developed countries, disease-specific differences in health outcomes have been demonstrated in developing countries. For example, the risk for lung cancer in Nepal has been shown to differ by ethnicity.[44] Data also demonstrate an increased risk for mental health disorders among racial and ethnic minorities in developing countries.[45]

The Causes of Health Disparities Among Disadvantaged Racial/Ethnic Populations

Because race and ethnicity are so intimately linked with socioeconomic status, it is difficult to fully tease out the contribution of race and ethnicity to population-level health outcomes. Nevertheless, studies have suggested that as much as one-half of mortality differences among racial and ethnic groups may be attributable to socioeconomic factors.[46] The corollary is the suggestion that a significant portion of health status is determined by factors specifically unique to race and ethnicity. This section explores the factors that may lead to disparities in health outcomes for disadvantaged racial and ethnic populations.

Research has suggested that many social variables likely contribute to racial and ethnic inequities in health. First among these includes determinants directly related to the neighborhoods in which these populations live. For example, as was discussed in Chapter 5, obesity is associated with poor access to healthful foods and neighborhood green space for people of lower socioeconomic status, an association more likely to affect minority groups due to their higher rates of poverty.[47] In the United States, African-American and Hispanic children are more likely to develop asthma in part due to their increased likelihood of living in public housing and the resultant exposure to such asthma triggers as cockroaches.[48] Disadvantaged racial and ethnic groups are also much more likely to be exposed to violence, with negative ramifications for physical and mental health.[49] Similarly, indigenous populations across the globe tend to experience higher injury and death rates due to accidents associated with cramped living conditions, unsafe housing, lack of space and facilities for safe play, and exposure to a high volume of fast-moving traffic.[50] The social environment in which disadvantaged racial and ethnic populations live and the associated self-perception of inequalities lead to an increase in risk taking and unhealthy behaviors.[51]

Social factors also likely contribute to racial and ethnic inequities in health outcomes as a result of their impact on access to care. Again, the case of the United States is instructive. As shown in Figure 6.2, racial and ethnic minorities in the United States have historically been less likely than whites to have health insurance coverage. As will be discussed in more detail

FIGURE 6.2 Percentage of Americans with Health Insurance Coverage, by Race and Ethnicity

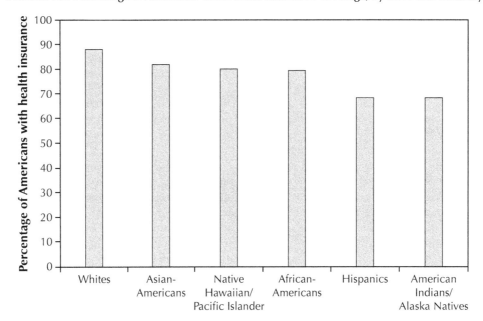

Source: Reproduced from Lesley Russell, "Fact Sheet: Health Disparities by Race and Ethnicity" (Center for American Progress, 2010). Available online at: http://www.americanprogress.org/issues/2010/12/disparities_factsheet.html.

in Chapter 10, this situation has existed due to a health care model that relies heavily on employer-based health insurance and does not provide universal coverage to all residents.

Consistent with this inequity in insurance coverage, racial and ethnic minorities are much less likely than whites to access the health care system. For example, African-Americans, Hispanics, and Asian-Americans are more likely to be without a regular doctor than are whites.[52] Additionally, racial and ethnic minorities are much less likely than whites to receive health care services, including preventive care, such as screening for colorectal cancer and prostate cancer.[53]

Even in countries where universal health care coverage is provided, inequities in access to care for disadvantaged racial and ethnic populations exist. For instance, certain immigrant populations in Australia have been shown to receive lower rates of orthopedic surgery for severe osteoarthritis.[54] Racial and ethnic minorities have been shown to have similarly decreased

access to therapies for end-stage renal disease in Venezuela.[55] Finally, in South Africa, a study revealed that, even after adjusting for other socioeconomic factors, black women were less likely than nonblack women to receive preventive care services during pregnancy and birth,[56] and another study revealed that 40.8 percent of blacks, as compared with 10.9 percent of whites and 6.9 percent of Asians, reported going without necessary medical care at some point in the previous year.[57]

These findings of racial and ethnic inequities in health care among countries with universal health care coverage suggest that factors other than health insurance status affect access to high-quality care. Some of these determinants are likely rooted in socioeconomic factors. For example, a 2008 study demonstrated that transportation barriers are significantly more often responsible for unmet medical care needs for children among Native Americans than for other racial groups.[58] Disparities in access to care can also result from inequities in educational attainment among racial and ethnic minorities. For example, lower levels of health literacy and educational attainment serve as a barrier to the receipt of preventive services such as screening mammography among racial and ethnic minorities in the United States.[59] Ethnic minorities in Vietnam occasionally forgo seeking care for their children because they have not been appropriately educated on recognizing the signs of illness.[60] Geographic determinants have also been associated with inequities in the quality of care delivered to disadvantaged racial and ethnic groups. In the United States, individuals living in predominantly racial and ethnic minority communities are much more likely than whites to report having little choice in where to seek medical care.[61] This inequity is further complicated by findings that show that racial and ethnic health disparities in the United States exist across hospitals rather than within individual facilities.[62] According to this study, whites and racial and ethnic minorities treated within the same hospital were shown to receive the same standard of care; minorities, however, were more likely to present to hospitals that provided lower-quality care.[63] Similar geographic disparities have been demonstrated in South Africa, where medications such as antimicrobials in rural primary facilities are often of lesser quality than in urban hospital-based centers.[64]

Because they are intimately linked with racial and ethnic status, socioeconomic determinants likely account for a significant portion of the inequities in health status and health care access seen among disadvantaged racial and ethnic populations. However, there are almost certainly factors specific to race and ethnicity that also contribute to these disparities. Biological differences in risk for developing certain conditions exist among racial and ethnic groups. For example, individuals of African heritage are much more likely to inherit the mutated gene responsible for causing sickle cell disease. Genetic factors also influence the predisposition of individuals of certain racial and ethnic groups to the development of conditions such as Type II diabetes mellitus and hypertension.

Racial and ethnic minorities may also experience inferior health outcomes as a result of language barriers. In the United States, individuals with limited English proficiency (LEP) often have limited access to care or receive a lesser quality of care. Though Title VI of the Civil Rights Act requires that any health care provider receiving federal funds, including providing Medicaid and Medicare services, must provide adequate language assistance to an LEP patient,[65] language discordance can still limit the quality of care provided. For example, in one study, Spanish-speaking Hispanics noted that communication difficulties made it more challenging to fully explain symptoms, ask questions of providers, follow through with filling of prescriptions, and fully understand physician recommendations; nearly 20 percent reported not seeking medical treatment due to language barriers.[66]

Disadvantaged racial and ethnic populations also tend to be more likely to exhibit mistrust toward health care providers. For example, Malay-Muslims in Singapore expressed concern about the potential for racial discrimination as well as the participant selection process for genetic research.[67] As a result of patient mistrust, disadvantaged racial and ethnic groups may be less likely to seek critical preventive care and treatment. For instance, patient mistrust contributes to lower prostate cancer screening among African-Americans in the United States.[68] Patient race and ethnicity can also influence physicians' perceptions of patients. Data from a 2000 study revealed that patient race was associated with physicians' assessment of patient intelligence, feelings of affiliation toward the patient, and beliefs about the patient's likelihood of risk behavior and adherence with medical advice.[69] These potential barriers of language discordance, patient mistrust of providers, and patient stereotyping by physicians likely exist in no small part due to the underrepresentation of disadvantaged racial and ethnic populations in the physician workforce. In the United States, although African-Americans, Hispanics, and Native Americans constitute more than 30 percent

UNDER THE MICROSCOPE

Reflections on Patient-Physician Language Discordance

I have worked as a primary care provider for pediatric and adult populations since 1995. During this time, I have had the opportunity to work in a variety of settings. I worked at three large academic health centers in Cincinnati and New York City that served a wide variety of patients, but I largely provided care for children and adults with public health insurance, the majority of whom were racial and ethnic minorities. I also worked at a community health center in Cincinnati, where many of the patients were uninsured minorities. Lastly, I worked briefly providing care to a population of patients who were mostly healthy, nonminority young adults with employment-based private health insurance while I was employed by a private practice in an affluent neighborhood in New York City. Prior to entering the workforce, I had the privilege as a medical student to work for a limited period of time with the Indian Health Services in Oklahoma caring for a population of Native Americans. Given this breadth of experience, I feel that I can offer a unique perspective on the challenges faced in accessing high-quality care for racial and ethnic minorities.

It has been my experience that racial and ethnic minorities are at a clear disadvantage when attempting to navigate the health care system. The challenges faced result not only from issues related to our current organization of health care in the United States but also from social and cultural factors. One important example is that of patient-physician language discordance.

Many of the patients for whom I have provided care, and continue to provide care, are individuals with limited English proficiency. I am limited in that I am fluent only in English. In our practice, we see patients who speak Spanish, French, Portuguese, Senegalese, Mandarin, Bengali, and Hindi, to name just a few. Many of my patient encounters, therefore, have language discordance as an obstacle that must be addressed to ensure the best possible delivery of care. To deal with this challenge, we have available to us, at a cost to our institution, language interpreter services. Given the volume of patients and

of the population, these groups accounted for only 8.7 percent of physicians, 6.9 percent of dentists, 9.9 percent of pharmacists, and 6.2 percent of registered nurses, according to 2007 data.[70]

Several overarching themes can be gleaned from this examination of the causes of health disparities faced by disadvantaged racial and ethnic populations. First, social determinants play a critical role in the development of racial and ethnic inequities in health. Only by addressing these disparities in the condition of daily life of disadvantaged racial and ethnic groups can greater equity in the health status of populations be achieved.[71] As concerns health care systems, measures must be taken to improve access, including expansion of health care coverage to the uninsured and underinsured members of the population. Education of patients to improve their understanding of disease processes, treatment options, and methods to most effectively access health care systems is important.[72] Additionally, it is critical to provide better education of health care the diversity of languages for which such services are required, on-site interpreters are impractical. Rather, we employ an off-site service accessed via telephone.

Communication in this manner is less than ideal, for both patient and provider. In a system that places a priority on seeing a high volume of patients in an efficient manner, the time intensity required to ensure mutual understanding of key elements of the patient's history and the provider's prescribed plan of care steals critical minutes from an already-limited visit. This is particularly troubling when providing care to patients with a complexity of medical problems. Additionally, a large portion of communication is subtle, in terms of both spoken word and nonverbal cues, and these subtleties are easily missed during language discordant evaluations. Given the inherent intimacy of the professional relationship between patient and physician, these missed opportunities for information gathering might negatively affect physician decision making. Lastly, even when language discordance is not, strictly speaking, an issue during a patient evaluation, ethnic and cultural differences in spoken word between provider and patient can also affect communication—if I ask for "a lift" in London, I may be surprised to be led to an elevator rather than to one's car.

Underscored in this reflection is the critical importance of effective communication between patient and physician. It is a common medical teaching, one that I have found to be confirmed in my years as a clinician, that 90 percent of arriving at a correct medical diagnosis is based on a detailed patient history of symptoms. How, then, can one provide the best possible care to his or her patients if the starting point is one of limited communication? To remedy this, it is imperative that, when necessary, clinicians be provided with language interpreter services. Also, having available culturally appropriate and language-specific reading materials for patients is critical. Providing education to expand provider language skills is helpful, though, as suggested, any one provider being able to gain fluency in the multitude of languages that may be encountered in practice is likely impractical. Thus, the ultimate goal should be to increase the diversity of trainees in the field of medicine to ensure the most appropriate care for the greatest breadth of patients seen in our health care systems.

—David E. DeLaet

professionals so that communication barriers, both cultural and linguistic, can be addressed and providers might more consistently exhibit cross-cultural competency in the care of patients. Implementing policies that will better ensure medical training for a greater diversity of health care providers would be of obvious benefit in eliminating these language and cultural barriers. Lastly, improving public awareness of the scope of the problem is likely to result in greater support and more realistic achievement of these goals.

Gender Inequities in Global Health

Health Disparities Between Men and Women in Global Health

The health status of men and women across the globe is characterized by significant differentials. Several indicators used to measure health status, including life expectancy, health-adjusted life expectancy (HALE), and disability-adjusted life years (DALYs), demonstrate the health disparities that exist between men and women.

In every region of the world and across all levels of economic development, women have a higher life expectancy than men. In 2007, the global average female life expectancy was 70 years, compared to 65 years for men. Women's higher average life expectancy is especially pronounced in the developed world, where more than twice as many women than men live past the age of 80.[73] A narrower gap between female and male life expectancy exists in low-income countries, where women can expect to live 58 years, compared to 55 years for men.[74] The female health advantage in life expectancy holds true across all regions of the world.[75] The starkest gap in life expectancy between women and men emerges in Central and Eastern Europe and the Commonwealth of Independent States, where women can expect to live roughly 74 years, compared to just 65 years for men. The gap between women and men is smallest in sub-Saharan Africa, where female life expectancy is 52.5, compared to 50.4 for men.[76] According to United Nations Development Programme (UNDP) data for 2007, male life expectancy was higher than female life expectancy in only two countries: Afghanistan (43.5 for women versus 43.6 for men) and Swaziland (44.8 for women versus 45.7 for men).[77] Taken together, World Health Organization (WHO) and UNDP data on life expectancy demonstrate a striking, if surprising, pattern of greater longevity for women that holds across the globe.

HALE estimates follow the same pattern as life expectancy indicators. Women can expect to live more years in full health in every region of the globe, and women's health advantage on this indicator holds across all levels of economic development. However, the gap between men and women is smaller in HALE estimates than in general estimates of average life expectancy. The 2007 HALE for women globally was 61 years compared to just 58 years for men. Women's advantage in HALE estimates is somewhat more pronounced in high-income countries, where females have a

HALE of 72 years compared to 68 years for males. As in the case of general life expectancy, the gap between men and women on HALE indicators narrows at lower levels of economic development. In lower-middle-income countries, females have a HALE estimate of 62 years compared to 60 years for men in good health. The gap is narrowest in low-income countries, where women can expect to live 49 years in full health compared to 48 years of expected good health for men.[78] The female advantage in HALE estimates again holds across all global regions, although the HALE gap between men and women is smaller than the gap in general life expectancy.

The most interesting discrepancies between life expectancy and HALE indicators show up in individual countries. Unlike life expectancy measures, which show a male advantage over females in only Afghanistan and Swaziland, HALE estimates are higher for males in a number of countries: Bangladesh, Botswana, the Central African Republic, Pakistan, Qatar, Tajikistan, Tonga, and Zimbabwe. In numerous other countries—Afghanistan, Bahrain, Benin, Cameroon, Chad, Kuwait, Mali, Mozambique, Nepal, Nigeria, Sudan, Swaziland, Tuvalu, United Arab Emirates, and United Republic of Tanzania—HALE estimates for men and women are identical. The male advantage in HALE is not large in the cases where it exists—typically just one or two years.[79] Nevertheless, the shift is notable and suggests that HALE estimates, which incorporate variables related to quality of life and not just longevity of life, are more likely to capture the effects of variables that have negative effects on women's health.

An examination of lost healthy life expectancy years, which is the difference between total life expectancy and HALE,[80] provides another lens for examining health differentials between men and women. In contrast to life expectancy and HALE indicators, data on lost years of full health suggest a health disadvantage for women. Globally, women lose an average of nine years of HALE compared to seven years for men. This pattern holds across all regions of the world and across all levels of economic

238

development. In every region of the world, women lose eight or nine years of full health compared to six to eight years for men.[81] The estimated number of lost years of full health for females is highest in upper-middle-income countries, where women lose an average of eleven years of good health and males lose an average of nine years. In low-income countries, the number of lost years of good health drops to nine for females and seven for males. Despite women's health advantage in longevity and HALE, these data show that women have higher morbidity than men and will spend a higher percentage of their lives in less than a state of full health.[82]

In addition to differentials in life expectancy measures, men and women experience different burdens of disease, as measured in DALYs, which indicate the number of years of healthy life lost due to particular diseases and injuries. As DALY data show, men and women suffer disproportionately from different kinds of illnesses. Table 6.1 shows the leading causes of burden of disease measured in DALYs by sex. In high-income countries, the top five causes of DALY losses in women include unipolar depressive disorders, migraines, health problems associated with alcohol use, bipolar disorders, and schizophrenia. In low-income countries, the major causes of DALY losses for women are HIV/AIDs, tuberculosis, abortion complications, schizophrenia, and maternal sepsis.[83] Conditions specific to women make up a significant proportion of women's burden of disease. Globally, maternal conditions (including maternal hemorrhage, maternal sepsis, hypertensive disorders, obstructed labor, obstetric fistula, and complications from unsafe abortions) contribute to 2.8 percent of women's DALY losses.[84] Cancers, including breast and cervical cancer, contribute to 1.1 percent of DALY losses for women.[85] Women also have higher disease prevalence for certain illnesses, such as Alzheimer's, osteoporosis, and arthritis, due, in part, to their average higher life expectancy.[86] Injuries contribute disproportionately to men's burden of disease, and men are also more prone to suffer from heart

TABLE 6.1 Leading Causes of Burden of Disease (DALYs) by Sex, 2004

Disease or injury	Percentage of total DALYs	
	Female	Male
Infectious and parasitic diseases	19.6	20.1
Neuropsychiatric disorders	13.9	12.4
Cardiovascular diseases	9.4	10.4
Unintentional injuries	7.1	10.9
Perinatal conditions	8.5	8.1
Sense organ disorders	6.2	5.3
Cancers	4.9	5.3
Maternal conditions	5.4	—
Respiratory diseases	3.6	4.2
Digestive diseases	2.5	3.1
Intentional injuries	1.8	4.6
Diabetes mellitus	1.5	1.1

Source: Adapted from the World Health Organization, *The Global Burden of Disease: 2004 Update*: 60–64. Available online at: http://www.who.int/healthinfo/global_burden_disease/GBD_report_2004update_full.pdf.

disease and coronary artery disease. A significant proportion of the global male burden of disease—2.7 percent of DALY losses—results from war and violence.[87] Men also have significantly higher prevalence rates of drug and alcohol disorders.[88]

The causes of death for males and females also shed light on disparities in the health status of men and women across the globe. Figure 6.3 illustrates the distribution of the major causes of mortality by sex. At the global level, cardiovascular disease is the major cause of death for both men (26.8 percent) and women (31.5 percent). Globally, other major causes of male mortality are infectious and parasitic diseases (16.7 percent), cancers (13.4 percent), unintentional injuries (8.1 percent), respiratory infections (7.1 percent), and respiratory disorders (6.9 percent). After cardiovascular disease, the major causes of death for females include infectious and parasitic diseases (15.6 percent), cancers (11.8 percent), respiratory

FIGURE 6.3 Distribution of Global Deaths by Leading Cause Groups, Males and Females, 2004

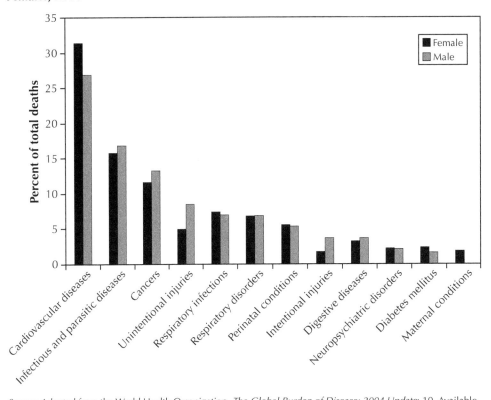

Source: Adapted from the World Health Organization, *The Global Burden of Disease: 2004 Update*: 10. Available online at: http://www.who.int/healthinfo/global_burden_disease/GBD_report_2004update_full.pdf.

infections (7.4 percent), and respiratory disorders (6.8 percent).[89]

Men have higher adult mortality rates across all regions, which can be attributed in large part to high male mortality due to injuries. Although this pattern holds across the globe, sex-based disparities in mortality rates are apparent across regions. Differences are most pronounced in Africa, where females have significantly higher mortality due to communicable illnesses and to maternal and nutritional conditions. Overall, HIV/AIDS causes 40 percent of female deaths in Africa compared to the 14 percent of deaths resulting from maternal conditions. Communicable illnesses are also the major cause of mortality for African men, but they are less likely to die from communicable illnesses than women. Males in Africa have a somewhat higher mortality resulting from injuries than

women. In Europe, cardiovascular disease and injury are major causes of male mortality. Men face much higher mortality rates than women in the Eastern Mediterranean Region due to injuries. In South-East Asia, minimal differences between men and women manifest in mortality rates due to communicable illnesses. Men have slightly higher mortality rates due to noncommunicable illnesses and injuries. In Latin America and the Caribbean, injuries are a major cause of death for men, contributing to higher male mortality rates in this region.

A final indicator that underscores a serious global health disadvantage for women is the surplus male population in the developing world. Approximately 50.3 percent of the world's 6.2 billion people are male, and roughly 49.7 percent are female. Records of live births across all societies indicate a "natural" sex ratio of 103–106 male births for every 100 female births. In China today, this ratio is 124 to 100 in favor of boys. India, South Korea, Singapore, and Taiwan have similarly distorted sex ratios. These sex ratios indicate a surplus male population. Globally, estimates suggest that 100 million women are "missing" from the total global population.[90] The discrepancy results from gender-biased practices in areas of the developing world, most notably sex-selective abortion and the killing of girl children in infancy. These practices stem from cultural preferences for boy children in many societies. The neglect of girl children, dowry violence, and other forms of domestic violence also contribute to surplus male population across the globe. This "gender paradox"—of longer average female life expectancy and HALE but a lower percentage of women in the world's total population—is largely concentrated in the developing world.[91] High-income countries have a higher proportion of women than men in the total population; this relationship is reversed in low-income countries, and it is especially pronounced in the region of South Asia.

The Causes of Health Disparities Between Men and Women in Global Health

The global health disparities between men and women have varying causes. In some cases, these disparities can be described as **sex differentials**. Here, health disparities are rooted in biological causes, including basic biological differences between males and females as well as genetic and hormonal factors. Other health disparities are better characterized as **gender differentials**, in which case men and women experience different health outcomes due to socially constructed norms of masculinity and femininity. Gender differentials in health outcomes between men and women result from health behaviors, cultural practices, and governmental policies shaped by **gender norms**—the culturally prevailing constructs of presumed "normal," "appropriate," or "ideal" behavior and identities of men (masculinity) and women (femininity.) Although it is helpful to distinguish between sex and gender differentials, divergent health outcomes for men and women, in many instances, represent a complex interplay of biology and gender.

Many health disparities between men and women can be attributed to sex differentials. Take women's longer average life expectancy as an example. Women have certain biological advantages that contribute to their greater average longevity. Scientists have offered a variety of potential explanations for the female longevity advantage. For one, sex chromosomes give females a health advantage. To understand this advantage, it is necessary to review some very basic fundamentals regarding sex chromosomes. Female offspring result from two X chromosomes, whereas male offspring are the product of an X chromosome and a Y chromosome. X chromosomes carry

---

KEY DEFINITIONS PERTAINING TO GENDER AND GLOBAL HEALTH

Gender Differentials: health disparities between men and women that are rooted in socially constructed norms of masculinity and femininity.

Gender Norms: the culturally prevailing constructs of presumed "normal," "appropriate," or "ideal" behavior and identities of men (masculinity) and women (femininity).

Sex Differentials: health disparities between men and women that are rooted in basic biological differences between males and females as well as genetic and hormonal factors.

more genes than Y chromosomes, and, as a result, more sex-linked traits, including illnesses, are carried on the X chromosome. Most sex-linked illnesses result from recessive genes carried on the X chromosome. Therefore, males have a 50 percent chance of getting a sex-linked illness if their mother carries one abnormal gene. Conversely, females would need to inherit a recessive gene from both the mother and the father in order to develop the condition. Hemophilia is a classic example of a sex-specific illness that is more common among males for precisely this reason. Women may have certain hormonal as well as chromosomal advantages that contribute to their longer average life expectancy. The male hormone testosterone may increase risk taking and aggressive behavior that lead to high rates of unintentional injury among men. Metabolic differences, which predispose men to higher levels of LDL ("bad cholesterol"), may also contribute to longevity disadvantages for men.[92] For instance, to the extent that metabolic differences lead to higher levels of bad cholesterol among men, they contribute to the higher rate of cardiovascular disease seen in men.

Although sex differentials produce certain health advantages for women, biological factors are responsible for a number of significant health challenges faced by women alone. For example, women's reproductive health issues are fundamentally rooted in biological differences between the sexes. Numerous examples fall under this category. Ovarian cancer, eclampsia, gestational diabetes, pregnancy and birth-related hemorrhage, obstetric fistula, and maternal death during childbirth all involve reproductive and maternal health conditions faced by women alone. Thus, these health challenges have roots in basic biology. Higher rates of depression and migraine headaches among women also can be attributed to hormonal and genetic factors fundamentally rooted in sex differentials. Additionally, autoimmune disorders, such as hypothyroidism and hyperthyroidism, as well as lupus and rheumatoid arthritis, are more common

among women and can be attributed to inherent biological differences.

Men also face a number of health challenges that are primarily biologically based. Obvious examples include prostate and testicular cancer. Males also have a much higher incidence of cardiovascular morbidity and mortality in young and middle adulthood, at least in developed countries. Higher rates of cardiovascular disease among men have been attributed in large part to hormonal differences between males and females. Interestingly, these hormonal differences are essentially neutralized after women become postmenopausal, and women experience a similar incidence of cardiovascular morbidity and mortality in late adulthood.[93]

As these examples illustrate, health disparities between men and women in global health can be partially attributed to sex differentials. However, gender differentials also contribute fundamentally to various disparities in health outcomes between men and women. For example, maternal conditions are sex-specific health challenges rooted in biology. Over 500,000 women die each year due to complications from pregnancy and childbirth; most of these deaths would be preventable with simple and affordable public health interventions.[94] The extent to which these maternal conditions contribute to burden of disease depends very much on socially constructed gender norms that partially determine women's access to perinatal and postnatal care as well as the general social and economic determinants that shape women's health status across the globe. As the example of maternal health suggests, divergent health outcomes in some areas reflect gender biases that lead to underfunding of women's health priorities.

Gender biases that prioritize men's health over women's health also manifest in different ways. Men in most societies have dominated political decision making over health care policy and budgets.[95] Male biases in medical research also have played a role here. For example, a great deal of medical research on cardiovascular disease has historically been based primarily on male subjects, which limits the applicability of research findings to female patients. Due to prevailing conceptions of femininity in many societies that lead women to prioritize the health of the male members of their families and communities more highly than their own health or that of their daughters, women are often less likely than men to seek necessary health care. The uneven distribution of financial resources within households also makes many women less likely to seek professional medical care even if they would otherwise be inclined to do so.[96] Gender differentials also contribute to underreporting of certain diseases for women. For example, due to social stigmas that place high value on sexual "purity" among women, women are often reluctant to undergo testing or to seek treatment for sexually transmitted diseases.

Gender norms also contribute to health disadvantages for women in other ways. In particular, gender norms that devalue girl children and women contribute to all sorts of harmful practices that threaten the health and lives of women and girls across the globe. These harmful practices include sex-selective abortion and female infanticide, feeding practices that prioritize giving more of scarce food to boy children and men, dowry violence, sexual violence, and other forms of domestic violence. Such practices lead to a wide range of health problems for girls and women, including debilitating injury, malnutrition, and death. Unlike maternal conditions, these health problems have no biological basis and are rooted almost entirely in discriminatory gender norms. Gender norms also shape the transmission, experience, and treatment of critical illnesses for women. HIV/AIDS is a case in point. Gender inequalities embedded within societies can make women more susceptible to contracting the disease. For example, gender inequalities can limit women's ability to control their sexuality or to use birth control in sexual relationships (especially within marriage) and, thus, contribute to high HIV prevalence rates among women in many societies. Sexual violence against women also exacerbates the spread of disease. Unequal economic and power relations within families and

societies at large also can limit women's ability to receive effective treatment for the disease.[97]

Additionally, women face gendered health challenges that undermine their well-being without necessarily constituting disease or disability. For instance, women in the developing world, especially in rural areas, commonly have primary responsibility for running households. Women are often responsible for child rearing, growing and cooking food for the family, obtaining water for the household (which often involves walking significant distances), caring for frequently sick children, and facing high mortality rates among their children. These burdens are especially pronounced in high-fertility countries where women are often pregnant and raising several young children at the same time. These sorts of socioeconomic burdens may negatively affect women's physical and mental health without necessarily resulting in diseases or disabilities that show up in general health indicators.[98]

Gender differentials also contribute to specific health challenges faced by men. Although women's longer average life expectancy can be attributed in part to biology, social factors also contribute to a lower average life expectancy for men. For example, fatal injuries are a major cause of male mortality in regions across the globe. Socially constructed gender norms contribute to this phenomenon. A form of masculinity that encourages aggressive, risk-seeking behavior results in a greater propensity of men to engage in behaviors (for example, fast or reckless driving) that could lead to life-threatening injuries. Prevailing forms of masculinity in most societies contribute to high mortality rates among men in other ways as well. High rates of male morbidity and mortality due to injuries result in large part from gendered social and economic norms that place many men at risk of occupational threats to their health. Occupational injuries are a major cause of morbidity and mortality for men in most societies across the globe. The fact that men are more likely than women to work in more dangerous occupations (for instance, construction, mining, or factory work involving heavy or dangerous equipment) can be attributed, at least in part, to socially constructed norms that treat such work as largely masculine endeavors.

Similarly, male burden of disease and mortality stemming from war-related violence is a highly gendered phenomenon resulting from the deep associations between prevailing forms of masculinity and military combat in most societies. For example, in countries with forced military conscription, such policies typically apply only to men. (The case of Israel, where women as well as men face compulsory military service, is a prominent exception.) As a result, men are more likely to be injured or killed as combatants even when they do not have a real choice about participating in military service. This phenomenon stems from gender norms that fundamentally tie responsibility for military service in national defense to a masculine conception of civic duty. Gender norms that presume men are potential combatants and women and children are innocent civilians also contribute to war-related morbidity and mortality for men during war.[99] Many civilian men are likely to be killed as *potential* soldiers simply because they are males of "fighting age."[100]

Many crucial questions remain about the relative effect of sex differentials versus gender differentials on health disparities between men and women. In some cases, it is clear that sex differentials are the primary cause of disparate health challenges. Maternal health conditions, experienced only by women, are a good example. In other cases, such as female infanticide and sex-selective abortion, discriminatory gender norms are obviously the primary determinant of this gender gap in health outcomes—neither practice is fundamentally rooted in biology.

However, in many cases it can be very difficult to disentangle the relative contribution of biological sex versus gender constructs in shaping health outcomes. For instance, high rates of unintentional injury among men are caused, in part, by risk-taking behavior shaped by prevailing conceptions of masculinity. At the same time, hormonal differences rooted in biology also contribute to such behavior. The same thing can be said of the higher rates of war-related injury and death for men. On the one hand, masculine norms that prioritize aggressive, self-sacrificing behavior among men shape these outcomes. On the other hand, we can ask ourselves how much of this behavior is influenced by fundamental biological differences between men and women. Some evidence exists that men are more prone to violence due to higher testosterone levels, biological propensity to greater size and strength, biologically rooted differences in cognition, and other biological or genetic factors.[101] Furthermore, there is evidence that suggests that aggressive behavior itself increases testosterone levels, indicating that the relationship between biological sex and gender works in both directions.[102]

Due to the complex interplay of biology and gender, we cannot reach definitive conclusions about what causes various gender gaps in global health. Clearly, both biology and gender play a role, and interactive effects of both biology and gender are important. Disentangling the relative influence of biological sex and gender goes well beyond the scope of this chapter. For the beginning student of global health, the important thing to remember is that both sex and gender differentials are responsible for the disparities in health outcomes between men and women.

Conclusion

This chapter provided an overview of a range of inequities in global health. These inequities are manifested across numerous borders— territorial, poverty-based, and social borders— that shape the international relations of global health. Territorial borders reveal distinct inequities between high-income countries with good aggregate population health outcomes and low-income countries with comparatively poor aggregate population health outcomes. The strength of this general correlation between levels of national wealth and population health reflects a larger North-South gap in global health that is rooted in broad systemic features and underlying structural inequities in the global economy.

Despite the importance of broad territorially based inequities between countries and between developed and developing regions in general, significant inequities within, between, and across territorial borders are also critical. Differences in population health outcomes across countries are not entirely rooted in levels of national income, and variations in national health systems (as will be discussed in Chapter 10) influence population health, as do social, political and cultural inequities within societies. In particular, poverty-based inequities are a fundamental source of disparities in population health outcomes, as are disparities rooted in socioeconomic inequities among racial and ethnic groups across and within societies. Across the globe, both women and men face important health disparities rooted in both sex and gender differentials. Notably, poverty-based, racial/ethnic, and gendered health disparities cut across national borders, suggesting transnational causes and trends, at the same time as they are manifested in unique ways in particular societies.

The economic, ethnic, and gender inequities in global health considered in this chapter do not represent isolated, discrete categories. Rather, considerable overlap exists in terms of both the disparities in health outcomes and the root causes of these disparities. Territorially based inequities have been shaped by racialized transnational processes and events, such as colonialism. Sexism on a global scale has contributed to poverty-related health challenges faced by women across the globe. The reverse is also true: Health disparities faced by disadvantaged racial and ethnic populations, as well as health disparities between men and women within particular societies, are rooted in broader, transnational economic forces and trends. As a result of the complicated intersections among poverty, race/ethnicity, and gender both within and across societies, it is difficult to disentangle the relative weight of each of these categories.

For our purposes, the critical point is to highlight the importance of all of these inequities. Students of public health need to be aware of the multiple sources and manifestations of economic, ethnic, and gender inequities in global health. The range of inequities in global health—and the complex interplay among various forms of inequities—underscores the importance of drawing on the knowledge of scholars and practitioners from many disciplines in seeking to promote global health. To mitigate inequities in global health, the insights and contributions of medical professionals, social workers, sociologists, economists, cultural anthropologists, public policy experts, and political scientists will be essential in efforts to address the underlying socioeconomic determinants of health in a comprehensive manner on a global scale.

NOTES

22. World Health Organization, Western
Pacific Regional Office, *Women, Girls,
HIV, & AIDS* (2004). Available online
at: http://www.wpro.who.int/NR/
rdonlyres/F1F88521-518C-4EAC-AF7E-
1F07A4E9FF0B/0/WAD2004_Women_
Girls_HIV_AIDS.pdf.

23. United Nations Children's Fund and World
Health Organization, *Diarhoea: Why Children
Are Still Dying and What Can Be Done*
(2009). Available online at: http://whqlibdoc.
who.int/publications/2009/9789241598415_
eng.pdf.

24. *Ibid.*: 23.

25. J.A. Schellenberg, C.G. Victora, A. Mushi,
D. de Savigny, D. Schellenberg,
H. Mshinda, and J. Bryce, "Inequities
Among the Very Poor: Health Care for
Children in Rural Southern Tanzania,"
Lancet 361: 9357 (2003): 561–566.

26. C.T. Sreeramareddy, R.P. Shankar,
B.V. Sreekuraman, S.H. Subba, H.S. Joshi,
and U. Ramachandran, "Care-seeking
Behavior for Childhood Illness—A
Questionnaire Survey in Western Nepal,"
*BMC International Health and Human
Rights* 6 (2006): 7–16.

27. J. Akin and P. Hutchinson, "Health Care
Facility Choice and the Phenomenon of
Bypassing," *Health Policy and Planning*
14: 2 (1999): 135–151; D. Chernichovsky
and O.A. Meesook, "Utilization of Health

Services in Indonesia," *Social Science & Medicine* 23: 6 (1986): 611–620.

28. D. Thomas, V. Lavy, and D. Strauss, "Public Policy and Anthropometric Outcomes in the Côte d'Ivoire," *Journal of Public Economics* 61: 2 (1996): 155–192.

29. F. Castro-Leal, J. Dayton, L. Demery, and K. Mehra, "Public Social Spending in Africa: Do the Poor Benefit?" *World Bank Research Observer* 14: 1 (1999): 66–74.

30. World Health Organization, *Health, Economic Growth, and Poverty Reduction* (2002): 37. Available online at: http://whqlibdoc.who.int/publications/9241590092.pdf.

31. J. Sachs and P. Malaney, "The Economic and Social Burden of Malaria," *Nature* 415 (2002): 680–685.

32. Jeffrey Long and Rick Kittles, "Human Genetic Diversity and the Nonexistence of Biological Races," *Human Biology* 75: 4 (2003): 449–471.

33. Kenneth D. Kochanek, Jiaquan Xu, Sherry L. Murphy, Arialdi M. Miniño, and Hsiang-Ching Kung, "Deaths: Preliminary Data for 2009," *National Vital Statistics Report* 59: 4 (2011): 1–51.

34. *Ibid.*

35. Glenn Flores and the Committee on Pediatrics Research, "Racial and Ethnic Disparities in the Health and Health Care of Children," *Pediatrics* 125: 4 (2010): e979–e1020.

36. Janet Smylie, Deshayne Fell, and Arne Ohlsson, "A Review of Aboriginal Infant Mortality Rates in Canada: Striking and Persistent Aboriginal/Non-Aboriginal Inequities," *Canadian Journal of Public Health* 101: 2 (2010): 143–148; Charles H. Wood, José A. Magno de Carvalho, and Cláudia J. Guimarães Horta, "The Color of Child Mortality in Brazil, 1950–2000: Social Progress and Persistent Racial Inequality," *Latin American Research Review* 45: 2 (2010): 114–139.

37. U.S. Centers for Disease Control and Prevention, "CDC Health Disparities and Inequalities Report—United States, 2011,"

Morbidity and Mortality Weekly Report 60: Suppl. (2011): 1–114.

38. Stacey Jolly, Eric Vittinghoff, Arpita Chattopadhyay, and Kirsten Bibbens-Domingo, "Higher Cardiovascular Disease Prevalence and Mortality Among Younger Blacks Compared to Whites," *American Journal of Medicine* 123: 9 (2010): 811–818; Tanisha D. Hill, LeRoy M. Graham, and Varada Divgi, "Racial Disparities in Pediatric Asthma: A Review of the Literature," *Current Allergy & Asthma Report* 11: 1 (2011): 85–90; Ganna Chornokur, Kyle Dalton, Meghan E. Borysova, and Nagi B. Kumar, "Disparities at Presentation, Diagnosis, Treatment, and Survival in African American Men Affected by Prostate Cancer," *Prostate* 71: 9 (2011): 985–997.

39. Holly Mead, Lara Cartwright-Smith, Karen Jones, Christal Ramos, and Bruce Siegel, "Racial and Ethnic Disparities in U.S. Health Care: A Chartbook," *The Commonwealth Fund* (2008). Available online at: http://www.commonwealthfund.org/Publications/Chartbooks/2008/Mar/Racial-and-Ethnic-Disparities-in-U-S—Health-Care—A-Chartbook.aspx.

40. Antonio A. Lopes, "End-stage Renal Disease Due to Diabetes in Racial/Ethnic Minorities and Disadvantaged Populations," *Ethnicity & Disease* 19: Suppl. 1 (2009): 47–51.

41. Morton N. Beiser and Feng Hou, "Ethnic Identity, Resentment Stress and Depressive Affect Among Southeast Asian Refugees in Canada," *Social Science & Medicine* 63: 1 (2006): 137–150; M. Kelaher, Sheila Paul, Helen Lambert, Waqar Ahmad, Yin Paradies, and George Davey Smith, "Discrimination and Health in an English Study," *Social Science & Medicine* 66: 7 (2008): 1627–1636; Margarita Alegria, Melissa Vallas, and Andres J. Pumariega, "Racial and Ethnic Disparities in Pediatric Mental Health," *Child and Adolescent Psychiatric Clinics of North America* 19: 4 (2010): 759–774.

42. Martin Brockerhoff and Paul Hewett, "Inequality of Child Mortality Among

Ethnic Groups in sub-Saharan Africa," *Bulletin of the World Health Organization* 78: 1 (2000): 30–41; Mats Målqvist, Nguyen T. Nga, Leif Eriksson, Lars Wallin, Dinh P. Hoa, and Lars Å. Persson, "Ethnic Inequity in Neonatal Survival: A Case-referent Study in Northern Vietnam," *Acta Paediatrica* 100: 3 (2011): 340–346.

43. David Mayer-Foulkes and Carlos Larrea, "Racial and Ethnic Inequities: Bolivia, Brazil, Guatemala, Peru," in Antonio Giuffrida, ed., *Racial and Ethnic Disparities in Health in Latin America and the Caribbean* (Washington, DC: Inter-American Development Bank, 2007): 131–137. Available online at: http://idbdocs.iadb.org/wsdocs/getdocument.aspx?docnum=1148586.

44. M. Hashibe, B. Siwakoti, M. Wei, B.K. Thakur, C.B. Pun, B.M. Shrestha, Z. Burningham, Y.C. Lee, and A. Sapkota, "Socioeconomic Status and Lung Cancer Risk in Nepal," *Asian Pacific Journal of Cancer Prevention* 12: 4 (2011): 1083–1088.

45. Brandon A. Kohrt, Rebacca A. Speckman, Richard D. Kunz, Jennifer L. Baldwin, Nawaraj Upadhaya, Nanda R. Acharya, Vidya D. Sharma, Mahendra K. Nepal, and Carol M. Worthman, "Culture in Psychiatric Epidemiology: Using Ethnography and Multiple Mediator Models to Assess the Relationship of Caste with Depression and Anxiety in Nepal," *Annals of Human Biology* 36: 3 (2009): 261–280.

46. Robert A. Hummer, Maureen R. Benjamins, and Richard G. Rogers, "Racial and Ethnic Disparities in Health and Mortality Among the U.S. Elderly Population," in Norman B. Anderson, Rodolfo A. Bulatao, and Barney Cohen, eds., *Critical Perspectives on Racial and Ethnic Differences in Health in Late Life* (Washington, DC: The National Academies Press, 2004): 53–94; Peter Franks, Peter Muennig, Erica Lubetkin, and Haomiao Jia, "The Burden of Disease Associated with Being African-American in the United States and the Contribution of Socio-economic Status," *Social Science & Medicine* 62: 10 (2006): 2469–2478.

47. Ana V. Diez-Roux and Christina Mair, "Neighborhoods and Health," *Annals of the New York Academy of Sciences* 1186: 1 (2010): 125–145.

48. Jennifer Northridge, Olivia F. Ramirez, Jeanette A. Stingone, and Luz Claudio, "The Role of Housing Type and Housing Quality in Urban Children with Asthma," *Journal of Urban Health* 87: 2 (2010): 211–224.

49. Julie L. Crouch, Rachelle F. Hanson, Benjamin E. Saunders, Dean G. Kilpatrick, and Heidi S. Resnick, "Income, Race/Ethnicity, and Exposure to Violence in Youth: Results from the National Survey of Adolescents," *Journal of Community Psychology* 26: 6 (2000): 625–641.

50. World Health Organization, *World Report on Child Injury Prevention* (World Health Organization, 2008): 1–211. Available online at: http://whqlibdoc.who.int/publications/2008/9789241563574_eng.pdf.

51. Kathy Sanders-Phillips, Beverlyn Settles-Reaves, Doren Walker, and Janeese Brownlow, "Social Inequality and Racial Discrimination: Risk Factors for Health Disparities in Children of Color," *Pediatrics* 124: Suppl. 3 (2009): S176–S186.

52. Mead et al.: 44.

53. Natalie D. Crawford, Camara P. Jones, and Lisa C. Richardson, "Understanding Racial and Ethnic Disparities in Colorectal Cancer Screening: Behavioral Risk Factor Surveillance System, 2002 and 2004," *Ethnicity & Disease* 20: 4 (2010): 359–365; William R. Carpenter, Paul A. Godley, Jack A. Clark, James A. Talcott, Timothy Finnegan, Merle Mishel, Jeannette Bensen, Walter Rayford, L. Joseph Su, Elizabeth T. Fontham, and James L. Mohler, "Racial Differences in Trust and Regular Source of Patient Care and the Implications for Prostate Cancer Screening Use," *Cancer* 115: 21 (2009): 5048–5059.

54. Yuanyuan Wang, Julie A. Simpson, Anita E. Wluka, Donna M. Urquhart, Dallas R. English, Graham G. Giles, Stephen Graves, and Flavia M. Cicuttini, "Reduced Rates of Primary Joint Replacement for Osteoarthritis in Italian and Greek Migrants

to Australia: The Melbourne Collaborative Study," *Arthritis Research & Therapy* 11: 3 (2009): R86.

55. Ezequiel Bellorin-Font, Nidia Pernalete, Josefina Meza, Carmen L. Milanes, and Raul G. Carlini, "Access to and Coverage of Renal Replacement Therapy in Minorities and Ethnic Groups in Venezuela," *Kidney International* Suppl. 97 (2005): S18–S22.

56. Sarah Burgard, "Race and Pregnancy-related Care in Brazil and South Africa," *Social Science & Medicine* 59 (2004): 1127–1146.

57. Zeida R. Kon and Nuha Lackan, "Ethnic Disparities in Access to Care in Post-apartheid South Africa," *American Journal of Public Health* 98: 12 (2008): 2272–2277.

58. Glenn Flores and Sandra C. Tomany-Korman, "Racial and Ethnic Disparities in Medical and Dental Health, Access to Care and Use of Services in US Children," *Pediatrics* 121: 2 (2008): e286–e296.

59. Ian M. Bennett, Jing Chen, Jaleh S. Soroui, and Sheida White, "The Contribution of Health Literacy to Disparities in Self-rated and Preventive Health Behaviors in Older Patients," *Annals of Family Medicine* 7: 3 (2009): 204–211.

60. Bussarawan Teerawichitchainan and James F. Phillips, "Ethnic Differentials in Parental Health Seeking for Childhood Illness in Vietnam," *Social Science & Medicine* 66: 5 (2008): 1118–1130; Målqvist et al.: 340.

61. Karen S. Collins, Allyson Hall, and Charlotte Neuhaus, "U.S. Minority Health: A Chartbook," *The Commonwealth Fund* (1999). Available online at: http://www.common wealthfund.org/Publications/Chartbooks/1999/May/U-S—Minority-Health—A-Chartbook.aspx.

62. Darrell J. Gaskin, Christine Spencer, and Patrick Richard, "Do Hospitals Provide Lower-quality Care to Minorities than to Whites?" *Health Affairs* 27: 2 (2008): 518–527.

63. *Ibid.*

64. Duncan Thomas, Victor Lavy, and John Strauss, "Public Policy and Anthropometric Outcomes in the Côte d'Ivoire," *Journal of Public Economics* 61: 2 (1996): 155–192.

65. U.S. Office for Civil Rights, *Guidance to Federal Financial Assistance Recipients Regarding Title VI and the Prohibition Against National Origin Discrimination Affecting Limited English Proficient Persons—Summary* (Washington, DC: U.S. Department of Health and Human Services, 2000). Available online at: http://www.hhs.gov/ocr/civilrights/resources/laws/summaryguidance.html.

66. Robert Wood Johnson Foundation, "Language Barriers Contribute to Health Care Disparities for Latinos in the United States of America," *Pan American Journal of Public Health* 11: 1 (2002): 56–58.

67. Mee L. Wong, Kee S. Chia, Sharon Wee, Sin E. Chia, Jeannette Lee, Woon P. Koh, Han M. Shen, Julian Thumboo, and Dickey Sofjan, "Concerns over Participation in Genetic Research Among Malay-Muslims, Chinese and Indians in Singapore: A Focus Group Study," *Community Genetics* 7: 1 (2004): 44–54.

68. Carpenter et al.: 5048.

69. Michelle van Ryn and Jane Burke, "The Effect of Patient Race and Socio-economic Status on Physicians' Perceptions of Patients," *Social Science & Medicine* 50: 6 (2000): 813–828.

70. Louis Sullivan and Ilana S. Mittman, "The State of Diversity in the Health Professions a Century After Flexner," *Academic Medicine* 85: 2 (2010): 246–253.

71. World Health Organization, *Closing the Gap in a Generation: Health Equity Through Action on the Social Determinants of Health* (2008). Available online at: http://whqlibdoc.who.int/hq/2008/WHO_IER_CSDH_08.1_eng.pdf.

72. Institute of Medicine of the National Academies, *Unequal Treatment: What Health Care System Administrators Need to Know About Racial and Ethnic Disparities in Healthcare* (Institute of Medicine of the National Academies, 2002). Available online at: http://www.nap.edu/openbook.php?record_id=10260&page=1.

73. Mayra Buvinic, André Médici, Elisa Fernández, and Ana Cristina Torres, "Gender Differentials in Health," in Dean T. Jamison,

Joel G. Breman, Anthony R. Measham, George Alleyne, Maria Claeson, David P. Evans, Prabhat Jha, Anne Mills, and Phillip Musgrove, eds., *Disease Control Priorities in Developing Countries*, 2d ed. (New York: Oxford University Press; Washington, DC: The World Bank, 2006): 197.

74. World Health Organization, *World Health Statistics 2009* (2009): 44. Available online at: http://www.who.int/whosis/whostat/EN_WHS09_Full.pdf.

75. Data on life expectancy from both the UNDP and the WHO confirm women's advantage in life expectancy in all regions. World Health Organization, *World Health Statistics 2009*: 44; United Nations Development Programme, "Statistics of the Human Development Report," *Human Development Report* 2009. Available online at: http://hdr.undp.org/en/statistics/.

76. *Ibid.*

77. *Ibid.*

78. World Health Organization, *World Health Statistics 2009*: 44.

79. *Ibid.*: 36–43.

80. Colin D. Mathers, Christopher J.L. Murray, and Joshua A. Salomon, "Methods for Measuring Healthy Life Expectancy," in Christopher J.L. Murray and David B. Evans, eds., *Health Systems Performance Assessment: Debates, Methods, and Empiricism* (Geneva: World Health Organization, 2003): 439.

81. World Health Organization, *World Health Statistics 2009*: 44.

82. Morbidity simply refers to illness "or any departure, subjective or objective, from a psychological or physiological state of well-being." Skolnik: 22.

83. World Health Organization, *The Global Burden of Disease: 2004 Update*: 46.

84. Buvinic et al.: 199.

85. *Ibid.*

86. *Ibid.*: 196.

87. *Ibid.*: note 2 at 209.

88. World Health Organization, "Disease Incidence, Prevalence, and Disability," in *The Global Burden of Disease: 2004 Update* (2008): 36.

89. World Health Organization, *The Global Burden of Disease: 2004 Update*: 10.

90. "Gendercide: The Worldwide War on Baby Girls," *The Economist*, March 4, 2010. Available online at: http://www.economist.com/node/15636231/.

91. Buvinic et al.: 197.

92. "Mars vs. Venus: The Gender Gap in Health," *Harvard Men's Health Watch* (January 2010). Available online at: http://www.health.harvard.edu/newsletters/Harvard_Mens_Health_Watch/2010/January/mars-vs-venus-the-gender-gap-in-health/.

93. In fact, the role of female hormones in reducing the risk of cardiovascular disease was sufficiently well established by the 1990s that doctors recommended hormone replacement therapy (HRT) for peri/postmenopausal women not solely for relief from the symptoms of menopause but also to decrease the incidence of coronary disease. However, in the early years of the 21st century, a large randomized controlled trial (the Women's Health Initiative) demonstrated just the opposite effect—an increased risk of stroke and heart attack in the first two years of HRT. Thus, the pendulum swung, and the medical profession quit routinely using HRT for symptomatic control of hot flashes, except in cases of severe menopausal symptoms not responsive to nonhormonal treatments, out of fear of this increased cardiovascular risk. Writing Group for the Women's Health Initiative Investigators, "Risks and Benefits of Estrogen Plus Progestin in Healthy Postmenopausal Women: Principal Results from the Women's Health Initiative Randomized Control Trial," *Journal of the American Medical Association* 288 (2002): 321–333.

94. United Nations Development Programme, "Millennium Development Goals: A Compact Among Nations to End Human Poverty," *Human Development Report 2003*: 9. Available online at: http://hdr.undp.org/en/reports/global/hdr2003/.

95. Buvinic et al.: 197.

96. *Ibid.*: 198.

97. Jelke Boesten and Nana K. Poku, *Gender and HIV/AIDS: Critical Perspectives from the Developing World* (Burlington, VT: Ashgate Publishers, 2009).

98. I would like to thank Dr. John Murray, a consultant on child and maternal mortality with the World Health Organization, for discussions that contributed to this insight.

99. Charli Carpenter, "'Women and Children First': Gender Norms and Humanitarian Evacuation in the Balkans: 1991–1995," *International Organization* 57: 4 (2003): 661–694.

100. Adam Jones, "Gendercide and Genocide," *Journal of Genocide Research* 2: 2 (2000): 185–211.

101. Joshua Goldstein, *War and Gender: How Gender Shapes the War System and Vice Versa* (Cambridge, UK: Cambridge University Press, 2001): 128–182.

102. Will Courtenay, "A Global Perspective on the Field of Men's Health: An Editorial," *International Journal of Men's Health* 1: 1 (2002): 4.

Understanding Social Problems
of Human Behavior

Drug Users through the Ages

When Did We Decide Addicts Were a Separate Category?

Exactly when the Othering of addicts began can be traced to the 18th century, probably to the gin epidemic of London. Prior to our concerted effort to find evidence of the concept of the addict in the writings of the ancients, we had always thought that it had been present since the discovery of intoxicating preparations. We could not, however, find it in any of those writings, from the Ghitas to the Gilgamesh epic, to the Torah, to Plato's *Symposium,* to the letters of Paul the Apostle. All of these sources made mention of strong drink, and most warned against drunkenness, but none attributed drunkenness as a chronic condition. In all of these venerable writings, the lone example of the habitual addict appears in Homer's *Odyssey*, in which Odysseus and his crew encountered and are enticed by the Lotus Eaters, whose lifestyle seemed to reflect an addicted condition. Nevertheless, because the described behaviors resembled no known addictive pattern, involving no known drug, the appearance of the lotus eaters in *The Odyssey* may be a product of an active imagination, or perhaps a story from another source, rather than an expression of personal experience. In order to trace when and where humankind came to "recognize" addicts and addiction, this chapter begins by positing humankind's ability to ingest toxins and derive something other than illness or death from them as a phenomenon with deep evolutionary precedents.

Only speculation, albeit backed by archaeological and ethnographic evidence, is possible with regard to the process of discovering plant-derived preparations that gave pleasure to their users. After laying out the fundamentals of drug use among humans, this chapter proceeds in its search for instances in which writers of ancient texts perceived some of the people they knew or observed as drunkards or addicts. It appears, as noted, that the concept of addiction (including alcoholism) received full articulation in the 19th century, and that articulation co-occurred with the widespread availability of truly concentrated intoxicants, especially alcohol, opioids, and cocaine. This chapter's narrative focuses on alcohol, because it has the longest documented history of human consumption. In our pursuit of instances where ancient writers attributed chronicity to the observed use of drugs, we also inspect the evidence on opioids since concentrated preparations made it relatively easy to become intoxicated, thereby increasing the likelihood of intoxication in individual users.

EVOLUTIONARY PRECEDENTS

Millennia before the first archaeologically detectable evidence that humankind consumed some plants or plant products to become intoxicated, humans were interacting with biospheres and discovering by accident the plants or plant-derived preparations that made their senses function differently. McGovern's (2003) research, for example, limits the hard evidence of wine and its use and storage to 7000 or 8000 years before the present. Nevertheless, we can assume that humans were exposed to fermented grapes and other fruit long before that. Likewise, across millennia of interaction with plants, paleolithic humans were likely to have tasted of plants, such as the flowers or fruit of datura, that caused them to have a variety of altered nerve functions, perhaps depressant, perhaps stimulant, perhaps hallucinogenic. The fact that humans willingly repeated these exposures tells us that on some very basic level, the human body was ready to process the toxins in wine and other plant material and then derive some kind of benefit from the plants' effect on the nervous system.

An understanding of how humans have come to use plant-derived drugs and how plants have come to produce drugs has emerged as neurobiology and botanical pharmacology have become increasingly sophisticated at the molecular level. The process of knowledge development began in the mid-1990s with the assertion that the concept of "evolutionary novelty" explained human use of plant-derived drugs (e.g., Nesse and Berrige 1997). Later theorists held that plants and animals constantly develop action-and-reaction features involving plant toxins and defenses against those toxins, leaving humans with some of the same defenses originally developed by herbivores millions of years earlier (e.g., Sullivan et al. 2008).

In the former argument, Nesse and Berrige (1997) excluded human beings, at least temporarily, from the influence of evolutionary process in the human response to psychotropic plants, holding that when humans got around to trying some psychoactive plants, they derived reward messages to the brain that bypassed other systems for processing the total effect of the toxins being ingested. In other words, whatever was negative or not useful in the experience of eating opium or chewing coca was essentially over-shadowed by the reinforcement that went straight to the pleasure centers of the mid-brain (Nesse and Berrige 1997). Consequently, humans liked and wanted this experience again, even though it did not really meet full criteria for being beneficial to the human consumer (e.g., providing nourishment or enhancing performance). Once they had discovered the "empty treat" of the drug high, humans began to seek the reward repeatedly.

The latter argument, forwarded by Sullivan, Hagen, and Hammerstein (2008), rests on the fact that plants and animals have been evolving for millennia at counter-purposes—plants developing aversive toxins to put animals off of eating them and animals developing metabolic mechanisms to filter out the plant-derived toxins so they could keep on eating. The characterization of the cytochrome P450 system, which resides in the human liver, but exists in many other animals as well, has fed this particular theory, because it provides strong evidence of the evolutionary universality of animals' internal mechanisms that counteract the effects of plant toxins. Drug plants present an array of alkaloids that often are toxic in high concentrations, but as they occur in plant material, they are not so toxic as to be intolerable to humans equipped with the cytochrome P450 mitigation system. At least that may be true for some humans, as the accumulated evidence on the workings of cytochrome P450 show considerable variation across human populations (Sullivan et al. 2008) regarding what toxins are metabolized and thoroughly excreted. So, for example, Asian populations may respond to the nearly universal plant-derived toxin alcohol differently from European populations, although most human populations have categorized alcohol in the form of fermented beverages as desirable and often a complement to other food.

The cytochrome P450 system aids in processing plant-derived toxins other than alcohol, helping to keep our omnivorous ancestors out of trouble and mitigating the impact of consuming plants that contain drugs or alcohol produced from plants. If we follow the logic of this particular speculative theory to its conclusion, the eventual elaboration of the human nervous system led to circumstances in which the creatures endowed with a complex brain might discover and derive gratification from plant material that did not necessarily nourish them but did make them feel different. If that feeling was pleasant, these creatures were smart enough to seek out ways to repeat it. Although the original authors of these theories did not engage in this level of description, one could imagine our pre-primate ancestors, for example, foraging for leafy vegetables and coming upon a succulent-looking proto-tobacco that had developed an emetic toxin—nicotine—that it contained in sufficient amounts to put our ancestors off by making them nauseous. Some of these ancestors, however, acquired by mutation or other genetic process a modification that enabled them to process modest amounts of nicotine without getting sick, and that allowed continued consumption of the proto-tobacco, which for some reason—perhaps its ability to revive a tired body—improved their survival chances within the species' total population.

Flash forward millions of years, and we find humans somewhat disengaged from the back-and-forth counter-adaptations suggested by Sullivan, Hagen and Hammerstein (2008), but they are a curious species, constantly discovering new components of nature's bounty and testing for nutritional or other value. As fully developed *Homo sapiens sapiens,* they now have brains that are so elaborately developed that they value far more than whether or not a plant material alleviates hunger and provides nourishment. A human may prize a plant or plant product if it makes him/her feel different—perhaps more energetic or somnolent, or if it alleviates pain. The combination of curiosity, the aptitude to store in their cultural warehouse vast amounts of environmental information, the capacity to appreciate a wide variety of effects associated with consumption, and the physiologic equipment to process safely a wide range of the toxins that may be involved makes the contemporary human being (i.e., anybody born after 20,000 BCE) the ideal explorer of plants and what they have to offer. These features of humanity also made it inevitable that the vast majority would discover something in their local environments to alter their consciousness and incorporate into cultural traditions. And this is precisely what occurred in global history.

Left out of this anthropocentric explanation is recognition that what appears to be nonhuman animal consumption of plants that contribute to what appear to be altered physiological states and states of consciousness (Huffman 2003). It is well known, for example, that cats are highly attracted to the valerian plant (*Valeriana officinalis*) and catnip (*Nepeta cataria*). Sniffing and consuming these plants appears to push cats into a state of observable satisfaction. Similarly, cattle will readily eat plants that contain alkaloids that seem to have a narcotic effect (Dudley 2002). Additionally, birds and various other animals have been observed seeking out and consuming highly fermented fruit and afterward showing signs of being drunk, such as stumbling and acting as if they are noticeably under the influence. All of these behaviors suggest that many species in addition to humans have long evolutionary histories consuming plants with psychoactive properties. In the assessment of ethnopharmacologist Ronald Siegel (2005:10), "ethnological and laboratory studies ... and analyses of social and biological history, suggest that the pursuit of intoxication with drugs is a primary motivational force in the behavior of organisms." Siegel labels this behavior "the fourth drive" in a list that includes the biologically based motivators of hunger, thirst, and sex. As this discussion suggests, human involvement with psychotropic plants builds on and constitutes a set of cultural elaborations of more broadly shared and evolutionarily far older behavioral patterns in diverse species.

HUMANKIND AND INTOXICATION

Wine and its consumption provide good starting points for discussing the beginnings of human intoxication because humankind has a documented continuous history of drinking wine and getting drunk from its effects that spans all of recorded history and reaches back into the realm of oral history that preceded it. This background story of wine and its consumption provides useful material on the formation of ancient peoples' attitudes about intoxication and altered states of consciousness.

Because the receptacles used by Paleolithic hunter-gatherers were likely to be made of organic material, such as animal skin and/or reed basketry, archaeologists hold out little hope of finding conclusive evidence of the very earliest instances of humans' consumption of fermented grapes, or proto-wine, which might easily have occurred over 10,000 years ago, given the climate shifts associated with the recession of the last Ice Age (McGovern 2003: 8). The availability of the fruit, Vitis vinifera sylvestris, that is ancestral to the grapes used in contemporary winemaking occurred in several different sites in what we now call the Middle East. Archaeologists have been able to find apparent wine residues in ancient pottery, pointing to the presence in ancient parts of contemporary Georgia, Turkey, and Iraq of traditions of wine production (McGovern 2003: 40–42) possibly as early as 8,000 years ago, but at least 7,000 years ago.[1]

The presence of this potentially intoxicating and addictive drink, however, did not necessarily lead to the establishment of a sub-population of consumers identified as problematic by the rest of their group. Rather, the ancients expressed a caution about wine's effects when drunk to excess (Grivetti 1995:10). In ancient India, China, and Egypt, physicians and men regarded as wise consistently expressed ambivalent opinions about the consumption of wine. The Ayurvedic physicians of India (ca.1400 BCE) were aware of wine's benefits, attributing, among other things, exhilaration, nourishment, and freedom from fear, grief, or fatigue to its consumption (Grivetti 1995). They also recognized a downside to wine drinking in excess:

One who saturates himself excessively with . . . fresh wine . . . and at the same time abstains from physical movements including day-sleep, suffers from diseases . . . such as diabetic boils, urticarial patches, itching, anemia, fever, leprosy, anorexia, drowsiness, impotency, over-obesity, disorders of consciousness, sleepiness, swelling, and other disorders (Grivetti 1995:10).

Despite the subtext of wine drinking as a chronic condition, however, they did not pathologize excessive drinking to the point of giving this behavior a separate name. That name did not enter the literature on alcohol consumption until the middle of the 19th century, when Magnus Huss wrote about alcoholism (Phillips 2000: 271). During the 3,300 years after the Ayurvedic writers recorded their opinions about wine, philosophers and physicians made various observations about the effect of wine drinking. Egyptians warned against wine's duality, noting that while it made the drinker feel good, its consumption in excess could lead to unacceptable behavior (Grivetti 1995:11). Similarly, Hippocrates noted wine's positive effects, going so far as to include wine in some of his remedies, even what sounds like a wine diet: "It is better to be full of wine than full of food." (Grivetti 1995:12) Nevertheless, he also recognized the potential harm of drinking wine in excess. Throughout the ancients' musings on wine and its influence, a pattern of duality emerges in which wine in moderation is seen as beneficial, and wine in excess is seen as harmful, or at least embarrassing. With the exception of the Ayurvedic physicians, however, the ancients' discussions focused on the acute intoxicating effects of wine, not on the long-term effect of addiction. We should also note that the ancient Egyptians, Greeks, and Romans almost always diluted wine with water, making the task of achieving an intoxicating dose more difficult than if it were consumed neat, or without dilution. Depending on how much water was added to the wine, the resulting drink may have had the rough equivalent of the proportion of alcohol found in beer (4–8 percent by volume).

Were there no people labeled as chronic drunks in the ancient world? If there were, the available literature does not tell us much about them. Perhaps they did not congregate in easily recognizable locales, such as present-day Seattle's Skid Road, New York's Bowery, or Miami's overpasses. Among the Greeks and Romans, in the writings of Plato about the Greek *symposium* and Plutarch and others on the Roman equivalent *convivium* there was a sense that the participants were not drunkards but men who intended to drink on the occasion of one of these gatherings (Standage 2005:78). Still, even in the passages describing people given to excess drink, it appears that the ancient writers focused not on chronicity so much as on the harm that excessive drinking sessions do to the drinker. For example, in Plato's *Symposium*, one participant suggests that after the previous night's excesses the group might adopt a drinking policy:

> … [T]hey were about to commence drinking, when Pausanias said, "And now, my friends, how can we drink with least injury to ourselves? I can assure you that I feel severely the effect of yesterday's potations, and must have time to recover; and I suspect that most of you are in the same predicament, for you were of the party yesterday. Consider then: How can the drinking be made easiest?" (MIT Classics 2011).

Pausanias wanted not a reprise of the previous night's excesses, but to establish some principles by means of which the same group who were drunk the previous night would drink but avoid excess on the night at hand. Ancient texts repeatedly give the reader the sense that each drunken occasion was to the participants and witnesses more significant than the frequency of these occasions.

Saint Augustine's writings on the subject of drunkenness (cf. Cook 2006:52–56) indicate that early Christian philosophy regarding intoxication with alcoholic beverages deplored drunkenness as a sin of the flesh that led to other fleshly sins, such as lust and gluttony. Again, Augustine emphasized the acute state of drunkenness as undesirable, especially as a result of consuming excessive wine in the context of Christian ritual. Apparently, he never made reference to drunkards, or chronically impaired drinkers.

Burton ([1621] 2000) provided some of the first indications that alcohol had a relationship with ongoing problems, and he asserted, somewhat incorrectly according to Abel (1999), that the ancients had identified "drunkards," or people given to excessive wine drinking. Informed by more accurate translation than that used by Burton, Abel indicates that, consistent with other information on the ancients' perceptions of wine and its consumption, the ancients' emphasis remained on the drunken episode rather than a chronic condition. The use of flawed translations may help explain why Keller (1979) so forcefully asserted in his overview of alcohol and alcoholism that the ancients understood alcoholism, but perhaps more influential in his interpretation of the ancients' writings about alcohol was his strong belief that alcoholism existed. Examples used by Keller to illustrate the ancients' concept of alcoholism (e.g., the fall from a rooftop of Odysseus's companion, Epenore, or a Greek eulogist's friend falling down) actually describe acute bouts of intoxication and their consequences, not chronic conditions of drunkenness.

Health and social ills associated with drinking alcoholic beverages appeared emphatically in William Hogarth's "Gin Lane" engraving released in 1751 (Rodin 1981:1238). The "gin mania" that swept the poor neighborhoods of London beginning about 1715 led to the development of patterned habitual drunkenness, abuse of families, and neglect and mistreatment of children. This response to high availability of gin was not lost on Hogarth, who sardonically depicted the alleged effects of that liquor on the poor people of London, including, it appears, facial deformities consistent with fetal alcohol syndrome. Even if the face of the poor baby being dropped to his death in that famous etching was only a product of Hogarth's outstanding observational acumen rather than any understanding of how the mother's drinking caused the baby's face to be misshapen, this point in Western history, one hundred years prior to Huss's introduction of the concept of alcoholism, marks the spot when alcohol use gained recognition in the West for its long-term consequences. If we also examine the social and economic conditions that produced Gin Lane, we find England making a transition to industrial capitalism with no constraints on the treatment of workers. Poor pay, squalid and overcrowded living conditions, and inter-class prejudice made the lives of people living in London's tenements sufficiently grim to warrant the consumption of very strong drink. A question raised by this development was how did the dominant sectors in society accept the increasingly inhuman conditions suffered by their fellow citizens? This question is fundamental to the purpose of this book as the Othering of the poor, expressed in the condemnation of their drug-using behaviors, served to justify their suffering as something they brought on themselves.

The beverage implicated in "gin lane" was qualitatively different from the wine and beer available to steady English drinkers before the introduction of distilled spirits by the Dutch in the seventeenth century (Fleming 1975). Whereas beer and wine provided the drinker with between four

Gin Lane (by William Hogarth, 1751)

and fourteen percent alcohol by volume, gin provided 40 percent, a truly efficient means of becoming intoxicated. Harkening back to the cytochrome P450 "shield" afforded by the herbivore forebears mentioned earlier, the availability of gin led to unprecedented stress on that system for processing alcohol in the liver. It is not surprising that astute observers such as Hogarth noticed poor health outcomes among the consumers of gin in his native England. He also contrasted gin lane with "beer street" in a second etching,

Beer Street (by William Hogarth, 1751)

showing prosperity, good health, and no endangered children in that illustration. In the relatively narrow span of 170 years, the bad reputation of distilled liquor, including blame for the dissolution of families, maltreatment of women and children, and ruination of personal finances had grown to the point where large numbers of people, particularly women, found the consumption of "hard" liquor intolerable and worthy of being eradicated. In fact, the time from when Magnus Huss gave a name to the condition of chronic drunk to the time when the United States ratified its 18th amendment prohibiting sale or production of alcoholic beverages only spanned 69 years, an astonishingly brief period in which a whole country (or at least two-thirds of the states) enacted prohibition of a widespread behavior. Given the rapidity with which it occurred after their introduction, one wonders if distilled spirits had not been invented and distributed whether prohibition would have happened at all.

OTHER DRUGS AND INTOXICATION

This question becomes a recurring theme as we examine the histories of other drugs in the human pharmacopoeia: Does the "refinement" of a drug's active ingredients always result in severe impact on the users? The beginnings of addiction as a concept appear to correspond in some cases to the refinement of certain basic drugs, including alcohol and tobacco, but the first important refinement of opioids, laudanum, pre-dates its acquiring a reputation for generating addicts by about three centuries. Paracelsus is credited with inventing this opium-based mixture in the early sixteenth century (Ball 2006), but use of opioid preparations in medicine can be traced to ancient Mesopotamia (Scarborough 2010:vii–4). The Greeks and Romans, including Hippocrates, Dioscorides, Nicander, Celsus, and Pliny all included opium in larger works that described various sectors of the ancient pharmacopoeia of their respective eras (Scarborough 2010:vii–5). Although the ancients apparently recognized the danger of poisoning from opium, and had fairly sophisticated methods for rendering it consumable, they did not report non-medical use of the drug. In England, as with distilled alcohol, public consciousness of laudanum as a problem lagged far behind its development as medicine. Thomas de Quincey's *Confessions of an English Opium Eater*, published in 1822, acknowledged that there were people in English society who had become habituated to a tincture of opium also called laudanum, but not the same as Paracelsus' formulation (Ball 2006:182-183), notably including some literati, as discussed in Chapter 4.

The production of the opium-alcohol tincture laudanum is credited to the British physician Thomas Sydenham (Davenport-Hines 2002:184). To make it, he prepared a concentration of the morphine alkaloid that was 25 times as potent as paregoric, achieving a potential for intoxication not possible through use of raw opium or other preparations available in the early 19th century. The fact that its invention did not engender a rapid rise in the number of impaired users is somewhat puzzling, considering the English response to gin and the uptake of cocaine in Europe within a couple of decades of the introduction of these concentrated drugs. Perhaps because laudanum's principal uses as anti-diarrhea and analgesic medicines, rather than pleasure-giving purposes, dominated medical applications, it simply did not occur to the recipients of laudanum in medical contexts to use the drug for anything other than alleviating symptoms. Concentrated alcohol in the form of rum or gin or brandy, on the other hand, went straight to the streets as a handy mitigation of stress and as a welcomed social lubricant. Despite its restricted medical pattern of use, potential addicts eventually "discovered" laudanum, although its heavy consumption never became as widespread as distilled ethyl alcohol.

THE "BIG FIVE" AND THEIR TRANSFORMATION INTO MORE DANGEROUS FORMS

The 19th century in Europe and the United States appears to have brought about a convergence of potent drug preparations which led ultimately to the development of the poly-drug configuration seen in present-day drug issues. In their concentrated forms, each presented new challenges to the metabolic capacities of their consumers, sometimes also producing patterns of highly recidivistic use. Five drugs in particular—alcohol, tobacco, opioids, cocaine, and cannabis became the principal components of Western drug consumption,[2] and all became, deservedly or not, associated with problems in the lives of their users. Each drug had a unique pathway toward widespread use and engendering problems among users. The following sections offer summaries of those pathways:

Alcohol. Distillation as a physical principle in the management of fluids was probably known to humans in the present-day Middle East as early as 1,100 years ago, but as noted earlier, its use in the production of preparations for general consumption did not become prevalent in Europe until sometime in the 17th century (Standage 2005: 94–95). Refinement of fermented liquids derived from sugar cane or grain became widespread as commerce with the West Indies and the rest of the world developed in Europe. Rum in particular became a currency in international trade with which slave traders plied their commerce in human misery and the British Empire compensated its sailors for services rendered and/or imposed. The New World bustled with activity in the invention, manufacture, distribution, and consumption of distilled beverages, including the sour mash concoctions of southern North America, rye whiskey in the north of that continent, and eventually, tequila in Mexico. The impact of their popularity, especially among males in the US populations, included the profusion of drinking houses, often called "saloons," and burgeoning social problems related to drunkenness that plagued the saloons' customers. The temperance movement in the United States was aimed at preventing the consequences of addiction to the powerful alcohol preparations sold in such establishments.

Tobacco. Nicotine is such a powerful drug that its dosage had to be reduced to make it a truly effective and heavily consumed commodity. The most widely used tobacco before the 19th century was in powdered form (snuff) as well as cut tobacco (which could be smoked in pipes, cigars, or hand-rolled cigarettes). Inhalation of pipe tobacco or cigars delivers such a jolt of nicotine that it induces nausea and dizziness. Hand rolling of small quantities of "mild" tobaccos into cigarettes required skill and patience that not many consumers had. In Spain in 1804, the introduction of hand-rolled "papeletes" constituted a first step in the eventual mass-production of ready-made tubes of cut tobacco from which smoke could be inhaled into the lungs, delivering a substantial dose of nicotine without dizzying toxic effects (Goodman 1993:90–99). These little vehicles of nicotine delivery could be carried around easily and consumed anywhere, and they were inexpensive enough to be used all the time. As the numbers of cigarette smokers grew and began in the 20th century to live long enough to incur cigarette-related illness, it became clear by 1964 that this product generated the most addictive tobacco consumption and the greatest hazard to the public health of any known drug.

Opioids. Opium, as we noted earlier, has been in the pharmacopoeia, beginning with people in the Fertile Crescent, for thousands of years, usually consumed as medicine for the treatment of pain, nausea, and diarrhea. It was a valuable medicine that could be used in very small quantities to treat patients for pain, coughing, or nausea. The introduction of water soluble preparations, including morphine sulfate and diacetyl morphine (heroin) in the 19th and 20th centuries eventually led to more widespread consumption of opioids (Musto 1987:1–3; Davenport-Hines 2002:184–187). Recently, nonmedical use of opioid analgesics of the next generation has emerged as a drug-use pattern of choice in many parts of the United States. Most prominent among these prescription preparations is Oxycontin, which is the brand name for a time-release version of the semi-synthetic preparation oxycodone, which in certain parts of the United States, has become popular and also dangerous, dominating emergency department statistics on accidental overdose.

Cannabis. Diffusion of this drug plant into the rest of the world traveled on two different historical tracks: (1) usage other than as a drug, and (2) use as a mind-altering drug. The former is apparently the more ancient, with some evidence of cannabis being used for food and fiber among the Chinese at least 3,500 years before the common era (BCE) (Booth 2003:17) The plant's long, pliant fibers constitute useful material for manufacturing cordage and clothing, and its fatty seeds are highly nutritious and totally devoid of the tetrahydrocannabinol that is the most pharmacologically active alkaloid in the plant. Almost as soon as the Spanish arrived in the New World, they attempted to encourage the planting of cannabis in most colonies (called Cáñamo). By the mid-sixteenth century, some cannabis plantations could be found as far south as Chile and as far north as Mexico (Carter et al. 1980:12). Nevertheless, in the New World, little evidence testifies to any form of cannabis use for mind-altering purposes until the 19th century. For psychotropic uses of cannabis, there was a different path, originating in India and traveling west into North Africa and Spain as the followers of Mohammed dominated the 8th through the 15th centuries in that part of the world. Reasons why it did not filter into Europe until the 19th century and never really became established in China are subject to conjecture, but alternative theories lack historical evidence. The European crusaders of the 11th through 13th centuries, despite the fact that many lived for extended periods in the "Holy Land" in the presence of hashish-smoking people, did not bring cannabis back to Europe with them. French soldiers under Napoleon, on the other hand, did. The wholesale shipping of indentured servants from India to Jamaica and Trinidad-Tobago provided another putative pathway for cannabis to enter the Western Hemisphere. Coming from an ancient tradition of cannabis use, the East Indians who were transferred to the West Indies likely brought their ganja with them, and, while they lived alongside African-descended populations, these immigrants imparted their patterns of drug consumption to their neighbors. All of the process described above is murky, because historians rarely attended to drug-using patterns of the poor and/or the populations of color. Nevertheless, by the beginning of the 20th century, the lands surrounding the Caribbean and the Gulf of Mexico were epicenters of diffusion of cannabis use into North America. Regarding potency of the preparations consumed, there was relatively little change between 800 and 1975, with a range of cannabis preparations' potency from bhang (drink made with bottom leaves of the plant) to ganja (tops and flowers of the female plant) to charas, or hashish (collected resin rich in THC). The latter form varied between 10 and 15 percent THC by weight. After 1975, as a broad market had been established, astute growers began to increase the THC content of cannabis through manipulation of hybrid strains and strategies to avoid formation of seeds (sinsemilla), edging the percentage of THC into content as high as 20 percent. It is uncertain whether this increase in potency has affected cannabis users in ways analogous to the apparent impact of distilled spirits, laudanum, and cocaine hydrochloride.

Coca/cocaine. As early as 1800 BCE, natives of South America were cultivating coca. The plant had attracted their attention because someone had discovered that chewing its leaves gave feelings of well-being and satiation (Carter and Mamani 1986:69–70). That pattern of coca consumption spread throughout the Andes region, so that it was pervasive among mountain-dwelling people at the time of the Spanish conquest. The Spanish colonial administrators regarded coca chewing as a nasty habit of benighted indigenous people (Burchard 1976, 1992) but the behavior attracted the attention of European tourists who, upon noticing the strength, endurance, and energy of Aymara- and Quechua-speaking natives of the Andes in surroundings of high altitude, asked how they were able to function so well in the thin mountain air. The natives replied that coca enabled them to do these things. European chemists set about trying to discover what chemicals in the coca leaf might be pharmacologically active enough to cause the energy and strength they had observed. They were looking for the pharmacologically most active of the component compounds in the coca leaf, and they found one that was highly active and named it cocaine. In order to make this compound more readily useful as an ingredient in medicines, the chemists who isolated cocaine added a hydrochloride radical to make the alkaloid water soluble. Cocaine hydrochloride became a pervasive ingredient in the European and North American pharmacopoeias, primarily in energizing elixirs. It also became useful as a local anesthetic for facial surgery. Before long, large numbers of North American housewives were addicted to the elixirs. Freud had briefly endorsed the drug as a treatment for depression and later re-canted. The short half-life of its acute effects and the spiraling patterns that its use engenders have caused various cocaine epidemics to wax and wane over the century-and-a-half that this drug has been available. Between 2009 and 2011 it again was object of a surge in popularity in both Europe and the United States among youth who came of age in the 21st Century.

In addition to the Big Five drugs mentioned above, methamphetamine emerged as a drug of choice in certain parts of the United States by the be - ginning of the 21st Century. It has a much shorter history than any of the big five, being isolated in 1893 and scheduled in 1944 as a pharmaceutical drug in the United States, specific for narcolepsy and exogenous obesity. Methamphetamine use as a recreational drug became pervasive in parts of the North American Midwest, West, and Southeast by the year 2000. In 2008, methamphetamine was about 6 percent of the drugs mentioned in emergency-department presentations that involved drugs (DAWN 2009). This figure places methamphetamine ahead of all other drugs in the second tier of drugs (those not part of the Big Five). Its potential for engendering addiction gained recognition during the 1960s, if not earlier. Along with its close relative, amphetamine, methamphetamine developed a following of devotees who earned a separate designation: "speed freaks" which gained common usage by the late 1960s. The people known to use these highly active stimulants acquired a reputation for obsessive, repetitive use of their drugs of choice, by any ingestion route possible, although the injection route appeared to be especially favored. The gloss that denoted this kind of drug user carried clear implications of ongoing use and extreme disruption of normal behavior patterns.

We cannot achieve the same precision in defining exactly when the drugs included in the Big Five (or Six) became associated specifically with a separate kind of human being involved in the obsessive pursuit of that particular drug. That, however, is exactly the kind of question that this chapter, and more broadly, this book seeks to answer. How and when did some human beings come to define a set of human beings as Others based on their long-term, regular consumption of a specific drug? In the preceding discussion, the evidence suggests that a concept of "addict" or "(fill in the addictive drug or activity)-holic" is not very old in the total history of humankind, perhaps as little as 200-years old, a phenomenon we here label *social externalization*. It is based on the identification of people within a social body who are defined on the basis of their use of drugs (or participation in other disapproved activities) as inherently different and as threatening and their subjection to rituals of social rejection and attacks on their social worth. In the case of drug-related addiction, the concept appears to be related to the refinement of drug preparations into highly concentrated forms capable of engendering craving and compulsive use. All of these developments seem to converge during the 19th century, so that, by 1900, it was possible to be recognized by your fellow human beings as an alcoholic or a person addicted to morphine and/or cocaine. At that time, tobacco cigarettes were gaining popularity and were on the verge of being mass manufactured by machines and promoted by governments and what were soon to be very wealthy national and transnational corporations (Singer 2008). Although some evidence indicates that people in North America and Western Europe began to recognize the addictive potential of tobacco long before the introduction of ready-made cigarettes (Goodman 1993), cigarettes became the most convenient method for ingesting nicotine and ultimately, the most deadly.

The most-refined forms of cannabis, charas and hashish, were already ancient by 1800, but were not well known outside of India and the Middle East. Cannabis did, however, migrate to Europe and the New World in the 19th century, eventually diffusing in a limited way from migration focal points in France and Jamaica, respectively. Those who took up cannabis use in France included the veterans of Napoleon's invasion of Egypt and eventually members of the literati, such as Dumas and Baudelaire (1971:70–71). In the case of Indian ganja and its migration to the Caribbean there is no evidence of any preparations other than teas, infusions (that were not mind altering but medicinal), and smokable plant material in any of the 19th century accounts of cannabis use in the New World. Ethnographic accounts of ganja use in Jamaica (cf. Dreher 1982; Rubin and Comitas 1975) report no forms of cannabis use other than either boiling or smoking the plant's leaves, tops, and flowers. Some evidence of a recent trend may appear in the statistics on drug-treatment presentations, in which cannabis is a leading drug of choice in the self-reports of new treatment patients (Schensul et al. 2000). Skepticism may be appropriate in interpreting these figures, however, because of the young (14–17) age of the presenting patients and the fact that they often are referred to treatment by their parents or their schools.

Regardless of the degree to which people who present for treatment of problems related to cannabis use can be assessed as addicts, it is clear that this particular drug did not develop as strong a reputation for causing drug-related problems as did alcohol, opioids, and cocaine during a key period of Western history between 1700 and 1900. In fact, cannabis was essentially absent from discussions of drug-induced impairment as the reputations for addictive problems of the other three were growing most rapidly. In Western Europe, Baudelaire's coterie hardly elicited a response other than bemusement at the outlandish reports of intoxicated experiences that they produced. Emerging news of "soldiers' disease," afflicting thousands of veterans who sustained war wounds in 19th-century wars, the widely read "confessions" by DeQuincey describing the life trajectory of an addict, and reports of cocaine-addicted housewives in the United States attracted much more public attention than a handful of French bohemians' dabbling in cannabis use. In fact, there has developed a certain degree of social expectation that artists and intellectuals will engage in borderline behaviors without suffering the full weight of opprobrium to which others are subjected, especially if they come from subordinated social classes. To a degree, it appears, they are allowed to walk on the wild side as a means of providing vicarious pleasure to the constrained masses.

Human susceptibility to habituation or addiction remains something of an enigma, yet it is highly relevant to the question of how people come to be perceived as addicts. Why are people affected so variously by the consumption of the drugs? Most people who ever use alcohol or opioids or cocaine do not become alcoholics or addicts, but some do. What sets those who do apart from those who do not? Ming Tsuang and colleagues (1998) attempted to investigate this question from the point of view afforded by the sector of behavioral genetics known as twin studies. Using data collected from 7,500 male twin pairs, this investigative team set out to determine how much of the potential to have problems with drugs involved heredity. Not surprisingly, they found that they could explain about half of the variance in the presence or absence of drug-related problems in terms of genetic background and half in terms of environment. This result was not surprising because studies going back to Vaillant (1983) have found more or less the same thing. For the present discussion, however, the more interesting part of Tsuang et al.'s findings is that the genetic component characterized by their studies was generic in terms of the addict's or problem user's drug of choice. In other words, people with exactly the same genetic makeup (i.e., monozygotic, or "identical" twins) could develop problematic use of any or all of the Big Five drugs in any configuration (e.g., cigarettes, alcohol, and cocaine, or marihuana, tobacco, and heroin). Social environment was found to influence specific drug choices, but genetic makeup helped determine whether or not the individual would have problems with his drugs of choice (Tsuang et al. 1998). In this sense, then, the addict or problematic drug user is in fact qualitatively unlike his/ her contemporaries in terms of genetic makeup, which in part causes him/ her to respond to psychotropic drugs differently, namely more intensely. If certain drug preparations were modified to deliver their key mind-altering ingredients (e.g., ethanol, morphine, or cocaine) in more concentrated form than they had ever done in the history of their use by humans, that concentration in combination with a genetic predisposition to feel that concentration intensely would be likely to produce a reaction beyond what had been possible previously. Tsuang et al. suggest that a subset of humans have the predisposition to feel drugs—any of the Big Five—more forcefully than the rest of us. The introduction of highly potent forms of the Big Five would have a high likelihood of matching drug consumption with this kind of predisposition.

Again, the biological part of the analysis only explains half of the variance (and, it should be noted, none of the social reaction to heavy drug use). Environmental factors explain the other half. Exposure to cultural contexts in which potent drugs are used is a crucial variable in the establishment of addictive patterns, especially if the use pattern itself is highly frequent and heavy. Clearly, inner-city London was such an environment by 1750. Harlem in the 1960s was also, as was East Harlem of the 1980s. In each of these places—and socially defined place is hence an important issue—people internalized a vague cultural idea that they were equal with everyone else in society, but yet their daily experiences in interaction with other people told them that they were in fact unequal and did not count. They received poor wages for hard work and had few prospects of transcending their social place because of clogged opportunity structures. In these conditions of social derogation, resorting to strong drink or potent drugs could be seen as a strategy to get through inevitably unpleasant days and self-recriminating nights. Adoption of heavy, chronic patterns of consuming cheap, abundant drugs became widespread, and the proliferation of heavy users invited generalizations about the nature of the drug-using population at large. Given the recently achieved potency of the drugs of choice, by the late 1800s, the stage was set for the identification of addicts, especially poor addicts, but to a certain extent all addicts as separate subpar categories of human being.

NOTES

1 Nothing of that antiquity has been found so far in the New World—probably because there were no fruits quite as sugar-laden as *Vitis vinifera sylvestris.* Corn and Agave were early contributors to the production of fermented beverages, but the evidence of their domestication is much later (ca. 1500 BCE, compared with 5000–6000 BCE for the Old World). The evidence also depends on residues in stone or clay containers, which appear later in the New World than the Old. In all likelihood humans discovered plant-derived preparations of some kind much earlier than the evidence for corn and agave would testify, but the accoutrements of these preparations left no trace from which to infer use.

2 Because they are 20th century drugs without the same historical background of being associated with problems of chronic use and addiction, we have not included LSD or methamphetamine in this group. By the time those drugs were synthesized and introduced into consumption, the concept of addiction was already well established. Otherwise, methamphetamine certainly would be a candidate for inclusion, based on its accelerating reputation as an addictive drug. LSD, on the other hand, is not really associated with addiction at all.

Crack in the News

This depiction of the female crack addict does not often appear in the news. Rather, according to Reeves and Campbell (1994), she has appeared within the context of an antifeminist and anti-social-welfare backlash that targets out-of-work people of color in the inner city and draws upon the myth of the Black matriarch "as the irrational nurturer of chaos" and the welfare mother as too dependent (p. 99). The journalistic view of crack mothers, they claimed, "often reduced women to their reproductive identities" (p. 192) while drawing on a hybrid of Collins's (1991) four controlling images of women – the mammy, matriarch, welfare mother and Jezebel. The result is "a composite 'she-devil'" fusing the image of the welfare mother with the sexually aggressive Jezebel who presents a particularly menacing image of Black fertility personified by out-of-control sexuality (Reeves and Campbell, 1994, p. 213). Berated "as an enemy to the innocent life within," the crack mother was demonized as a monster while her children, the crack babies, were demonized as future delinquents and a burden on society (Reeves and Campbell, 1994, p. 208). The news linked a so-called "epidemic" of crack babies to a "'poverty of values' crippling America's largely black inner cities" (Reeves and Campbell, 1994, p. 209).

This view is consistent with that of critical cultural studies scholars, who emphasize that the news represents the interests of a ruling elite within a hierarchy of competing social formations. By presenting the views, values and opinions of those in power as natural, commonsensical and inevitable, the news builds consensus around this "dominant ideology" so that it appears grounded in everyday reality. For example, Hall et al. (1978) found that media portrayals of racial violence tend to legitimate the criminal justice system, building support for a law-and-order state while simultaneously portraying Black youth as a threat to social order.

The representation of African Americans – adults as well as youths – as criminals, a common theme within the news, does the ideological work of supporting the dominant power structure (Campbell, 1995; Campbell, LeDuff, Jenkins and Brown, 2012; Dixon, 2006a, 2006b, 2008b, 2011; Entman, 1990, 1992, 1994; Entman and Rojecki, 2000; Ferguson, 1998). As part of this work, the news creates and sustains "moral panics" through the portrayal of certain groups and activities as tearing at the fabric of an orderly and lawful society. Moral panics are characterized by copious news coverage of the group or activity in question, followed by public outcry, increased law enforcement activity, political posturing and policy formation. Cohen (1972), who pioneered the concept of moral panics in his study of British Mods and Rockers during the 1960s, found they were portrayed in the news as folk devils whose activities inevitably would lead to disaster. Young Black males also have been targeted for moral panics (Hall et al., 1978), as have "sex fiends" and "drug scares," the latter of which involves a period during which numerous social problems, such as crime, illness and educational failure, are blamed on a chemical substance (Reinarman and Levine, 1997).

Crack surfaced as a drug scare in the 1980s. According to Potter and Kappeler (1998) news magazines, television and newspapers, in particular, worked with the state to create a moral panic around crack use as a means of continuing and extending the Reagan administration's "war on drugs" (pp. 8–9). Reeves and Campbell (1994) similarly claimed news coverage of the war on drugs was co-opted by the Reagan administration. While they blamed TV journalism "for its role in legitimating a reactionary political agenda in its knee-jerk support of the war on drugs," they concluded that the primary culprit was "the New Right operating under the banner of Reaganism" (p. 2). Drug experts and journalists:

> benefited personally and professionally from producing a series of moral panics that centered on "controlling" crack and its users: journalistic recruitment in the anticocaine crusade was absolutely crucial to converting the war on drugs into a political spectacle that depicted social problems grounded on economic transformations as individual moral or behavioral problems that could be remedied by simply embracing family values, modifying bad habits, policing mean streets, and incarcerating the fiendish enemies within.
>
> (p. 3)

The construction of the crack scare linked crack cocaine use to inner-city Blacks, Hispanics and youths, all of whom had been the previous targets of moral panics. Potter and Kappeler (1998) pointed out that during the 1970s, when an expensive form of powdered cocaine was popular among affluent Whites, "both the media and the state focused their attention on heroin, seen as the drug of the inner-city poor" (p. 9). It was only when cocaine became available in the inexpensive form of crack, they added, that "the scapegoating common to drug scares" began, starting in 1986 with media hype that contained highly inflated estimates of crack use and dire warnings of impending disaster from a crack epidemic (p. 9). In fact, crack use, having peaked four years earlier, was declining at the time, and media reports about its highly addictive nature and related health dangers were widely exaggerated. Nevertheless, new laws were created to increase prison sentences for crack use and sale.

Potter and Kappeler (1998) claimed that this link between race and cocaine is not accidental: "Starting with the crack panic of the 1980s, both the state and the media have gone to extraordinary lengths to tie illicit drug use to African Americans while ignoring heavy drug use among affluent whites" (p. 13). They add that false beliefs about crime "play a disproportionate role in the formulation of government and law enforcement policies" (p. 12), diverting "attention away from the social and cultural forces that cause crime to individual pathologies: they reinforce stereotypes of minorities, poor people, and people who are 'different'" (p. 15).

However, even when the news attempts to present a compassionate, positive portrayal of minority communities, it is unable to evade the negative stereotypes that accompany "'dysfunctional' social activities, such as crime, drugs and out-of-wedlock births" (Parisi, 1998b, p. 239). Particularly problematic is the narrative convention of personalization, which draws on individual profiles and anecdotes. As Parisi (1998b) noted, when the fragmented stories of individuals are presented as sufficient to explain life, society becomes defined as "an aggregate of separate individualities" divorced from social, political and economic realities (p. 242). When combined with social problems such as drugs and crime, personalization encourages racist stereotyping by treating individuals "as objects, who embody social problems, rather than subjects and centers for consciousness" (p. 242).

In constructing cocaine use as either a criminal pathology or moral disease, the user becomes a "super deviant" whose demographic profile on the evening news is "predominantly black or Latino, young, male, poor, and isolated in the inner city" (Reeves and Campbell, 1994, p. 26). The news created and legitimated Reagan's war on drugs from 1981 to 1988 as a political spectacle in three phases of coverage, during which the cocaine narrative told by the news changed "from a white, upper- and middle-class addiction tale to a black, inner-city horror story" (Reeves and Campbell, 1994, p. 64) and from a therapeutic narrative to a pathologic/criminal narrative as it shifted emphasis from class to race and from White people to people of color. During the first phase, which centered on the drug's use by the White middle class, these offenders were offered therapeutic intercession. The second phase focused on race and class to evoke images of urban chaos. During the third phase, the war on drugs became a major issue in the 1988 presidential campaign.

Reeves and Campbell (1994) also found that the cocaine narrative involved four major social types: (1) primary definers of the problem – the experts and authorities in law enforcement or drug recovery; (2) transgressors, consisting of private citizens, who can be rehabilitated, and delinquents, who are beyond redemption; (3) representatives of common sense – the private citizens' or on-the-street voice of consensus; and (4) well-informed journalists. Over the course of the three phases of their study, the chief definers changed from the treatment industry to law enforcement and politics; increasingly, transgressors were defined as people of color. In addition, Reeves and Campbell pointed out that the narrative was created by reporters and news sources who were "overwhelmingly male" (p. 64).

Beginning in 1987, Reeves and Campbell (1994) noted, a kind of revisionist coverage drawing on a fatalistic "discourse of doom" rehumanized cocaine transgressors as tragic victims "of the 'slings and arrows of outrageous fortune' whose 'fate' is to make bad choices and pay the consequences" (p. 233). This discourse ignores the inequality of material and social resources that provide a breeding ground for the desperate conditions that encourage drug use.

So What Is the Answer?

It is clear that we will never truly know "why" these events have happened. The people who can answer such a question are not here. The Virginia Tech shooter, Cho, left a detailed manifesto in which he rambled on about his disdain for wealthy kids and hedonism (Schildkraut 2012b). For Columbine, there potentially is a similarly documented response straight from the killers. These tapes, infamously dubbed "The Basement Tapes," have been sealed from the public and won't be released until 2026 (at the earliest) out of fear of copycat attacks (Schildkraut 2012b). So until we can hear it straight from the killers' mouths, we are left to speculate as to their motive. Sandy Hook, however, presents an even greater challenge, as Adam Lanza doesn't appear to have left the same video diary as his predecessors. This gap appears to only fuel the fire of speculation, rather than allowing society to focus elsewhere.

Given the reliance of the public discourse on media reporting of such tragedies, we are perhaps left with more questions than answers regarding the potential causes (and therefore implied remedies) for such cases. Clearly, the three-ring circus of violent media, guns, and mental illness are insufficient, even in combination, to explain the complexity of school massacres. The following quote from an editorial by Maureen Dowd illustrates the ridiculous simplicity of characterizing an event such as Columbine as solely related to gun availability and policies (regardless of whether the argument is that there are too many or too few restrictions on firearms):

> As Jesse Ventura said, if only the concealed weapons law had passed in Colorado, students and teachers secretly packing heat could have cut down those

two outcasts. The problem is not that bad guys have guns; it's that good guys don't. (Dowd 1999)

Similarly, in combination, violent and fantasy media, guns, and uncontrolled rage cannot be fingered as the cause, as illustrated in another quote from Dowd's op-ed:

Just blame Marilyn Manson, Oliver Stone, the Internet, video games, Magic cards, Goths. Here's a good sound bite: Software makes people go nuts, not hardware. Guns don't kill people; trench coats kill people. Guns don't kill people; people who have not reached closure with their anger kill people. (Dowd 1999)

It is not our position simply to point the finger at the news media or politicians, and it is obviously pointless to expect the media industry and political apparatus to disregard the relevance of shocking school massacres. As self-reflective media personnel commented after the Columbine incident, it's impossible for media *not* to cover such cases.

[T]he Sheriff speaks directly with a female reporter at KUSA [unnamed in transcripts] and he suggests that the media coverage sparks the possibility of copycat attacks. "Well, you just wonder how much—when the attention like this media attention gets on it, that this is broadcast all over the United States and other people get the same idea...." The reporter responds, "And the conflict is that you can't not cover it. But then again, you know, the dilemma is that 15 seconds of fame of whatever the motive is." Stone concludes, "Yes, I understand." (Savidge et al. 1999)

Similarly, the public expects its leaders to comment on such cases, and therefore public leaders walk a similar line in their responsibility to step up as leaders and spokespersons for their constituencies, and perhaps also to advance their political agendas. After all, public figures will frequently attempt to connect their agendas rhetorically to the events, an action which capitalizes on the affective intensity of a riveted audience. As John Velleco commented, "Unfortunately, there are going to be politicians who are going to climb over the bodies of the victims and pursue an agenda" (in Brooke 1999). Clearly the news media and politicians are both necessary to the functioning of civil society; however, such cases also make both their necessity and limited nature clear.

Even for academicians, the complex causes of school massacres are extremely difficult to pinpoint, for various reasons. First, there are relatively few cases of school massacres, and therefore it is impossible to identify a set of nomothetic causes from the examination of a small number of cases. Second, in the case studies that have been conducted, the causes seem to vary from case to case. Therefore, no set of causes has been identified as sufficient to produce a school massacre.[7] It is true that the "big three" of violent media, guns, and mental illness often figure into the situation; however, these are insufficient to explain school massacres in themselves. Case in point is the fact that millions of persons may consume violent media, own firearms, and have mental illnesses, often at the same time, yet school massacres are rather rare.

How, then, to clarify the causes of these troubling events? We argue that what is needed is a protracted, extended discourse about school shootings and related massacres, one that explores their cultural meaning and causes. Given the new media's relatively short attention cycle for any specific issue, this examination apparently cannot take place in the news media. In addition, given the wide array of areas on which politicians must comment, it is unrealistic to expect such public figures to spend a long time on violence, as it will always be superseded in short order, with public attention and/or media attention shifted elsewhere.

However, such a slow and protracted exploration of relevant issues is taking place in various scholarly disciplines in the social sciences, education, and humanities (see Muschert 2007a and 2010 for a review). But if such exploration is going on in the academic realms, why does it not then bleed over into the popular, mass-market discourse of news media and politicians? The divide persists more sharply in the United States between the so-called ivory tower and more popular modes of public discourse. In part, the academic discourse in the United States is frequently divorced from the public and political discourse, and academics are rarely professionally rewarded for informing news media and politicians. In short, these parties simply do not converse with one another very frequently, and therefore there is little opportunity for academics to inform journalists and politicians as to their findings and thinking about issues, just as there little chance for the opposite conversation to take place. What is needed in the case of school massacres is a discussion among these parties regarding the complex individual, community-level, and sociocultural causes of school massacres (and violence more generally) (see Henry 2000 and 2009; Muschert 2007a and 2010; Muschert et al. 2014).

Nonetheless, there may be glimmers of hope. Over the last decades, many academic disciplines have taken strides to make their expertise more public, and politicians and policymakers are increasingly insisting on evidence-based policies and/or independent evaluation of policy outcomes. It is our hope that this trend toward sharing information and cross-fertilizing academic, media, and political discourses will continue, especially in the case of mass violence in various locations, including schools. Such an extended and protracted discussion is necessary, because without intelligent and informed analysis of social problems such as school violence, policies may be ineffective (or even counterproductive) in preventing and mitigating the issue, without which we are in danger of continuing to live in disproportionate fear of such tragedies.

Notes

1. In this event, twenty-year-old Adam Lanza forcefully entered Sandy Hook Elementary School in Newtown, Connecticut, and opened fire. The shooting left twenty first-grade students and six educators, including the school's principal, dead. Lanza also had shot and killed his mother Nancy prior to the rampage.

2. On April 20, 1999, Columbine seniors Eric Harris (age eighteen) and Dylan Klebold (age seventeen) opened fire on their school. They shot and killed twelve students and one teacher before committing suicide in the school's library.

3. On April 16, 2007, Virginia Tech senior Seung-Hui Cho (age twenty-three) shot and killed two students in the West Ambler Johnston dormitory on campus. After a two-hour break, during which he mailed his now infamous multimedia manifesto to NBC, Cho opened fire in Norris Hall, killing an additional thirty students and faculty. He killed himself as police gained entry to the building.

4. For a discussion of the complexities of assigning culpability to youthful offenders, see Cerulo (1998), Muschert and Janssen (2012), Spencer (2005), and Spencer and Muschert (2009).

5. In Warner and Curtiz (1942).

6. An ouroboros is an ancient symbol that represents cyclicality. In its current form, it is the idea that there is no beginning or end to a discussion following school shootings, and that this discussion does not lead to any progress toward a solution.

7. Muschert (2007a) points out that individual access to guns are the only necessary cause for school shootings to occur. However, similar attacks have taken place without guns, and have involved bombs (as in the 1927 Bath, Michigan, school massacre) or knives (as occurred in various places in China in 2012, on the same day as the Sandy Hook massacre).

The Problem of Closeness in Relationships

Moushumi Roy, PhD

Michigan State University

Introduction

Close relationships are forms of interdependent behaviors marked by social influences. Frequently, people use the word "close" to imply strong social ties that can potentially exist between neighboring nations, within the community, neighborhood, family or between two individuals. Yet, the closeness that defines these relationships has the potential to spur conflict within them. For instance, neighboring nations, communities, neighborhood, family are the collectives that manifest a sense of closeness, yet are not devoid of conflict within them. The definition of "closeness," a socially constructed phenomenon, however, generally dissuades people from picturing the risk of conflict such as between neighboring nations, or in a family. Closeness can be found in various social processes and intersectionalities. While examples, such as neighboring nations or family, are in themselves socially constructed, the ways in which their respective interactions operate within and between each of them further builds and expands the social construction process. Some of the social processes and intersectionalities that are considered in this study include geographical patterns, immigration processes, gender, age, time, socioeconomic status, family, and health. These intersectional identities may form close relationships within and across each other, yet at the same time, may generate conflict as well.

The negative attitudes and behaviors of any close interaction may manifest in poor and impulsive emotions and behaviors, such as irritation, aggression, violence, dehumanization, jealousy, and competitiveness. The health outcomes associated with these kinds of conflict are most likely to be poor—such as chronic illnesses and mortality. The severity of negative attitudes and behaviors can lead to serious health conditions and hospitalization. Furthermore, the association between closeness and conflict is linked to social condemnation, yet the symptoms of negativity within closeness have rarely been understood as being linked with social denunciation.

The goal of this text is to unfold some of the complexities associated with closeness at the nexus of geographical proximity, immigration, gender, age, time, socioeconomic status, family, and health. To meet this goal, this text will identify some ways that conflict is associated with closeness. I argue that conflict in closeness is an objective problem that is further complicated by social condemnation. For example, research has found that blaming the survivors of domestic abuse by their healthcare providers or emergency nurses is associated with a rise in poor mental and physical health conditions in addition to the experiences of domestic violence (Thapar-Björkert and Morgan, 2010). Victim blaming in the form of social condemnation assumes a structural relationship. This study will use the lens of social condemnation to understand how conflict within closeness is a health issue.

Closeness, Conflict, and the Boundaries of Nation States at the Nexus of Immigration

Consideration of 'closeness' in the process of immigration has been noted as frequently occurring and problematic in many cases. For instance, immigration across the borders of Mexico and the U.S. or Bangladesh and India are a few examples that capture this dynamic. The negative markers in this context of geographical proximity and immigration are associated with poor attitudes and dehumanizing immigrant populations. Immigrants are perceived as criminalizing the destination country, overusing the health care system, taking away jobs that "rightfully" belong to natives, living on welfare, and lacking in assimilative tendencies. The stereotypical obsessions that responsible administrative units (including governments) rely on, believe in, and follow to implement actions towards immigrant population have been described in social health scholarship as bordering on disorder syndrome. This pandemic disease is evident in the current socio-political system in the ways it is engaged in promoting and instilling xenophobic attitudes enmeshed within policy frames. These socially condemning socio-political framings inflict suffering toward opportunity-seeking immigrants/migrants from close borders. Consequently, immigrants endure harsh health conditions. In sum, based on several examples, the whole process of immigrants' experiences when crossing neighboring nation states border can be explained through the relationship between closeness and negativity. Furthermore, the policies ignoring the poor experiences of immigrants or migrants contribute to developing a social structure formed with condemnation. These dehumanizing policies pose extra challenges for the vulnerable opportunity seeking immigrants. Consequently, this intensifies the pain of survival among people living close together.

In the post-colonial society, globalization was primarily defined by immigration, while in pre-colonial times trade relationships were the foundation of globalization. Compared to trading linkages, which are fundamentally more economic, immigration, which is more social, has often resulted in some form of condemnation against immigrants at their destinations. Entry of people from close borders has often been viewed as problematic. For instance, some have deemed it appropriate to raise walls in response to migrants entering from neighboring countries. The most outstanding example of this relationship development shaping immigration is found along the U.S. and Mexico border. The obsession with curbing immigration from Mexico has now assumed the catchall agenda of raising a gigantic disciplinary wall that has drawn attention from multiple directions: social, economic and political. The negativity associated with immigration has grown to the point that migrants who bypass approved immigration channels may be denied basic needs such as water and food because within the highly charged socio-political atmosphere they are considered "illegal." Media reports even suggest incidents of arrests among advocates engaged in serving water and food to migrants (Silva, 2018).

While social convergence can be understood through both the processes of social construction and deconstruction of closeness, we can also comprehend the ways in which closeness stands in opposition to its meaning. For instance, the paradoxical linkage of closeness and conflict described as nation-state boundary and social-process formation can also extend to domestic spaces. While at the national level it is defined by boundary-raising across nation-states, on another level, it takes the shape of domestic violence within households. Although the social meaning assigned to family formation is bounded by closeness, domestic violence (DV) and intimate partner violence (IPV) and child abuse are examples of conflict within the family. Closeness is situated at the nexus of dependence on intimacy and yet independent from it as part of conflict. Clearly, experiences of domestic violence and sexual assaults within families have implications for physical and mental health disorders. Added to this, experiences of social condemnation, such as victim and survivor blaming both by the public at large and by healthcare providers complicates the situation. While closeness in its semantic form thrives naturally as a positive health marker, some social constructions of closeness may result in negative behaviors.

While the consequences of closeness have been found in general within any population, immigrants face additional burdens of closeness when subjected to forms of negativity that are likely to emerge out of socially constructed closeness. The socially constructed closeness is loosely bounded by its differing interpretations. Among immigrant populations, closeness affects are born out of multidimensional and multiscale social characteristics. Investigating the narratives of domestic violence advocates, Kapur & Zajicek (2018) found that closeness linked by marital relationship among South Asian immigrants experience multidimensional influences of negativity. When closeness and negativity connection influences a vulnerable population, such as immigrant women of color, closeness and negativity assume an intersectional dimension. In this situation, the likelihood of negativity increases within closeness. Addressing the data dearth in this intersectional form of closeness may find strong relationship between "closeness" and health and wellbeing. Furthermore, the use of intersectionality separates out the nuances associated with closeness and experiences of negativity among immigrants. These identified intersectional determinants are social in nature that include race, class, age, and gender. For example, several studies on domestic abuse and violence within the South Asian communities in the U.S. have shed light on how women continue to suffer in abusive relationships (Kapur & Zajicek, 2018; Mahapatra, 2012; Midlarsky, Venkataramani-Kothari & Plante 2006; Mehrotra, 1999). If critically assessed, it will be found that the responsible factors of domestic violence within the South Asian population are born out of closeness.

Often, learned beliefs and behaviors are used in victimizing women in a close relationship. Verma et al. (2006) note that among adolescent boys in India, socialized instilled inequitable gender ideals are widely prevalent. Using the lens of gender equity and examining gender attitudes, they found that adolescent boys conform to ideology that men possess the right to discipline their wives or intimate partners. Furthermore, wife beating is viewed as a normal consequence of women's refusal to obey men. Boys are socialized by these violent behaviors starting at an early age. Verma and colleagues argue that regardless of what is learned during socialization, within the context of South Asian origin, attitudes toward gender inequity affect women of caste, class, and age placed at the lower end of the social hierarchy. Culture-specific behaviors targeted toward dehumanizing and objectifying women as part of the socialization process is still a gendered learning for men from their family or association. As part of this cultural group, men have been conditioned to develop trust in and practice the values of their close associates. In any situation of weak closeness, these values, attitudes, and beliefs translate into domestic violence and intimate partner violence.

Other factors associated with conflict in closeness is the consciousness of maintaining masculine-specific power and control among men. Studies have found that in the South Asian culture, there is a systematic linkage of power and control with domestic and intimate partner violence. The extent to which power and control informs masculinity is the result of a significant preference for a son in the South Asian culture. Nonetheless, higher outcomes of power and control in intimate relationships between men and women is found among young adults and individuals of low class and caste statuses. The social condemnation toward these problems is exacerbated by ignoring the need for intervention among men which contributes to normalization of this aspect of masculinity. Consequently, accumulation of gender-inequitable attitudes including objectification and dehumanization of women increases among men.

As immigrants are the carriers of their origin, among immigrant families who have been socialized to conform to the ideals of patriarchal power and control, the experiences of acculturative stress are negotiated using domination and oppression tactics toward women in the family. Accordingly, men assume the role of protector and are the responsible member who has more right to maintain family orderliness. For the past two decades since the development of intersectionality, the discussion of intimate partner violence emerging out of the feminist literature has focused on how various hierarchies of power structures intersect with each other. These power structures, age, gender, class, and space not only overlap, or build each other mutually, but they multiply along with the reinforced matrix of hierarchies. The stages included within this multiplication process spread across many dimensions such as unearned privileges, domination, and oppression (Erez, Adelman, & Gregory, 2009). Often the coping mechanisms among men who have been socialized to uphold patriarchal values are exercised in the form of violence. More so, these men specifically target intimate partners or spouses as victims. Intimacy and marriage as forms of dependency and closeness provide limited opportunity for women to overcome their vulnerabilities and escape from perpetrators. Often broken families are the results of these multifold conflicts. However, when women continue to live with domestic violence and intimate partner violence, the level of conflict continues to increase, often leading to injuries.

Among immigrant families, closeness also raises other issues. In many immigrant families financial need forces women to work outside home. Shifting roles within the families may produce extra burdens on women, especially if they are expected to both manage the home and maintain outside employment. Erez and colleagues note that job demands may contribute to the weakening of family bonds. Despite the demands of working and maintaining the household, both men and women in a family often try to disguise a rough relationship and portray a smoother surface on the outside.

The earlier immigrant groups and older generations of Asian origin perceive themselves as community guardians who have carried the traditions of South Asian culture. Measuring by their own social mobility and success, these leaders of the community from earlier immigration cohorts assume that maintaining the cultural values and beliefs leads to achieving immigrants' success. Women who are victims of domestic violence find it to be of absolute necessity to remain silent and suffer in the hope of receiving the reward by measuring up to the desired model for Asian immigrants. Following the socialization pattern among immigrants of Asian origin, strict obedience to traditional gender roles has been maintained within Asian immigrant households. Following such strict measures means women are typically more responsible for household work and caregiving than men who are bounded by the hours for their employment. Reversal from this gender pattern, if any, means disobedience to the tradition of masculine power as well as systematic disruption to the orderly flow in the household. While men work outside home is theoretically labeled as a job, for women caregiving is considered household work. Women with children may bear extra burdens of domestic violence when they self-regulate to prioritize the interest and wellbeing of their children. The fear of disrupting the preferred family model and thoughts about welfare of children may force victims to suppress evidence of violence. The lack of knowledge and awareness including internalization factors among the weakly powered partner leads to self-control and submission to the control of the stronger partner. Multiple external pressures can restrict women from avoiding and moving away from experiencing conflicts as part of their closeness.

Another example of closeness and conflict found among immigrant families is parent and adolescent conflict. This conflict is not simply the byproduct of intergenerational outcomes. It is, instead, related to post-immigration situations compromising the relationship between parents and children. For example, evidence from Mexican immigrant families shows that in the post-immigration phase and during the settlement period in the U.S., parents' employment outside the home leads to experiences of isolation among children that are then associated with violent behavior among the children (Espiritu & Wolf, 2001). Intergenerational conflicts may also raise negative feelings within households. Furthermore, while stress associated with immigration and post-immigration settlement affects closeness, negative family dynamics have been shown to influence children's psychological health problems.

Discussion Conclusion and Limitations

Relationships are central to human life. Generally, closeness has primarily been understood as being associated with unproblematic interactions and positive interrelationships. Hence, the assumption of closeness is inherently situated as a positive phenomenon. However, closeness also may reflect social nuances that are associated with severe public health issues. As simple and affable as it may sound due to its semantic positioning, the closeness construct can be riddled with complexities and negative associations. For example, intimate partner violence (IPV), domestic violence (DV), and sexual abuse continue to be monitored by the World Health Organization (WHO, 2010). These forms of violence mostly victimize women. The relationship between intimate partner violence and emergency room visits has been found to have significant association with external injuries treated in urgent care units (Peisenhofer & Seibold, 2007). Closeness issues are rarely discussed in the context of immigrants and their relationship with the structure formed linking bordering nations and within families. The existing closeness complexities in the context of immigrants have been investigated implicitly and explicitly as the phenomena of family relationships. The scales of closeness within immigrant populations have been rarely discussed as a social problem. To gain better understanding of closeness and its association with negativity requires developing multidimensional sociological constructs that include a variety of approaches to understanding the relationship between closeness and conflict.

Acknowledgement: I would like to convey my gratitude to Dr. Ralph Pyle and other anonymous reviewers from Michigan State University for their helpful comments and suggestions on the initial draft of this paper.

REFERENCES

Dasgupta, S. D. (2007). Body evidence: intimate violence against south Asian women in America. Retrieved from https://ebookcentral-proquest-com.proxy2.cl.msu.edu

Erez, E., Adelman, M., & Gregory, C. (2009). Intersections of Immigration and Domestic Violence: Voices of Battered Immigrant Women. *Feminist Criminology. 32 (4)*, 31-56.

Espiritu, Y. L., and Diane, L. Wolf., (2001). The Paradox of Assimilation: Children of Pilipino Immigrants in San Diego. In R. G. Rumbaut and A. Portes (eds.) *Ethnicities: Children of Immigrants in America. (pp.157-176) SanDiego, CA.: University of California and Russell Sage.*

Kapur, S. & Zajicek, A. (2018). Constructions of Battered Asian Indian Marriage Migrants: The Narratives of Domestic Violence Advocates Violence Against Women, 1–21 https://doi-org.proxy2.cl.msu.edu/10.1177/1077801218757373

Kapur, S. A., Zajicek, A., & John, G. (2017). Nonprofit Organizations Serving Domestic Violence Survivors: Addressing Intersectional Needs of Asian Indians Journal of Women and Social Work vol. 32(1) 50-66

Mahapatra, N. (2012). South Asian women in the U.S. and their experience of domestic violence. *Journal of Family Violence, 27*(5), 381-390. doi:http://dx.doi.org.proxy1.cl.msu.edu/10.1007/s10896-012-9434-4

Mehrotra, M. (1999). The social construction of wife abuse: Experiences of Asian Indian women in the United States. *Violence Against Women*, 5, 619-640. 10.1177/10778019922181400

Midlarsky, E., Venkataramani-Kothari, A., & Plante, M. (2006). Domestic violence in the Chinese and South Asian immigrant communities. Annals New York Academy of Sciences, 1087, 279-300. https://doi-org.proxy2.cl.msu.edu/10.1196/annals.1385.003

Peisenhofer, S., & Seibold C. (2007). Emergency department care of women experiencing intimate partner violence: are we doing all we can? Contemp Nurse. Feb;24(1):3e14. http://dx.doi.org/10.5172/conu.2007.24.1.3

Silva, D. (2018). Volunteer arrested after giving food, water to undocumented immigrants in Arizona. Retrieved from https://www.nbcnews.com/news/latino/volunteer-arrested-after-giving-food-water-undocumented-immigrants-arizona-n840386

Thapar-Bjo¨ rkert S & Morgan K (2010)"But sometimes I think they put themselves in the situation": exploring blame and responsibility in interpersonal violence. Violence Against Women 16 (1), 32–59.

Verma, R.K., Pulerwitz, J., Mahendra, V., Khandekar, S., Barker, G., Fulpagare, P., & Singh, S.K. (2006). Challenging and changing gender attitudes among young men in Mumbai, India. Reproductive Health Matters, 14(28), 135–143.

WHO. (2010). Preventing intimate partner and sexual violence against women: taking action and generating evidence http://www.who.int/violence_injury_prevention/violence/activities/intimate/en/

Participation and Claiming of Social Problems: Voices of Activism

This article demonstrates the political strategies of two groups of South Asian Muslim women. The study reveals the ways in which members embody the idea of bicultural feminism in their identity movement by using what has been a stigmatized image of veiling as a major tool for their activism. Taking advantage of the visibility of their dress code, they attempt to publicize positive images of Islam while increasing their solidarity. Their narratives suggest that these forms of activism are elaborate strategies that result from embracing their multicultural identity as U.S.-born Muslim women. They reflect a strong sense of mission to bring social justice to the lives of "unseen" or "imagined" Muslim sisters in the United States and other nations. Such resilience underpins the fact that difference and deviance can be translated into a symbol of strength, as well as a driving force for Asian women to cope with social adversity stemming from cultural sexism and imperialism.

The implications of this study are that the future orientation of political boundaries and activism associated with South Asian women, especially Muslims, will be along the lines of their religious identity, in contrast to previous generations. Many studies of the Asian-American movement in the late 20th century have noted that rising anti-Asian violence has often spurred panethnic solidarity among diverse Asian groups (Espiritu, 1993; Chang, 2001; Lien, 2001; Wei, 1993, 2004). Also, many South Asian feminist leaders have sought to reduce ethnic and religious disparities among members by emphasizing their shared social experiences and histories of immigration and colonization (Aguilar-San Juan, 1994; Shah, 1994; Leonard, 2003; Takhar, 2003). Contrary to these trends, in the aftermath of September 11 the Muslim women studied here believe their social experiences, issues, and consequent political strategies have significantly departed from those of other groups of South Asians. Instead, the emergent generation of South Asian Muslim women may expand their membership to other Muslim women's groups nationally and internationally, as increasing media attention is devoted to the political tension between the United States and Middle Eastern (as well as other Islamic) nations in the post-September 11 global age.

NOTES

1. All of the names of individuals have been changed to protect their anonymity.

2. For examples, see U.S. Department of Justice (2002). For a list of hate crimes by state, see Tolerance.Org (2002). Also, see Burson (2001), Saada (2003), Ahmad (2006), and Melwani (2005).

3. The data for this study are derived from my participant observation in over 100 activities of these groups on and off campus, from 40 in-depth interviews with their group leaders and affiliates, and from analysis of websites and newsletters. As a group member, I participated in their religious meetings, including prayers and Quran reading circles, as well as in nonreligious events such as general body meetings and anti-war protests. I also attended leisure activities such as weekend trips, parties, and inner-peer-group gatherings. The interviewees were selected using snowball sampling. Each of the interviews was conducted individually on campus or at their residence and lasted from one to three hours. All interviews were tape recorded and transcribed.

REFERENCES

Abraham, M.
1995   "Ethnicity, Gender, and Marital Violence: South Asian Women's Organizations in the United States." *Gender and Society* 9: 450–468.
Aguilar-San Juan, K. (ed.)
1994   *The State of Asian America: Activism and Resistance in the 1990s.* Boston: South End Press.
Ahmad, Shomial
2006   "Seeking Peace, Fair Portrayals." *Newsday* (August 12).
Alba, R. and V. Nee
2005   *Remaking the American Mainstream: Assimilation and Contemporary Immigration.* Boston: Harvard University Press.
Alcoff, L.
2005   *Visible Identities: Race, Gender, and the Self.* New York: Oxford University Press.
2000   "Habits of Hostility on Seeing Race." *Philosophy Today* 44: 30–40.
Anderson, B.
1983   *Imagined Communities: Reflections on the Origin and Spread of Nationalism.* New York: Shocken Books.
Bacon, J.
1999   "Constructing Collective Ethnic Identities: The Case of Second Generation Asian Indians." *Qualitative Sociology* 22: 141–160.
Burson, Pat
2001   "America's Ordeal/Fear Grips Muslim Community." *Newsday* (September 23).
Chang, G. (ed).
2001   *Asian Americans and Politics: Perspectives, Experiences, Prospects.* Stanford, CA: Stanford University Press.
Chiang, P., M. Cho, E. Kim, M. Lui, and H. Zia
1997   "On Asian America, Feminist, and Agenda-Making: A Roundtable Discussion." *Dragon Ladies: Asian American Feminists Breathe Fire.* Cambridge, MA: South End Press: 57–72.

Chin, J. (ed.)
    2000   *Relationships Among Asian American Women*. Washington, D.C.: American Psychological Association.

Cho, M.
    1994   "Losing Face for a Living." *Glamour* (November): 78–81.

Espiritu, Y.
    1997   *Asian American Women and Men: Labor, Laws and Love*. Thousand Oaks, CA: Sage Publications.

    1993   *Asian American Panethnicity: Bridging Institutions and Identities*. Philadelphia: Temple University Press.

George, S.
    2005   *When Women Come First: Gender and Class in Transnational Migration*. Berkeley: University of California Press.

Goffman, E.
    1963   *Stigma: Notes on the Management of Spoiled Identity*. New York: Simon and Schuster.

Gordon, M.
    1964   *Assimilation in American Life: The Role of Race, Religion and National Origins*. New York: Oxford University Press.

Khandelwal, M.
    2003   "Opening Spaces: South Asian American Women Leaders in the Late Twentieth Century." S. Hune and G. Nomura (eds.), *Asian/Pacific Islander American Women: A Historical Anthology*. New York: New York University Press: 350–364.

Kibria, N.
    2006   "South Asian Americans." P.G. Min (ed.), *Asian Americans: Contemporary Trends and Issues*. Thousand Oaks, CA: Pine Science Press: 206–227.

Lee, J. and M. Zhou (ed).
    2004   *Asian American Youth*. New York: Routledge.

Leonard, K.
    2003   *Muslims in the United States: The State of Research*. New York: Russell Sage Foundation.

    1997   *The South Asian Americans*. Westport, CT: Greenwood Press.

Lien, P.
    2001   *The Making of Asian America Through Political Participation*. Philadelphia: Temple University Press.

Lu, L.
    1997   "Critical Visions: The Representation and Resistance of Asian Women." S. Shah (ed.), *Dragon Ladies: Asian American Feminists Breathe Fire*. Cambridge MA: South End Press: 17–28.

Melucci, A.
    1996   *Challenging Codes: Collective Action in the Information Age*. Cambridge, U.K.: Cambridge University Press.

    1995   "The Process of Collective Identity." H. Johnston and B. Klandermans (eds.), *Social Movements and Culture*. London, U.K.: UCI Press: 41–63.

Melwani, Lavina
    2005   "The New New Yorkers." *Newsday* (August 17).

Min, P.
    2002   *The Second Generation: Ethnic Identity Among Asian Americans*. Lanham, MD: Alta Mira Press.

Mohanty, C.
    1991   "Cartographies of Struggle: Third World Women and the Politics of Feminism." C. Mohanty, A. Russo, and L. Torres (eds.), *Third World Women and the Politics of Feminism*. Bloomington: University of Indiana Press: 1–47.

Nagata, D.
    2000   "World War II Internment and the Relationships of Nisei Women: Relationships Among Asian American Women." J. Chin (ed.), *Relationships Among Asian American Women*. Washington, D.C.: American Psychological Association: 49–70.

Portes, A. and R. Rumbaut (eds.)
    2001   *Legacies: The Story of the Immigrant Second Generation*. Berkeley, CA: University of California Press.

Purkayastha, B., S. Raman, and K. Bhide
    1997   "Empowering Women: SHNEHA's Multifaceted Activism." S. Shah (ed.), *Dragon Ladies: Asian American Feminists Breathe Fire*. Boston, MA: South End Press: 100–107.

Saada, Laila
    2003   "Piece of Cloth." *Newsday* (November 30).

Shah, S.
    1997   *Dragon Ladies: Asian American Feminists Breathe Fire*. S. Shah (ed.). Boston, MA: South End Press.
    1994   "Presenting Blue Goddess: Toward a National, Pan-Asian Feminist Agenda." K. Aguilar-San Juan (ed.), *The State of Asian America: Activism and Resistance in the 1990s*. Cambridge, MA: South End Press: 147–158.

Shandhu, S.
    2004   "Instant Karma: The Commercialization of Asian Indian Culture." J. Lee and M. Zhou (eds.), *Asian American Youth: Culture, Identity, and Ethnicity*. New York: Routledge: 131–141.

Takhar, S.
    2003   "South Asian Women and the Question of Political Organization." N. Puwar and P. Raghuram (eds.), *South Asian Women in the Diaspora*. New York: Berg: 215–226.

Tan, H.
    1997   "Building Shelter: Asian Women and Domestic Violence." S. Shah (ed.), *Dragon Ladies: Asian American Feminists Breathe Fire*. Cambridge, MA: South End Press: 108–120.

Tolerance.Org
    2002   "Violence Against Arab and Muslim Americans." At *www.tolerance.org/news/ article_hate.jsp?id=412*.

Tuan, M.
    1999   *Forever Foreigners or Honorary Whites? The Asian Ethnic Experience Today*. New Brunswick, NJ: Rutgers University Press.

U.S. Department of Justice
    2002   *Annual Hate Crime Report 2001*. Washington, D.C.: U.S. Department of Justice.

Wei, W.
    2004   "A Commentary on Young Asian American Activists from the 1960s to the Present." J. Lee and M. Zhou (eds.), *Asian American Youth*. New York: Routledge: 299–312.
    1993   *The Asian American Movement*. Philadelphia: Temple University Press.

Epilogue
"Where the Bad Guys Are"

IN NOVEMBER 1989, PRESIDENT GEORGE H. W. BUSH supported General Colin Powell's order to establish Joint Task Force 6 (JTF-6) at Fort Bliss, Texas.[1] The task force's original mission was to "to serve as the planning and coordinating operational headquarters to support local, state, and federal law enforcement agencies within the Southwest border region to counter the flow of illegal drugs into the United States."[2] JTF-6's original area of operations consisted of the four border states of California, Arizona, New Mexico, and Texas. In February 1995, by directive of the commanding general of US Army Forces Command, JTF-6's area of responsibility was expanded to include the entire continental United States, Puerto Rico, and the Virgin Islands. In June 1997, responsibility for Puerto Rico and the US Virgin Islands transferred to US Southern Command.[3] JTF-6 was created amid a flurry of protests by political and civic groups who felt that the military outfit violated the law of *posse comitatus*, which forbade the use of the military for law enforcement activities. By restricting the military's role to surveillance and technical backup, legal consistency prevailed.[4] Nevertheless, social and political pressure to win the "War on Drugs" in the late 1980s and early 1990s encouraged President Bush to form JTF-6 and expand governmental role in law enforcement.[5]

In 1991, at least six hundred troops from the Army's Seventh Infantry Division conducted Operation Block It in the southwestern corner of New Mexico in Hidalgo County.[6] At the same time, a contingent of US Marines assisted Doña Ana County officers with the arrest of drug smugglers in southern New Mexico.[7] In 1997, JTF-6 would see their services called to Redford, Texas, a small border town of roughly one hundred inhabitants in Presidio County that the United States Border Patrol had identified as a major drug corridor.[8]

On the evening of May 20, 1997, seventeen-year-old Esequiel Hernández Jr. of Redford, Texas, took his modest herd of goats out to the Rio Grande. Hernández took along with him a World War I–era .22 caliber rifle because some wild dogs had harassed the goats on a previous occasion. At some point while the goats grazed, Hernández fired two shots. Although it is not clear why Hernández fired into the desert bushes, the consequences were severe.[9] Unbeknownst to the young man, Hernández had fired in the direction of US Marines from JTF-6 who were in their third day of a reconnaissance mission in the area and were heavily camouflaged and largely undetectable to the common civilian.[10] The soldiers were each wearing clothing that rendered their presence "unclear whether they were shrouded by land bunkers or vegetation cover."[11] Marine Corporal Clemente Banuelos interpreted Hernández's inadvertent fire as an aggressive attack against his company by a suspected drug trafficker and responded with a single shot, striking Hernández's chest. The four densely camouflaged United States Marines approached their target only to find seventeen-year-old Esequiel Hernández Jr.'s dangling feet; he had fallen into a well after being shot. They soon discovered that the man they believed to be a menacing drug trafficker was in fact a young American high school student, tending to his goats and shooting at what many law enforcement and military experts concluded were wild dogs or the vacant desert breeze.[12]

Hernández's family heard the helicopters and sirens wailing near their property. Esequiel's father hopped in his truck and searched for his son, unaware that he had been killed. A deputy informed Mr. Hernández that Esequiel died of a gunshot wound after having been fired on by US Marines. An investigation by the Texas Rangers, Department of Defense, and local law enforcement ensued, raising several questions including the justification for the shooting. For example, at the time of the shooting, Corporal Banuelos and the three other privates in the patrol never identified themselves to Hernández. However, Marine Colonel Thomas Kelly said later that the Marines responded within the Joint Chiefs of Staff's peacetime rules of military engagement.[13]

The Department of Defense and military officials quickly went on the defensive following the incident. Local, state, and national media outlets descended upon the small border town of Redford, causing a hailstorm of criticism throughout the Southwest and beyond. Public outcry and an official "review" of the military's role in border patrol activities forced JTF-6 to suspend all operations in the Marfa sector and, eventually, all along the US-Mexico border.[14] Corporal Banuelos and his Marine comrades were subject to a grand jury investigation to determine the legality of the shooting. After an exhaustive process, the Texas grand jury cleared the Marines of any wrongdoing in August 1997.[15] Not long after Esequiel Hernández Jr. was gunned down by US Marines, in May 1998, the US House of Representatives voted and authorized enlisting the military to help patrol US borders in the war against drug smuggling and illegal immigration.[16] The federal government would continue the policy of militarizing the border in the fight against drug trafficking well into the twenty-first century.

It is not the objective of this book to provide a detailed account of the contemporary militarization of the US-Mexico border. Rather, the consequences of border militarization are most revealing. Jack Zimmerman, the defense attorney for Corporal Banuelos, stated that "an armed man on foot, walking behind a herd of goats" fit the profile of a drug trafficker, a threatening figure that undermined the country's efforts in the "War on Drugs" and the enforcement of federal immigration policies.[17] In other words, a young man of Mexican descent along the US-Mexico border with a .22-caliber rifle, tending to his goats, "fit the profile" of the enemy the military, law enforcement, and politicians sought in their "War on Drugs" campaign. The Esequiel Hernández murder in May 1997 served as a climactic event that epitomized the conflictive and complicated legacy of militarization efforts along the US-Mexico border that started in the late nineteenth century.

The Hernández murder suggests that ethnic Mexicans continue to be categorized as an enemy and threat to United States society regardless of their citizenship or social standing. Not only did Zimmerman's description of Esequiel Hernández Jr. paint a picture of an enemy combatant, but also the intelligence the Border Patrol provided that portrayed Redford as a center for drug traffickers with 70 to 75 percent of the population involved in the illicit trade, framed the "criminal portrait" perfectly.[18] Criminalizing members of Redford's mostly Mexican population categorically labeled them as enemies of the state. Or, as borderlands scholar Joseph Nevins contends:

> Seen from Washington, the border region—Redford included—is to a highly significant degree an area of existential threats to the larger national body, an area that needs to be secured—whether against "illegal" migrants crossing the boundary to "steal" jobs, drug cartels, or would-be terrorists.[19]

Ethnic Mexicans residing in the United States, regardless of status, are guilty by association and, because of border militarization, are identified as enemies of the state. Since the establishment of JTF-6, the US-Mexico border has experienced a continuing and expanding presence of military personnel. The increased militarization of state and local law enforcement further complicates ethnic Mexican integration into the larger socioeconomic fold. In other words, the militarization of local authority and the expansion of its powers to enforce federal law draw in the marginal borders to the center of policy and social debate. The once "existential threat" is assumed a mainstream reality, especially in the post-9/11 era.[20]

In September 2009, Texas Governor Rick Perry dispatched a team of specially trained Texas Rangers, called Recon Rangers, to the "hostile border wilderness near the Rio Grande to maintain a constant vigil for 'bad guys' from Mexico."[21] According to newspaper reports, the Recon Rangers resembled more a "military-style commando unit in a foreign war zone."[22] Members of the recon force, who trained at Texas military bases and were taught advanced military skill sets, were sent to the "foreign war zones" of West and South Texas where desolate areas were difficult for undermanned sheriff's departments to patrol.[23] The Texas Department of Public Safety (DPS), the umbrella agency of the Texas Rangers, reported that the entire Ranger force consisted of only 144 officers, and Governor Perry was not clear on how many of those would patrol the 1,254-mile Texas-Mexico border.[24] Governor Perry's mobilization of the Rangers for border duty would evoke a mythical past that would garner the political support he so desired in a hotly contested primary race for the Republican nomination for governor with Senator Kay Bailey Hutchinson.[25] However, for some in the Mexican community, mobilization of the Rangers brought back the vividly horrid memories of lynchings, violence, terrorism, and marginalization represented by the iconic agency and its civilian supporters in the early decades of the twentieth century.[26] Governor Perry's politicization of the international boundary was a page out of the old political book; however, the organization of a special Ranger team did more than win Perry a few votes. Perry's border security campaign mobilized the civilian sector in a manner reminiscent of the old

Home Guard of the 1910s and eerily foreshadowed by the Arizona "Minute-men" project.

Perry's border security campaign explicitly sought and encouraged civilian involvement. In addition to Rangers patrolling the border, the governor authorized the "Virtual Border Watch Program." It was a hi-tech system of cameras placed along the border that created a virtual online patrol presence and allowed the public to view and report suspicious activity to law enforcement. Members of the public were encouraged to assist law enforcement and register with the Virtual Border Watch program online.[27] The governor's recruitment of the public in assisting law enforcement followed a relatively popular wave of vigilantism that began in Arizona in 2005 and spread to neighboring border states.

Perry's program of civilian "activism" runs parallel in 2005 when civilian participation in the militarization of the international boundary line came to a head in Arizona. In April 2005, James Gilchrist of California and Chris Simcox formed "The Minuteman Project" to "get a neglectful US government to simply enforce existing immigration laws."[28] They soon splintered into two separate groups. The group Simcox led hoped to "embarrass the government" into action by keeping watch on the Arizona-Sonora (Mexico) border with hundreds of armed and unarmed volunteers.[29] In response to growing public and political pressure, President George W. Bush ordered nearly six thousand National Guard troops to the US-Mexico border in May 2006 under Operation Jump Start to provide intelligence, surveillance, and other support.[30] Under the order, National Guard troops provided mobile communications, transportation, logistics, training, and construction support to the US Border Patrol for a security fence along the southern border.[31] After two years and millions of dollars in drug seizures and thousands of apprehended illegal immigrants, Operation Jump Start ended on July 15, 2008.[32] Although Operation Jump Start was politically popular, according to border scholar Timothy Dunn, "the rate of return on the use of the National Guard in immigration enforcement [was] not spectacular and costs appear high."[33] Initial forecasts believed it would take up to one-third of the National Guard's total force to staff the border. A great undertaking and burden, according to Dunn, for a force already spread thinly in Afghanistan and Iraq. In addition, he argues that increased numbers do not necessarily result in more apprehensions or reduction in illegal crossings.[34] Despite data suggesting that increased militarization is too costly and largely ineffective, in May 2010, President Barack Obama announced the deployment of at least 1,200 National Guard troops to the southern border, again, amid public and political pressure stemming from unprecedented drug violence in northern Mexico, illegal immigration flow into the United States, and state governments, like Arizona, challenging federal border policy.[35]

In April 2010, Arizona Governor Jan Brewer signed Senate Bill 1070, also known as the "Support Our Law Enforcement and Safe Neighborhoods Act," into law.[36] For any lawful contact made by a law enforcement official of the State of Arizona where a "reasonable suspicion exists that the person is an alien who is unlawfully present in the United States, a reasonable attempt shall be made . . . to determine the immigration status of that person."[37] Local police wielded broader power to detain anyone suspected of being in the United States illegally. Opponents of Senate Bill 1070 argued that vague wording, such as "reasonable suspicion" and "reasonable attempt," provided an open invitation for harassment and discrimination against Latinos, particularly against Mexican Americans, regardless of their citizenship status.[38] Moreover, the law served to further marginalize ethnic Mexicans as the very presence of ethnic Mexicans became questionable, indeed, virtually and practically vilified. In her press conference following the bill signing, Governor Brewer categorically linked all criminal activity to immigrants simply by emphasizing that the bill, "protects all of us, every Arizona citizen and everyone here in our state lawfully. . . . Border-related violence and crime due to illegal immigration are critically important issues to the people of [Arizona]."[39] Governor Brewer obviously did not refer to immigrants from Europe, Asia, or Africa in these border issues. Criminal activities and illegal immigration were inextricably understood to refer to ethnic Mexicans and Mexico.

Ironically, the 2009 crime data report published by the Federal Bureau of Investigation showed that violent crime in Arizona declined dramatically in the pervious two years; the crime rate was significantly lower than average crime rates across the United States.[40] Despite contradictory evidence that clearly dismisses Governor Brewer's claims of increased crime rates because of illegal immigration, the governor understood the power of xenophobia and the historical deep-seated racism that would make immigration and the politicization of the border discourse into election-winning rhetoric. The broadening of federal policing powers to include city police suggests a dire set of circumstances unfulfilled by federal agencies, including the Border Patrol and military. The apparent desperate state of affairs attributed to the border thus requires full protection from an outward threat, the ethnic Mexican. Again, the combination of harsh social and political rhetoric as well as stricter immigration enforcement further criminalizes not only migrants but also their ethnic brethren and communities.

Border militarization finds itself center stage one hundred years after the Mexican Revolution. New multiagency and military operations continue under the tutelage of President Barack Obama. The lingering effects of border militarization and the role it plays on the social stratification of ethnic Mexicans in the United States continue to render identity formation a fragile and precarious process. "¡Pobre México! Tan lejos de Díos, tan cerca a los Estados Unidos (Poor Mexico! So far from God, so close to the United States), the classic Mexican proverb rings ever more true today.[41] A reinterpretation of the phrase could just as well be applied to the borderlands, a region so far from Washington, DC, so close to Mexico. People in political and economic centers of power, such as Washington DC, Phoenix, Austin, and such, view the border as an "area of existential threat to the larger national body, an area that needs to be secured."[42] As Joseph Nevins argues:

> The U.S.-Mexico borderlands has increasingly become a society comprised substantially of "police and thieves" . . . one in which civil and human rights

are effectively less than they are elsewhere in the United States, making it a zone of exception . . . a site in which the state acts in a manner outside of normal constraints and takes extreme measures for the declared safe of security. In doing so, the federal [and state] government has normalized various forms or violence in the name of fighting threats . . . thus requiring mobilization of U.S. society as a whole.[43]

Because of the proliferation of security measures along the border since 9/11, ethnic Mexicans have emerged as criminals of the state due to persistent concerns over illegal immigration and drug smuggling. National security concerns naturally assumed the highest priority after 2001. A narrowed focus toward a porous border consequently positioned migrants from Mexico and ethnic Mexicans residing in the United States as potential terrorists.[44] Militarization efforts along the United States' southern border contribute to Mexican otherness and more specifically to Mexicans' criminalization despite citizenship or social standing.[45]

The United States' approach to border enforcement follows a well-established modus operandi that includes reactive policies to social, economic, and political pressures. These restrictive policies are then followed by enforcement details that are ineffective due to topographical obstacles, lack of manpower and financial resources, and economic demands that require looser enforcement. Moreover, the impetus for such policies falls short of long-term objectives. Why? According to political scientist and borderlands scholar Peter Andreas, federal and state governments continue to perform an "audience-directed" nature of border enforcement:

> Audience-directed border enforcement draws from sociological insights about the role of images and symbols in public interaction . . . the border as a political stage, state actors continuously engage in 'face work' and the 'art of impression management.'"[46]

Law enforcement officials and politicians are engaged in what Andreas calls a "double performance," having to assure the populace that the border is open to legal commercial trade while reassuring others that the border is sufficiently closed to illegal flows. An inherent contradiction exists within the infrastructure of border enforcement. Those entrusted with its integrity are forced to concede to the undermining demands of the border's major actors, employers' dependency on cheap migrant labor, and the populace's demand for illicit drugs.[47] However, the consequence of this melodrama has real effects on ethnic Mexicans on both sides of the border. Like with any classic narrative, actors are categorized as protagonists and antagonists. Border militarization defines these roles, and ethnic Mexicans are typecast as "those bad guys." The never-ending cycle of identifying the villain that hails from the US-Mexico borderlands and retaliating with militarization reinforces the categorization of ethnic Mexicans as the enemy. With every passing decade ethnic Mexicans struggle to find their place in the American social, political, and economic mainstream.

In 2008, General Motors aired a series of television commercials for its Chevrolet brand titled, "This Is Our Country," promoting their Silverado truck line. The commercials are laden with iconic "Americana": images of farming communities, rock 'n' roll, firemen, cowboys, and other iconic symbols. Included in the string of images are photographs of Rosa Parks, Muhammad Ali, and a clip of Dr. Martin Luther King's "I Have a Dream" speech. The basic racial binary of white and black flashes across the screen, symbolizing the face of America. In this idyllic postracial America, African Americans are, too, the face of America. Noticeably absent in most of the commercials is the Latino. In a separate commercial but still part of the "This Is Our Country" series is the "My Truck" advertisement. In this short piece, various men give a short anecdote about their Chevrolet trucks and how the trucks either represent them or help them improve their communities. One of the featured men is a Spanish-speaking man whose grandsons explain that their Chevy has been passed down from generation to generation. In the last ten to fifteen seconds of the commercial each featured speaker states, "This is my truck," except for the Spanish-speaking man. He proudly states, "esta es mi troca/this is my truck."[48]

The Chevy commercial series "This Is Our Country" reveals a vivid and homogenous image of what "our country" should look like in the twenty-first century. In three of the four commercials the vast majority of images that depict America are largely of white males and children, while only a handful of images are of African Americans. Latinos are visibly absent from the commercial series, with the sole exception of the "my truck" commercial. The commercial that specifically spoke to brand loyalty featured the only obvious Spanish-speaking customer. A serious disconnect emerges out of this commercial series. "Our country" is made of whites, mostly male, with a sprinkling of African Americans. Latinos are absent, nonexistent, not members of "our country," but are welcomed as consumers. Are ethnic Mexicans a part of "our country?" Can they be the face of "America?" The multipronged authority structure that includes federal, state, and local law enforcement, xenophobic legislation, increased militarization along the US-Mexico border, and organized civilian resistance suggests that ethnic Mexicans are not a part of "our country." If they are not a part of the United States, are they in turn an enemy of America? Perhaps. A comprehensive review of the history of ethnic Mexicans in the United States suggests that their full inclusion in the American sociopolitical fabric has not been fully realized. As one observer of Texas race relations once said, "It is difficult to convince these people that a Mexican is a human being. He seems to be the Texan's natural enemy."[49] The struggle continues.

EPILOGUE: "WHERE THE BAD GUYS ARE"

The title for the epilogue is taken from "Texas Rangers' Deployment to Mexico Border a Military-Style Effort," Ft. Worth Star-Telegram, September 15, 2009, Governor Rick Perry Homepage, http://www.rickperry.org/media -articles/texas-rangers-deployment-mexico-border-military-style-effort (accessed June 21, 2010).

1. In 1989, General Colin Powell was the commanding general of the US Army's Forces Command. After September 28, 2004, Joint Task Force 6 became known as Joint Task Force North. "History of Joint Task Force North: Joint Task Force Originally Established in 1989," Joint Task Force North homepage, http://www.jtfn.northcom.mil/subpages/history.html (accessed June 18, 2010).

2. Ibid.

3. Ibid.

4. "Family Doubts Marines' Account," El Paso Times, May 23, 1997, 2A, "Border Patrol" Vertical File, BHC-EPPL.

5. Ibid., 1A. For more on America's "War on Drugs," see Dan Baum, Smoke and Mirrors: The War on Drugs and the Politics of Failure (New York: Back Bay Books, 1997); Mike Gray, Drug Crazy: How We Got into This Mess and How We Can Get Out (New York: Routledge, 2000); Tony Payan, The Three U.S.-Mexico Border Wars: Drugs, Immigration, and Homeland Security (Westport, CT: Praeger Security International, 2006); Douglas Valentine, The Strength of the Wolf: The Secret History of America's War on Drugs (London: Verso, 2006).

6. "Border Patrol Brings in Marines," El Paso Times, August 8, 1992, "Border Patrol" Vertical File, BHC-EPPL.

7. Ibid.

8. Julia Prodis, "Fatal Shooting of Goat Herder by Marines Enrages Border Town," Associated Press, June 29, 1997, http://www.dpft.org/hernandez/ ap_062997.html (accessed June 22, 2010).

9. "Family Doubts Marines' Account," El Paso Times, May 23, 1997, "Border Patrol" Vertical File, BHC-EPPL.

10. Prodis, "Fatal Shooting of Goat Herder by Marines Enrages Border Town," Associated Press, June 29, 1997, http://www.dpft.org/hernandez/ap_062997 .html (accessed June 18, 2010).

11. "Family Doubts Marines' Account," *El Paso Times*, May 23, 1997, 1A–2A, "Border Patrol" Vertical File, BHC-EPPL.

12. Many law enforcement officials including Texas Ranger Captain Barry Caver speculated that Hernández "might have thought he was shooting at a wild animal rustling in the brush." Julia Prodis, "Fatal Shooting of Goat Herder by Marines Enrages Border Town," Associated Press, June 29, 1997, http://www.dpft.org/hernandez/ap_062997.html (accessed June 18, 2010).

13. "Family Doubts Marines' Account," *El Paso Times*, May 23, 1997, 2A, "Border Patrol" Vertical File, BHC-EPPL.

14. "Border Patrol Cuts Military's Drug Fight Role," *El Paso Times*, July 11, 1997, 1A, "Border Patrol" Vertical File, BHC-EPPL; "Troops Pulled from Anti-Drug Patrols," *Washington Post*, July 30, 1997, http://www.dpft.org/hernandez/wp_073097.html (accessed June 18, 2010).

15. The grand jury believed that Corporal Banuelos and the other Marines were following the rules of engagement when they pursued Hernández; the grand jury believed that Esequiel fired first but did not conclude that he shot at the Marines intentionally. "Marine Avoids Indictment," *Dallas Morning News*, August 15, 1997, http://www.dpft.org/hernandez/dmn_081597.html (accessed June 28, 2010).

16. Representative James Traficant, sponsor of the bill, clarified that the bill only authorized the deployment of the military and did not require it. "Military Authorized to Return to Border Patrol Duty," Associated Press, May 22, 1998, http://www.dpft.org/articles/militaryokd.htm (accessed June 18, 2010).

17. Jack Zimmerman, *The Ballad of Esequiel Hernández* (2008), DVD, directed by Kieran Fitzgerald (Taos, NM: Heyoka Pictures, LLC, 2008).

18. Joseph Nevins, *Operation Gatekeeper and Beyond: The War on "Illegals" and the Remaking of the U.S.-Mexico Boundary*, 2nd ed. (New York: Routledge, 2010), 171; Enrique Madrid, *The Ballad of Esequiel Hernández* (2008), DVD, directed by Kieran Fitzgerald (Taos, NM: Heyoka Pictures, LLC, 2008).

19. Nevins, *Operation Gatekeeper and Beyond*, 172.

20. "9/11" is a popular reference to the terrorist attacks on September 11, 2001, in New York City, Washington, DC, and Pennsylvania.

21. "Texas Rangers' Deployment to Mexico Border a Military-Style Effort," *Ft. Worth Star-Telegram*, September 15, 2009, Governor Rick Perry Homepage, http://www.rickperry.org/media-articles/texas-rangers-deployment-mexico -border-military-style-effort (accessed June 21, 2010).

22. Ibid.

23. Ibid.

24. "Perry Sending Rangers, Guard to the Border," *Texas Tribune*, September 10, 2009, http://www.texastribune.org/texas-mexico-border-news/texas-mexico -border/perry-sending-rangers-guard-to-the-border/ (accessed June 21, 2010).

25. "Texas Governor Sends Rangers to Mexico Border," Associated Press, September 11, 2009, http://www.msnbc.msn.com/id/32793136/ns/us_news -security (accessed June 21, 2010).

26. One of the comments listed below the article announcing Perry's deployment of Rangers stated: "Rangers were overtly lynching Mexicans until just a few decades ago. It is very dangerous to be Mexican American around one. Ten cuidado! (Be Careful!)." "Texas Rangers to Get Border Duty," MySanAntonio .com (San Antonio Express News), September 10, 2009, http://www.mysan antonio.com/news/local_news/Texas_Rangers_to_get_border_duty.html? c=y&viewAllComments=y (accessed June 21, 2010).

27. Press Release from the Office of the Governor Rick Perry, "Gov. Perry Announces Highly Skilled Ranger Recon Teams as Texas' Latest Efforts to Enhance Border Security," Office of the Governor Rick Perry, http://www .governor.state.tx.us/news/press-release/13577 (accessed June 23, 2010).

28. "About Us," Jim Gilchrist's Minutemen Project Website, http://www.minute manproject.com/organization/about_us.asp (accessed June 22, 2010); "The

Angry Patriot," Salon.com, May 11, 2005, http://dir.salon.com/news/feature/
2005/05/11/minuteman/index.html (accessed June 22, 2010).

29. "Minuteman's goal: To Shame Feds Into Action," USAToday.com, May 25,
2006, http://www.usatoday.com/news/nation/2006-05-24-minuteman
-goals_x.htm (accessed June 22, 2010).

30. "Bush Ordering Up to 6,000 in Guard to Border," MSNBC.com, May 15,
2006, http://www.msnbc.msn.com/id/12796688/ (accessed June 22,2010).

31. The "Secure Fence Act of 2006 (H.R. 6061)" authorized the Department of
Homeland Security to spend $1.2 billion for the construction of a 700-mile
fence along the US-Mexico border. 109th Congress, 2nd sess., H.R. 6061,
United States Congress, September 14, 2006; "Operation Jump Start Jumps
into Gear along Southwest Border," American Forces Press Service (Department of Defense), June 15 2006, http://www.defense.gov/news/newsarticle
.aspx?id=16033 (accessed June 23, 2010).

32. "Operation Jump Start Officially Ends," ABQNews.com (Albuquerque
Journal), July 16, 2008, http://www.abqjournal.com/abqnews/index.php?
option=com_content&task=view&id=7954&Itemid=2 (accessed June 23,
2010); "Operation Jump Start Ends on Quiet Note," The Monitor Online
(McAllen, Texas), July 12, 2008, http://www.themonitor.com/articles/border
-14503-set-patrol.html (accessed June 23, 2010).

33. Timothy Dunn, *Blockading the Border and Human Rights: The El Paso Operation
That Remade Immigration Enforcement* (Austin: University of Texas Press, 2009),
226–27.

34. Ibid.

35. "Obama to Send up to 1,200 Troops to Border," *New York Times*, May 25, 2010,
http://www.nytimes.com/2010/05/26/us/26border.html (accessed June 23,
2010); "Obama Relents, Send National Guard to Arizona Border," *The Examiner* (Washington, DC), May 26, 2010, http://www.washingtonexaminer.com/
politics/white-house/Obama-relents_-sends-National-Guard-to-Arizona
-border-94877654.html (accessed June 23, 2010); "Mexico under Siege," Los
Angeles Times Online, News series, http://projects.latimes.com/mexico
-drug-war/#/its-a-war (accessed June 23, 2010).

36. Governor Jan Brewer signed Senate Bill 1070 into law on April 23, 2010. State
of Arizona, Senate, Forty-Ninth Legislature, Second Regular Session, 2010,
http://www.azleg.gov/legtext/49leg/2r/bills/sb1070s.pdf; "Arizona Enacts
Stringent Law on Immigration," *New York Times*, April 23, 2010, http://www
.nytimes.com/2010/04/24/us/politics/24immig.html (accessed June 21,
2010).

37. State of Arizona, Senate, Forty-Ninth Legislature, Second Regular Session,
2010, http://www.azleg.gov/legtext/49leg/2r/bills/sb1070s.pdf (accessed
June 21, 2010).

38. "Arizona Enacts Stringent Law on Immigration," *New York Times*, April 23,
2010, http://www.nytimes.com/2010/04/24/us/politics/24immig.html (accessed June 21, 2010).

39. "Official Statement by Governor Jan Brewer: SB 1070," *Sonoran Weekly Review*,
April 23, 2010, http://sonoranweeklyreview.com/statement-by-governor
-jan-brewer-sb1070/ (accessed June 21, 2010).

40. "Crime in the United States," *Preliminary Annual Uniform Crime Report, January-
December 2009, Report* issued by Robert S. Mueller III, Director, Federal
Bureau of Investigation, United States Department of Justice, Washington,
DC, May 24, 2010, http://www.fbi.gov/ucr/prelimsem2009/index.html (accessed June 23, 2010); Christopher Dickey, "Reading, Ranting, and Arith-
metic," *Newsweek*, May 27, 2010, http://www.newsweek.com/2010/05/27/
reading-ranting-and-arithmetic.html (accessed June 22, 2010).

41. Attributed to Porfirio Díaz (b. 1830 Oaxaca; d. 1915 Paris), president of the
Republic of Mexico (1877–80; 1884–1911).

42. Nevins, *Operation Gatekeeper and Beyond*, 172.

43. Ibid.

44. Payan, *The Three U.S.-Mexico Border Wars*, 87–111; Monica Miller, "La Raza,

Mexican Terrorist Organization," *Canada Free Press* (canadafreepress.com), August 3, 2009, http://www.canadafreepress.com/index.php/article/13357 (accessed June 25, 2010); Malcolm Beith, "Are Mexico's Drug Cartels Terrorists Groups?" Slate (slate.com), April 15, 2010, http://www.slate.com/id/2250990 (accessed June 25, 2010).

45. "Arizona to birther the entire world, starting with this truck driver," Rachel Maddow Show, April 26, 2010, http://maddowblog.msnbc.msn.com/_news/2010/04/26/4206306-arizona-to-birther-entire-world-starting-with-this-truck-driver (accessed June 25, 2010).

46. Peter Andreas, *Border Games: Policing the U.S.-Mexico Divide* (Ithaca, NY: Cornell University Press, 2000), 10.

47. Ibid., 8–10.

48. General Motors' "This Is Our Country" television ad featuring the Chevrolet Silverado 2006, http://www.youtube.com/watch?v=QVVT-wumaLk (accessed July 17, 2010); General Motors' "This is my truck" television ad featuring the Chevrolet Silverado, http://www.youtube.com/watch?v=qriNbVCIsow&feature=related (accessed July 17, 2010).

49. William D. Carrigan, *The Making of a Lynching Culture: Violence and Vigilantism in Central Texas, 1836–1916* (Urbana: University of Illinois Press, 2004), 28.

Bibliography

GOVERNMENT PUBLICATIONS

"Crime in the United States." *Preliminary Annual Uniform Crime Report, January–December 2009*. Federal Bureau of Investigation. Report issued by Robert S. Mueller III, Director.

Records of Boundary and Claims Commission, Arbitrations, 1923–1937. "Motion on Behalf of the United States to Strike Out Portion of Brief on Behalf of United Mexican States," Special Claims Commission, United States and Mexico, The United States of America on behalf of (17 defendants) v. The United States of Mexico, Docket No. 449, Record Group 76, National Archives and Records Administration, Washington, DC.

———. "Memorial of the Cusi Mining Company to the Secretary of State, Supplemental to the Affidavits and the Brief Heretofore Submitted to the Department of the State for its Interposition with the Carranza Government of Mexico." Records Relating to the Santa Ysabel Cases, 1924–1936, Record Group 76, National Archives and Records Administration, College Park, MD.

———. "In the Matter of the Killing of C. R. Watson, Manager of the Cusi Mining Company, and Others, Near Santa Ysabel, in the State of Chihuahua, Mexico, January 10, 1916," Affidavit of J. O. H. Newby, June 27, 1916.

———. "Answer to Memorial Before the Special Claims Commission Mexico and the United States," The United States of America on behalf of Matilda Symansky Bodine Administration of the Estate of Manuel Bonifacio Romero vs. the United Mexican States, The Santa Ysabel Cases, no. 7.

Records of the Department of State Relating to Internal Affairs of Mexico, 1910–1929. National Archives Microfilm, National Archives and Records Service, Washington, D.C.

State of Arizona Legislature. Senate. *Support Our Law Enforcement and Safe Neighborhoods Act of 2010*. SB 1070. 49th Legis., 2nd regular session. (April 23, 2010).

Sworn Testimonies. *Proceedings of the Joint Committee of the Senate and House Investigation of the Texas State Ranger Force*, 36th Legislature, Regular Session, 1919, Legislative Papers, Texas State Library and Archives Commission, Austin, Texas.

Texas Adjutant General Department. *Adjutant General Thomas Scurry, General Order No 62, July 3, 1901*. Archives and Information Services Division, Texas State Library and Archives Commission. Austin, Texas.

———. *General's Report, June 1870–December 1870*. Austin, Texas, 1870.

———. *General's Report, 1903–1904*. Austin, Texas, 1904.

———. *Company 'D,' Monthly Returns, November 30, 1908*. Ranger records, Texas Adjutant General's Department. Archives and Information Services Division, Texas State Library and Archives Commission, Austin, Texas, 1908.

———. *Ranger Force Correspondence, 1917*. Ranger records, Texas Adjutant General's Department. Archives and Information Services Division, Texas State Library and Archives Commission, Austin, Texas, 1917.

Texas Governor James Edward Ferguson. *Telegram from Secretary of State, Newton D. Baker to Texas Governor, James E. Ferguson, May 1, 1916*, Records, Archives and Information Services Division, Texas State Library and Archives Commission, Austin, Texas.

Texas Governor O. B. Colquitt. *Correspondence*, Records, Archives and Information Services Division, Texas State Library and Archives Commission, Austin, Texas.

Texas State Legislature. *Proceedings of the Joint Committee of the Senate and House Investigation of the Texas State Ranger Force*, 36th Legislature, Regular Session, 1919,

Legislative Papers, Texas State Library and Archives Commission, Austin, Texas.

US Army. Post Returns, 1910–1916. Fort Bliss, Texas (El Paso, Texas).

US Bureau of the Census. *Population of Principal Cities [Texas] from earliest Census to 1920*, Bureau of the Census. Washington, DC, 1920.

———. *Special Census of the Population of El Paso, Texas*, January 15, 1916, Bureau of the Census. Washington, DC, 1916.

———. United States Department of the Interior. *Statistics of the Population of the United States, 1880*, Census Office. Washington, DC, 1882.

———. United States Department of the Interior, *Report on Population of the United States, 1890*, Census Office. Washington, DC, 1895.

———. United States Department of the Interior. *Census Reports, Volume I: Population of the United States, 1900*. Prepared under the supervision of William C. Hunt, Census Office. Washington, DC, 1901.

———. United States Department of Commerce. *Population 1910: General Report and Analysis*. Prepared under the supervision of William C. Hunt, Bureau of the Census. Washington, DC, 1913.

———. United States Department of Commerce. *Population of the United States, Volume I & III, 1920*. Prepared under the supervision of William C. Hunt, Bureau of the Census. Washington, DC, 1921, 1922.

———. United States Department of Commerce. *Population of the United States 1930, Volume I & III*. Prepared under the supervision of Leon E. Truesdell, Bureau of the Census. Washington, DC, 1931, 1932.

US Congress. *Emergency Quota Act of 1921*, 57th Cong., 1st sess., 42 Stat. 5; 8 U.S.C. 22.

———. *Immigration Act of 1917*, 39 Stat. 874; 8 U.S.C.

US Congress. Hearings before the Committee on Immigration and Naturalization. 69th Cong., 1st sess., January 12, 1926.

US Congress. *The Secure Fence Act of 2006*, 109th Cong., 2nd sess., September 14, 2006.

US Congress. House. Committee on Immigration and Naturalization. *Restriction of Immigration*. 69th Cong., 1st sess., January 12, 1926.

———. *Immigration Border Patrol*. 70th Cong., 1st sess., March 5, 1928.

———. *El Paso Troubles in Texas*. 45th Cong., 2nd Sess., March 1877–1879.

US Congress. Senate. Subcommittee of the Committee on Foreign Relations. *Investigation of Mexican Affairs*. 66th Cong., 2nd sess., December 6, 1919.

US Congress. Senate. Subcommittee of the Committee on Foreign Relations. "Investigation of Mexican Affairs, 1920: Partial Report of Committee, Abstracts of Testimony, and Index." 66th Cong, 2nd sess., 1920. Committee Print.

US Department of Labor. *U.S. Immigration Service Bulletin*. Commissioner General of Immigration. Washington, GPO, April 1, 1918–August 1, 1919.

US First Brigade. First Provisional Infantry Division. *Circular Letter Regarding Neutrality*, January 8, 1917, Headquarters, Brownsville District, Benjamin F. Delamater Collection, Archives of Texas Military Forces Museum, Austin, Texas.

———. *Bulletin Number 11, copy of sections 12, 13 and 14 of 'Emergency Army Bill Against Liquor and Disorderly Resorts*, May 28, 1917, Headquarters, Brownsville District. Brownsville, Texas.

———. *Bulletin Number 12, May 30, 1917*, Headquarters, Brownsville District. Brownsville, Texas.

———. *General Orders Number 4, May 27, 1916*, Headquarters, Brownsville District. Brownsville, Texas.

———. *General Orders Number 7, June 10, 1916*, Headquarters, Brownsville District. Brownsville, Texas.

———. *General Orders Number 22, February 10, 1917*. War Department, Washington, D.C.

———. *General Orders Number 26, August 17, 1916*, Headquarters, Brownsville District. Brownsville, Texas.

ARCHIVAL AND OTHER PRIMARY SOURCES

Adjutant General Papers. Texas State Library and Archives Commission, Austin, Texas.

American Defense Society Records. The New York Historical Society, New York University Digital Library, http://dlib.nyu.edu/eadapp/transform?source=nyhs/americandefsoc.xml&style=nyhs/nyhs.xsl&part=body (accessed April 29, 2010).

Border Heritage Center, Southwest Collection, El Paso Public Library, El Paso, Texas.

Border Patrol Vertical Files. Border Heritage Center, Southwest Collection, El Paso Public Library, El Paso, Texas.

Cano, Tony. Papers. Personal Notes and Archives, Canutillo, Texas.

Casey Collection. Archives of the Big Bend, Bryan Wildenthal Memorial Library, Sul Ross State University, Alpine, Texas.

C. L. Sonnichsen Special Collections Department, University of Texas at El Paso.

"Columbus Raid" Vertical File. Columbus Historical Society, Columbus, New Mexico.

El Paso Historical Society.

Institute of Oral History, University of Texas at El Paso.

"Maude Wright" Vertical File. Columbus Historical Society, Columbus, New Mexico.

National Archives and Records Administration, College Park, Maryland and Washington, DC.

"National Guard in Texas" Vertical File. Benjamin F. Delamater Collection, Archives of Texas Military Forces Museum, Austin, Texas.

Otis A. Aultman Photo Collection Online. Border Heritage Center, El Paso Public Library, El Paso, Texas.

Papers Read at the Meeting of Grand Dragons, Knights of the Ku Klux Klan. New York: Arno Press, 1977.

Roy W. Aldrick Collection. Archives of the Big Bend, Bryan Wildenthal Memorial Library, Sul Ross State University, Alpine, Texas.

Smithers (W. D.) Collection. Dolph Briscoe Center for American History, University of Texas at Austin.

Southwest Collections/Special Collections, Texas Tech University.

Swancutt, Dale. Papers. National Border Patrol Museum, El Paso Texas.

Texas Governor James E. Ferguson Papers. Texas State Library and Archives Commission, Austin, Texas.

Texas Governor Oscar B. Colquitt Papers. Texas State Library and Archives Commission, Austin, Texas.

Texas Ranger Research Center, Texas Ranger Hall of Fame and Museum, Waco, Texas.

Texas Ranger Vertical Files. Border Heritage Center, Southwest Collection, El Paso Public Library, El Paso, Texas.

Warren, Harry. Papers. Archives of the Big Bend, Bryan Wildenthal Memorial Library, Sul Ross State University, Alpine, Texas.

Wright, E. A. "Dogie." Papers. Dolph Briscoe Center for American History, University of Texas at Austin.

ORAL HISTORIES
Archives of the Big Bend, Bryan Wildenthal Memorial Library, Sul Ross State University, Alpine, Texas.

E. A. Wright oral history, interview no. 86

Institute of Oral History, University of Texas at El Paso

Mario Acevedo, interview 153.2

Epitacio Armendaríz, interview no. 551

George E. Barnhart, interview no. 282

Chester Chope, interview no. 27
Mauricio Cordero, interview no. 250
Alice B. Cummings, interview no. 426
Brigadier General S. L. A. Marshall, interview no. 181
Edwin Reeves, interview no. 135
E. W. Rheinheimer, interview no. 427
Armando A. Sanchez, interview no. 270
Wesley E. Stiles, interview no. 756
Estella Duran Vega, interview no. 308
Hortencia Villegas, interview no. 235

Southwest Collection/Special Collections, Texas Tech University
Dorothy Massey, September 23, 1982

With Author
Tony Cano
Jane Brite White (with Tony Cano)

PERIODICALS

Albuquerque Journal
Armed Services Press Service
Associated Press
Canada Free Press
Dallas Morning News
El Paso Herald Post
El Paso Morning Times
El Paso Times
El Paso World News
Fort Worth Star-Telegram
Houston Chronicle
Labor Advocate
Los Angeles Times
Mesilla Valley Independent
National Republic
Newsweek
New York Times

Pioneer News Observer
Salon.com
San Antonio Express
Slate.com
Sonoran Weekly Review
Texas Tribune
The Cattleman
The Examiner
The Literary Digest
The Monitor Online
The Southwesterner
USAToday
U.S. Immigration Service Bulletin
Washington Post

FILMS AND DOCUMENTARIES

The Ballad of Esequiel Hernández. Taos, NM: Heyoka Pictures, LLC, 2008.
The Hunt for Pancho Villa. Boston: WGBH Educational Foundation, American Experience, 1993.

ELECTRONIC SOURCES

"Arizona to Birther the Entire World, Starting with This Truck Driver." *Rachel Maddow Show,* April 26, 2010. At http://maddowblog.msnbc.com/_news/2010/04/26/4206306-arizona-to-birther-entire-world-starting-with-this-truck-driver (accessed June 25, 2010).
General Motors. "This Is Our Country." Television ad featuring the Chevrolet Silverado 2006. At http://www.youtube.com/watch?v=QVVT-wumaLk (accessed July 17, 2010).
———. "This is my truck." Television ad featuring the Chevrolet Silverado. At http://www.youtube.com/watch?v=qriNbVCIsow&feature=related (accessed July 17, 2010).
"Governor Perry Announces Highly Skilled Ranger Recon Teams as Texas' Latest

Efforts to Enhance Border Security." Office of the Governor Rick Perry. At
http://www.governor.state.tx.us/ (accessed June 21, 2010).

Tuck, Jim. "The Mexican Revolution: A Nation in Flux, pt. 1 and pt. 2." *mexconnect*
.com, October 9, 2008. At http://www.mexconnect.com/articles/296-the
-revolution-a-nation-in-flux-part-1-1910-20 (accessed April 5, 2011).

US Customs and Border Protection. "United States Border Patrol—Protecting Our
Sovereign Borders." At http://www.cbp.gov/xp/cgov/border_security/
border_patrol/history.xml (accessed April 11, 2007).

ARTICLES, BOOKS, AND DISSERTATIONS

Acuña, Rodolfo. *Occupied America: A History of Chicanos.* San Francisco: Canfield Press,
1972.

Army Historical Series. "American Military History." Center of Military History, US
Army, Washington, DC, 1989.

Alonso, Ana Maria. *Thread of Blood: Colonialism, Revolution, and Gender on Mexico's
Northern Frontier.* Tucson: University of Arizona Press, 1995.

Anders, Evan. *Boss Rule in South Texas: The Progressive Era.* Austin: University of Texas
Press, 1982.

Anderson, Gary Clayton. *The Conquest of Texas: Ethnic Cleansing in the Promised Land,
1820–1875.* Norman: University of Oklahoma Press, 2005.

Andreas, Peter. *Border Games: Policing the U.S.-Mexico Divide.* Ithaca, NY: Cornell University Press, 2000.

Baker, T. Lindsay. *Ghost Towns of Texas.* Norman: University of Oklahoma Press,
1986.

Batchelder, Roger. *Watching and Waiting on the Border.* Boston: Houghton Mifflin,
1917.

Baum, Dan. *Smoke and Mirrors: The War on Drugs and the Politics of Failure.* New York:
Back Bay Books, 1997.

Beezley, William H. *Insurgent Governor: Abraham González and the Mexican Revolution in
Chihuahua.* Lincoln: University of Nebraska Press, 1973.

Beezley, William H., and Colin M. MacLachlan. *Mexicans in Revolution, 1910–1946:
An Introduction (The Mexican Experience).* Lincoln: University of Nebraska Press,
2009.

Benton-Cohen, Elizabeth. *Borderline Americans: Racial Divisions and Labor War in the Arizona Borderlands.* Cambridge, MA: Harvard University Press, 2009.

Braddy, Haldeen. *Cock of the Walk, Qui-Qui-Ri-Qui!: The Legend of Pancho Villa.* Albuquerque: University of New Mexico Press, 1955.

———. *Pancho Villa at Columbus.* El Paso: Texas Western College Press, 1965.

Brenner, Anita. *The Wind That Swept Mexico: The History of the Mexican Revolution, 1910–
1942.* Austin: University of Texas Press, 1984.

Brown, Richard Maxwell. "Violence and Vigilantism in American History." In *American Law and the Constitutional Order: Historical Perspectives,* edited by Lawrence M.
Friedman and Harry N. Scheiber, 173–90. Cambridge, MA: Harvard University Press, 1978.

Buenger, Walter L. *The Path to a Modern South: Northeast Texas between Reconstruction and
the Great Depression.* Austin: University of Texas Press, 2001.

Bush, Ira Jefferson. *Gringo Doctor.* Caldwell, ID: Caxton Printers, 1939.

Calderón, Roberto R. *Mexican Coal Mining Labor in Texas and Coahuila, 1880–1930.* College Station: Texas A&M University Press, 2000.

Callahan, Manuel. "Mexican Border Troubles: Social War, Settler Colonialism, and
the Production of Frontier Discourses, 1848–1880." PhD diss., University of
Texas at Austin, 2003.

Calleros, Cleofas. *El Paso . . . Then and Now.* El Paso: American Printing Company,
1954.

Calvert, Peter. *The Mexican Revolution, 1910–1914: The Diplomacy of Anglo-American Conflict.* Cambridge: Cambridge University Press, 1968.

Camarillo, Albert. *Chicanos in a Changing Society: From Mexican Pueblos to American Barrios in Santa Barbara and Southern California, 1848–1930. Cambridge, MA: Harvard University Press, 1979.

Cano, Tony, and Ann Sochat. Bandido: The True Story of Chico Cano, the Last Western Bandit. Canutillo, TX: Reata Publishing, 1997.

Carrigan, William D. The Making of a Lynching Culture: Violence and Vigilantism in Central Texas, 1836–1916. Urbana: University of Illinois Press, 2004.

Carrigan, William D., and Clive Webb. "The Lynching of Persons of Mexican Origin or Descent in the United States, 1848–1928." Journal of Social History 37 (Winter 2003): 411–38.

Castillo, Pedro, and Albert Camarillo, eds. Furia y muerte: Los bandidos Chicanos. Los Angeles: Aztlán Publications, 1973.

Chalkley, John F. Zach Lamar Cobb: El Paso Collector of Customs and Intelligence during the Mexican Revolution, 1913–1918. El Paso: Texas Western Press, 1998.

Chan, Sucheng, ed. Entry Denied: Exclusion and the Chinese Community in America, 1882–1943. Philadelphia: Temple University Press, 1991.

Clendenen, Clarence C. Blood on the Border: The United States Army and the Mexican Irregulars. London: Macmillan, 1969.

———. The United States and Pancho Villa: A Study in Unconventional Diplomacy. Ithaca, NY: Cornell University Press, 1961.

Coerver, Don M., and Linda B. Hall. Texas and the Mexican Revolution: A Study in State and National Policy, 1910–1920. San Antonio: Trinity University Press, 1984.

Collins, Michael L. Texas Devils: Rangers and Regulars on the Lower Rio Grande, 1846–1861. Norman: University of Oklahoma Press, 2008.

Cool, Paul. "El Paso's First Real Lawman, Texas Ranger Mark (Marcus) Ludwick." Quarterly of the National Association for Outlaw and Lawman History (October–December 2001): 1–9.

———. Salt Warriors: Insurgency in the Rio Grande. College Station: Texas A&M University Press, 2008.

Coolidge, Dane. Fighting Men of the West. New York: E. P. Dutton, 1932.

Cunningham, Eugene. Triggernometry: A Gallery of Gunfighters. Caldwell, ID: Caxton Printers, 1958.

Darrah, Jason T. "Anglos, Mexicans, and the San Ysabel Massacre: A Study of Changing Ethnic Relations in El Paso, Texas, 1910–1916." Master's thesis, Texas Tech University, 2003.

De Grazia, Sebastian. "What Authority Is Not." American Political Science Review (June 1959): 321–31.

De León, Arnoldo. Mexican Americans in Texas: A Brief History. 3rd ed. Wheeling, IL: Harlan Davidson, 2009.

———. They Called Them Greasers: Anglo Attitudes toward Mexicans in Texas, 1821–1900. Austin: University of Texas Press, 1983.

———. War Along the Border. College Station: Texas A&M University Press, 2012.

Diener, Alexander C., and Joshua Hagen. Borderlines and Borderlands: Political Oddities at the Edge of the Nation-State. Lanham, MD: Rowman and Littlefield, 2010.

Douglas, Claude Leroy. The Gentlemen in the White Hats: Dramatic Episodes in the History of the Texas Rangers. Dallas: Southwest Press, 1934.

Dunn, Timothy. Blockading the Border and Human Rights: The El Paso Operation That Remade Immigration Enforcement. Austin: University of Texas Press, 2009.

———. The Militarization of the U.S.-Mexico Border, 1978–1992. Austin: University of Texas Press, 1996.

Estrada, Richard. "The Mexican Revolution in Ciudad Juárez–El Paso Area, 1910–1920." Password (Spring 1979): 69.

Foos, Paul. A Short, Offhand, Killing Affair: Soldiers and Social Conflict during the Mexican-American War. Chapel Hill: University of North Carolina Press, 2002.

Fregoso, Rosa Linda. MeXicana Encounters: The Making of Social Identities on the Borderlands. Berkeley: University of California Press, 2003.

Frost, H. Gordon. The Gentlemen's Club: The Story of Prostitution in El Paso. El Paso: Mangan Books, 1983.

Ganster, Paul, and David E. Lorey, eds. *Borders and Border Politics in a Globalizing World*. Lanham, MD: SR Books, 2005.

García, Mario. *Desert Immigrants: The Mexicans of El Paso, 1880–1920*. New Haven, CT: Yale University Press, 1981.

Garnett, William Edward. "Immediate and Pressing Race Problems of Texas." In *Proceedings of the Sixth Annual Convention of the Southwestern Political and Social Science Association*, edited by Caleb Perry. Austin: Southwestern Political and Social Science Association, 1925.

Gillett, James B. *Six Years with the Texas Rangers, 1875–1881*. New Haven, CT: Yale University Press, 1925.

Gilly, Adolfo. *The Mexican Revolution: A People's History*. New York: New Press, 2006.

Gómez-Quiñones, Juan. "Plan de San Diego Reviewed." *Aztlán: Chicano Journal of the Social Sciences and Arts* 1 (Spring 1970): 125.

———. "Toward a Perspective on Chicano History." *Aztlán: Chicano Journal of the Social Sciences and Arts* (Fall 1971): 1–51.

Gonzalez, Gilbert. *Guest Workers or Colonized Labor?: Mexican Labor Migration to the United States*. Boulder, CO: Paradigm Publishers, 2007.

Gould, Lewis. *Progressives and Prohibitionists: Texas Democrats in the Wilson Era*. Austin: University of Texas Press, 1973.

Gray, Mike. *Drug Crazy: How We Got into This Mess and How We Can Get Out*. New York: Routledge, 2000.

Griswold del Castillo, Richard. *The Treaty of Guadalupe Hidalgo: A Legacy of Conflict*. Norman: University of Oklahoma Press, 1990.

Gutiérrez, David. *Walls and Mirrors: Mexican Americans, Mexican Immigrants, and the Politics of Ethnicity*. Berkeley: University of California Press, 1995.

Habermeyer, Christopher Lance. *Gringo's Curve: Pancho Villa's Massacre of American Miners in Mexico, 1916*. El Paso: Book Publishers of El Paso, 2004.

Harris, Charles H., III, and Louis R. Sadler. *The Border and the Revolution: Clandestine Activities of the Mexican Revolution: 1910–1920*. Silver City, NM: High-Lonesome Books, 1988.

———. "Pancho Villa and the Columbus Raid: The Missing Documents." *New Mexico Historical Review* (October 1975): 335–46.

———. *The Secret War in El Paso: Mexican Revolutionary Intrigue, 1906–1920*. Albuquerque: University of New Mexico Press, 2009.

———. *The Texas Rangers and the Mexican Revolution: The Bloodiest Decade, 1910–1920*. Albuquerque: University of New Mexico Press, 2004.

———. "The 'Underside' of the Mexican Revolution, 1912." *The Americas* (July 1982): 69–83.

Harris, Larry. *Pancho Villa: Strong Man of the Revolution*. Silver City, NM: High-Lonesome Books, 1955.

Hart, John Mason. *Revolutionary Mexico: The Coming and Process of the Mexican Revolution*. 10th ed. Chapel Hill, NC: University of North Carolina Press, 1997.

Hernández, Kelly Lytle. "Entangled Bodies and Borders: Racial Profiling and the U.S. Border Patrol, 1924–1955." PhD diss., University of California at Los Angeles, 2002.

———. *Migra!: A History of the U.S. Border Patrol*. Berkeley: University of California Press, 2010.

Hobsbawm, Eric J. *Bandits*. London: Weidenfeld and Nicolson, 1969.

Hoffman, Abraham. "Mexican Repatriation Statistics: Some Suggested Alternatives to Carey McWilliams." *Western Historical Quarterly* (October 1972): 391–404.

———. "Stimulus to Repatriation: The 1931 Federal Deportation Drive and the Los Angeles Mexican Community." *Pacific Historical Review* (May 1973): 205–19.

———. *Unwanted Mexican Americans in the Great Depression: Repatriation Pressures, 1929–1939*. Tucson: University of Arizona Press, 1974.

Hurst, James W. *Pancho Villa and Black Jack Pershing: The Punitive Expedition in Mexico*. Santa Barbara, CA: Praeger Publishers, 2007

———. *Villista Prisoners of 1916–1917*. Las Cruces, NM: Yucca Tree Press, 2000.

Husk, Carlos. "Typhus Fever." *Bulletin of the El Paso County Medical Society* (1916): 75–79.

Johnson, Benjamin Heber. *Revolution in Texas: How a Forgotten Rebellion and Its Bloody Suppression Turned Mexicans into Americans.* New Haven, CT: Yale University Press, 2005.

Joint Task Force North. "History of Joint Task Force North: Joint Task Force Originally Established in 1989." At http//:www.jtfn.northcom.mil/subpages/history.html (accessed June 18, 2010).

Jordan, David Starr. *The Days of a Man: Being Memories of a Naturalist, Teacher, and Minor Prophet of Democracy.* New York: World Book, 1922.

Judson, Pieter M. *Guardians of the Nation: Activists on the Language Frontier of Imperial Austria.* Cambridge, MA: Harvard University Press, 2006.

Justice, Glenn. *Little Known History of the Texas Big Bend: Documented Chronicles from Cabeza de Vaca to the Era of Pancho Villa.* Odessa, TX: Rimrock Press, 2001.

———. *Revolution on the Rio Grande.* El Paso: Texas Western Press, 1992.

Katz, Friedrich. *The Life and Times of Pancho Villa.* Stanford, CA: Stanford University Press, 1998.

———. *Pancho Villa y el ataque a Columbus, Nuevo México.* Chihuahua, Mexico: Sociedad Chihuahuense de Estudios Históricos, 1979.

Keil, Robert. *Bosque Bonito: Violent Times along the Borderland during the Mexican Revolution.* Alpine, TX: Sul Ross State University Press, 2002.

Ku Klux Klan. *Papers Read at the Meeting of the Grand Dragons, Knights of the Ku Klux Klan: Together with Other Articles of Interest to Klansmen.* 2nd ed. New York: Arno Press, 1977.

Lau, Estelle T. *Paper Families: Identity, Immigration Administration, and Chinese Exclusion.* Durham, NC: Duke University Press, 2007.

Lay, Shawn. *War, Revolution, and the Ku Klux Klan: A Study of Intolerance in a Border City.* El Paso: Texas Western Press, 1985.

Lee, Erika. *At America's Gates: Chinese Immigration during the Exclusion Era, 1882–1943.* Chapel Hill: University of North Carolina Press, 2003.

Lemay, Michael, and Elliot Robert Barkan, eds. *U.S. Immigration and Naturalization Laws and Issues: A Documentary History.* Westport, CT: Greenwood Press, 1999.

Levario, Miguel Antonio. "Cuando vino la mexicanada: Authority, Race, and Conflict in West Texas, 1895–1924." PhD diss., University of Texas at Austin, 2007.

———. "The El Paso Race Riot of 1916." In *War along the Border*, edited by Arnoldo De León. College Station: Texas A&M University Press, 2012.

López, Ian Haney. "Race and Colorblindness after *Hernández* and *Brown.*" In *"Colored Men" and "Hombres Aquí,"* edited by Michael A. Olivas, 41–52. Houston: Arte Público Press, 2006.

Luibhéid, Eithne. *Entry Denied: Controlling Sexuality on the Border.* Minneapolis: University of Minnesota Press, 2002.

Margo, A. *Who, Where, and Why Is Villa?.* New York: Latin-American News Association, 1917.

Markel, Howard. *When Germs Travel: Six Major Epidemics That Have Invaded America since 1900 and the Fears They Have Unleashed.* New York: Pantheon Books, 2004.

Martin, Jack. *Border Boss: Captain John R. Hughes, Texas Ranger.* Austin: State House Press, 1990.

Martin, John L. "Can We Control the Border? A Look at Recent Efforts in San Diego, El Paso, and Nogales." Washington DC: Center for Immigration Studies, May 1995. At http://www.cis.org/articles/1995/border/index.html (accessed April 12, 2007).

Martínez, Oscar J. *Border Boom Town: Ciudad Juárez since 1848.* Austin: University of Texas Press, 1975.

———. *Mexican-Origin People in the United States: A Topical History.* Tucson: University of Arizona Press, 2001.

———. *Troublesome Border.* Tucson: University of Arizona Press, 1988.

Mayhall, Mildred P. *Indian Wars of Texas*. Waco: Texian Press, 1965.

McElhaney, Jacquelyn Masur. *Pauline Periwinkle and Progressive Reform in Dallas*. College Station: Texas A&M University Press, 1998.

McWilliams, Carey. *North from Mexico: The Spanish-Speaking People of the United States*. New York: Greenwood Press, 1948.

Means, Joyce E. *Pancho Villa Days at Pilares: Stories and Sketches of Days-Gone-By from the Valentine Country of West Texas*. El Paso: Joyce E. Means, 1976.

Metz, Leon Claire. *Border: The U.S.-Mexico Line*. El Paso: Mangan Books, 1989.

———. *Desert Army: Fort Bliss on the Texas Border*. El Paso: Mangan Books, 1988.

———. *El Paso Chronicles: A Record of Historical Events in El Paso, Texas*. El Paso: Mangan Books, 1993.

Meyer, Marshall W. "Two Authority Structures of Bureaucratic Organization." *Administrative Science Quarterly* (September 1968): 211–28.

Molina, Natalia. *Fit to Be Citizens?: Public Health and Race in Los Angeles, 1879–1939*. Berkeley: University of California Press, 2006.

Montejano, David. *Anglos and Mexicans in the Making of Texas, 1836–1986*. Austin: University of Texas Press, 1987.

Montejano, David, ed. *Chicano Politics and Society in the Late Twentieth Century*. Austin: University of Texas Press, 1999.

Moore, Alvin Edward. *Border Patrol*. Santa Fe: Sunstone Press, 1988.

Myers, John M. *Border Wardens*. Englewood Cliffs, NJ: Prentice-Hall, 1971.

Nevels, Cynthia Skove. *Lynching to Belong: Claiming Whiteness through Racial Violence*. College Station: Texas A&M University Press, 2007.

Nevins, Joseph. *Operation Gatekeeper and Beyond: The War on "Illegals" and the Remaking of the U.S.-Mexico Boundary*. 2nd ed. New York: Routledge, 2010.

Ngai, Mae M. *Impossible Subjects: Illegal Aliens and the Making of Modern America*. Princeton, NJ: Princeton University Press, 2004.

Nunnally, Michael. *American Indian Wars: A Chronology of Confrontations between Native Peoples and Settlers and the United States Military, 1500s–1901*. Jefferson, NC: McFarland, 2007.

Omi, Michael, and Howard Winant. *Racial Formation in the United States: From the 1960s to the 1990s*. 2nd ed. New York: Routledge, 1994.

Paredes, Américo. *With His Pistol In His Hand: A Border Ballad and Its Hero*. Austin: University of Texas, 1958.

Payan, Tony. *The Three U.S.-Mexico Border Wars: Drugs, Immigration, and Homeland Security*. Westport, CT: Praeger Security International, 2006.

Perkins, Clifford Allan. *Border Patrol: With the U.S. Immigration Service on the Mexican Boundary, 1910–1954*. El Paso: Texas Western Press, 1978.

Prodis, Julia. "Fatal Shooting of Goat Herder by Marines Enrages Border Town." *Associated Press*, June 29, 1997, http://www.dpft.org/hernandez/ap_062997.html.

Purcell, Allan R. "The History of the Texas Militia, 1835–1903." PhD diss., University of Texas at Austin, 1981.

Raht, Carlysle Graham. *The Romance of Davis Mountains and Big Bend Country: A History*. Odessa, TX: Rahtbooks, 1963.

Rak, Mary. *Border Patrol*. Boston: Houghton Mifflin, 1938.

Reisler, Mark. "Always the Laborer, Never the Citizen: Anglo Perceptions of the Mexican Immigrant during the 1920s." *Pacific Historical Review* (May 1976): 231–54.

Reséndez, Andrés. *Changing National Identities at the Frontier: Texas and New Mexico, 1800–1850*. Cambridge: Cambridge University Press, 2004.

Rice, Harvey F. "The Lynching of Antonio Rodríguez." Master's thesis, University of Texas at Austin, 1990.

Rocha, Rodolfo. "The Influence of the Mexican Revolution on the Mexico-Texas Border, 1910–1916." PhD diss., Texas Tech University, 1981.

Rodriguez, Jaime E. *Common Border, Uncommon Paths: Race, Culture, and National Identity in U.S.-Mexican Relations*. Wilmington, DE: Scholarly Resources, 1993.

Romo, David Dorado. *Ringside Seat to a Revolution: An Underground Cultural History of El Paso and Juárez, 1893–1923*. El Paso: Cinco Puntos Press, 2005.

Samora, Julian, Joe Bernal, and Albert Peña. *Gunpowder Justice: A Reassessment of the Texas Rangers*. Notre Dame, IN: University of Notre Dame Press, 1979.

Sánchez, George J. *Becoming Mexican American: Ethnicity, Culture, and Identity in Chicano Los Angeles, 1900–1945*. New York: Oxford University Press, 1995.

Sandos, James A. *Rebellion in the Borderlands: Anarchism and the Plan of San Diego, 1904–1923*. Norman: University of Oklahoma Press, 1992.

Schrag, Peter. *Not Fit for Our Society: Nativism and Immigration*. Berkeley: University of California Press, 2010.

Shipman, Jack. "Texas Rangers." Photocopy, Border Heritage Center, Southwest Collection, El Paso Public Library, El Paso, Texas.

Smedley, Audrey. *Race in North America: Origins and Evolution of a Worldview*. 3rd ed. Boulder, CO: Westview Press, 2007.

Sonnichsen, Charles Leland. *The El Paso Salt War of 1877*. El Paso: Hertzog, 1961.

———. *Pass of the North*. El Paso: Texas Western Press, 1968.

St. Clair, Robert, Guadalupe Valdés, and Jacob Ornstein-Galicia, eds. *Social and Eduational Issues in Bilingualism and Biculturalism*. Washington, DC: University Press of America, 1981.

Stern, Alexandra Minna. "Buildings, Boundaries, and Blood: Medicalization and Nation-Building on the U.S.-Mexico Border, 1910–1930." *Hispanic American Historical Review* (February 1999): 64.

———. *Eugenic Nation: Faults and Frontiers of Better Breeding in Modern America*. Berkeley: University of California Press, 2005.

Stopka, Christina. "Partial List of Texas Ranger Company and Unit Commanders," At http://www.texasranger.org/ReCenter/Captains.pdf. Publication date unknown (accessed June 7, 2007). Texas Ranger Research Center, Waco, Texas.

Stout, Joseph. *Border Conflict: Villistas, Carrancistas, and the Punitive Expedition, 1915–1920*. Fort Worth: Texas Christian University Press, 1999.

Timmons, Wilbert H. *El Paso: A Borderlands History*. El Paso: Texas Western Press, 1990.

Tompkins, Frank. *Chasing Villa: The Last Campaign of the U.S. Cavalry*. Silver City, NM: High-Lonesome Books, 1934.

Turner, Frederick C. "Anti-Americanism in Mexico, 1910–1913." *Hispanic American Historical Review* (November 1967): 502–18.

Tyler, Ronnie C. *The Big Bend: A History of the Last Texas Frontier*. Washington, DC: Office of Publications, 1975.

Utley, Robert M. *Lone Star Justice: The First Century of the Texas Rangers*. New York: Oxford University Press, 2002.

———. *Lone Star Lawmen: The Second Century of the Texas Rangers*. New York: Oxford University Press, 2007.

Valdés, Guadalupe, ed. *Social and Educational Issues in Bilingualism and Biculturalism*. Washington, DC: University Press of America, 1981.

Valentine, Douglas. *The Strength of the Wolf: The Secret History of America's War on Drugs*. London: Verso, 2006.

Vanderwood, Paul J. *Disorder and Progress: Bandits, Police, and Mexican Development*. Wilmington, DE: Scholarly Resources, 1992.

Vila, Pablo. *Crossing Borders, Reinforcing Borders*. Austin: University of Texas Press, 2000.

———. "Everyday Life, Culture, and Identity on the Mexican-American Border: The Ciudad Juárez–El Paso case." PhD diss., University of Texas at Austin, 1994.

Webb, Walter Prescott. *The Texas Rangers: A Century of Frontier Defense*. Austin: University of Texas Press, 1935.

Weber, C. Edward. "The Nature of Authority: Comment." *Journal of the Academy of Management* (April 1961): 62–63.

Welsome, Eileen. *The General and The Jaguar: Pershing's Hunt for Pancho Villa: A True Story of Revolution and Revenge*. New York: Little, Brown, 2006.

Wilson, Thomas M., and Hastings Donnan, eds. *Border Identities: Nation and State at International Frontiers.* Cambridge: Cambridge University Press, 1998.

Winders, Richard B. *Mr. Polk's Army: The American Military Experience in the Mexican War.* College Station: Texas A&M University Press, 1997.

Zamora, Emilio. *Claiming Rights and Righting Wrongs in Texas: Mexican Workers and Job Politics during World War II.* College Station: Texas A&M University Press, 2009.

———. *The World of the Mexican Worker in Texas.* College Station: Texas A&M University Press, 1993.

Zillich, Emily Tessier. "History of the National Guard in El Paso." Master's thesis, Texas Western College (University of Texas at El Paso), 1958.

Figure 1.1

May Day 2006: A Day Without an Immigrant.

Source: Photo by Jonathan McIntosh, posted to Wikimedia.org at http://commons
.wikimedia.org/wiki/File:May_Day_Immigration_March_LA03.jpg (licensed CC-BY-
2.5).

A Day Without an Immigrant: Social Movements and the Media Ecology

The image in figure 1.1 depicts the streets of downtown Los Angeles on May 1, 2006. This scene was mirrored in cities across the country as millions of new immigrants, their families, and their allies joined the largest protest in U.S. history.[1] They left their homes, schools, and workplaces, gathered for rallies and mass marches, and took part in an economic boycott for immigrant rights. This chapter explores the May Day 2006 mobilization, known as A Day Without an Immigrant, through the lens of the changing media ecology.[2]

Our media are in the midst of rapid transformation. On the one hand, mass media companies continue to consolidate, more and more journalists are losing their jobs to corporate downsizing, and long-form, investigative journalism is steadily being replaced by less costly recycled press releases and entertainment news.[3] Public broadcasters remain one of the most trusted information sources, but their funding is under attack. As audiences fragment across an infinite-channel universe, the agenda-setting power of even the largest media outlets wanes. On the other hand, regional consolidation has produced new channels that speak from the former peripheries. For example, Latin American media firms now reach across the United States, and Spanish-language print and broadcast media draw larger audiences and wield more influence than ever before.[4] At the same time, widespread (though still unequal) access to personal computers, broadband Internet, and mobile telephony, as well as the mass adoption of social media, have in some ways democratized the media ecology even as they increase our exposure to new forms of state and corporate surveillance.

Social movements, which have always struggled to make their voices heard across all available platforms, are taking advantage of these changes. The immigrant rights movement in the United States faces mostly indifferent, occasionally hostile, English-language mass media. The move- ment also enjoys growing support from Spanish-language print newspapers and broadcasters. At the same time, commercial Spanish-language mass media constrain immigrant rights discourse within the framework of neo- liberal citizenship. Community media outlets that serve new immigrant communities, such as local newspapers and radio stations, continue to provide important platforms for immigrant rights activists. Increasingly, social movement groups also self-document: they engage their base in participatory media-making, and they circulate news, information, and culture across many platforms, especially through social media. In the spring of 2006, the immigrant rights movement was able to take advantage of opportunities in the changing media ecology to help challenge and defeat an anti-immigrant bill in the U.S. Congress.

Immigration policy, border militarization, domestic surveillance, raids, detentions, and deportations are all key tools of control over low-wage immigrant workers in the United States. These tools are not new. They have been developed over the course of more than 130 years, at least since the Chinese Exclusion Act of 1882, the first major law to restrict immigra- tion. This law, the culmination of decades of organizing by white suprema- cists, barred Chinese laborers from entering the United States and from naturalization.[5] Immigration policy, surveillance, detention, and deporta- tion have long been used to target "undesirable" (especially brown, yellow, black, left, and/or queer) immigrants[6] and thereby to maintain whiteness, heteropatriarchy (the dominance of heterosexual males in society),[7] and capitalism.[8] The past decade, however, has been particularly dark for many immigrant communities. After the September 11, 2001, attacks, the con- solidation of Immigration and Naturalization Services into the Department of Homeland Security was followed by the "special registration" program, then by a new wave of detentions, deportations, and "rendering" of "sus- pected terrorists" to Guantánamo and to a network of secret military prisons for indefinite incarceration and torture without trial.[9] In 2006, Immigration and Customs Enforcement (ICE) increased the number of beds for detainees to 27,500, opened a new 500-bed detention center for families with children in Williamson County, Texas, and set a new agency record of 187,513 "alien removals."[10] By the spring of that year, it had become politically feasible for the Republican-controlled House of Repre- sentatives to pass H.R. 4437, better known as the Sensenbrenner bill.

Sensenbrenner would have criminalized 11 million unauthorized immigrants by making lack of documentation a felony rather than a civil infraction. It would also have criminalized the act of providing shelter or aid to an undocumented person, thus making felons of millions of undocumented folks, their families and friends, and service workers, including clergy, social service workers, health care providers, and educators.[11] The Republican Party used the bill and the debates it provoked to play on white racial fears in an attempt to gain political support from the nativist element of their base. The Sensenbrenner bill abandoned market logic: a Cato Institute analysis found that reducing the number of low-wage immigrant workers by even a third would cost the U.S. economy about $80 billion. By contrast, the same study found that legalizing undocumented workers would grow the U.S. economy by more than 1 percent of GDP, or $180 billion.[12]

The response to the Sensenbrenner bill was the largest wave of mass mobilizations in U.S. history. A rally led by the National Capital Immigration Coalition on March 7 brought 30,000 protesters to Washington, D.C.; soon after, on March 10, 100,000 attended a protest in downtown Chicago.[13] Yet these events were only the tip of the iceberg. March, April, and May 2006 saw mass marches in every U.S. metropolis, as well as in countless smaller cities and towns. In the run-up to May Day (May 1), a date still celebrated in most of the world as International Workers' Day, immigrant rights organizers called for a widespread boycott of shopping and work. The economic boycott, also a de facto general strike, was promoted as "A Day Without an Immigrant," a direct reference to the 2004 film *A Day Without a Mexican*. The film (a mockumentary by director Sergio Arau) portrays the fallout when immigrant Latin@s disappear from California en masse, leaving nonimmigrants to do the difficult agricultural, manufacturing, service-sector, and household work that is largely invisible, but provides the foundations for the rest of the economy. Participation in the Day Without an Immigrant mobilizations was immense: half a million people took to the streets in Chicago, a million in Los Angeles, and hundreds of thousands more in New York, Houston, San Diego, Miami, Atlanta, and other cities across the country. In many places, these marches were the largest on record.[14]

What produced such a powerful wave of mobilization? The surging strength of the immigrant rights movement was built through the hard work of hundreds of organizations, including grassroots groups, nonprofit organizations, regional and national networks, and policy-focused Beltway groups.[15] At the same time, the rapidly changing media ecology provided crucial opportunities for the movement to grow, attract new participants, reach an unprecedented size, and achieve significant mobilization, cultural, and policy outcomes.[16]

A Day Without an Immigrant

English-language TV news channels have long played important roles in the information war that swirls around human migration. However, in the spring of 2006, all major English-language media outlets completely failed to anticipate the strength of the movement and the scale of the mobilizations. By contrast, Spanish-language commercial broadcasters, including the nationally syndicated networks Telemundo and Univision, provided constant coverage of the movement. Spanish-language newspapers, TV, and radio stations not only covered the protests but also played a significant role in mobilizing people to participate.[17] This was widely reported on in the English-language press after the fact.[18] Indeed, by most accounts, commercial Spanish-language radio was the key to the massive turnout in city after city. In L.A., Spanish-language radio personalities, or *locutores*, momentarily put competition aside in order to present a unified message: they urged the city's Latin@ population to take to the streets against the Sensenbrenner bill. Media scholar Carmen Gonzalez describes a historic meeting and press conference held by the *locutores*:

On March 20th all of the popular Spanish-language radio personalities gathered at the Los Angeles City Hall to demonstrate their support for the rally and committed to doing everything possible to encourage their listeners to attend. Those in attendance included: Eduardo Sotelo "El Piolín" & Marcela Luevanos from KSCA "La Nueva" 101.9FM; Ricardo Sanchez "El Mandril" and Pepe Garza from KBUE "La Que Buena" 105.5FM; Omar Velasco from KLVE "K-Love" 107.5FM; Renan Almendarez Coello "El Cucuy" & Mayra Berenice from 97.7 "La Raza"; Humberto Luna from "La Ranchera" 930AM; Colo Barrera and Nestor "Pato" Rocha from KSEE "Super Estrella" 107.1FM.[19]

These and other *locutores* across the country had a combined listener base in the millions. They ran a series of collaborative broadcasts during which they joined each other physically in studios and called in to one another's shows. They focused steadily on the dangers of H.R. 4437, the need to take to the streets, and the demand for just and comprehensive immigration reform. Gonzalez surveyed mobilization participants in the streets of L.A. and found that, after face-to-face conversations, Spanish-language commercial radio was the most important platform in terms of motivating march turnout (friends and family were the primary source of protest information, followed by radio).[20] One of the community organizers I later interviewed reiterated this point:

We saw it with the 2006 marches, where the radios had, some would say ... most of the push. Not the organizations that were organizing. They've been doing their work for a long time, but that whole thing of being able to be on the radio in front of millions of people really motivated the majority of people to participate in the economic boycott, and in the walkouts.[21]

While immigrant rights groups in L.A. organize yearly May Day marches that tend to turn out several thousand people, in the spring of 2006 the marches were ten to a hundred times larger than usual. The threat of the Sensenbrenner bill, combined with the involvement of the commercial *locutores*, produced this massive shift.[22]

The Walkouts

Figure 1.2
Silver Lake area students walk out for immigrant rights on March 29, 2006.
Source: Photo by pseudonymous poster "jlr-builder123," posted to L.A. Indymedia at http://la.indymedia.org/news/2006/03/152082_comment.php.

While the mass marches were largely organized through broadcast media, especially Spanish-language talk radio, text messages and social networking sites (SNS) were the key media platforms for the student walkouts that swept Los Angeles and some other cities during the same time period.[23] As the anti-Sensenbrenner mobilizations provided fuel for the fires of the (mostly Anglo, middle-class) blogosphere, walkout organizers enthusiastically turned to MySpace and YouTube to circulate information, report on their own actions, and urge others to join the movement. At the same time, text messaging (also called SMS, or short messaging service) was used as a tool for real-time tactical communication. Student organizers I interviewed made it clear that both text messaging and MySpace played important but not decisive roles in the walkouts.[24] Pre-existing networks of students organized the walkouts for weeks beforehand by preparing flyers, meeting with student organizations, doing the legwork, and spreading the word. Some said that text messages and posts to MySpace served not to "organize" the walkouts but to provide real-time confirmation that actions were really taking place. For example, one student activist told me about checking her MySpace page during a break between classes. She said that it was when she saw a photograph posted to her wall from a walkout at another school that she realized her own school's walkout was "really going to happen."[25] That gave her the courage to gather a group of students, whom she already knew through face-to-face organizing, and convince them that it was time to take action.[26] Another high school student activist explained:

It was organized, there was flyers, there was also people on the Internet, on chat lines and MySpace, people were sending flyers also. So that's also one of the ways that it was organized. The thing is that students just wanted their voice to be heard. Since they can't vote, they're at least trying to affect the vote of others, by saying their opinion towards H.R. 4437 affecting their schools and their parents or their family.[27]

This student activist, like many of those I worked with and interviewed, emphasized the pervasive and cross-platform nature of movement media practices during the spring of 2006. Staff at community-based organizations repeatedly described radio as the most important media platform for mobilizing the immigrant worker base. By contrast, student activists often mentioned SNS (specifically MySpace, the most popular SNS at the time) as a key communication tool during the walkouts. A few also mentioned email (especially mailing lists) and blogs, but most emphasized that organizing took place through a combination of face-to-face communication with friends, family, and organized student groups, printed flyers, text messages, and MySpace. I discuss the walkouts in more detail in chapter 2; for now it is enough to say that media organizing during the walkouts involved pervasive all-channel messaging, as young people urged one another to take action to defeat Sensenbrenner and stand up for their rights.

Analyzing A Day Without an Immigrant and the student walkouts side by side, we can see the contours of the overall media ecology for the immigrant rights movement in 2006. Although ignored, if not attacked, by English-language mass media and bloggers, the movement against the Sensenbrenner bill was able to grow rapidly by leveraging other platforms. Commercial Spanish-language broadcast media reported on the movement in detail, and, in the case of Spanish-language radio hosts, actively participated in mobilizing millions. At the same time, middle school, high school, and university students combined face-to-face organizing and DIY media-making, and used commercial SNS and mobile phones to circulate real-time information about the movement, coordinate actions, and develop new forms of symbolic protest. As these practices spread rapidly from city to city, the mobilizations continued to grow in scope and intensity. The vast scale of the movement was reflected in the slogan, "The sleeping giant is now awake!" The movement's power briefly caught the opposition off guard, and the Sensenbrenner bill died, crushed by the *gigante* (giant) of popular mobilization.

Movements and the Media Ecology: Looking across Platforms

We've seen, briefly, how the changing media ecology presented opportunities for the immigrant rights movement during the 2006 mass mobilization wave. Next, we will explore how immigrant rights activists engage across all available media platforms, including English-language mass media, Spanish-language mass media, community media (especially radio), and social media. The immigrant rights movement can teach us a great deal about how social movement media strategy today extends across platforms, despite the recent turn in the press, the academy, and activist circles toward a nearly exclusive emphasis on the latest and greatest social media platforms. At the same time, cross-platform analysis helps us understand what is really new in social movement media practices. For example, in the past, the main mechanism for advancing movement visibility, frames, and ideas was through individual spokespeople who represented the movement in interviews with print or broadcast journalists working for English-language mass media. This mechanism is now undergoing radical transformation. For the immigrant rights movement, increasingly powerful Spanish-language radio and TV networks provide important openings. At the same time, social media have gained ground as a crucial space for the circulation of movement voices, as the tools and skills of media creation spread more broadly among the population. I begin, however, by looking at the tense relationship between the movement and what activists call "mainstream media."

English-Language Mass Media

Many immigrant rights organizers express frustration with "mainstream media." By mainstream media they usually mean English-language newspapers and TV networks, especially those with national reach. Their feelings about unfair coverage are supported by the scholarly literature. For example, a recent meta-analysis of peer-reviewed studies of immigration framing in English-language mass media (by Larsen and colleagues) found that when immigrants are covered at all, they are usually talked about in terms that portray them as dangerous, threatening, "out of control," or "contaminated."[28] Despite some recent gains, such as the Drop the I-Word campaign that, in 2013, convinced both the Associated Press and the *Los Angeles Times* to stop using the terms "illegal immigrant" and "illegal alien," professional journalists generally continue to use dehumanizing language to refer to immigrants who lack proper documentation.[29] Indeed, a 2013 study by the Pew Research Center found that, despite some recent shifts toward the use of "undocumented immigrant" and away from "illegal alien," "illegal immigrant" remains by far the most common term used in the English-language press.[30]

Nonetheless, by focusing on lifting up the voices of immigrants and portraying them as full human beings, the immigrant rights movement has sometimes been able to shift public discourse. For example, immediately after the 2006 mobilizations, a research group led by Otto Santa Ana at UCLA conducted a critical discourse analysis of mainstream newspaper reporting on immigration policy, immigration, and immigrants. The group gathered one hundred key newspaper articles from two time periods: first, immediately after the May 2006 mobilizations, and second, in October 2006, after public attention had moved on. The authors found and categorized approximately two thousand conceptual metaphors used to refer to immigrants in English-language newspaper coverage during these time periods. They determined that the discursive core of the immigration debate is about the nature of unauthorized immigrants: on one side, there is a narrative of the immigrant as a criminal or animal, and on the other there is a narrative of the immigrant as a worker or a human being. Through a quantitative analysis of metaphor frequency, they found that, during coverage of the mass mobilizations in the spring of 2006, newspapers did shift toward a balance between the use of humanizing (43 percent) and dehumanizing (57 percent) metaphors about immigrants. However, by October, after the mobilizations had faded from public memory, newspapers switched back to employ dehumanizing metaphors more than twice as frequently as humanizing ones (67 percent of the time).[31] The discursive battle in English-language mass media is thus a long, slow, and painful process for immigrant rights organizers and for the communities they work with.

Many organizers say they occasionally do manage to gain coverage in mainstream media, but only in exceptional circumstances. One, who works with indigenous migrant communities, put it this way: "It's rare that we get the attention of the mainstream media unless there's blood or something. Then they'll come to us if it's related to indigenous people."[32] She feels that she is called on to speak as an expert about indigenous immigrants, but only in order to add color to negative stories about her community. She also mentioned that the difficulty seemed specific to L.A., and to the *Los Angeles Times* in particular; she feels that local partners of her organization in some other Californian cities have more luck with mainstream media. Many also express frustration that movement victories in particular are almost never covered. They find it especially galling that the mass media flock to cover the activities of tiny anti-immigrant groups while ignoring the hard day-to-day work done by thousands of immigrant rights advocates. One said, "I feel like a lot of the great work that's going on with organizations, say day laborers won a huge settlement or claim, you're not going to hear about it in the mass media. What we do hear about immigrant rights is anti-immigrant rights and anti-immigrant sentiment. That's pretty [much] across the board, that's how it's presented."[33] A few feel that anti-immigrant rights activists get more coverage because they are more savvy about pitching their actions to journalists, and that the immigrant rights movement could do a much better job of placing its stories and frames in English-language mass media.[34] Others feel that mainstream outlets consistently reject even their best media strategies.[35]

A few activists, mostly those who participate in more radical social movement groups, shared an explicit analysis of the mass media as a powerful enemy. One said, "We have an understanding that the media is not on our side. The corporate media is not on the side of the people, and they're actually an extension of the state, of these corporations."[36] The same activist, however, also talked about how the corporate media can occasionally be used to the movement's advantage:

We know they can reach way more people than we can at this point. Until we take over their TV stations, we're not going to be able to trust them. But around specific cases of police murder, for example an incident that happened in East L.A. recently was Salvador Cepeda, who was an eighteen-year-old, [who was] murdered by the sheriffs in the Lopez Maravilla neighborhood. We put out a press release and they came out to the vigil that we had. We try to encourage the families to speak out, to get it out there, but we're not going to be dependent on them.[37]

Whether they believe mass media to be actively antagonistic to the immigrant rights movement or not, most are frustrated by the way that they feel the media either ignore them or twist their words. Both activists' experiential knowledge and qualitative and quantitative scholarly studies demonstrate the systematic difficulties immigrant rights organizers face as they try to shape public discourse. Yet most continue to engage the mass media. Only two activists I interviewed, both from a collective called Revolutionary Autonomous Communities (RAC), said they had moved beyond anger and frustration and decided to stop speaking to "the corporate media:" "RAC has the position that as RAC, we're not going to rely on the corporate media at all. We're not going to speak to them. Anything we do, it's not going to be popularized through the corporate media. Because they're going to try to tell our stories their way."[38] One of the reasons RAC decided to stop speaking to corporate media was to avoid what they described as the problem of media "creating movement leaders" through selective decisions about whom to interview for the movement's perspective, a dynamic I return to below.

Most immigrant rights organizers, however, desire more and better coverage from English-language print and broadcast media. To achieve this, they emphasize the importance of personal relationships with reporters.

Some talked about specific reporters with whom they had developed a rapport. For example, one online organizer with a national group described how journalists who have a personal connection to immigration, especially those who come from immigrant families themselves, are easier to work with and more likely to report on the movement in a positive light:

It's a lot easier to get your message across through someone who has a personal connection to it.... I have a relationship with a writer from the Associated Press, he's of Mexican descent, he loves us. I pitched him this piece about us going to donate blood as undocumented students, and he wrote an article about it.... It was really well written and just put us in a really positive light, there's these students going out all across the nation, and going to donate blood around Christmas time, and so it was kind of like, is their blood illegal or something?[39]

Despite occasional examples of excellent coverage in English-language mass media outlets, often based on the long-term cultivation of connections with reporters and sometimes facilitated by the relative ease of contacting journalists through social media (especially Twitter), immigrant rights activists generally find themselves turning to other outlets that are more receptive: Spanish-language mass media, community radio, and the "ethnic press."

Spanish-Language Mass Media

Spanish-language mass media, especially commercial radio *locutores* (or announcers), played a key role in supporting the 2006 mobilizations against the Sensenbrenner bill. This was by no means a new development. Spanish-language media in Los Angeles have historically provided support for the immigrant rights movement, as Elena Shore has extensively documented.[40] More broadly, Juan Gonzales and Joe Torres have recently written a detailed popular history of the U.S. media that traces the role of the black press, the Spanish-language press, and the Chinese American press in the long struggle toward racial justice.[41] These accounts provide important context for the experiences of many in today's movement, who intimately understand the importance of Spanish-language mass media to their organizing efforts. For example, savvy immigrant rights organizers recognize that Facebook and Twitter are crucial for reaching immigrant youth, but they also know that to reach the broader Latin@ immigrant community, Univision and Telemundo are the most important channels to target:

When talking about immigrant youth, definitely, I would say [email, Facebook, and Twitter are] probably the biggest mediums. But when you're talking about the immigrant community broadly, Univision and Telemundo are huge. They're some of the most watched TV channels in this country.[42]

Immigrant rights organizers across the spectrum share this opinion. Students, labor organizers, indigenous community activists, staff at independent worker centers, and members of radical collectives all agree that commercial Spanish-language media frequently provide coverage where English-language media are nowhere to be found.[43] When they talk about the media used by the communities they organize, some mention not only the largest Spanish-language newspapers (*La Opinión*) and television channels (Univision, Telemundo) but also outlets focused on migrant workers' city, state, or community of origin. For example, many Oaxacans follow the major pan-Latin@ media but also read the Oaxacan newspapers *El Oaxaqueño* or *El Impulso de Oaxaca*[44] (I return to this dynamic, also known as *translocal media practices*, in chapter 4.) These patterns are also generational: younger indigenous people, especially those born in L.A., are more likely to "go to MySpace, listen to Rage Against the Machine, everything else."[45] Media use, in particular the adoption of SNS, is also related to how long the person has been a resident of the United States, although this is changing as SNS use rates increase in the home countries of migrant workers.[46]

The Spanish-language press is not the only important media ally for immigrant rights activists in L.A. To some degree, similar dynamics apply across all immigrant communities. For example, organizers from the Koreatown Immigrant Workers Alliance (KIWA) discussed gaining coverage in Korean-language media outlets during their supermarket workers' campaign, which ultimately secured a living-wage agreement in five different supermarkets in L.A.'s Koreatown.[47] Strategies for gaining newspaper coverage, whether the newspaper is in English, Spanish, Korean, or any other language, include building relationships with individual reporters, calling in favors from high-status allies, and the use of timely or familiar frames.[48] In the case of KIWA's Koreatown supermarket campaign, these strategies were highly effective in generating attention from Korean-language media, which covered the campaign "every step of the way."[49] KIWA's experience of positive coverage by Korean-language media thus mirrors many Latin@ activists' experience with the Spanish-language press. However, there are important differences. Spanish-language media in the United States have grown into nationwide, and in some cases transnational, networks that now reach a massive pan-Latin@ market.[50] The reach and power of Spanish-language mass media thus dwarf that of other minority-language outlets.

Leveraging this power does not come without complications. While commercial Spanish-language radio stations provide important opportunities, many activists feel that these stations are also sensationalist, materialistic, sexist, racist, and homophobic.

Those are very commercial outlets. They're in favor of immigrant rights but in kind of a very general way. And then sometimes they'll talk about raids and things like that, which is a big concern in the immigrant community and in the immigrant rights community. But they don't do what I would want them to do, which would be very proactive about warning people, having people call in when they see ICE vans, warning people where they see them, that's what I would really like to see those media outlets do.... They're as bad or worse as the mainstream media in English.[51]

Many immigrant rights organizers have mixed feelings about the role of Spanish-language mass media. Their experiential knowledge is again supported by critical scholarship, such as work by Beth Baker-Cristales, who analyzed the role of Spanish-language mass media in the 2006 marches.[52] Baker-Cristales provides rich detail about the key media personalities and networks involved in supporting the protests. She argues that, even as they played an important role in mobilizing Spanish-speaking immigrants to participate, print newspapers, TV, and radio networks also shaped the protests in ways that reproduced the dominant post-9/11 ideology of neoliberal citizenship. In other words, Spanish-language mass media successfully shaped protesters' ideas, language, and protest tactics to conform to the narrative of immigrants as ideal citizens, hard workers, and consumers who primarily desire cultural and political assimilation into mainstream, 'all-American' (Anglo, middle-class, heteronormative, U.S. nationalist) values.[53] Protesters were encouraged to portray themselves as "good immigrants," as opposed to the negative (and racially coded) categories "criminals" and "terrorists." Additionally, Baker-Cristales shows how the media chastised those who engaged in nonsanctioned forms of protest, such as the high school (and middle school) walkouts. Spanish-language broadcasters also heavily discouraged protesters' attempts to assert their own cultural or national identities alongside their desire for immigration policy reform. Most visibly, this took place through repeated calls for immigrant rights protesters to abandon flags from their own countries of origin and replace them with U.S. flags. This was meant to demonstrate "undivided" loyalty, despite the reality that many migrants do feel connected both to their communities of origin and to their new homes, and do participate meaningfully in binational or translocal citizenship.[54]

Community Radio

While Spanish-language commercial radio *locutores* with daily audiences of millions played the most important role in catalyzing the marches of 2006, their support for the immigrant rights movement overall has been sporadic. Community radio stations, on the other hand, reach fewer people at any one time but play an ongoing role in covering, supporting, and strengthening the movement. This should not be surprising. From Bolivian miners' radio[55] to the first pirate station in the United States, linked to the black power movement,[56] from the struggle for civil rights in the U.S. South[57] to the international feminist radio collective FIRE, community radio has long been a core tool of social movement communication.[58] Movement-based radio played a key role in the Algerian national liberation struggle,[59] the rise of the antiwar counterculture in the United States during the Vietnam War, and the Italian labor and social struggles of the 1970s, to name a few examples among many.[60] Today, the number of community radio stations continues to climb, even as the number of firms that control hundreds (or thousands) of full-power stations shrinks. Since the reregulation of radio in the United States in 1996, the radio giant Clear Channel has snapped up more than 1,200 stations. At the same time, however, the World Association of Community Radio Broadcasters counts 3,000 member stations across 106 countries.[61] In the United States, community radio activists such as Philadelphia's Prometheus Radio Project have struggled for, and won, expanded access to legal low-power FM licenses.[62] These and other battles have led some to theorize community radio as a social movement in and of itself.[63] Indeed, despite the recent wave of enthusiasm for social media as the key strategic tool for social movements, there is little doubt that community radio continues to play a critical role. In general, radio remains the primary news source for many of the world's poorest people. This is true everywhere, but it is most marked in parts of Latin America, Africa, and Asia, particularly where illiteracy rates are high and where there are communities of indigenous language speakers who are marginalized from national-language media.[64] These conditions describe low-wage immigrant workers on the margins of global cities everywhere, including Los Angeles.

In L.A., a number of community radio stations support social movements on a daily basis. These stations include the Pacifica affiliate KPFK, which carries Spanish-language movement programming such as *Mujeres Insurgentes* (Insurgent Women), *Voces de Libertad* (Voices of Freedom), and others; the streaming Internet station Killradio.org, originally a project of L.A. Indymedia; an unlicensed station run by Proyecto Jardín (Garden Project), an unlicensed station run by La Otra Campaña del Otro Lado (the Zapatista-affiliated Other Campaign from the Other Side); and *Radio Sombra* (Radio Shadow) in East L.A. Other radio stations linked to the immigrant rights movement include Radio Campesina, the network of local stations run by the United Farm Workers, which started in 1983 with KUFW in Visalia and now includes stations in Bakersfield, Fresno, Lake Havasu (Arizona), Phoenix, Salinas, Tri-Cities (Washington), and Yuma (Arizona). Many, if not all, of these radio stations and networks participated extensively in immigrant rights organizing in 2006. A study by Graciela Orozco for the Social Science Research Council analyzed coverage of the 2006 mobilization wave by Radio Bilingue (Bilingual Radio), a more than two-decades-old nonprofit network of Latin@ community radio stations with six affiliates in California and satellite distribution to over one hundred communities in the United States, Puerto Rico, and Mexico. She found that the nonprofit network played an important role in circulating information and encouraging people to join the mobilizations.[65]

Some immigrant rights organizations have developed relationships with specific community radio outlets over time. For example, the Frente Indígena de Organizaciones Binacionales (Indigenous Front of Binational Organizations, FIOB) has a long-standing relationship with Radio Bilingue. The network will often air audio content, interviews, and public service announcements (PSAs) provided by FIOB. For a time, FIOB ran a regular public affairs show called *Nuestro Foro* (Our Forum).[66] In similar fashion, KIWA was able to secure a monthly hourlong radio show called *Home Sweet Home* on Radio Seoul, a Korean-language radio station that broadcasts in Koreatown.[67] Similar dynamics play out in many locales; for example, one immigrant rights organizer in Boston described community radio as an important outreach avenue: "Radio's huge for a lot of different types of immigrant communities. I'm working not only with the Spanish-speaking immigrant community, but there's Haitian radio, there's Brazilian radio, that's the way people get a lot of their news."[68] Community-based, minority-language radio thus remains a key part of the media ecology for many in the immigrant rights movement.

Streaming Radio and Internet-Enabled Distribution

As I note throughout this book, the most dynamic social movement media practices often take place across platforms. By 2006, at the time of the mass mobilizations against the Sensenbrenner bill, many movement-based radio stations were operating live streams over the Internet. Activists use streaming radio to transmit audio to remote listeners, who may listen via a computer linked to speakers, a mobile phone with a data connection, a stereo in the home, or a portable music player. Movement radio producers throughout the world also use the net to share and distribute both audio files and streams, which are picked up by community radio stations for local transmission on AM or FM bands. Examples in Los Angeles include Kill Radio, Radio Sombra, and Radio Insurgente, the EZLN station in Chiapas that is rebroadcast locally by pirate radios throughout the Americas (http://radioinsurgente.org). Several activists I worked with and interviewed were involved in movement radio projects, and all were quite familiar with live streaming radio over the net.

We have a show on killradio.org.... We're able to do our own reporting, interviews with people that are in different cities, organizing around ICE raids, immigration, indigenous rights, police brutality, other things that are happening, which is a good thing. Eventually I think we want to maybe even do it where—I know one of our members from Copwatch, he has raisethfist.org, where he has an Internet news show and then it's through FM dial. He's going to rebroadcast some of our shows, too. It's heard throughout Compton, Long Beach, Southeast L.A.[69]

As this activist describes, pirate radio stations now operate their studios in one location, then stream live over the Internet to a radio transmitter (or to multiple transmitters) for FM broadcast. This is known as a streaming studio-to-transmitter link (STL). The increasingly common use of this approach in the United States is confirmed by FCC reports, which indicate that in the majority of FCC raids on pirate broadcasters, the seized transmitters are remotely controlled.[70]

Movement-based audio production and distribution networks include the Latin American Association of Radiophonic Education (http://aler.org), which distributes programming across the hemisphere via satellite and Internet, with eight uplinks, 187 satellite receivers, and 117 affiliates. Free Speech Radio News (FSRN, http://fsrn.org) counts over two hundred journalists from fifty-seven countries around the world and is broadcast on the five Pacifica Network stations and more than fifty community stations in the United States, as well as in 120 countries via the Internet, shortwave, and community radio stations.[71] Workers' Independent News Service (WINS, http://laborradio.org) produces syndicated daily headline news segments, in-depth features and stories, economic reports, and raw audio archives that are used by radio stations and print publications. The content is created by local unions and allied activists, gathered together, edited, and repackaged, then distributed by audio streaming and podcast. The Internet has thus facilitated the growth of distribution networks that gather audio material from movement-based radio producers, package it, and amplify its impact through online streaming and delivery to network affiliates for AM or FM broadcast.

Community Media

Commercial Spanish-language media, including large-circulation newspapers and major TV networks, are key allies of the immigrant rights movement. They regularly report on immigration as an issue, follow immigration policy debates, and send reporters to cover immigrant rights activism. Sometimes, as in the spring of 2006, they also participate in efforts to mobilize the Latin@ community to take political action. At the same time, Spanish-language commercial media shape and constrain the language, strategy, and tactics of the immigrant rights movement. In addition, not every immigrant community is Spanish-speaking, and so not every immigrant community can count on access to the same kind of amplification. However, to some degree, every immigrant community does have access to community media, sometimes in its mother tongue, sometimes in English, and often bi- or multilingual. Indeed, the history of the U.S. media system is largely a history of newspapers and radio stations founded to serve the needs of new immigrant communities. This field is sometimes referred to as the ethnic press. Although the term is used by many immigrant rights activists, I avoid it, since it tends to mask the ethnicity of the Anglo (white) press.[72] In any case, ethnic/community media outlets such as newspapers, radio stations, and, increasingly, websites continue to play a crucial role in the immigrant rights movement. Many immigrant rights organizers see a presence in these media as essential:

Ethnic media has been one of our biggest resources. *El Mundo, El Planeta,* the *Brazilian Times,* and all the Brazilian media outlets, because they get the narrative out there. And they usually use the narrative that we want them to use, which is different from the American media.[73]

Print newspapers especially still provide legitimacy for activists. For example, student organizers in Boston mentioned that newspaper coverage produces credibility in working-class immigrant communities:

It makes people trust us. When they see us in *El Planeta,* they're like, "Oh, I saw you in *El Planeta,* so that's why I want to be involved," or "I saw you in the *Brazilian Times* and I heard so much about you guys, here's a hundred dollars, I want to donate to the campaign." So in terms of getting more support from your own community, it's a good resource, 'cause it almost makes you more legit, you know. Even though it's your community, when they see you in the paper they're like, "Oh, these kids are real."[74]

Community media thus act as legitimators of immigrant rights activists, and cover them far more frequently than mainstream English-language papers. Although community media have far less reach than either English- or Spanish-language mass media, the content they publish circulates across outlets through both formal and informal distribution networks. In particular, some activists cited the community media content network New American Media as a key media ally.[75]

The strength of local community media outlets has direct impacts on the strength of local organizing efforts. One activist who works as an online organizer for a national immigrant rights organization noted that the movement in Wisconsin has been consistently able to turn out large numbers of people for marches and mass mobilizations. He attributed the high turnout to the presence of a number of community media outlets, including newspapers and radio shows, produced by the immigrant community.[76] In the Boston area, the same organizer mentioned an AM radio station that sells hourly time slots. Organizations such as Centro Presente and Better Youth Boston take advantage of this and help members produce their own radio programs.

There is a long history in the United States of new immigrants creating media for their community of national origin, published in their mother tongue. However, many immigrant rights activists point to a shift in the past decade toward increased access to these outlets. For example, one described how what she termed "ethnic media" have emerged over the past decade as a key space for community-based organizations to gain coverage, where previously English-language print journalists and broadcasters ignored them:

For us, we always have to stop and think, "What's the best way?"... And even till now, we still hit that mainstream newspaper, and then we realize other things that work because the mainstream doesn't show up, but the ethnic does. So for us ethnic media was this huge opening.... We eventually learned how to navigate ethnic press—really, pretty soon the mainstream were going to the ethnic press to get the information.[77]

The ethnic press is thus important not only because it covers stories that mainstream media ignore but also because it has become a source of stories for the mainstream press. This closely mirrors the more widely heard argument that the mass media now regularly draw stories from blogs and social media. The same organizer described the press strategy around a campaign to gain increased fares for taxi workers in New York:

So I worked on a project in New York, with Taxi Workers, and pitched it to the *New York Times*.... The reporter bought it, and he was totally down with it, had the cover of the local news, you know, "Taxi drivers can't support their families." And we're like, "Could it have been more perfect?" That morning that it came out is when we sent out the press release for the wider "report comes out today." We got thirty media, local radio, TV, newspaper, tons of ethnic press, and that led to both *New York Daily News* and the *New Yorker*, the two smaller, the weeklies, to actually write editorials that support[ed] taxi workers in getting a fare increase. They never, ever, ever, ever say anything nice about the drivers. Which led to the fare increase victory.[78]

This story reveals the continued importance of the mainstream print media (the *New York Times*). At the same time, it illustrates how coverage by a major media outlet is situated within a changed media ecology that savvy organizers have learned to exploit. The initial story in the *Times* provided important momentum and credibility to the campaign, which organizers then leveraged to increase visibility for a report release about conditions in the industry, thereby generating a flurry of coverage across local and community media and ultimately securing a fare increase for immigrant taxi drivers.

Social Media

In the current media ecology, the immigrant rights movement is generally denied access to the English-language mass media, but is able to find openings in Spanish-language commercial media, as well as in community media outlets. In addition, despite deeply unequal levels of digital media access,[79] many grassroots media activists, immigrant rights organizers, and movement participants do use the Internet extensively to promote, document, and frame their activities. By 2006, the time of the Sensenbrenner mobilizations, social movements everywhere, including the immigrant rights movement, had widely adopted SNS. The first SNS to gain significant visibility was Friendster, soon followed by MySpace, then Facebook and Twitter (as well as a host of other, nationally specific SNS, such as Orkut in Brazil, Cyworld in Korea, and Sina Weibo in China). Social movements have used each of these SNS to advance their goals. For example, MySpace was originally marketed as a site for independent musicians to promote their music and connect with fans, but it soon became the most popular SNS for young people in the United States.[80] By 2006, a wide spectrum of activist networks and social movement groups, including anarchists, environmentalists, and feminists, all had MySpace profiles.[81] Activists use SNS as tools to announce meetings, actions, and events, distribute movement media, and reach out to Internet-savvy demographics.[82] Some SNS focus explicitly on facilitating face-to-face meetings based on shared interests. For example, in 2004, Howard Dean's campaign recognized that MeetUp could help the candidate's base self-organize during Dean's bid for the Democratic Party presidential nomination.[83] The use of MeetUp emerged first from the base of Dean supporters and was then encouraged and fostered by campaign leadership.[84] This case, and the social media–savvy strategy of the Obama campaign in 2008 and again in 2012, illustrate how participatory media practices have been used to revitalize vertical political organizational forms. Movement appropriation of SNS takes place even while these sites are also spaces where users replicate gender, class, and race divisions—for example, see danah boyd on how Indian Orkut users replicated the caste system, and on teens' class- and race-based discourse about MySpace versus Facebook.[85]

Movements extensively use the Internet and mobile phones as tactical mobilization tools. For example, we have seen how students in the L.A. Unified School District used MySpace and SMS to help coordinate walkouts that saw 15,000 to 40,000 students take the streets during the week following the March 25, 2006, marches.[86] I return to the walkouts in chapter 2.

Almost all the immigrant rights activists I worked with and interviewed said that social media are important organizing tools that can be used to connect with and inspire new activists, even as they repeatedly emphasized that the core work of movement building takes place through face-to-face connection. Movements are about relationships, and in-person communication is essential.[87] At the same time, many organizers also note that social media can be used to develop or extend relationships not only with the networks of other activists but also with reporters. Personal relationships with reporters, in turn, are essential to garner positive coverage in print and broadcast media. For example, several DREAM activists talked about developing Twitter relationships with reporters. They found that Twitter produces higher response rates and faster response times from reporters than traditional press releases: "I could send a Twitter message to a reporter and that reporter will respond ten times faster than if I send a press release. And it's ten times less work."[88]

Mobile phones are also key. Many organizers who talk about Facebook, Twitter, and email lists as important tools for connecting with immigrant youth emphasize that mobile phones are a crucial platform in new immigrant communities:[89]

Folks that grew up in this country mostly, they use a lot of the newer tools, like Facebook and Twitter, and e-mail lists is a way a lot of people communicate. But I work in a community [which] broadly uses cell phones a lot more. So for instance I just sent out this tweet to ask people to sign a mobile petition to stop deportation, and I actually tried to get them to send me their emails, to get them to formally sign the petition. Also, I'll hopefully follow up with them through email so I can explain the case more broadly; it's a little bit hard to do it with 140 characters. A lot of people signed, or wanted to sign, the petition and not as many sent the email. I mean, it shows that more people use mobile phones than emails,... so that's where I think the future is for our community.[90]

Widespread access to mobile phones has also produced an important shift over the last few years, from the use of the web to document past actions and mobilizations to real-time social media practices. As one interviewee stated,

I think right now we're at this point where suddenly we're kind of moving into this ... different area of real-time web.... I mean I'm finding with video, for example, how feasible it is to make a video and put it up the day that it happens.... In the past, I think in 2006, we wouldn't really have thought like that.[91]

He said that a few years earlier, activists would have mostly relied on commercial TV stations to provide video coverage of an action or mobilization, then recorded the TV broadcast and perhaps used it later to point to evidence of successful organizing. Today, by contrast, social movements are increasingly able to provide real-time or near real-time coverage of their own actions. It is not uncommon, for example, for movement media-makers to document a day's action, then post the video to the web within a few hours. Increasingly, movement media-makers also broadcast their own actions via commercial live-streaming sites. For example, DREAM activists used UStream to provide real-time feeds from sit-ins at Department of Homeland Security (DHS) offices, congressional offices, and Obama campaign headquarters in 2012. Most famously, media activists with Occupy Wall Street used UStream, Livestream, and other services to broadcast everything from General Assemblies to the violent displacement of protest camps by riot police.[92]

Some immigrant rights activists feel that the assumption that social media makes organizing easier is not necessarily true. For example, one online organizer who works for a national media-savvy organization described both positive and negative aspects of what he calls "new media" in the context of community organizing. On the "good side," he felt that social media allow rapid list building and getting in touch with many people quickly, and he offered the example of Occupy Wall Street. He also pointed to the ability to "control and tell your own story, which is extremely powerful. The power of narrative, public narrative is amazing…. It's huge to be able to say now, they don't have to tell our story, we're going to tell our own story."[93] On the other hand, he described social media as having three main drawbacks. First, it produces a mode of activism that he calls "reactionary as opposed to intentional"; in other words, activists end up responding to online debates about various events rather than "sitting down and figuring out what you're going for." Second, it blurs the boundaries of public and private, which he sees as potentially harmful. Organizers who default to public by posting everything on social media end up making mistakes and "putting out all these fires that you don't necessarily want to be putting out." Third, he is concerned about social media's ability to produce the illusion of making a difference. His example of this dynamic: "Someone puts out a Facebook status update 'Call your senator,' and then you click 'Like,' and you're like 'Ah, I just did something good today.' If you click 'Like' and you didn't call a senator, you just did absolutely nothing."[94]

Immigrant rights activists also see great potential for the amplification of their voices in digital space but are frustrated by the current lack of realization of that possibility. For example, many feel that progressive English-language bloggers don't spend a lot of time engaging immigration issues.[95] They see this as a crucial problem, especially since right-wing and anti-immigrant frames and language are widespread across the blogo-sphere. One interviewee noted that phrases like "What part of illegal don't you understand?" often dominate the comment sections of articles, blog posts, and other online spaces.[96] At the same time, he noted that the rela-tively small but highly motivated group of older white racists who system-atically post negative comments are more familiar with "older technology like forums, but they're not good at using some of the newer tools that we have."[97] Some online platforms are thus seen (if only temporarily) as friendlier to immigrant rights advocates than others.

Activists also note that social media can be used to reinforce power inequality. For example, one online organizer observed that although revo-lutionary uses of social media have been widely covered and discussed in the wake of the so-called Arab Spring, social media are primarily used by elites. Those who have greater access to digital media tools and skills tend to be those who have class or educational privilege. He gave an example from Guatemala, where an elite lawyer recorded a YouTube video critical of the left-leaning president just before committing suicide. The video was circulated widely via SNS and then amplified by right-leaning news web-sites, in a context in which only the wealthy have broadband Internet access. Elites used the video as a rallying tool against the democratically elected president, almost to the point of constitutional crisis.[98] Ultimately, none of my interviewees argued that social media or the Internet per se have a transformational impact on organizing or social movements. Instead, they see them as tools that can be applied to organizing but are currently underutilized by their communities.

The Power of Fox News: "We Know the Law's Racist But We Still Support It Anyway"

Changes in the media ecology provide important new opportunities for the immigrant rights movement. However, these changes should not be overestimated. Even as the movement gains visibility, as activists develop

339

new relationships with journalists, and as movement participants increasingly self-document their struggles, the media system remains dominated overall by language, frames, and metaphors that systematically dehumanize immigrants.[99] Many activists also emphasize that they still face daunting opposition in the form of powerful right-wing broadcast media. Even as the immigrant rights movement wins certain kinds of victories, both symbolic and political, it can be very difficult to withstand concerted attacks from the anti-immigrant media machine:

When we get the full force of the media outlets, we generally get our asses kicked. I think a good example of that is [Arizona State Bill] SB-1070. We came out very strong, framing that through our story of racial profiling and oppression.... The best image I had was the image of the Phoenix Suns wearing the "Los Suns" jersey, 'cause they were saying "solidarity with the Latino community." But you know, after Fox News and all these folks started going after us, the polling changed on it. It was the worst polling ever, 'cause they were like, "We know the law's racist but we still support it anyway."[100]

In the fight against Arizona's SB 1070 (key components of which have now been struck down as unconstitutional), even support from a major sports team was not enough to counter the force of a sustained attack from Fox News and right-wing talk radio. The changed media ecology, while it provides many important opportunities, is still often hostile terrain for the immigrant rights movement.

The Immigrant Rights Movement and the Media Ecology: Conclusions

In the spring of 2006, the immigrant rights movement burst out of the shadows and into the streets. The Sensenbrenner bill was crushed by a massive protest wave, the largest in U.S. history. Organizers were successful in part because they leveraged new opportunities in a changing media ecology.

The dominant component of the media ecology, English-language mass media, remains challenging terrain for the immigrant rights movement. When activists do receive coverage in English-language print and broadcast media, they are often framed in ways that do not help them achieve their goals. Occasionally, however, the English-language press does tell immigration stories in ways that humanize immigrants. Organizers feel that cultivating relationships with individual sympathetic reporters is key to increasing the frequency of favorable frames. They also note that this can sometimes be more easily achieved with reporters who have a personal connection to immigration.

In general, the movement enjoys better access to commercial Spanish-language radio and television, even as these outlets grow in reach and political power. Yet commercial Spanish-language media constrain the immigrant rights movement within "safe," and often deeply problematic, assimilationist narratives of neoliberal citizenship: "good" versus "bad" protesters and "hard workers" versus "criminals" and "terrorists." Over the past few years, organizers have become more savvy about how to generate coverage in community media (the ethnic press), and how to further push such coverage until it bubbles up to wider circulation via the mainstream media. Community media also provide access to more recent immigrants, and help legitimize immigrant rights activists within their own communities. As we shall discuss in chapter 4, translocal media practices also facilitate movement building, as migrants increasingly access and sometimes create content for media outlets in their hometowns, cities, or communities of origin.

At the same time, the explosion of access to social media helps organizers more directly involve movement participants, allies, and supporters in the production and circulation of their own rich media texts. The rise of Spanish-language commercial media and the spread of social media both provide important openings for the insertion of movement narratives into public consciousness. In addition, English-language mass media outlets sometimes pick up and amplify stories that begin in social media, community media, or Spanish-language mass media. More recently, movement participants have begun to produce real-time or near real-time self-documentation of their struggles. Yet even as social media have steadily grown in importance, according to organizers, nothing displaces the power of face-to-face communication.

Overall, the media ecology is evolving: where once there were only a few pathways to public visibility, there are now more, and more flexible, routes. However, activists can effectively leverage this flexibility only if they recognize the opportunities available in the new media ecology rather than remain focused solely on gaining access to English-language print and broadcast media. The next chapter describes how the immigrant rights movement uses what I call *transmedia organizing* strategies to become visible across platforms, to open up the movement narrative to participatory media-making, to link attention to action, and to do all this in ways that remain accountable to the movement's social base.

Notes

1. Jesse Díaz, "Organizing the brown tide: *La gran epoca primavera* 2006, an insiders' story," PhD diss., University of California, 2010, http://www.escholarship.org/uc/item/3m92x4nb (retrieved August 1, 2013).

2. Communication scholars have long used the term "media ecology" to examine the relationship between media technologies, media content, and social structure. In this book I use the term in its more popular sense, as a synonym for "media system" or "media across all channels and platforms." This is how the term is usually deployed by the activists and organizers I interviewed. I use it to highlight flows of information across multiple channels, including mass, community, and social media. Readers interested in the scholarly literature on media ecology should explore Harold Adams Innis, *The Bias of Communication* (Toronto: University of Toronto Press, 2008); Neil Postman, "The humanism of media ecology," *Proceedings of the Media Ecology Association* 1 (2000): 10–16; and Lance Strate, *Echoes and Reflections: On Media Ecology as a Field of Study* (Creskill, NJ: Hampton Press, 2006).

3. Robert W. McChesney and John Nichols, *Our Media, Not Theirs: The Democratic Struggle against Corporate Media* (New York: Seven Stories Press, 2011).

4. Arlene Dávila, *Latinos, Inc.: The Marketing and Making of a People: Updated Edition with a New Preface* (Berkeley: University of California Press, 2012).

5. Erika Lee, "The Chinese exclusion example: Race, immigration, and American gatekeeping, 1882–1924," *Journal of American Ethnic History* 21, no. 3 (2002): 36–62.

6. Andreas Peter, *Border Games: Policing the US-Mexico Divide* (Ithaca, NY: Cornell University Press, 2000).

7. For more on heteropatriarchy, see Andrea Smith, "Heteropatriarchy and the three pillars of white supremacy," in *Color of Violence: INCITE! Women of Color Against Violence,* ed. Andrea Smith, Beth E. Richie, and Julia Sudbury, 66–73 (Cambridge, MA: South End Press, 2006).

8. Ibid.

9. Wahab Twibell and Ty Shawn, "The road to internment: Special registration and other human rights violations of Arabs and Muslims in the United States," *Vermont Law Review* 29, no. 2 (2005): 407–553; Rachel Ida Buff, "The deportation terror," *American Quarterly* 60, no. 3 (2008): 523–551.

10. Immigration and Customs Enforcement, "Fact Sheet: ICE Office of Detention and Removal," Washington, D.C., ICE, 2006. http://www.ice.gov/pi/news/factsheets/dro110206.htm (retrieved August 20, 2007).

11. Immigrant Legal Resource Center, "Dangerous immigration legislation pending in Congress," Immigrant Legal Resource Center, San Francisco, December 23, 2005.

12. Peter B. Dixon and Maureen T Rimmer, *Restriction or Legalization? Measuring the Economic Benefits of Immigration Reform,* Trade Policy Analysis 40, Cato Institute, Washington, D.C., August 13, 2009, http://www.cato.org/publications/trade-policy-analysis/restriction-or-legalization-measuring-economic-benefits-immigration-reform (Retrieved April 7, 2014).

13. Otto Santa Ana, Sandra L. Treviño, Michael J. Bailey, Kristen Bodossian, and Antonio De Necochea, "A May to remember: Adversarial images of immigrants in U.S. newspapers during the 2006 policy debate," *Du Bois Review: Social Science and Research on Race* 4, no. 1 (2007): 207–232.

14. Laura Pulido, "A Day Without Immigrants: The racial and class politics of immigrant exclusion," *Antipode* 39, no. 1 (2007): 1–7.

15. Díaz, "Organizing the brown tide."

16. Suzanne Staggenborg, "Can feminist organizations be effective?," in *Feminist Organizations: Harvest of the New Women's Movement,* ed. Myra Marx Ferree and Patricia Yancey Martin, 339–355 (Philadelphia: Temple University Press, 1995).

17. Adrián Félix, Carmen González, and Ricardo Ramírez, "Political protest, ethnic media, and Latino naturalization," *American Behavioral Scientist* 52, no. 4 (2008): 618–634.

18. Mandalit Del Barco, "Spanish-language DJ turns out the crowds in LA," National Public Radio, April 12, 2006, http://www.npr.org/templates/story/story.php?storyId=5337941 (retrieved September 1, 2007).

19. Carmen Gonzalez, "Latino mobilization: Emergent Latino mobilization via communication networks," Unpublished paper, Annenberg School for Communication & Journalism, University of Southern California, Los Angeles, 2006.

20. Ibid.

21. Interview, NB.

22. Interviews, NB, XD, KB, BH, DH, CX.

23. Wayne Yang, "Organizing MySpace: Youth walkouts, pleasure, politics, and new media," *Educational Foundations* 21, nos. 1–2 (2007): 9–28.

24. Interviews, BH, XD, NB.

25. Interview, EN.

26. Ibid.

27. *Source Code*, "Students Unite in LA," Season 3, Episode 10: "Immigration emergency?," 2006, video, http://www.archive.org/details/freespeechtv_sourcecode3_10 (Retrieved April 6, 2014).

28. Knud Larsen, Krum Krumov, Hao Van Le, Reidar Ommundsen, and Kees van der Veer, "Threat perception and attitudes toward documented and undocumented immigrants in the United States: Framing the debate and conflict resolution," *European Journal of Social Sciences* 7, no. 4 (2009): 115–134.

29. A letter signed by more than one hundred psychologists in support of the Drop the I-Word campaign and the AP changes describes in detail the way this term functions on a cognitive level to dehumanize those it is applied to.

30. Emily Guskin, "'Illegal,' 'undocumented,' 'unauthorized': News media shift language on immigration," FactTank, Pew Research Center, Washington, D.C., June 17, 2013, http://www.pewresearch.org/fact-tank/2013/06/17/illegal-undocumented -unauthorized-news-media-shift-language-on-immigration (retrieved October 13, 2013).

31. Santa Ana et al., "A May to remember."

32. Interview, PS.

33. Interview, NB.

34. Interview, XD.

35. Interview, TX.

36. Interview, KB.

37. Ibid.

38. Interview, RF.

39. Interview, LC, online organizer.

40. Elena Shore, "What is the role of Hispanic media in immigrant activism?," *Social Policy* 36, no. 3 (2006): 8.

41. Juan González and Joseph Torres, *News for All the People: The Epic Story of Race and the American Media* (New York: Verso Books, 2011).

42. Interview, LC.

43. Interviews, DH, PS, LC, BH, EQ.

44. Interview, PS.

45. Ibid.

46. Interview, LC.

47. Interview, EQ.

48. William A. Gamson and Gadi Wolfsfeld, "Movements and media as interacting systems," *Annals of the American Academy of Political and Social Science* 528 (July 1993): 114–125.

49. Interview, EQ.

50. Dávila, *Latinos, Inc.*

51. Interview, CY.

52. Beth Baker-Cristales, "Mediated resistance: The construction of neoliberal citizenship in the immigrant rights movement," *Latino Studies* 7, no. 1 (Spring 2009): 60–82.

53. Ibid.

54. Ibid.; Alvaro Lima, "Transnationalism: What it means to local communities," Boston Redevelopment Authority, Boston, Winter 2010. http://www.bostonre developmentauthority.org/getattachment/40c9373f-d170-4ed7-91bf-300f2b7 daeb9/ (Retrieved April 6, 2014).

55. Alan O'Connor, *Community Radio in Bolivia: The Miners' Radio Stations* (Lewiston, NY: Edwin Mellen Press, 2004).

56. Timothy B. Tyson, *Radio Free Dixie: Robert F. Williams & the Roots of Black Power* (Chapel Hill: University of North Carolina Press, 1999).

57. Brian Ward, *Radio and the Struggle for Civil Rights in the South* (Gainesville: University Press of Florida, 2004).

58. Lawrence Soley, *Free Radio: Electronic Civil Disobedience* (Boulder: Westview, 1999).

59. Frantz Fanon, "This is the Voice of Algeria," in *Studies in a Dying Colonialism,* trans. Haakon Chevalier, 69–98 (New York: Monthly Review Press, 1965). First published 1959, in French.

60. John Downing, *Radical Media: Rebellious Communication and Social Movements* (Mountain View, CA: Sage, 2001).

61. See the website of the World Association of Community Radio Broadcasters (AMARC), an international nongovernmental organization serving community radio, at http://amarc.org.

62. Andy Opel, *Micro Radio and the FCC: Media Activism and the Struggle over Broadcast Policy* (Westport, CT: Praeger, 2004).

63. Kevin Howley, "Remaking public service broadcasting: Lessons from Allston-Brighton free radio," *Social Movement Studies* 3, no. 2 (2004): 221–240.

64. For examples, see Alfonso Gumucio Dragon and Thomas Tufte, *Communication for Social Change: Anthology: Historical and Contemporary Readings* (South Orange, NJ: CFSC Consortium, 2006).

65. Graciela Orozco, "Understanding the May 1st immigrant rights mobilizations." (New York: Social Science Research Council, 2007).

66. The FIOB coordinator in Santa Maria, Jesus Estrada, was also able to secure a regular TV show on Telemundo at one point (interview, PS).

67. Interview, KZ.

68. Ibid.

69. Interview, KB.

70. See DIYMedia.net's FCC Enforcement Action Database at http://www.diymedia .net/fccwatch/ead.htm.

71. See the website of Free Speech Radio News, at http://fsrn.org.

72. Simon Cottle, *Ethnic Minorities and the Media: Changing Cultural Boundaries* (Philadelphia, PA: Open University Press, 2000).

73. Interview, SU.

74. Ibid.

75. Interview, LC.

76. Ibid.

77. Interview, TX.

78. Ibid.

79. To be explored in more depth in chapter 5.

80. danah boyd, "Why youth (heart) social network sites: The role of networked publics in teenage social life," in *Youth, Identity, and Digital Media,* ed. D. Buckingham, 119–142 (Cambridge, MA: MIT Press, 2007).

81. See http://myspace.com/infoshopdotorg (anarchist infoshop), http://myspace.com/gpus (Greenpeace), and http://www.myspace.com/feminists for examples.

82. Kara Jesella, "The friendster effect," AlterNet, January 29, 2006, http://www.alternet.org/story/31103 (retrieved June 29, 2010).

83. Araba Sey and Manuel Castells, "From media politics to networked politics: The Internet and the political process," in *The Network Society: A Cross-Cultural Perspective,* ed. M. Castells, 363-384 (Cheltenham, UK / Northampton, MA: Edward Elgar, 2004).

84. Joe Trippi, *The Revolution Will Not Be Televised* (New York: HarperCollins, 2009).

85. danah boyd, "White flight in networked publics? How race and class shaped American teen engagement with MySpace and Facebook," in *Race After the Internet,* Eds. Lisa Nakamura and Peter Chow-White, 203–222 (New York: Routledge, 2011); boyd, "Why youth (heart) social network sites."

86. Jenna M. Loyd and Andrew Burridge. "La Gran Marcha: Anti-racism and immigrants' rights in Southern California," *ACME: An International E-Journal for Critical Geographies* 6, no. 1 (2007): 1–35.

87. Interviews, SU, MO.

88. Interview, ON.

89. Interviews, BH, LC, QK.

90. Interview, LC.

91. Interview, XD.

92. Sasha Costanza-Chock, "Mic check! Media cultures and the Occupy movement," *Social Movement Studies* 11, nos. 3–4 (2012): 375–385.

93. Interview, LC.

94. Ibid.

95. Interviews, LC, ZD, LN.

96. Interview, LC.

97. Ibid.

98. Ibid.

99. Otto Santa Ana, "'Like an animal I was treated': Anti-immigrant metaphor in US public discourse," *Discourse & Society* 10, no. 2 (1999): 191–224.

100. Interview, LC.

Constructing Social Movement: Transformation of Social Change

SOCIAL DYNAMICS

The Change Process and Models of Change

Sociology examines the parts of society, how they are arranged in space, and how they influence each other. Parts of society are usually thought of as individuals, groups, institutions, social structure, roles, norms, power, stratification, tradition, and so on. This approach to understanding society is what August Comte (one of the first sociologists) called *social statics*. It is a continuation of the ancient Greek view (from Parmenides) of the world as "a motionless continuum of matter and space" (Harper 1993, 4).

Another way to examine society is to look at motion. The study of movement is the study of change. Comte called this approach to society *social dynamics*. It is in line with the Greek philosopher Heraclitus, who saw everything as constantly changing. "One never steps into the same river twice," he said. There is a dichotomy between these two approaches. Sociologists have focused on the parts rather than motion because studying movement is more complicated (Sztompka 1993).[1] Examination of structure is more in line with Western thinking. Social research includes some aspects of social dynamics, but it is not a commonly studied area.

---

1. A traditional correlation of two or more social components draws inferences of the effect of one component on the other based on changes observed at two or more specific points in time. While this is superior to the understanding of the components at a single point in time, it does not take into account feedback loops and other influences on all of the social components. A comprehensive model that accurately captures the confluence of influences in all directions is mathematically very challenging. Some analysts have concluded that the laws of social science can only be of the second stage in deterministic type, hence verification "exceeds by orders of magnitude all previous efforts expended on the natural sciences" (Stent 1978, 57).

PROBLEMS ADDRESSED THROUGH EDUCATION AND PUBLIC AWARENESS, INTERPERSONAL INTERACTION, REPARATION, APOLOGY, AND INDEPENDENT INDIVIDUAL ACTION

Social order in a peaceful society is based on the voluntary behavior of its citizens—whether out of responsibility, courtesy, conviction, or other reasons.[1] Convincing people to act in the interest of social harmony and their own well-being requires dissemination of information that is framed in a positive and convincing way. Education and public awareness are important to the resolution of social problems, even if they are not the only ameliorating action.

Laws can be an important part of voluntary behavior, such as regulating what is available—taking soda vending machines out of schools or prohibiting the sale of alcohol to minors. They can sanction consequences to some extent—ticketing drunk drivers or charging drug users. But excessive regulation, which is characteristic of a police state, generally leads to dissatisfaction.

To get full cooperation from a community, its members need to be informed of the consequences, or, to the contrary, of situations where their assistance is needed. A simple example of a public awareness measure occurred in Texas during the summer of 2011, when temperatures stayed above 100 degrees for more than forty days. The excessive heat caused electricity use to peak, and providers appealed to residents and businesses to cut back on usage to prevent outages. The appeal was made primarily through the news media,

---

1. The environmental sections of this chapter were written with Candace Halliburton.

Another example of a media campaign to inform people of an issue is the seatbelt campaign in the 1980s. For the first time since cars were invented, seatbelts were mandatory, to reduce accident fatalities and severe injuries. But many people had not yet gotten in the habit of using them, having gone many years without using them. They had to be informed, hence the Click It or Ticket campaign.

Yet another example is the situation of women during World War II. There were hundreds of vacancies in the war industries and in other essential areas after the men went off to the military. But most women were not accustomed to working outside the home. So the government organized a campaign appealing to women to help the war effort by taking those jobs. Magazines, museums, and other public institutions all participated. Rosie the Riveter—icon of the campaign—is still popular (Sorensen 2004; Thompson n.d.).[2]

For most of the problems discussed in this chapter, information campaigns and individual independent action are important to their resolution. Both are very important to environmental concerns. Without information, people would not be compelled to act. However, as important as legislation is in some areas—the Clean Water Act or Clean Air Act, for instance—it takes concerted effort on the part of many individuals to make a change. People must be conscious of the problems and do their part in avoiding actions that contribute to pollution, or refraining from wasting precious natural resources. Without cooperation from a large segment of the population, environmental concerns cannot be addressed successfully.

2. More details of this campaign can be found at www.adcouncil.org/default.aspx?id+128.

Credits

Sara Towe Horsfall, "What is a Social Problem?" Social Problems: An Advocate Group Approach, pp. 3-26. Copyright © 2012 by Perseus Books Group. Reprinted with permission.

Darin Weinberg, "The Social Construction of Social Problems," Contemporary Social Constructionism: Key Themes, pp. 113-123. Copyright © 2015 by Temple University Press. Reprinted with permission.

Steven M. Buechler, "How to Think Sociologically," Critical Sociology, pp. 3-7. Copyright © 2014 by Taylor & Francis Group. Reprinted with permission.

Simon Reid-Henry, "The Way of Wealth," The Political Origins of Inequality: Why a More Equal World Is Better for Us All, pp. 113-123, 201-202. Copyright © 2015 by University of Chicago Press. Reprinted with permission.

Stephen Caliendo, "Income and Wealth," Inequality in America: Race, Poverty, and Fulfilling Democracy's Promise, pp. 39-64, 206-215. Copyright © 2014 by Perseus Books Group. Reprinted with permission.

Heather Johnson, "Wealth Privilege," The American Dream and the Power of Wealth: Choosing Schools and Inheriting Inequality in the Land of Opportunity, pp. 149-154. Copyright © 2014 by Taylor & Francis Group. Reprinted with permission.

Ernesto Castañeda, "Places of Stigma: Ghettos, Barrios, and Banlieues," Ghetto: Contemporary Global Issues and Controversies, pp. 181-190. Copyright © 2011 by Perseus Books Group. Reprinted with permission.

Jeff Ballinger , "How Civil Society Can Help: Sweatshop Workers as Globalization's Consequence," Harvard International Review, pp. 54-59. Copyright © 2011 by Harvard International Relations Council. Reprinted with permission. Provided by ProQuest LLC. All rights reserved.

John Iceland, "Racial and Ethnic Inequality," A Portrait of America: The Demographic Perspective, pp. 138-160, 223-225. Copyright © 2014 by University of California Press. Reprinted with permission.

Allan Johnson, "Sociology as Worldview: Where White Privilege Came From," The Forest and the Trees: Sociology as Life, Practice, and Promise, pp. 149-159, 174. Copyright © 2014 by Temple University Press. Reprinted with permission.

Krystal Beamon, "The Native American Experience: Racism and Mascots in Professional Sports," The

CPSIA information can be obtained
at www.ICGtesting.com
Printed in the USA
LVHW061725201222
735562LV00006B/41

59. Frantz Fanon, "This is the Voice of Algeria," in *Studies in a Dying Colonialism,* trans. Haakon Chevalier, 69–98 (New York: Monthly Review Press, 1965). First published 1959, in French.

60. John Downing, *Radical Media: Rebellious Communication and Social Movements* (Mountain View, CA: Sage, 2001).

61. See the website of the World Association of Community Radio Broadcasters (AMARC), an international nongovernmental organization serving community radio, at http://amarc.org.

62. Andy Opel, *Micro Radio and the FCC: Media Activism and the Struggle over Broadcast Policy* (Westport, CT: Praeger, 2004).

63. Kevin Howley, "Remaking public service broadcasting: Lessons from Allston-Brighton free radio," *Social Movement Studies* 3, no. 2 (2004): 221–240.

64. For examples, see Alfonso Gumucio Dragon and Thomas Tufte, *Communication for Social Change: Anthology: Historical and Contemporary Readings* (South Orange, NJ: CFSC Consortium, 2006).

65. Graciela Orozco, "Understanding the May 1st immigrant rights mobilizations." (New York: Social Science Research Council, 2007).

66. The FIOB coordinator in Santa Maria, Jesus Estrada, was also able to secure a regular TV show on Telemundo at one point (interview, PS).

67. Interview, KZ.

68. Ibid.

69. Interview, KB.

70. See DIYMedia.net's FCC Enforcement Action Database at http://www.diymedia .net/fccwatch/ead.htm.

71. See the website of Free Speech Radio News, at http://fsrn.org.

72. Simon Cottle, *Ethnic Minorities and the Media: Changing Cultural Boundaries* (Philadelphia, PA: Open University Press, 2000).

73. Interview, SU.

74. Ibid.

75. Interview, LC.

76. Ibid.

77. Interview, TX.

78. Ibid.

39. Interview, LC, online organizer.

40. Elena Shore, "What is the role of Hispanic media in immigrant activism?," *Social Policy* 36, no. 3 (2006): 8.

41. Juan González and Joseph Torres, *News for All the People: The Epic Story of Race and the American Media* (New York: Verso Books, 2011).

42. Interview, LC.

43. Interviews, DH, PS, LC, BH, EQ.

44. Interview, PS.

45. Ibid.

46. Interview, LC.

47. Interview, EQ.

48. William A. Gamson and Gadi Wolfsfeld, "Movements and media as interacting systems," *Annals of the American Academy of Political and Social Science* 528 (July 1993): 114–125.

49. Interview, EQ.

50. Dávila, *Latinos, Inc.*

51. Interview, CY.

52. Beth Baker-Cristales, "Mediated resistance: The construction of neoliberal citizenship in the immigrant rights movement," *Latino Studies* 7, no. 1 (Spring 2009): 60–82.

53. Ibid.

54. Ibid.; Alvaro Lima, "Transnationalism: What it means to local communities," Boston Redevelopment Authority, Boston, Winter 2010. http://www.bostonre developmentauthority.org/getattachment/40c9373f-d170-4ed7-91bf-300f2b7 daeb9/ (Retrieved April 6, 2014).

55. Alan O'Connor, *Community Radio in Bolivia: The Miners' Radio Stations* (Lewiston, NY: Edwin Mellen Press, 2004).

56. Timothy B. Tyson, *Radio Free Dixie: Robert F. Williams & the Roots of Black Power* (Chapel Hill: University of North Carolina Press, 1999).

57. Brian Ward, *Radio and the Struggle for Civil Rights in the South* (Gainesville: University Press of Florida, 2004).

58. Lawrence Soley, *Free Radio: Electronic Civil Disobedience* (Boulder: Westview, 1999).